August Wilson's American Century

AUGUST WILSON'S AMERICAN CENTURY

Life as Art

LAURENCE A. GLASCO

UNIVERSITY OF PITTSBURGH PRESS

A John D. S. and Aida Truxall Book

Published by the University of Pittsburgh Press, Pittsburgh, Pa., 15260
Copyright © 2026, University of Pittsburgh Press
All rights reserved
Manufactured in the United States of America
Printed on acid-free paper
10 9 8 7 6 5 4 3 2 1

Cataloging-in-Publication data is available from the Library of Congress

Hardcover: 978-0-8229-4854-4

Cover photo: August 14, 2001, playwright August Wilson phoographed at the bar of W. A. Frost, a restaurant on Selby Avenue in St. Paul, where he chain smoked cigarettes while working on his plays when he lived in St. Paul. Tom Sweeney / Minneapolis Star Tribune / TNS via ZUMA Wire / ZUMA Press, Inc. / Alamy

Cover design: Alex Wolfe

Publisher: University of Pittsburgh Press, 7500 Thomas Blvd., 4th floor, Pittsburgh, PA 15260, United States, www.upittpress.org

EU Authorized Representative: Easy Access System Europe, Mustamäe tee 50, 10621 Tallinn, Estonia, gpsr.requests@easproject.com

To Ingrid, my always supportive wife

CONTENTS

August Wilson's American Century

Introduction

The Power of Place

August Wilson occupies a unique place in the history of American theater. His main body of work, the so-called Pittsburgh Cycle, consists of ten plays, each set in a different decade of the twentieth century and all but one set in Pittsburgh. Looked at individually, the plays are notable for featuring unforgettable characters and compelling dialogue. Looked at collectively, the Pittsburgh Cycle is a remarkable, century-long theatrical history. Although the plays are not an exhaustive interpretation of Black life in America, Wilson consciously sought to have each play in the cycle—*Gem of the Ocean, Joe Turner's Come and Gone, Ma Rainey's Black Bottom, The Piano Lesson, Seven Guitars, Fences, Two Trains Running, Jitney, King Hedley II*, and *Radio Golf*—delve into "one of the most important questions that blacks confronted" in a specific decade.[1] No other playwright—certainly none in the United States—has written a comparable set of excellent plays set in the same place and treating a common topic over an extended period of time. Eugene O'Neill once attempted such a feat, but ultimately abandoned the effort.[2] Wilson's success in fulfilling such an ambitious project is unprecedented, and has enshrined him in the pantheon of American playwrights.

Through his plays, Wilson gave dignity and respect to the lives of Pittsburgh's working-class Black residents that he carefully observed and came to value. In his plays, those residents demand respect and understanding. They burn down a mill in protest of a fellow worker's unnecessary death. They reclaim their racial identity by participating in African-based rituals. They argue vigorously about when certain trains did and did not pass through the city. A blues performer believes fame and fortune will soon be his, a former star of the Negro Leagues complains about not getting the chance to play in the majors, and a waitress scars her legs so that men will focus more on her personality than on her looks. Unlicensed cab drivers worry about losing their station to urban renewal, pessimism about the future causes women to obtain abortions, and politicians scheme to "redevelop" the neighborhood by bringing in a Starbucks and other "amenities."

In making Pittsburgh the setting for his plays, Wilson put his hometown on the world-cultural map, doing for Pittsburgh what William Faulkner did for Oxford, Mississippi, and James Joyce for Dublin, Ireland. Today, thanks to the Pittsburgh Cycle, the city occupies an iconic place in the story of America in general and of Black America in particular. Among theatergoers and many others, Pittsburgh's Hill District has challenged Harlem as the metaphorical site of the urban Black experience. This book explores how Pittsburgh influenced both Wilson's identity and his accomplishments—the life experiences that generated them, and the consequences for Wilson himself, his work, and his literary career.

Pittsburgh profoundly shaped both Wilson and his literary output. Without question, the city meant a lot to him. It is where he was born, where he spent almost all the first thirty-three years of his life, where he first fell in love, married, and started a family, where he began his literary career, and where he acquired much of what he knew about life. The city furnished Wilson with memories of people, places, and events that became raw material for his plays. Just as importantly, through his early life and experiences in Pittsburgh, Wilson acquired a set of set of identity traits that defined who he was and who he would become, both personally and professionally: outsider, warrior, race man, and poet. Being an outsider made him a close observer of others, being a warrior taught him to persevere in the face of setbacks, being a race man gave him a central theme for his writings, and being a poet gave him the ability to create compelling dialogue that amounted to free-verse poetry. This fourfold set of identity traits became crucial to his later success, and Wilson embedded them in the personas of the leading characters of his play.

Despite thousands of books, articles, dissertations, and videos about Wilson's literary output,[3] Wilson himself has been the subject of only one previous book-length biography, Patti Hartigan's *August Wilson: A Life*. Published in 2023, it is a detailed, engaging examination of Wilson's life by the longtime theater critic of the *Boston Globe*. While Hartigan's biography offers gripping detail, it provides little in the way of an overarching theme, little concerted effort to define, simply and convincingly, who Wilson was, how he got that way, and how his own persona shaped his plays. Moreover, and perhaps relatedly, the majority of Hartigan's book focuses on the period after Wilson achieved national fame and fortune.[4] An understanding of Wilson's relationship with Pittsburgh provides the key to understanding both the playwright and the plays.

Happily, there is no shortage of material relating to Wilson and Pittsburgh. The archives at the University of Pittsburgh hold Wilson's personal papers as well as the papers of several of his friends and colleagues. There are numerous public documents to draw upon, including census records, city directories, and legal documents. Opportunely, Wilson's friend Lee Kiburi interviewed both him and others in the 1990s as part of an investigation of Pittsburgh's Black Power movement. Those detailed interviews are of central importance in telling the story of Wilson and his hometown. Most importantly, there still are many individuals who knew Wilson personally and remember him well. Many of his former neighbors, friends, relatives, classmates, girlfriends, and wives were willing to talk about a person they knew and admired. For this biography, I interviewed some sixty or so individuals from those days, interviews that add greatly to an understanding of Wilson's personal life and literary development.

To appreciate the power of a place, one first needs to know something about the place itself. For our purposes, that would be Pittsburgh's Hill District. The setting of nine of the plays in the Pittsburgh Cycle, the Hill District is the neighborhood where Wilson lived as a young boy, and he returned to it as a young man when he was beginning his career as a writer. Wilson's story is tied up in the neighborhood's story, which begins early in the nineteenth century, when African Americans became the first to settle the rolling hills just east of downtown. The Hill's natural beauty and favorable location soon attracted white professionals and businessmen, who settled among these original Black residents. A local newspaper praised the industriousness and work ethic of these Black settlers. "In repeated instances, they have dug the cellars of their abodes with their own hands and have made brick of the clay upon the spot." The paper went on to praise local Black settlers for their "orderly conduct, sobriety, and [respect for] the civilities of life." It added that their behavior was "appreciated and warmly approved by their white neighbors." The paper

closed by hoping the neighborhood's Black residents would "continue to pros-
per and outlive the many prejudices which have existed against them."[5]

These early settlers were an unusual group who had benefited from an
unusual history. They came largely from Virginia's Shenandoah Valley, some
two hundred miles to the south. In the valley, enslaved Black people worked
on the area's small wheat farms. As such, their lives differed markedly from
those of their counterparts who toiled elsewhere on larger, highly regimented
tobacco and cotton plantations. Valley Black people worked side by side with
their owners, performing a variety of tasks and in the process acquiring a
range of valuable job skills.[6] In the off-season, some were hired out to area
ironworks, further expanding their psychological horizons as well as their
range of job skills. Interracial mixing was common in the valley, as evidenced
by the 1850 US Census, which classified most of Pittsburgh's African American residents as "mulattoes," or persons of mixed-race ancestry.

While Black people made up most of the Hill's original settlers, over
time, the neighborhood's demographic makeup changed markedly. In the
mid-nineteenth century, Irish and German immigrants turned it into a working-class neighborhood. In the latter part of the century, Jewish immigrants
from Eastern Europe further increased its ethnic diversity. And in the early
twentieth century, a massive influx of Poles, Serbs, Slovaks, Italians, Syrians,
Lebanese, Greeks, and Chinese made it the city's most racially and ethnically
diverse neighborhood.

Race relations in Pittsburgh were characterized by less tension and violence than in places like New York City and Philadelphia. However, as was
true throughout the North, Black people were confined to a narrow range
of jobs, working mainly as day laborers and in such service occupations as
waiters, cooks, barbers, domestics, and boat stewards. Despite these limited
opportunities, Black people retained their penchant for hard work and the
"civilities of life." A. B. Hall, editor of "Afro-American Notes," a weekly
column in the *Pittsburgh Press*, described the late-nineteenth century Black
community as dominated by "an aristocracy of genteel families and cliques
from Virginia and Maryland." Maintaining their generations-long pursuit of
gentility and the "civilities of life," they supported a remarkable number of
concert orchestras, choirs, and musicians specializing in European classical
music.[7]

Despite residents' efforts at respectability, the Hill acquired an increasingly negative image. In 1905, newspaper columnist Hartley Phelps penned
a series of articles blaming the neighborhood's decline on its residents. "The

Hebrews," Phelps wrote, "transformed Wylie Avenue," the neighborhood's main retail corridor, "into a sort of Bowery . . . the East Side of New York City transplanted."[8] Phelps castigated the Hill also for suffering "throngs of greasy, unkempt Italians [who] stand around in front of crazy little grocery stores, jabbering or smoking."[9] As one might expect, he also had things to say that were critical of the Hill's Black residents, including their patronage of "open lunch counters . . . where . . . bums and others sit in slouchy fashion, eating 'short orders' at 3 cents a plate."[10]

Alas, Phelps's comments reflect more than simple prejudice. The Hill's housing was, in fact, the city's oldest and most dilapidated. Typically over-crowded and lacking running water and indoor toilets, homes there had been divided and subdivided to accommodate the desperate search of Black and white newcomers for a cheap place to stay. By the turn of the century, most upper-class residents had left the Hill. Pittsburgh's *Blue Book* listed 114 socially prominent families residing there in 1887; by 1904, it listed only three.[11]

Although Black people had been the Hill's original residents, lack of job opportunities kept their numbers low. The city's industries were booming, but for the most part industries hired Black people only as temporary strike-breakers and fired them once the strike was broken. In the early twentieth century, the setting for *Gem of the Ocean*, the earliest play in Wilson's Cycle, Pittsburgh's booming steel-, glass-, and aluminum-based economy created a labor shortage acute enough that Black people began finding work as self-employed haulers and carters, who earned a decent living leveling the city's hilly terrain. Other job opportunities attracted an increasing number of Black migrants—again, mainly Virginians—such that by 1910, Black people numbered some twenty-five thousand residents and made up 5 percent of the city's overall population. Some ten thousand resided in the Hill, with the rest dispersed into outlying neighborhoods such as East Liberty, Homewood, the North Side, and Beltzhoover.

Virginians and their descendants long made up the bulk of Pittsburgh's African American community. However, things changed dramatically in 1917 when the United States entered World War I. Germany vowed to sink any ship found crossing the Atlantic, and the threat quickly ended most transatlantic shipments and virtually ended European immigration to the United States. The cutoff of immigration immediately created a severe labor shortage in the United States—so severe that, for the first time in history, Northern indus-tries in places like Pittsburgh began hiring Black people and making them a permanent part of their labor force.

To be sure, manufacturers confined Black people to the hottest, most dangerous, and lowest-paying jobs. But industrial wages in the North still were better than almost anything available down South. Understandably, Black workers and their families rushed north in a massive movement known as the Great Migration. Between 1910 and 1930, this unprecedented movement of people doubled Pittsburgh's Black population to over fifty thousand. And, for the first time in history, most came not from Virginia (and, to a lesser extent, Maryland) but from the Deep South, particularly Alabama and Georgia. The newcomers settled not in the Lower Hill, long inhabited by Virginians, but in the Middle Hill, from where they could easily walk to the Jones & Laughlin Steel mills that lined both sides of the Monongahela River. The Great Migration of 1917 quickly ended the Virginians' long dominance of the Hill District's population. With the massive arrival of migrants from Alabama, Georgia, and North Carolina, the blues joined classical music as an important part of cultural life in the Hill.

The same job shortage that brought Black people north also propelled white people up the occupational ladder. Many who moved up also moved out—Jews to Oakland and Squirrel Hill, Italians to Oakland and Bloomfield. As a result, between 1910 and 1940, the Hill's white population declined by some twenty thousand and its Black population increased by about the same number. In 1930, Black people constituted half of the Hill's residents; thereafter, the neighborhood became increasingly majority Black. Because Black people had always lived in the Hill, white people did not perceive their arrival as an "invasion," and so their arrival did not generate the sort of violence that wracked Chicago and over twenty other cities. In 1920 one third of the Hill's Black residents still had a white neighbor—often Jewish—residing nearby. Schools had desegregated in the 1870s—far earlier than in most Northern cities—and Urban League investigators found relatively little racial fighting among pupils.[12]

The newcomers made the Hill more vibrant than ever. The neighborhood had a long tradition of Black-operated concert orchestras; now it also featured the liveliest jazz scene between New York and Chicago. Prominence in jazz stemmed in no small measure from the blues brought in by Alabamans and Georgians fusing with the Virginians' tradition of European classical music. Jazz thrived in Hill District bars and nightclubs like the Humming Bird, the Leader House, Derby Dad's, the Harlem Show Bar, the Crawford Grill, the Harlem Casino, the Flamingo, the Hurricane, Stanley's Lounge, and the Musician's Club. The Hill District's Pittsburgh Crawfords and the nearby Homestead Grays fielded two of the finest baseball teams in the Negro Leagues, home to such future Hall of Famers as Satchel Paige, "Cool Papa" Bell, and Josh Gibson. The *Pittsburgh Courier*, edited and printed in the Hill, became the finest and largest-circulation Black newspaper in the nation.[13]

The Great Depression brought suffering in its wake, so much so that a 1939 study by the Federal Writers' Project cited the Hill as an example of "the worst that a fiercely industrial city like Pittsburgh can do to human beings." The Writers' Project deplored the Hill's many impoverished Jews, Italians, and Black people, as well as depressing scenes of "slump- shouldered men with hungry eyes; Negro women, spindle-legged from childhood rickets; spine-sagging, down-at-heal, listless men and women."[14] However, Black people who worked for wealthy white families or operated elevators downtown usually kept their jobs and their income. In Wilson's play *The Piano Lesson*, set in the midst of the Great Depression, Berniece, one of the play's leading characters, works as a maid for a family in the well-off neighborhood of Squirrel Hill. Berniece's boyfriend Avery works downtown as an elevator operator at Gulf Oil.

Happily, things improved dramatically in the 1940s. The war against the Nazis in Europe softened racial attitudes at home. In addition, as the United States geared up for World War II, Pittsburgh's mills became part of the so-called Arsenal of Democracy. Operating virtually nonstop, mill owners placed ads in the *Pittsburgh Courier* for workers of any skill level, apparently signaling they were ready to upgrade Black people into semiskilled and skilled positions. With steady jobs and money in their pockets, Black-owned businesses thrived as never before. Without question, the 1940s—the decade in which Wilson was born—became the most prosperous decade in the history of the Hill, and indeed of Black Pittsburgh more generally. A robust job market and rising wages enabled middle-class Black people to begin moving into the fine homes of the Upper Hill, a neighborhood known popularly as "Sugar Top" because life there was supposedly so sweet. Families of limited means benefited from the 1940 opening of the Terrace Village public housing project in the southern Hill. Shortly afterward, Bedford Dwellings, another housing project, opened in the northern Hill. Public housing later became stigmatized, but at the time, these attractive, well-built units were sources of pride and hope.[15] Full employment and new housing generated visions of success.

Wilson benefited from both the prosperity of the time and the racial harmony of his childhood neighborhood—especially the four blocks of Bedford Avenue in the Hill District between Crawford and Roberts Streets, which were quiet, safe, neighborly, racially diverse, and racially integrated. "The street I lived on," he said years later, "was a *community* of people. I remember coming home from school, and all of the parents would be sitting on the stoops, talking and exchanging recipes, talking about what they were cooking for dinner, talking about their kids. That was a nice neighborhood," he added, "in the sense that anyone . . . was your social parent."[16]

Wilson's childhood home was a small apartment in one of the neighborhood's oldest and most dilapidated homes. Located in the rear of 1727 Bedford Avenue, it sat well back from the street, hidden behind a grocery store, and accessible only by way of a long, narrow walk that was closed off by a gate. But the family's small, cramped apartment was located in a supportive, racially diverse neighborhood. Just down the street, Saint George Syrian Orthodox Church served the neighborhood's many Middle Eastern congregants. Next door resided the Buteras, a family of Italian descent who ran a shoe- and watch-repair business. In front lived the Sigers, a Jewish couple who operated Bella's Market, a neighborhood grocery. Another Jewish family, the Goldblums, lived across the street, and next to them resided the Burleys, an African American family that played an important role in Wilson's formative years.

During Wilson's childhood, Wylie Avenue—the Hill's main retail corridor—featured a large variety of stores that generated pride among residents. Lillian Allen, a local beautician, says the Hill had so many stores, and such a variety of stores, that residents seldom needed to go elsewhere for shopping. On Sundays, Allen says:

> There was a line waiting to eat at Nesbit's [Pie Shop]. Around the corner on Center Avenue was . . . Robert L. Vann's *Pittsburgh Courier*, our weekly newspaper. The Hill was very proud of the New Granada and Roosevelt Theaters, where uniformed ushers seated you, like downtown. . . . On Fullerton Street was . . . a nightclub in the basement called The Bambola . . . [which was] the haunt of the nightlife people. . . . The Halloween night party [there] was a time when the lesbians and the gays could come out of the closet. . . . Among the popular places to go was William Stanley's bar on Fullerton and Wylie . . . The Crawford Grill [was] a place to relax over a drink and enjoy good food and jazz. [Jewish-owned stores like] Fireman's Department Store . . . filled the needs of the average family and Gordon's Shoes fitted the feet of all sizes and types.[17]

When Wilson was eleven years old, the Hill suffered a devastating setback. In 1956, in the name of urban renewal, the city razed the area around Wylie

Avenue, the commercial, residential, and institutional heart of the Hill. Doing so eliminated over four hundred businesses, mostly owned by white people, and displaced some eight thousand residents, most of whom were African American. The city hoped that replacing Wylie Avenue and the Hill's decrepit housing with a gleaming Cultural District would change its "Smoky City" image and stanch the outflow of downtown corporations.

Originally, Black people supported urban renewal because the city promised them new housing and good jobs rebuilding the area. Ultimately, they received only a large arena, a massive parking lot, and a luxury apartment building too expensive for them to live in. Worse, the city operated through eminent domain, which let it raze any property they desired after compensating owners the property's assessed value. The compensation was often generous, and so owners were content. But renters were livid that they were given little assistance in relocating and no jobs rebuilding the neighborhood. Not surprisingly, the threat of urban renewal figures prominently in three of Wilson's plays: *Jitney*, *Two Trains Running*, and *Radio Golf*.[18]

Centre Avenue quickly replaced Wylie as the Hill's main retail corridor, as displaced owners on and around Wylie often used their compensation checks to relocate to Centre. In 1965, when Wilson moved back to the Hill at the age of twenty after spending his teen years with his family in Hazelwood, he rejoiced at how Centre Avenue would "shimmer" with activity, its sidewalks crowded with shoppers, loiterers, and families out for a stroll. By this time an aspiring poet, he explored the Hill looking for material to write about, taking daily walks along the busy retail corridor, observing residents as they passed by. On these walks, Wilson often stopped in at one or more of the neighborhood's many bars, diners, restaurants, and shops. He wrote poetry in Eddie's Diner, surrounded by the sort of folks he would write about later in his plays: migrants, housewives, waitresses, conjure women, preachers, blues singers, boardinghouse dwellers, garbage collectors, baseball players, jitney drivers, undertakers, restaurant owners, politicians, real estate developers, alcoholics, drug addicts, ex-convicts, and half-crazed old men.

In the spring of 1968, Centre Avenue's vibrant scene came to a sudden, tragic end. It happened a few days after the assassination of Martin Luther King Jr., when angry residents torched many of the avenue's stores. The results were devastating. Unlike urban renewal, the city did not compensate owners for their losses. Even more devastating, insurance companies stopped issuing policies for businesses in the Hill. Most devastating of all, many white merchants lost their appetite for operating there. In just a few years, the 120 retail shops that once made Centre a lively retail corridor dropped to 66—and many of those were struggling to survive.[19] Years later, when New York theater critic Ben Brantley visited Wilson, he found Centre a depressing streetscape of empty lots and scattered buildings that Brantley likened to "the last teeth in an old man's smile."[20]

The Hill as a place of energy and celebration gave way to one of gloom and foreboding. In 1973 the *Pittsburgh Courier* tasked reporter Greg Mims with learning whether there might be any riots that year. Mims reported in the negative—not because residents were content, but because they felt hopeless and powerless.[21] Wilson's play *Two Trains Running*, set one year after the riots, echoes Mims's report. The play's characters have concluded that nonviolent protest does not yield racial equality, and that violence only makes things worse. As the title of the play, drawn from the lyrics of an old blues song, puts it: "Two trains running, neither going my way." Adding to the sense of despair, a surge in illicit drug use and street crime frightened away shoppers, particularly women, further reducing avenue foot traffic and business.

Just as the 1940s marked the Hill's high point, the 1970s and 1980s, with the influx of cocaine, the collapse of the steel industry, and the rise of violent crime, marked the city's low point. Fortunately, the 1990s saw the beginnings of a revival. Crawford-Roberts, a government-private partnership, began erecting new townhouses along and around Centre Avenue. Many residents still had qualms about urban renewal, evident in the threatening way Wilson depicts it in *Radio Golf*. Happily, however, the new housing initiative did not seize properties, evict tenants, or—as feared—gentrify the neighborhood. Rather, it created attractive homes with green space and, in some cases, commanding views of downtown. The local press began referring optimistically to what it called "The Rebirth of the Hill."[22] Over the following years, a number of existing properties were restored. These included Wilson's childhood home on Bedford Avenue, which opened to the public in 2023. The new housing—some available at market rates, others subsidized for lower-income residents—attracted white and Asian residents as well as African Americans. Indeed, the Hill may be coming full circle back to what it had been two centuries earlier—an attractive, bustling, racially integrated neighborhood.

Wilson's frequent walks through the Hill District as a young man, observing and interacting with residents, enabled him to depict Black life and culture with accuracy and sensitivity. Ironically, it was only after he had left Pittsburgh and was living in Saint Paul, Minnesota, that Wilson found his way. It happened one evening when he saw a book of paintings by Romare Bearden, the nation's leading Black artist. In what proved a career-changing epiphany, Wilson saw that Bearden achieved success by depicting the patterns of daily life among everyday people. He excitedly realized that this was something he could do himself. For years he had observed everyday residents of the Hill as they went about their lives. He had just never made the daily life of such people the subject of his poetry and plays. Bearden showed Wilson the way forward. Henceforth, he would harness the power of place by writing about everyday life in Black Pittsburgh.

After Saint Paul, Wilson moved to Seattle, where he spent the final fifteen years of his life. Although he never again lived in his hometown, he returned often. And his heart and his memories never left. After the success of *Fences*, he told a local radio interviewer who asked about his having left, "I never really left. I don't know if one can do that because you carry your home with you wherever you go. I carry [Pittsburgh] around in my heart with me."[23] Coming of age in Pittsburgh exposed Wilson to a rich assemblage of social types. It shaped his identity as an outsider, warrior, race man, and poet, enabling him to imbue his plays' leading characters with those same qualities. Wilson was keenly aware of his debt to the city. As he told the interviewer, "You can only write what you know, and I guess what I know best is Pittsburgh from my thirty-three years of living here and the experiences that I've had."[24] The result is both a tribute to Pittsburgh and a shining example of the power of place.

1

From Plumtree to Pittsburgh

Friday, April 27, 1945, dawned cool and drizzly, but that meant little to Daisy. At 6:42 that morning, in Pittsburgh's Magee Women's Hospital, she gave birth to her first son. After three girls in a row, Daisy was desperate for a boy.[1] Her daughter Donna said that, if need be, she "would have had eleven girls—she didn't care—she would have kept trying till she had a son."[2] Daisy named the boy Frederick August Kittel in honor of his father, a German-speaking immigrant from a village near Dresden in what today is the Czech Republic. Daisy had high hopes for the boy's future, but she could scarcely have imagined that, under the name August Wilson, he would become a world-famous playwright. "Freddy," or "Little Freddy Kittel," as he was known to family and friends, occupied a special place in her heart, and she in his. Years later, Freddy described the high esteem in which he held his mother. "The content of my mother's life," he said, "her myths, her superstitions, her prayers, the contents of her pantry, the smell of her kitchen, the song that escaped from her sometimes-parched lips, her thoughtful repose and pregnant laughter—all are worthy of art."[3]

Daisy was born on March 12, 1920, in Plumtree, an unincorporated hamlet in Avery County, North Carolina. Situated high in the Blue Ridge Mountains, about fifty miles from Asheville,[4] Avery's natural beauty has made it the setting for two movies and an upscale destination for outdoor enthusiasts.[5]

However, during Daisy's time there, Avery was a poverty-stricken locale with an economy dominated by mica, a silicate mineral used in making electrical equipment and the viewing windows of coal stoves. Mica, like asbestos, often leaves a debilitating, deadly fibrosis in the lungs of those who mine it. Most residents of Avery, including the family of Daisy's mother, either worked in the mica mines or eked out a living as subsistence farmers. Many did both.[6]

African Americans residing in the mountainous regions of western North Carolina had little in common with their counterparts who worked the tobacco plantations in the eastern lowlands. In 1920 Black people made up only 2 percent of Avery's overall population. Three fourths of even that small number were classified by the census as "mulattoes," persons of mixed racial heritage. In the mountainous regions of Kentucky, Tennessee, West Virginia, and North Carolina, anthropologists classified such isolated pockets of mixed-race residents as triracial isolates; locals often referred to them as Melungeons. Either way, they were the product of the region's long history of racial mixing.[7] Like the Creoles of Louisiana, they stayed largely to themselves in an effort to maintain their precarious identity as neither Black nor white. [8]

Daisy had a light complexion and wavy hair but was not Melungeon. Her mother Zonia Cutler—sometimes known as "Zona" or "Arizona"—was the daughter of one of Avery's few families that the census classified as Black rather than "Mulatto." Daisy got her complexion and hair texture from her father, a man she seldom talked about. Years later, she confided to a friend that she didn't know her father and it didn't matter. "He didn't raise me," she said, "so that was just something that happened." In fact, Daisy did know her father. Years later, on her marriage license she listed him as Friel Vance.[9]

To be the daughter of Friel Vance connected Daisy to one of North Carolina's wealthiest, most prominent families. In 1909 Friel's father David founded the Tar Heel Mica Company, which quickly became one of the world's leading producers of that valuable mineral.[10] It may be relevant that in 1920 Friel was studying engineering at North Carolina State University and that Daisy was born nine months after the start of the school's summer vacation, a time when Friel may well have been home. Daisy's family says she was the result of Zonia being raped while working as a maid for the Vances.[11] If so, it may be relevant that, three years later, Zonia gave birth to a second light-skinned child, known sometimes as Ray and other times as Detroit.[12]

Whatever Zonia's relation—or nonrelation—with Friel, in 1928 she married Bynum Wilson, a dark-skinned farm laborer from the rural area outside Charlotte. Bynum's family says he went up in the high mountains looking for work and was never heard from again. We know that Bynum did find work. The 1930 US Census shows him employed as a coal loader in Rock, West Virginia, and living with his wife "Zony."[13] Life would have been hard for the couple since loading coal was an extremely demanding, low-paying job.

In 1934, at the age of fourteen, Daisy's life changed forever. Sometime that year, a car pulled into Spear, a hamlet next to Plumtree. The car would have drawn attention because in those years few mountain people, Black or white, owned cars. The new arrival was Bynum's brother Arthur, who had come to pick up the family and drive them to Pittsburgh. There, they were to stay with him and his wife Minerva while they got on their feet. Arthur and Minerva had a small apartment in the city's Hill District, so taking in Bynum and his family would make things very crowded. But at least Arthur could afford to house them. He had a good job as porter at the city's marquee hotel, the William Penn. The pay there was less than in the mills, but the work was steady, and the tips were good.[14]

In those days Pittsburgh was one of the nation's preeminent manufacturing centers, home to such behemoths as US Steel, Jones & Laughlin Steel, Alcoa Aluminum, Westinghouse Electric, Pittsburgh Plate Glass, and Heinz Foods. Arthur had traveled there in 1923, during the Roaring Twenties when job opportunities were plentiful. He started out as a common laborer, but in 1931 secured a position as porter at the William Penn Hotel.[15]

Arthur's brother Bynum had the misfortune of arriving in 1934, in the midst of the Great Depression, the greatest economic collapse in the nation's history, a time when things got so bad that white people began leaving the city in search of work. Black people like Bynum continued coming because things back home were even worse.

Pittsburgh was a dramatic change for Bynum and his family. In 1930 the city's Black population numbered 55,000, far more than anything Daisy had ever experienced. Unlike Avery, Pittsburgh was large and ethnically diverse. In 1930 it was the tenth largest city in the nation, with some 670,000 residents, mostly of Slavic, Jewish, Italian, Greek, Irish, German, and Syrian descent.

Bynum and his family squeezed into Arthur's small apartment on Logan Street, a narrow, cobblestoned passageway in the Lower Hill known affectionately as "Jew Town." Its stores attracted shoppers of all ethnic and racial backgrounds.

Bynum needed several years to get on his feet. He worked a series of low-paying jobs as janitor, laborer, and parking lot attendant until 1937, when he found an affordable place not far from Arthur. However, Bynum's situation remained insecure, evidenced by the fact that, between 1937 and 1942, his family changed residence almost every year.[16] Hard times undermined Daisy's chance to gain an education. She had been in the sixth grade when the family left North Carolina, but after moving to Pittsburgh apparently never attended school again. Rather, she worked as a janitor in downtown office buildings, no doubt to augment the family's meager income.[17]

In 1940, at the age of twenty, Daisy moved into her own apartment, located on Townsend Street, a few blocks from her parents. One day, it is said, while shopping at a nearby grocery, Daisy met a handsome, German-speaking stranger. She was shy at that first encounter, but at the urging of her mother became flirtatious the next time the two met.[18]

The stranger was Frederick August Kittel, a German-speaking immigrant and pastry chef twenty-five years her senior. Fred's relatives say the two did not meet at a grocery store, but rather while Daisy was working as a housekeeper for Fred and his wife in the South Hills.[19] Regardless of how they met, this marked the beginning of a relationship that would endure some twenty-five years.

Fred hailed from Dreihunken—a Bohemian village about forty miles south of Dresden in what today is the Czech Republic.[20] His family was relatively well-off, as evidenced by their substantial, attractive house, which still stands in good repair.[21] Fred's parents must have had high hopes for their son, for they named him after Frederick Augustus ("the Strong"), the famous Elector of Saxony who was chosen to become king of Poland and Grand Duke of Lithuania. Anton, Fred's father, was a blacksmith, but Fred apprenticed as a pastry chef, a high-status trade in the Austro-Hungarian Empire.

In 1913, at the age of eighteen, Fred immigrated to the United States, ultimately settling in Pittsburgh. He had been preceded by his brother Emil, who came in 1911, followed by Erdmann in 1914 and Rudolph in 1920. These four brothers remained in the Pittsburgh area, but a fifth brother, Anton, moved to California, and then to South America, and was never heard from again.[22] Fred was fortunate that he emigrated in 1913, for it let him avoid the mass conscription of young men for World War I. He also was fortunate that he was never called up to serve in the American forces, which spared him from fighting against his own countrymen.[23]

Fred adjusted well to life in Pittsburgh. His training as a pastry chef let him find work in such prominent downtown hotels as the Fort Pitt and William Penn, as well as in such leading bakeries as Waldorf's in the affluent Jewish neighborhood of Squirrel Hill.[24] In 1919 in St. Stanislaus Church,

Fred married Maryanna Jodzis, a Polish-Russian immigrant often known as Jennie.[25] In 1920 Fred acquired US citizenship, and in 1924 he purchased a one-acre lot at 1004 Stewart Avenue in the Overbrook neighborhood.[26] There, with the help of brothers Rudy and Emil, Fred erected a handsome Craftsman-style house. A few years later, he acquired an additional piece of property, and in 1936, his wife Jennie gave birth to the couple's first son, Fred C.

Despite these signs of a successful adjustment, other indicators suggest that Fred's life was not going well. On several occasions between 1933 and 1944, he disappeared from the city directory, unlike his brothers, who appeared each year like clockwork. And his son Fred C., after appearing in the 1940 US Census as a four-year-old, is not to be found again, either in public records or church records.[27] All this suggests instability, likely related to a problem that plagued Fred for the rest of his life: alcoholism.

In 1940, around the time when Daisy first met Fred, she became pregnant. The city directory for that year lists her as "Mrs. Daisy Wilson" and describes her as residing by herself on Townsend Street, a congested, largely commercial thoroughfare not far from Logan Street. In 1941, Daisy gave birth to her first child. Fred never accepted the child as his own, although Daisy named her Freda—pronounced "Fred-ah," presumably in his honor.[28]

In 1942, Daisy's life changed once again. That year, she moved out of her apartment on busy Townsend Street and onto Bedford Avenue, a much quieter thoroughfare. Bedford Avenue, especially the four or so blocks between Crawford and Roberts Streets—Daisy's immediate neighborhood—featured a number of handsome, well-maintained homes. Built around the turn of the century, many boasted Italianate, Second Empire, and Romanesque revival architectural styles, with detailing at the windows and brick corbels at the roofline. Barely getting by on government aid, Daisy could not afford those homes. But no doubt she valued the neighborhood's quiet, family-based, interracial atmosphere. In the end, she made do with what she could afford: a two-room cold-water flat in an unpretentious, hundred-year-old house badly in need of repair and updating. The house was situated in the rear of 1727 Bedford, at the intersection of Roberts and some four blocks east of Crawford Street.[29] It is a tribute to Daisy that, on her limited income, she managed to secure an apartment in one of the Hill's quietest, best-maintained, interracial neighborhoods.

It was in this stretch of Bedford that, over the next sixteen years, Daisy would raise her growing family. In 1942 she gave birth to a second daughter, Linda Jean; two years after that she gave birth to another daughter, Donna; and in 1945 she gave birth to Freddy, her first son. Two years after

Freddy's arrival, Daisy gave birth to her fourth daughter, whom she named Barbara Jean. Whereas Freddy was born in Magee Women's, the city's premiere maternity hospital, Barbara was delivered in the Roselia Foundling Asylum and Maternity Hospital, operated by the Sisters of Charity and located on Bedford, only a couple of blocks from Daisy's home. Barbara's hair texture and honey-almond complexion signaled that she was not Fred's daughter. Asylum records show that Daisy loved the child and visited her regularly, but in one of the most painful decisions of her life, she asked Faye, her sister in New York, to take Barbara and raise her as her own.[30] As a result, Barbara never met her father. Today, she treasures what little she knows about him—that his name was Charles Barton, that she was named Barbara in his honor, and that he was a light-skinned African American who had wanted to marry Daisy.[31] After Barbara, Daisy had two additional children, both boys: Edwin Anton, born in 1951, and Richard Louis, born in 1954.

The house lacked architectural features and was badly in need of repairs, maintenance, and updating.[32] It lacked a toilet, requiring the family to make do with an outdoor privy. It also lacked hot running water, requiring the family to bathe in the kitchen. Fortunately, Daisy was strong enough to lift a large tub of water onto and off the stove. Things improved in the late 1940s when Mr. Rand, the landlord, installed an indoor toilet, a water heater, and a bathtub in the basement. Space was always a problem. Daisy and her five children—Freda, Linda Jean, Donna, Freddy, and Edwin—were crammed into two small rooms on the first floor. Of necessity, each room had multiple functions.[33] The one closer to the street served as a combination living room, dining room, and children's bedroom. The one toward the back doubled as a bedroom and kitchen. Things improved in 1952, when the upstairs tenants, Louise and Hedley, moved out, giving the Wilsons two additional rooms. Despite its physical drawbacks, the location of Daisy's apartment in a congenial, diverse neighborhood counted for a lot. When Julia Burley moved into the neighborhood in 1948, she felt like she was "movin' on up," as in the theme song of the popular 1970s TV sitcom *The Jeffersons*.[34] Daisy probably felt the same way. Certainly, she did things to make the apartment as pleasant and attractive as possible. For example, she used a maroon-colored wallpaper with an attractive cream flower motif to cover the living room walls.[35]

That the neighborhood was racially and ethnically diverse made it an ideal place for Daisy to raise her family.[36] African Americans made up about half the residents in the stretch of Bedford Avenue between Crawford and Roberts streets. White residents were largely of Jewish, Italian, and Syrian/Lebanese descent. East of Roberts, Bedford Avenue became increasingly African American, especially as one got closer to Bedford Dwellings, a large public housing complex six or so blocks up Bedford that was occupied almost exclusively by African Americans. In the 1940s, Bedford Dwellings was regarded as a highly desirable place to live, featuring nicely furnished kitchens, well-maintained facilities, and lawns on which the children could play in safety.

The most common occupation among Black men in Daisy's part of Bedford was that of mill worker, typically at the Jones & Laughlin Steel works about a mile away in the Oakland neighborhood. Other common jobs for Black people included garbage collector and janitor. Many white people on Bedford also worked in the mills, but they enjoyed a wider range of jobs, such as working in stone quarries and railroad yards. A few white people operated their own business, including a bar, a grocery, a confectionary, and a combination watch-and-shoe repair shop.[37]

Daisy's section of Bedford was congenial as well as diverse. The front of 1727 Bedford housed a Jewish couple, Lou and Bella Siger, who operated Bella's Market, a mom-and-pop grocery store. A friendly woman, Bella occasionally let the Wilson girls Freda and Linda Jean "work" behind the counter.[38] Bella also collected rent for Mr. Rand, the Wilsons's Jewish landlord and owner of the New Bedford Bakery a few doors down the street. Next door to Bella lived an Italian family, the Buteras. Johnny Butera ran a watch-repair business and his brother Louis repaired shoes in the same space.[39] Johnny loved life on Bedford, where he had lived since being born there around the time of World War I. When asked about the neighborhood's race relations, Johnny says they did not socialize much, but were neighborly and "could be counted on in a pinch."[40]

The Goldblums, a Jewish family who operated a tavern nearby, called 1710 Bedford home. On holidays, Anna Goldblum would bring baked goods to the Wilsons and other neighbors. The family had four sons—Albert, Jacob, Abe, and Ray—all of whom became physicians. Albert, in particular, became a beloved fixture when he opened a medical practice in the family's Bedford Avenue home.[41] The Wilson's closest friends were the Burleys, an African American family who moved into the neighborhood in 1948, settling in an attractive row house across the street at 1712 Bedford. Charley was the son of a Black coal miner and an Irish immigrant mother. He hailed from eastern Pennsylvania, and in Pittsburgh was idolized as a legendary prize fighter. Residents often said that Charley should have been a world champion, having defeated Archie Moore, the world light-heavyweight champion, in

1944.[42] Charley's wife Julia—or "Aunt Julie" as she was called by Freddy and the other Wilson kids—was the daughter of a Syrian father and an African American mother. Raised on lower Bedford Avenue among Syrians, Jews, and Black people, Julia retained fond memories of life there. On lower Bedford, she says, Black people, Syrians, and Jews were impoverished but sociable. The women there would gather in a big courtyard and chat while pumping water. And, Julia says, Lower Bedford had a lot of "interracial" children, adding for emphasis, "*a lot of them.*"[43]

Julia became Daisy's closest friend, one of the few people in whom Daisy confided. The friendship began one day while the two women were shopping at Bella's Market. The outgoing and gregarious Julia struck up a conversation with Daisy, who normally kept to herself. Once the ice was broken, Julia invited Daisy to her house and taught her how to play the card game *Tonk*. This began years of sociable card games played in the afternoon before the children came home from school.[44] Julia invited several other neighbors to these afternoon gatherings, notably Minnie Abraham, a Syrian neighbor up the street, and Jenny Butera, Daisy's next-door neighbor. Occasionally, Pearl McClanahan, a Black woman from West Virginia who lived just down from the Buteras, would come over, as did Julia's Aunt Lil, who ran a gambling operation on Townsend Street. The games were highly sociable and entertaining, and the stakes were "high." Julia laughs: "We didn't play just for pennies. Heck no, we played dimes and quarters."

The relationship deepened when Daisy asked Julia if she could take in her mother Zonia, who was in poor health and missing her husband Bynum, who had left Pittsburgh and moved to someplace in the Midwest. To Daisy's eternal gratitude, Julia rented out her upstairs to Zonia and her grown son George, who had been injured in a fall that left him with some sort of mental disability. Julia says Zonia and George were friendly but, like Daisy, stayed to themselves.[45] Zonia passed away two years later, in 1950.

Fred Kittel was father to most of Daisy's children, but he did not live with them on Bedford. Years later, when interviewers would ask Freddy about his father, his replies were short and evasive—"he didn't live with us," or "he wasn't around very much." Freddy's reluctance to talk about his father made some interviewers fear that they were stepping on family secrets.[46] In fact, Freddy's response to questions about his father were misleading but technically correct. Fred did not live with the family and so, as far as the children were aware, was "not around very much." He worked the night shift at the William Penn Hotel, baking bread and pastries for the next day's shoppers.

He got off work around eight in the morning and, navigating a gauntlet of drinking establishments, made his way toward Daisy's. On the way, he often stopped for drinks at Sarasky's Tavern, a block or so down Roberts from the Wilsons's apartment. Before getting to Daisy's, Fred often would stop by the Burleys for an extended chat. By the time he arrived at Daisy's—around nine in the morning—the children had left for school. Fred would spend much of the day at Daisy's and, before the kids arrived home from school, he had taken the trolley back to his home in Overbrook. On weekends, however, Fred stayed overnight, and on Saturday would take Freddy and his younger brother Edwin to the Oyster House Restaurant, a popular eatery downtown on Market Square. There, in a tradition Freddy forever cherished, Fred had drinks at the bar while Freddy and Edwin sat at their favorite table and ate a fish sandwich.[47]

Fred suffered from alcoholism, it being said he drank Muscatel "by the gallon."[48] His talents as a pastry chef made it easy for him to find a job, but his drinking made it difficult to hold on to one. And his public inebriation was an embarrassment for the entire family. It was said that Freddy did not dislike his father so much as he did not respect him, considering him weak and unable to keep a job.[49]

Fred had a deep affection for Daisy. When asked whether he loved her, Julia says emphatically, "Oh, yes *indeedy*. Oh, he loved her, oh my gosh."[50] The attraction was mutual. Fred's drinking exasperated Daisy, but she returned his affection. Fred was handsome. A picture taken in 1914, shortly after his arrival in the United States, shows a handsome, clean-cut nineteen-year-old with dark hair and a boyish face. World War I induction papers describe him as five feet eight inches tall and a trim 140 pounds. Over the years, Fred kept his trim figure and good looks. In addition, he was well-mannered and a bit dapper. Julia describes him as "a nice-looking German guy. . . . . clean shaven . . . tall and very thin . . . straight hair . . . a neat dresser . . . wore slacks rather than overalls and was soft-spoken. He spoke good English, had a good sense of humor, and loved to regale you with stories from work." Julia hoped that some of Fred's stories were tall tales, such as the one about rats falling into the soup during the night and cooks pulling them out in the morning and reheating the soup.[51]

Occasionally, Julia found Fred to be a nuisance. Some mornings he would arrive at Daisy's quite inebriated, and she would not let him in. When that happened, Fred would go back to the Burleys and plead with Charley to "go and tell Daisy to let me in." Or he might ask Julia, plaintively, "Would

Donna"—his term of endearment for Daisy—"let me in?" Sometimes Julia would tell him sharply, "You go and find out." Fred would go back, hollering, "Donna, Donna." Sometimes Daisy became exasperated and chased him away. Usually, however, she let him in, partly to keep him from making a scene that would alert Nellie, the next-door neighbor. Dubbed "Nebby Nose Nellie," she would head to the outdoor privy and listen. Sometimes, Daisy let Fred in out of pity. "After all," Julia says, "she's human and he's human." However, Julia warned her, "You keep letting him in, and that's why you keep getting those babies."[52] Daisy's affection for Fred had no ulterior motive since, other than bringing over rolls and pastries from work, he provided little in the way of financial support.[53]

Daisy never met Fred's wife, although on one occasion she saw her from a distance.[54] Fred and Jennie lived in Overbrook, a blue-collar, white neighborhood in the South Hills. They lived in an attractive Craftsman-style house with gray stucco, hand-built by Fred and his brothers. The home featured hardwood floors, beautiful woodwork, an attractive fireplace, and a long living room. Emil Kittel, grandson of one of Fred's brothers, recalls visiting the house in 1947 when he was about eight years old. Emil liked the house and found Fred more easygoing and fun than the rest of the family. But he also felt that Fred's relaxed mannerisms distanced him from others in the family and caused him to be "pushed to the side." Emil suspects that his visit to Fred's home was the last time a family member saw him before he died some eighteen years later.[55]

Doris Cuddy, one of Fred's neighbors in Overbrook, remembers him and Jennie as "strange" people who lived on a large, wooded lot and kept to themselves. Doris and the other kids dreaded retrieving baseballs that accidentally went into the Kittel's yard because "Old Man Kittel" would angrily chase them away. Doris says Fred's wife Jennie seldom left the house. In addition, Jennie was disheveled, and had "wild" hair. Doris was surprised that Fred and Jennie had a four-year-old son. As far as she knew, they had no children. And certainly, no one knew about Fred's second family in the Hill District. "Oh, my," Doris says, startled. "I never knew that."[56]

Emil remembers Fred as easygoing and fun to be around, but also as someone with an explosive temper. Linda Jean says her father often brought rolls and pastries to the house, but when angry, he might throw the bags on the floor and stomp on them. During his tantrums, the children stayed out of the way, sometimes hiding behind the bed. One Thanksgiving, Fred yanked the door off the oven and Daisy had to prop it up with a stick so that the turkey could finish roasting.[57] On another occasion, an argument ended with Fred standing outside and heaving bricks at the house.[58] Despite these emotional outbursts, Fred never struck Daisy or the children. He was not strong, Julia says, and he definitely was not violent.[59] In fact, Julia is amused at the thought of Fred striking Daisy. "Nobody ever hit Daisy," she says with a laugh. "She would've killed him. She was big."[60] Julia had a soft spot for Fred, but sometimes found him irritating. She describes him as a "happy person" and a "good guy," but also someone who could be "kind of loud . . . a drunk . . . something else." And, she adds, he also could be "full of it."[61]

Although Fred loved Daisy, he showed little outward affection for the children. He seldom came over to celebrate their birthdays and was not the sort of parent who would hug their kids. He enforced a type of old-world regimen in which children were meant to be seen and not heard. While he was reading the paper, the kids had to sit down, be quiet, and not talk or play.[62]

In short, Fred was different things to different people. To his neighbors in Overbrook, he was a mystery. To his grand-nephew Emil, he was a lot of fun. To Julia and Charley Burley, he was a handsome and affable "good guy" who could sometimes be a nuisance. To Linda Jean, he was a caring father whom she dearly loved. To Daisy, he was the father of her children, someone she loved and who loved her in return. To Freddy, he was a source of mixed feelings, someone who could not keep a job and someone who did not fully accept him, but also someone who left him with fond memories of trips on Saturday to the Oyster House Restaurant.

Freddy's mixed feelings about his father caused him to look elsewhere for a father figure. He found one in Charley Burley. Where Fred was weak and struggled to hold a job, Charley was a legendary boxer who had defeated Pittsburgh icon Fritzie Zivic and earned the respect of Archie Moore, the world's long-reigning light-heavyweight champion. Where Fred was physically and emotionally distant, Charley treated Freddy like a son. He and Julia would invite the Wilsons over to watch television, and sometimes would ask them to stay for dinner. Charley became Freddy's idea of what a man should be. "Yeah," Freddy says, "Charley was the first image I had of a man. . . . The way Charley would dress and put that Stetson hat on. And his shoes, his mustache, that's what a man was, and I was going to be like that. I was gonna get some of them Florsheim shoes, get me a hat, you go out. I don't know what the hell you do when you go out. . . . I was just gonna do that."[63]

When Charley walked up Centre Avenue, he was greeted with a chorus of cheers. "Hey Champ, Hey Champ," admirers would call out. Freddy thought so highly of Charley that he would endure anything, including pain, to win his favor. "Charley'd take his knuckles, run 'em on your head, 'Hey champ,' and it'd hurt like hell, but you couldn't let him know it hurt."[64] Freddy admired the way Charley handled disappointment. Once his boxing career was over, he worked as a garbage hauler for the city—similar to Troy Maxson in the play *Fences*. Unlike Troy, however, Charley handled the situation with poise and composure. In fact, a garbage collector's job in those days was not something that most Black men sneered at. But for a potential boxing champion, the job must have been a painful disappointment. Freddy admired Charley for not being bitter as well as for getting along well with his two sons, Charles and David.[65] Charley's example taught Freddy that a champion fights hard but does not hold a grudge or become consumed with bitterness. He is a warrior who gets up off the mat and stays in the ring throwing punches.[66] Charley became the father figure Freddy needed. In fact, Freddy often said he wished Charley were his father.[67] Of course, a father figure can never fully replace a father.

In addition to being neighborly, Bedford Avenue had many places that the Wilson kids could explore and enjoy. They played cowboys and Indians at "Tombstone Rock," the name they gave to a hilly, wooded area at the corner of Webster and Crawford. When feeling adventurous, they might go over to "Redstone Canyon," their name for a wooded area off Cliff Street where the Hill drops precipitously to the Strip District. Sometimes, they would visit "Old Faithful," their name for an area off Arcena Street that had a similarly sharp drop-off. Sometimes they would ogle the nearby incline that transported coal and people between the Hill and the Strip District. Daisy forbade the kids to venture that far from home, but on their way back from school, they sometimes sneaked off and went there anyway.[68]

Schools, churches, and other institutions added to the neighborhood's texture. Connelley Vocational School, which Freddy attended briefly, was one of the most modern and well-equipped trade schools in the nation. Letsche, located near Connelley, was a kindergarten and elementary school with handsome art deco detailing and a playground. Saint George Syrian Orthodox Church, located next to Letsche, boasted an impressive onion dome and front steps where neighborhood kids often hung out. The large and impressive Roselia Foundling Asylum and Maternity Hospital was a source of neighborhood gossip and wonder.[69] Finally, the number 85 Bedford Avenue streetcar squealed and thumped as it went by. As it did, the Wilson kids would wave, and passengers would smile and wave back.

2

Bedford Avenue Outsider

Bedford Avenue was an ideal place for Freddy to spend his childhood.
Quiet, safe, and neighborly as well as racially diverse and racially integrated,
Bedford appealed to Freddy. He loved the neighborhood and considered it a
fine place in which to grow up. "The street I lived on," he said years later, "was
a community of people. I remember coming home from school, and all of the
parents would be sitting on the stoops, talking and exchanging recipes, talking
about what they were cooking for dinner, talking about their kids. That was
a nice neighborhood, in the sense that anyone . . . was your social parent."[1]

Despite the neighborhood's many attractive features, Freddy's years there
left him feeling like an outsider, someone who did not fully belong. As he
reminisced years later, toward the end of his life, he said a bit sorrowfully that
"even on a Saturday, when the rest of the kids would go to the movies, I'd
shoot marbles in my backyard. . . . I was sort of a loner, kept to myself, would
rather read a book."[2] Julia Burley confirms Freddy's self-assessment. She describes him as a "loner" who "just stayed to his self."[3] Loner, or outsider, was
Freddy's earliest and most defining identity.

A number of things contributed to Freddy's outsider identity. His house
made for an isolating experience. Located in the rear of 1727 Bedford Avenue,
it sat well back from the street, hidden behind Bella's Market and accessible

only by way of a long narrow walk and closed off by a gate.[4] Julia pitied the Wilsons for residing in what she disparagingly referred to as "that alley."[5] In addition, the house had a peculiar orientation. It was set at a ninety-degree angle to the street, such that the front door appeared to be a side entrance and the front yard like a side yard. Finally, the house was around a hundred years old and in need of major repairs and maintenance.

Daisy was another factor contributing to Freddy's feeling like an outsider. A very private person, Daisy did not welcome visitors. Julia describes her simply as "not sociable," someone who "stayed to herself."[6] Embarrassment over her relationship with a married man may have been one reason Daisy cut herself off. But Julia does not think so. She and Jenny Butera were the only neighbors who knew about Fred's marital status. In fact, Julia blames Fred more than Daisy for the situation. Sighing in resignation, she says "That's how men do. They have a wife, and then they have a woman on the side."[7] Nor does Julia think that Daisy was embarrassed that Fred was white. In the Hill, she says, there were many mixed-race couples. Julia's father was Syrian, Jenny Butera's son had an African American wife. A Syrian man up the street lived openly with his African American girlfriend. Neighbors did not express disapproval of those relationships.[8] Daisy's strong sense of privacy may have been a family trait. Julia says that when Daisy's mother Zonia lived with her, she seldom came down from her room and was not interested in socializing. In addition, Daisy's brothers John, Frank, and Ray (the latter also known as Detroit) lived on the North Side, but almost never visited Daisy.[9]

Card games at Julia's gradually helped make Daisy more sociable. After a while, she began inviting her upstairs neighbors, Louise and Hedley, to join her and other neighbors in the yard for an afternoon card game, typically pinochle or bid whist. Hedley was a West Indian—or at least someone from the Georgia/South Carolina Low Country, for he spoke with what Julia calls a "Geechee" accent. Sometimes in those afternoon card games, Daisy, Louise, and Hedley were joined by Bobby Lippi and his girlfriend Jeanie, a young Italian American couple who lived in the neighborhood. Daisy and the others would sit around eating fried chicken while Freddy and the other Wilson kids watched in awe as Louise cracked the chicken bones with her teeth and ate the marrow.[10] However, unlike in Wilson's play *Seven Guitars*, the card games took place in the afternoon, and Hedley did not sell chicken sandwiches to those in attendance.

Daisy encouraged the kids to play among themselves in their own back-yard, partly so that she could keep an eye on them from the kitchen window.

And she discouraged other children from coming over to play, even the Butera children who lived next door.[11] Julia's children—Angeline, David, and Charles—were pretty much the only ones who came over regularly to play with the Wilsons. Whereas neighborhood kids rode their bicycles up and down Bedford Avenue and played basketball at Letsche School, Freddy and his siblings (except Richie, the youngest) typically stayed home. Freddy seldom played sports with the other kids, preferring to shoot baskets by himself at Letsche School playground. As Julia says, he "just stayed to his self."[12]

Freddy's main playmate was his sister Linda Jean. The two loved to climb trees, shoot marbles, flip baseball cards, and toss pennies against the house. When the Wilson kids ventured out, they stayed largely to themselves. Freda's son Paul Ellis says the kids "moved as a self-contained tribe, catching caterpillars and lightning bugs in jars, tossing rocks down from Cliff Street toward the Heinz factory and Allegheny River far below, or walking to the library on Wylie Avenue."[13] Sometimes, Daisy had good reasons for keeping Freddy home. Jerry Rhodes, a neighbor and occasional playmate, recalls asking Freddy once why he hadn't been around lately. "Well," Freddy replied, "I used to throw stones at cars, and so my mom would bring me in all summer long . . . to keep an eye on me."[14]

Daisy compensated for her children's social isolation by creating family-centered rituals that gave them something to look forward to. They would sit down to dinner at a certain time. While eating, they would gather around the radio and listen to a set of programs. "Monday at seven the Rosary came on the radio," Freddy recalled. "We said the Rosary . . . Art Linkletter's 'People Are Funny' was Tuesday. . . . Then there was the Top Forty. Everyone got to pick a song. If your song got to No. 1, you got a nickel. Each one would root for his or her song."[15] Daisy loved gardening and grew colorful sunflowers and four o'clocks. She kept a grape arbor for making jelly, and she grew green peppers, tomatoes, and greens in order to have fresh vegetables for dinner. And she joined the kids in games, including *Parcheesi*, Chinese checkers, jacks, bingo, and *Pokeno*. Occasionally, Daisy even played dodgeball and baseball (or at least catch) with them. At Christmas, she would put up a tree and make sure all the children received gifts. A visitor noted that Daisy would wait until Christmas Eve and purchase a $1 tree that she could afford.[16]

Daisy had only a sixth-grade education, but she nurtured the children's intellectual development. She made sure they read every day. She got them secondhand copies of *Grimm's Fairy Tales*, Nancy Drew mysteries, and the Hardy Boys.[17] She taught Freddy to read when he was only four years old and was especially proud of his intellectual development. She called him her "genius son," made him the man of the house, and assured him he could achieve anything he wanted.[18] As Freddy said later, his mother stressed that people who knew how to read could choose their own profession—"a lawyer, a doctor, anything you wanted to be." When Freddy was five, his mother got him a library card, which he cherished. "I wore out my library card," he says, "and cried when I lost it." Daisy was pleased that the Hill Branch of Carnegie Public Library, located nearby, became Freddy's second home, a place where he loved to spend the day reading. When he got home, Freddy would tell the others what he had learned. He did not avoid difficult readings. "I started on the Bible in the fifth grade," he says, "and, skipping the begats, figured I could finish it by the time I was grown." Freddy's reading skills developed to the extent that his kindergarten teacher had him read to the second graders.

Reading helped Freddy escape—at least psychologically—his confining home environment. He would picture himself as part of the stories he read, whether fairy tales, mysteries, or adventures. He especially loved stories about Napoleon Bonaparte, whom he admired as a self-made man who had grown up poorer than his classmates and was teased for talking like a peasant. Freddy played the role of the future emperor so often that playmates nicknamed him "Napoleon."[19] At night, Freddy would lie in bed next to the wall, pick off peeling paint chips, and create stories about the figures that "magically" appeared. Freddy's imagination was further stimulated by his mother's belief in haunts. According to Daisy, a howling dog foretold someone's imminent death. One night, the family heard a dog's mournful howl, followed by footsteps on the stairs leading upstairs to their apartment. They waited nervously for a knock. When none came, they cautiously opened the door but found no one there. However, the mystery put everyone on edge and was never forgotten.[20] Indeed, it may have been the inspiration for the frightening appearance of Sutter's ghost in Wilson's play *The Piano Lesson*.

In addition to helping shape Freddy's identity as an outsider, Daisy bequeathed him a second identity trait. Freddy later termed it a "warrior spirit," meaning persistence in the face of disappointments and standing up for oneself when attacked. Daisy had a ready smile and a twinkle in her eyes, but she had zero tolerance for disrespect. Freddy was proud of the time she rejected a consolation prize of a used washing machine after having won a new Speed Queen in a radio contest. The announcer said that the washer would be given to the first person who called in with the correct answer to a question. Daisy knew the answer, gave a dime to Freda, and told her to run to Bella's store, telephone the station, and say, "Morton Salt!" Not long afterward, the announcer reported they had a winner. Later, however, when the station learned that Daisy was African American, it offered her only a used washing machine from the Salvation Army. Furious, Daisy rejected the offer, despite entreaties from Julia about how badly she needed a washer. Freddy long remembered his mother's rationale for refusing the prize: "Something is not always better than nothing." After this disappointment, Daisy saved up nickels and quarters and, with the help of Herb Glickman, a neighborhood freelance merchant, bought herself a new washing machine. It took years, but Freddy considered it an example of Daisy's "warrior spirit," a trait he acquired from his mother and cultivated in himself.[21]

Daisy was resilient. When asked if she used salty language, Julia says, "Like a sailor!" She adds, sheepishly, "We both did." Daisy was not afraid of physical confrontation. On one occasion she got into a heated argument with a woman who brought charges against one of the children, most likely Freddy. Fortunately, Julia's husband Charley was in the vicinity, or things might have gotten out of hand. Indeed, Daisy later told Julia, "I would'a killed [that woman] if Charley hadn't been there."[22] Despite Daisy's combativeness, she discouraged Freddy from fighting, advising him to do so only when attacked. Freddy usually followed his mother's wishes, but he too harbored a volatile temper. One time, he hit his sister Donna so hard that he broke her jaw.[23] Some believe Freddy inherited his temper from his father, but Julia insists he got it from Daisy.[24]

Freddy's light complexion and biracial background contributed to his sense of being an outsider. Freddy admired his mother for insisting on her identity as African American, correcting anyone who mistook her for an Italian or Syrian.[25] Later in life, Freddy emphasized his own racial identity as Black. He did this partly by downplaying his father's importance and insisting that his African American mother raised him in a fully Black environment. "I learned Black culture at my mother's knee," he told an interviewer. "The cultural environment of my life, the forces that have shaped me, the nurturing, the learning, have all been black ideas about the world that I learned from my mother."[26] Years later, in his most famous public address, "The Ground on Which I Stand," he described his mother as part of a chain of culture bearers binding together Africa and African America. "Growing up in my mother's house," he emphatically intoned, "I learned the language, the eating habits, the religious beliefs, the gestures, the notions of common sense, attitudes towards sex, concepts of beauty and justice, and the responses to pleasure and pain that my mother had learned from her mother, and which you could trace back to the first African who set foot on the continent."[27]

Such assertions were more aspirational than factual. Daisy was born in the South, but hailed from a part that was overwhelmingly white, both numerically and culturally. She cooked Southern dishes, but not chitterlings. She did not speak "Black English" and did not even have much of a Southern accent.[28] She preferred Top 40 radio songs to blues, jazz, or gospel music.[29] She forbade the children to attend services at Reverend Green's Holy Temple Church of God in Christ, an African American Pentecostal church located just a few doors from the family's residence. The church's emotional services fascinated the Wilson kids, but they had to listen to them while standing outside on the sidewalk.[30]

Despite Daisy's pride in her racial identity, she often exhorted Freddy, "Don't go out there and show your color." Freddy knew his mother simply meant for him to behave well in public, but he resented the racial implication. As he complained, "If you say showing your color is bad, you're saying, 'don't go down there and act . . . black.' Why would you tell a black kid that?"[31] The barbershop was one of the few places where Freddy was exposed to Black culture. He loved listening to the men there banter and tell wonderful stories.[32]

Growing up in a racially mixed environment enabled Freddy to see white people as individuals rather than through a strictly racial prism. After Daisy's unhappy experience with the washing machine, it was Herbert Glickman, a white salesman from the neighborhood, who helped her get a new washer. "Herbert Glickman," Wilson said, "God bless him."

> He did not have the money to pay for a washing machine . . . he'd go get some customers, and he'd go down to the store and say, "Look, I want to buy five washing machines, let me owe you"—because he *could* get credit. And then he would come around, and he would charge you—and of course he'd charge you, naturally, a little more than he'd pay for it. But he was willing to take a dollar a week or a dollar a month, so you could pay him on credit. . . . And had it not been for him, there was a whole lot of blacks who wouldn'ta had *nothin'*. We wouldn'ta had no radio. We wouldn'ta had no washing machine. We wouldn'ta had God knows what else without Herb Glickman—and people like him. He was an honest man—and a hard-working man, at that.[33]

Freddy's complexion and hair texture also contributed to his outsider identity. Four of his siblings—Linda Jean, Donna, Edwin, and Richard—appeared unambiguously "white." Two others—Freda and Barbara—had caramel complexions that identified them as African American. However, it was difficult to visually determine Freddy's race. His complexion marked him as white, but his hair texture proclaimed him as African American. His sisters Linda Jean and Donna did not help matters. They teasingly called him a "nappy-headed nigger," the sort of taunt that, at an early age and coming from within one's family, can raise painful issues of identity and belonging.[34] In addition, Freddy and his sister Freda were never fully accepted by their father. Fred Kittel's favorite child was Linda Jean, whom Julia terms a "daddy's girl."[35] Fred had little interest in Freda, the oldest daughter. Among the boys, he favored Edwin and was distant from Freddy. One of the few stories Freddy tells about his father is the time he took him downtown to get some Gene Autry cowboy boots. On the way, he gave Freddy some coins and told him to "jingle it" so people would know he had money.[36]

One likely reason that Fred was not close to Freddy and Freda was that their hair texture and/or complexion made them the only Wilson children identifiable as African American and not Fred's offspring. Julia never saw signs that Fred harbored racial prejudice, but Freda did. "I don't think [dad] ever accepted black people," she says.[37]

At school, racial identity and racial acceptance bedeviled Freddy and his sisters. Kindergarten classmates were puzzled by the girls' appearance and would ask them, "What are you?" Uncertain how to reply, they asked their mother, who advised them to say, "I'm a light-complexioned colored girl."[38] That did not work. Questioning turned into bullying, with the girls and Freddy ultimately being called "white crackers" and chased home from school. To put an end to such harassment, Daisy one day hid beside the long, narrow walk to her house and doused the pursuers with a tub of cold water. The next day, a contingent of mothers came by to protest, but left when Daisy stood her ground. A few days later, the kids returned with older friends. These too retreated when Daisy confronted them, but as they left, one heaved a brick through the Buteras's window next door.[39] Freddy and his sisters no longer were chased home, but the experience undoubtedly left him feeling less than fully accepted.

Freddy's experience was not unique. Melvin Williams grew up nearby on Cassatt Street and attended Letsche a few years before Freddy. Like Freddy, Williams got chased home by darker-skinned classmates. His parents complained, but the school did nothing about it.[40] Wali Jamal, a noted Wilsonian actor, says that when he was growing up in Homestead and Arlington Heights, he innocently joined others in harassing light-skinned and mixed-race kids. "We were very, very mean to them," Jamal says, something he regrets to this day.[41]

Partly to avoid such harassment, Freddy transferred to St. Brigid, a parochial school located nearby on Wylie Avenue. The transfer was partly the result of efforts by Sarah Degree, a Black woman in the neighborhood who made it her mission to convert Black children to Catholicism. Indeed, every Catholic that Freddy knew in the Hill had been brought to the church by way of "Miss Sarah," as she was called. Sometime in 1951, Miss Sarah saw Freddy and his sisters playing in front of their house. "Where you live?" she asked them. "I want to go talk to your mother." Sarah asked Daisy for permission to take her children to church. Daisy had no objections because she herself had no church affiliation and Miss Sarah was highly regarded in the neighborhood. Residents had often seen her, dressed in white and leading Black children down Webster Avenue in perfect order, two by two.[42]

"For Miss Sarah," Wilson recalled later, "everything was the Church and God. She had a thousand statues in her house." In 1954, when Daisy spent a week in the hospital after giving birth to Richard, Miss Sarah let the Wilson children stay with her. While there, Wilson later said, "We had Sunday School every day. At six o'clock, there's Miss Sarah teachin' us about the Bible. We had to sit there in this hot room in the middle of the summer with Miss Sarah . . . teachin' us stories from the Bible and makin' us say the Rosary every night at seven o'clock."[43] Miss Sarah became very special to Freddy. "If there was ever a saint," he said years later, "it was Miss Sarah."[44] Ultimately, Sarah became the inspiration for Aunt Ester, the woman he regarded as the most important character in his cycle of plays. Because of Miss Sarah, Freddy and his sisters Freda and Linda Jean converted to Catholicism and began attending to St. Brigid. Not long afterward, Daisy joined them and converted to Catholicism.[45]

Freddy and his sisters converted partly because Catholic schools had strict behavior codes that made harassment much less common than in public schools like Letsche.[46] Still, although St. Brigid spared Freddy color-based harassment, it did not change his identity as an outsider. A photograph taken inside to St. Brigid Church shows someone in the fourth pew who looks like Freddy, sitting forlornly by himself, reading.[47]

In the early 1950s, at the time of Freddy's conversion to Catholicism, St. Brigid was located at 1839 Wylie just behind the parish church. Like other Catholic churches in the Hill, it was falling on hard times. Established as an Irish parish, its congregation was dwindling as parishioners moved out to other neighborhoods. By the mid-1950s, the parish had ninety-six Black families and seventy-eight white.[48] As the numbers declined, the diocese invested fewer resources in to St. Brigid, causing a deterioration in the physical condition of both the church and the school.[49] Trying to save to St. Brigid may have been why Miss Sarah had begun recruiting African Americans.[50]

Not long after enrolling at St. Brigid, Freddy transferred to Holy Trinity, a large, better-maintained church that today is known as St. Benedict the Moor. Located at the intersection of Centre Avenue and Crawford Street, Holy Trinity had been erected in the 1890s to serve the Hill's German community. By the 1950s, however, Germans had largely left the Hill. As a result, the parish began recruiting Black congregants like Freddy. In 1952 he became part of Holy Trinity's small but growing African American student body.[51]

At Holy Trinity, where he spent the third and fourth grades, Freddy formed a friendship with Samuel Howze (later Sala Udin)—a Black student two years his senior. Both boys were proud to attend Holy Trinity. They ignored snide remarks made by other Black students about the "spooky" habits worn by nuns. They insisted they were getting a good education and learning to speak "proper" English.[52] At Holy Trinity, Freddy performed well, earning A's in all his courses.[53] However, in class he was shy and reserved, often hesitating to speak up. And in play period, he would stand back and not join in games with the other students.[54]

In 1955, as urban renewal was preparing to take down Holy Trinity's parish school, Freddy transferred to St. Richard, located a dozen or so blocks up Bedford Avenue from his home.[55] Freddy spent the fifth through seventh grades at St. Richard, where he remained a shy outsider. However, in the fifth grade, Freddy's shyness turned into a form of rebelliousness that led him to challenge teachers. "I would ask questions," Wilson said, "and [the nuns] would say 'Shut up. Sit down' because they didn't know the answers. So, I'd go to the library to find out."[56] When a teacher said that the Holy Trinity was an unfathomable mystery that could not be comprehended by man, Freddy asked himself "Why not?" and went to the library in search of proof to the contrary.[57] Over time, he became increasingly obstreperous, given to yelling answers out of turn.[58] Doing so was partly a sign of a questioning spirit, but also an indicator of an emerging rebellious edge, something he later called a "warrior spirit." As he put it, "I questioned everything, especially religion. In fifth grade, they taught us the Adam and Eve story. They said the serpent lied to Eve. I got the Bible, and I read where God said the serpent didn't lie. I thought I'd made a great discovery. I thought they were gonna' call up the Pope and send me to Rome. Sister Mary Eldephonse said, 'Sit down.' I was crushed."[59]

Despite his rebelliousness, Freddy became an altar boy, a coveted position that signaled one's enthusiastic embrace of the Catholic faith. Teachers and staff at St. Richard were caring, congenial, and unbiased. The school's principal, Father Connare, was admired by Black people as someone who was strict but did not tolerate racial discrimination.[60] The school's teachers, moreover, did not fit the stereotyped notion of nuns. For example, Sister Christopher played basketball in full nun's habit and could drive to the hoop like a professional.[61]

Black children constituted some two thirds of St. Richard's student body, a much larger proportion than at St. Brigid and Holy Trinity. Many of the white students were of Slavic descent and resided in the nearby neighborhood known as Polish Hill. Black students came from two distinct neighborhoods.[62] Some, like Freddy's friend Samuel Howze, came from blue-collar families in the Bedford Dwellings public housing project. Others were the children of Black middle-class families, many of whom lived in the Upper Hill, a neighborhood far removed from Freddy's part of Bedford, socially and economically. Nicknamed "Sugar Top" for the sweet life residents there presumably enjoyed, the Upper Hill housed much of the Hill District's Black elite.

Soon after enrolling at St. Richard, Freddy acquired a friend in the person of fellow student Tony Kirven. Tony certainly was well-off. His family vacationed on Martha's Vineyard, his stepfather owned the Star Pharmacy on Wylie, his uncle had a dental practice on Centre Avenue, and his cousin Birdie Dunlap owned the Hurricane Bar, a popular, highly respected night club on Centre Avenue. Quite naturally, Tony lived in Sugar Top.

Despite the socioeconomic differences in their background, Tony and Freddy got along well. This was partly because both were outstanding students. Freddy had always gotten A's in school and teachers regularly assured his mother that he could be anything he wanted.[63] Tony also excelled academically and enjoyed competing. He relished the time at St. Richard when he bested Freddy and received the top marks on the school's combined history, geography, and science test.[64] Freddy may not have gotten the top marks on the test, but his embrace of Catholicism gave him bragging rights. Teachers and staff loved that he had been an altar boy at Holy Trinity and that he continued as one at St. Richard. Freddy gained additional prestige when he underwent confirmation and let it be known that he planned to become a priest. In that respect, Freddy was echoing similar desires of his sisters Freda and Linda Jean, who wanted to become nuns.[65] Tony was not interested in a career with the church but resented that Freddy's embrace of Catholicism had displaced him as the school's unofficial "teacher's pet."[66]

At St. Richard, Freddy's interest in girls bloomed. He fixated first on Cathy Moran, a white classmate he had come to know at Holy Trinity. The infatuation blossomed during the school's Christmas pageant, in which Freddy was assigned the task of clanging the cymbals that announce the arrival of the Three Wise Men. During rehearsals, Freddy took notice of Cathy, whom he describes as a "small waiflike girl [with] jet-black hair and deep black eyes." Simply looking into her eyes unnerved him. Cathy came to occupy his every thought. On the day of the pageant, Freddy went into the cloakroom to retrieve the cymbals. Cathy was there and handed them to him. Freddy says it was like "handing Lancelot his sword." In the heat of the moment, he kissed her. In the pageant, Freddy remained so distracted thinking about Cathy that he forgot to bang the cymbals.

Freddy next fixated on Nancy Ireland, a blonde girl to whom he wrote what is the earliest known example of his poetry.

> I would I could mend my festering heart
> Harpooned by Cupid's flaming dart
> But too far the shaft did penetrate
> Alas, it is too late.[67]

Rather than sign the poem, Freddy surreptitiously left it on Nancy's desk. Unfortunately, Nancy assumed that Tony was the poem's author because his desk sat directly across from hers. Ultimately, Freddy's crush on Nancy ended his desire to become a priest when he realized marriage and the priesthood were not compatible.[68]

Years earlier, during Freddy's time at Letsche, his light complexion had gotten him chased home after school. At St. Richard, it strengthened his relationship, at least with Tony. "Back then," Tony says, "you figured that if a kid was light-skinned, the parents are trying to move up the ladder." Tony had a combination of light complexion and "good" hair that made him passably white. Such traits conferred prestige in some circles, but at St. Richard, they made Tony the target of resentment by darker-skinned classmates. As a result, Tony says, "I was more or less a loner because I refused to hang around people who didn't accept me."[69]

Freddy, however, identified exclusively as African American. He didn't fraternize much, but when he did, it was mostly with the school's darker-skinned students.[70] He tried especially to make friends with the "roughest" of those students—Robert Jenkins, Robert Ayers, and J. D. Penny, the brother of Freddy's later friend Rob Penny. Many students at St. Richard feared those three. Sala Udin says Jenkins and Penny were "rough," and Ayers was "rough *for real*."[71] During recess, Ayers, Jenkins, and Penny would pick on middle-class kids from Sugar Top, taking their lunch money and sometimes beating them up.[72]

But no one harassed Freddy. Things had changed from his time in kindergarten. At St. Richard, he proved quite capable of defending himself. "Freddy wasn't anybody to play with," Tony says. "I mean Freddy could *fight*."[73] Sala's brother, Reggie Howze (later known as Abdullah) confirms Tony's assessment. Reggie says people knew better than to "mess with" Freddy. If they did, he would "just go off," turn red in the face, put his tongue between his teeth, and make "some kind of wild sound like an animal." Students knew that "unless you were really ready for some big chaos, you would leave Freddy alone."[74] However, despite his physical prowess, Freddy never gained acceptance among the school's "rough" students. "That's the way it went," Tony says. "The darker-skinned kids thought that we were too snooty [and] trying to be white."[75]

The problem was more than complexion. Freddy's unfamiliarity with African American street culture undercut his acceptance by the rougher students. Like others in his family, he did not speak Black vernacular. And he did not play the "dozens," a game of ritualized insults, often told in rhyme, that was popular among young Black men and boys.[76] Tony says that Freddy was rejected by the "rough guys" but was not interested in hanging out with middle-class Black children. For example, he turned down an invitation to join the Boy Scouts, a popular organization in Sugar Top.[77] Freddy would run with a couple of kids for a while, Tony says, but he remained "basically an outsider" and "just didn't socialize that much."[78] Freddy existed in what could have been a dangerous no-man's-land, although Tony thinks that staying unaffiliated provided him a form of emotional protection. "To survive in the Lower Hill," Tony says," you had to have a hard shell around you and stay the outsider."[79] Even had Freddy wanted to make friends with kids from Sugar Top, it would not have been easy. His father was white and his mother was unmarried—realities that broke two key rules for membership in the Black middle class.[80] Freddy's hygiene also would have been a problem. His teeth had a greenish-yellow cast, which, Tony concluded, was the result of attitude more than finance. "How much does a toothbrush cost?" Tony asks.[81] Finally, the isolated location of Freddy's house and its deteriorated condition created additional barriers. Tony's parents had told him that the Lower Hill was "off-limits" for him. One day he decided to defy them and visit Freddy at his home. But when he got there, he found the house "so beat up" that he changed his mind. "Oh, hell no!" he told himself, "I'm not going in there."[82]

Freddy's warrior spirit—a trait he admired in his mother and nurtured in himself—manifested itself at St. Richard in ever-stronger acts of truculence. The movies he most wanted to see were those the Catholic Church had banned.[83] He cut class so often that the school filed truancy charges. Thelma Lovette, a social worker for the school district, investigated the charges and found that Freddy had been cutting class mainly to go to the public library, where he spent his time reading, no doubt to challenge something a teacher had said.[84] As Freddy admitted later, he was a "smartass" who enjoyed provoking the nuns.[85]

Freddy may have been a smartass, but he was not antisocial. Rather, he was polite, soft-spoken, and always tried to find the good in people.[86] He wanted to be popular, and so would do wacky things to win the attention of others. Almost every day, classmates asked each other excitedly, "What is Freddy going to do next?" Sometimes, Tony said, it seemed like Freddy was becoming "unhinged,"[87] displaying a zaniness that was hard to distinguish from simple agitation. In class, he had trouble sitting still and keeping quiet. When not in class, he spoke nervously, in an agitated, rapid way. And he had small, intense eyes that projected what Tony describes as "an unforgettable fierceness."[88] Tony thinks Freddy "probably should have been on Ritalin."[89]

A student acting out like Freddy was doing often signals that something is wrong at home. In fact, a new man had entered the family's life: David Bedford. Thirteen years older than Daisy and with a checkered past, "Dave," as he was called, hailed from Houston, Texas, where his father was an attorney and realtor.[90] Around 1920, Dave's parents separated and Dave and his mother moved to Pittsburgh, where they settled in the Lower Hill. Dark, stout, and muscular, Dave had difficulty adjusting. He played on the Fifth Avenue High School football team, but in 1923, at the age of sixteen, he dropped out of school and began working as a general laborer.[91] The next year, Dave was arrested as a "suspicious person"—a common charge against Black people during police sweeps. Like Floyd Barton in Wilson's play *Seven Guitars*, he served thirty days in the workhouse. The following year, Dave was charged with disturbing the peace; two years later, he was arrested for being in a cabaret that served alcoholic beverages; the year after that he was arrested for gambling.[92]

By 1931, things seemed to have settled down. Dave married, found work as a janitor, and was living with his wife, Ethel, on Centre Avenue.[93] However, one summer day his world turned upside down. In an attempt to rob the downtown Walgreen Drug Store where he worked, Dave shot and killed the manager. At his trial, he said the robbery was part of a "desperate search" for money after being told that he was about to be laid off because he was too large to work behind the soda fountain. He hid in the cellar until he thought everyone had left. But, unbeknown to him, the store manager and another person had not left. Panicked, Dave shot the manager and ran out.[94] He was arrested a few days later and tried for murder. Dave would not have had the money to hire good legal counsel, but someone, possibly a parent, hired Robert Vann, prominent editor of the *Pittsburgh Courier*, to defend him. Vann won Dave life in prison, which at the time was an unusually mild sentence for a Black man convicted of killing a white person.[95]

Sentenced to Pittsburgh's Western Penitentiary, Dave proved to be a model prisoner. He studied tailoring, coached the football team, and refereed basketball games. In 1954, after serving twenty-three years, he was paroled, partly because in 1953 he had not participated in a massive riot at the prison.[96] It also helped that influential figures spoke on Dave's behalf. Again, this may have been the influence of Dave's parents. Whatever the reason, Dave secured the services of Paul Jones, one of the city's leading Black attorneys, to represent him before the parole board. Howard McKinney, the highly respected African American head of the Hill City Boys Club, promised to serve as Dave's sponsor if he was released, and Charlie Solomon, the powerful white leader of the Hill's Democratic Party, pledged to find Dave steady employment.[97] That Dave could garner such high-profile support is as unusual as his original life sentence.

Placed on ten-year probation, Dave got a job through Charlie Solomon cleaning sewers for the water department. It was not pleasant work, but it provided a decent, steady income.[98] After he got out of prison, Dave led a quiet, law-abiding life. He moved in with his mother, Mary Noble, at 1824 Bedford, a block up the street from the Wilson family. A year later, in 1955, Dave married Viola Thaxton, a twenty-six-year-old widow. The wedding was covered in the *Pittsburgh Courier*'s society section, evidence that Dave had become a respectable figure in the community.[99] Because Dave's mother lived just a block from Daisy, it was almost inevitable that the two would meet. We don't know how or when that happened, but at some point, Dave separated from Viola and moved in with Daisy.

As a protégé of Solomon, Dave became active in local politics. He served as ward committeeman for the Lower Hill. In that capacity, he worked alongside

Louis "Hop" Kendrick, a political activist, businessman, county detective, and later *Pittsburgh Courier* columnist.[100] Dave and Hop held political meetings at Daisy's home, much to her annoyance. Daisy had never liked visitors and she generally made things unpleasant for the men. "I remember it like it was yesterday," Hop says angrily. "She never let us in the house. In fact, she would never open the door! We would knock on the door, and she would come, look out and see who it is, and say 'Bedford! Its Hop and Tony and them!' [Dave] would come and open the door and we would go straight down to the cellar. . . . We had to go down in the cellar! It wasn't a game room; it was the cellar!"[101]

Daisy may have been impatient with Dave's political meetings, but she was more than ready for a change. She was thirty-eight years old, and life with Fred had been confining and financially unrewarding. Julia said a bit sarcastically that Fred was "just interested in coming over." And, as a "good Catholic," he could not divorce Jennie.[102] In addition, Daisy was tired of her home on Bedford, having lived in its cramped, unpleasant quarters for sixteen years. Dave had a modest but decent income, earning $4,595 a year, equivalent to about $40,000 today. He was married, but in 1958 he left Viola and informed his probation officer that he intended to file for divorce.[103] Shortly thereafter, Dave moved Daisy and the children to Hazelwood, a predominantly white, blue-collar neighborhood about four miles from the Hill. Hazelwood opened a new chapter in the story of Daisy, Freddy, and the other children. Freddy would spend his teen years in Hazelwood, where he acquired a second identity trait: that of warrior.

3

Hazelwood Warrior

During his years in Hazelwood, Freddy retained his identity as an outsider. But he also acquired a second identity, one he described as that of a "warrior," someone with a combative mentality who won't quit in the face of setbacks and who won't tolerate disrespect. During his time at St. Richard, Freddy evinced the beginnings of a warrior mentality. He regularly challenged his teachers and made himself something he termed a "smartass." But in Hazelwood, Freddy's combativeness increased severalfold, provoking clashes with teachers and students alike. These clashes resulted in his withdrawing from two schools—Central Catholic and Connelley Vocational. Ultimately, at the age of sixteen and still in the ninth grade, Freddy's warrior spirit resulted in his quitting school altogether, to the bitter disappointment of his mother.

Freddy's heightened rebelliousness reflects the degree to which life in Hazelwood differed from what he had known in the Hill. Certainly, things were better financially. Dave Bedford's steady job enabled the family to secure much better housing,[1] allowing them to move into a well-maintained duplex at 185 Flowers Avenue. In addition to having an attractive, tree-lined yard, the duplex boasted a dining room, a kitchen, and separate bedrooms for the boys, the girls, and the parents.[2] In other ways, however, Hazelwood presented new challenges. For decades, the neighborhood's massive Jones & Laughlin Steel works had provided residents ample job opportunities—Italians on the railroad, Slavs and Black people in the mills. With plentiful jobs, the neighborhood enjoyed relatively harmonious race relations. However, in the 1950s, the steel industry entered a long-term decline, one that caused jobs to vanish and resentful white people to move out. As white people moved out, Black people were moving in, the latter a by-product of Pittsburgh's extensive urban redevelopment initiatives when, beginning in 1956, the city razed much of the Lower Hill. Thousands of Black residents were in desperate search of housing elsewhere. Many moved into the neighborhoods of Homewood and Hazelwood.

As Black people moved in, relations became tense not just between Black people and white people, but even between Black newcomers and their long-established counterparts. Marva Scott-Starks, the daughter of Hazelwood's most prominent Black minister, came from a family that had long resided in Hazelwood. She was critical of the newcomers. "I'm not saying that all the people who lived in the Hill District were poor," she says, "just that the ones that came to Hazelwood were. Hazelwood used to be a very desirable neighborhood. Now it's a different story."[3] Marva says Daisy would have preferred that earlier Hazelwood, which was pleasant and quiet, with good jobs and little crime, a place where residents could go to sleep at night and never lock their doors.[4]

Hazelwood's most serious tensions had a racial dimension. In 1958, the year the Wilsons moved in, Gladstone High School began accepting transfer students from Squirrel Hill and the South Side, two predominantly white neighborhoods whose children had little experience interacting with nonwhite people. When school opened in the fall, racial fighting broke out around Gladstone High School. *The Pittsburgh Courier* blamed the fighting partly on aggressive white parents and bullying white youth. It also blamed it on aggressive Black students who, it said, were "hijacking" white students' lunch money.[5] Daisy and her family had not moved to Hazelwood because of urban renewal, but nonetheless they became the first Black people to reside on Flowers Avenue. Not long after they moved in, a rock came crashing through their window bearing a note that read: "Nigger stay out."[6] Given that the word *nigger* was used in the singular, it probably referred to Dave, the only dark-skinned and recognizably African American member of the household. The rock incident was Freddy's first encounter with overt racism. Already something of a warrior, he quickly became feistier and much more racially sensitive. In Hazelwood, he began to see life through the prism of race.

Seeking a less racially charged neighborhood, the Wilsons moved into a duplex at 4738 Sylvan Avenue, four or so blocks from Flowers. There were drawbacks to the family's new residence. It sat across the street from Gladstone High School, which had recently endured racial conflict. Moreover, despite its name, Sylvan was not tree lined. Rather, it lay only a few blocks from the massive, highly polluting J&L Steel works that lined both sides of the nearby Monongahela River. Happily, the new duplex was spacious, featuring separate bedrooms for the girls, the boys, and the parents.[7] And, largely because most white people on Sylvan had already moved out or were planning to do so, it had less racial tension than Flowers.[8] The Wilsons's apartment had previously housed a family from Hungary, who had immigrated to the United States following that country's large anti-Communist uprising in the mid-1950s. When the Hungarians moved out, the landlord rented the duplex to two Black families—the Wilsons and the Crenshaws.[9] The duplex on the other side of the Wilsons housed a white family; the one on the side of the Crenshaws housed Marva Scott-Starks, the prominent, longtime resident of Hazelwood. Marva and her family had moved onto Sylvan two years previously, becoming one of the first Black families on the street.[10]

On Sylvan, Daisy showed signs of embarrassment regarding her marital status. The city directory, which came out annually, designated "Fred Kittel" as head of the household and "Daisy Kittel" sometimes as Fred's "wife," sometimes as his "widow."[11] The way the family was listed also may have been because Daisy wanted to give herself and the children the same last name. On Bedford, the directory had listed the children's family name as Kittel and Daisy's as Wilson. On Sylvan, the directory gave the family name of them all as Kittel.[12]

Daisy and the children quickly settled into life on Sylvan. However, neighbors there were a bit slow in warming up to Dave. Some were puzzled by the color difference between him and the rest of the family. Others were intimidated by Dave's stocky build and stern demeanor. "He never had a smile on his face," Marva says critically. Dave gradually won over the neighbors, though. Marva liked that he was soft-spoken and did not use foul language around the children. She also liked that she did not hear any quarreling at their duplex. And she especially liked that when Dave went to the grocery, he would ask her mother if there was anything she wanted him to bring back.[13] Finally, Marva was stunned by the way Dave treated Daisy.[14] She exclaims, "There wasn't anything he wouldn't do for her," whispering excitedly, "Daisy really ran the household!"[15]

Marva was not the only one impressed by the way Dave treated Daisy.[16] Julia Burley says in awe, "He gave her everything." Especially impressive,

Fred taught Daisy to drive and gave her free use of his car, a handsome, late-model, light-blue Cadillac. Daisy treasured the car, both for its beauty and for the sense of freedom it gave her. In order to protect the car's finish from the sulfurous coating deposited every night by the nearby mills, Daisy enlisted Freddy and some of the other children to help her wash the car almost on a daily basis.[17] On weekends, she sometimes drove Julia to Warren, Ohio, to visit her mother. Fondly remembering her own childhood in rural North Carolina, Daisy liked to walk around the garden and gaze fondly at the vegetables.[18] Although Julia admired the way Dave treated Daisy, she never fully warmed to him. The two had once worked together on ward political matters, and Julia had found Dave overbearing and opinionated. In addition, Julia may have harbored a bit of color prejudice. "He had this big yellow woman," she says sharply, "so he was happy."[19]

Freddy admired Dave, even though his arrival in the household displaced him as the man of the house.[20] In fact, all the children liked Dave because he treated them fairly. Dave's caring, supportive attitude showed Freddy that a former convict can also be an admirable person, something he later would depict in his plays. Freddy came to think of Dave as a warrior who had broken the law because he refused to accept society's racial injustices.

Not long after Daisy and the family moved onto Sylvan Avenue, Freddy acquired a new friend. It happened one wintry day when Earl Horsley, Marva's nephew and Freddy's next-door neighbor, heard a steady thump on Gladstone High School's outdoor basketball court.[21] As on Bedford, Freddy was shooting hoops by himself. Earl walked over and asked him his name. "Freddy Kittel" came the reply, followed by a startling announcement: "I hate that name." That assertion was followed by the even more startling announcement that one day he would change his name to August. Earl had never known anyone with a name such as "August." At a loss for words, Earl simply replied, "Oh," and let it go.[22] Despite the abrupt introduction, the two boys quickly became friends.

Freddy had a good jump shot and liked to play forward. Simply playing, however, was not good enough for Freddy. He regarded basketball as an expression of the warrior spirit, and so he practiced hard, all year long. Most kids quit playing when it snowed, but Freddy would shovel off the snow and spend hours shooting hoops by himself.[23] Now that he knew Earl, though, the two played against each other regularly. Occasionally, they even traveled around the city looking for pickup games.[24] Their radius expanded when another neighbor, Denny Hollis, joined in. The three pooled their money, came up with thirty-five dollars, and bought an old Dodge automobile so that they could compete in pickup games around the city. Because they were too young to have a license, they would park the car some distance from Sylvan in order to keep their parents from finding out what they had done.

Freddy loved baseball as well as basketball. As usual, being good was simply not good enough. He needed to excel. "I was going to hit 756 home runs," he vowed to himself. "It was going to be me and Hank Aaron."[25] Freddy played left field in Hazelwood's Prep League, proud that he was the only sixteen-year-old good enough to earn a spot on the starting team. Freddy was not a good fielder, and he couldn't hit a curveball. But he realized that crowding the plate made him the team's home-run champion. It was a big no-no for the pitcher to hit a batter, and so rather than risk hitting someone who crowded the plate, pitchers threw fastballs—which Freddy knew how to hit.[26]

Freddy's competitive streak was obvious to everyone. His sister Freda called him "a sorry loser" who always played to win. "Not winning was just highly unacceptable," she says.[27] Along with a determination to win came an emotional vulnerability that soon ended his baseball career. Freddy and the coach's son both struck out twice in a game. The third time Freddy came up to bat, the coach's son told him that he had been designated to bat in Freddy's stead. Freddy refused to relinquish the bat, and the two began arguing. Fans yelled for Freddy to sit down, but pride and determination got in the way. Finally, Freddy dropped the bat and walked toward center field. He was simply exiting the playground, but his appearance was so fierce that the pitcher ran off the mound, worried that Freddy was coming to beat him up. In reality, Freddy says, "I couldn't even see the pitcher because I was crying." When Freddy got home, his mother told him that the coach wanted his uniform. "He can have it," Freddy replied, ending his hopes of becoming the next Hank Aaron.[28]

Being kicked off the baseball team was especially painful because sport was Freddy's only social outlet. "He did not run the streets with the guys," Earl says. Nor did he go to the movies with other kids. And, except on rare occasions, he did not attend neighborhood parties and dances.[29] Moreover, kids didn't go over to Freddy's house like they did with other families.[30] Occasionally, Freddy attended events at the Glen Hazel Recreation Center, but would spend the evening there sitting by himself in the corner, scribbling.[31]

Sports helped reduce Freddy's sense of being an outsider, but other things worked to reinforce it. Without the benefit of Julia's card games, Daisy socialized less than before, and almost never had visitors. Marva says that even though she lived next door to the Kittels, there were few conversations. Most interactions consisted simply of a quick "good morning."[32] In addition, Hazelwood's Black community was small, clannish, and slow to accept newcomers. The community consisted largely of six or seven extended families who had lived there for generations—the Campbells, Trambles, Godfreys, Kings, Pingers, Williams, and McGruders. Joann Brown, a long-term resident, says locals considered Freddy and his family "newbies" and outsiders.[33] Because of this, Freddy was "very much a loner." Joann's cousin adds that local Black people felt Freddy "didn't belong there [and] made it known that he didn't."[34]

In addition to being excluded by Black people, Freddy was treated by local white people with the same disdain they accorded other African Americans. His siblings Linda Jean, Donna, Edwin, and Richard were accepted by locals because their light complexions and smooth hair texture that made them "white." Freddy, however, suffered racial discrimination that most of his siblings were spared.[35] White people in Hazelwood even had trouble distinguishing Freddy from clearly dark-skinned Black people. Once, to protest a white club's discriminatory policy, Earl and a friend put sand in members' gas tanks. Someone saw them do that and called the police. Freddy was picked up as a suspect and, although Earl and his friends had dark complexions, club members identified Freddy as one of the perpetrators. The case was dropped only when Freddy proved he had been somewhere else at the time.[36]

Race relations in Hazelwood were not always hostile.[37] Earl had grown up next to the mills in the impoverished, racially diverse Kansas Street neighborhood. There, Earl had a number of Italian friends, and sometimes ate over at their house. Racial tolerance even extended to neighborhood gangs. "White, black, no name-calling or nothing," Earl says. However, when Earl's family moved onto Sylvan Avenue, he could feel the tension.[38] Black people there had rocks thrown at them and were physically assaulted. "You had to just about fight your way out," Earl says, adding with a touch of pride, "We were a little tougher. We were outnumbered but we probably never lost any fights out there."[39]

Just as Hazelwood was giving Freddy his first dose of racial discrimination, the Hazelwood Public Library exposed him to books that discussed America's history of racial discrimination. Located just behind Freddy's house, the library featured a "Negro Books" section of thirty or so volumes. Freddy says that, at the age of fourteen, he walked into the library on his way home from Louis Field with a basketball under his arm and it changed his life.[40] He was thrilled to learn that Black people had written books. He devoured writings by such luminaries as Ralph Ellison and Langston Hughes. There and then, Freddy decided he wanted to be a writer. "I knew it was my strong suit," he says.[41] But not just any writer. Freddy wanted to be famous and influential. "I wanted my book up there too," he said. "I used to dream about being part of the Harlem Renaissance."[42]

Freddy read everything in the library—editorials, essays, advertisements, instruction manuals, magazines, comic books, and newspapers.[43] He read about the Civil War, about theology and anthropology. He did not avoid difficult books, but he put Ruth Benedict's *Patterns of Culture* back on the shelf, promising himself that one day, when he was older, he would be able to understand it.[44] He kept books past their due date. Years later, during a speaking engagement at the Carnegie Library of Pittsburgh, Freddy returned *The Collected Poems of Paul Laurence Dunbar*, which he had checked out from the Hazelwood branch twenty-eight years earlier.[45]

Dunbar was not the only poet Freddy read. In the 1950s, when the Beats came to prominence, Allen Ginsberg's poem "Howl" horrified elders, as did Jack Kerouac's 1957 novel, *On the Road*. But Ginsberg and Kerouac fascinated America's rebellious youth, Black as well as white.[46] Derisively called "beatniks," these bohemian rebels rejected middle-class values, disdained cleanliness and neatness, and idolized jazz and the "hipster" lifestyle of Black people. Their rebelliousness appealed to Freddy, who had shown his own signs of rebelliousness back in elementary school. Not brushing his teeth and not tending to personal hygiene may have been part of an early effort to define himself as a nonconforming rebel. Tony Kirven says that at St. Richard Freddy was "kind of in that Beatnik stage," adding, "We were all in that, but I think [Freddy] was further along."[47]

Freddy differed from the Beats in at least one important way: he admired hard work. "I've worked hard all my life," he later told an interviewer. "Hard work was no problem. I worked for my uncle for a dollar a day. At the end of the week, I had five dollars, a lot of money for an eight-year-old."[48] In Hazelwood, Freddy sold newspapers, shoveled snow, and did virtually anything to make a little change. At fourteen, he happened upon a sociological text that spoke glowingly of the "Negro's power of hard work." The phrase made a lasting impression. "I had never seen those words together . . . Negro [and] power," Freddy says.[49] Years later, those words led Freddy to the related concept of "Black Power." But in Hazelwood, he applied the concept to his part-time jobs. He and his younger brother Edwin cut grass for Herbert Douglas Sr., a blind neighbor and one of Hazelwood's early Black residents.[50]

"After he read about the 'Negro's power of hard work,'" Freddy didn't so much cut Douglas's lawn as "plow it."[51] After a heavy snowfall, he and Earl would leave home before dawn, walk two or three miles to Squirrel Hill, and shovel snow, sometimes until midnight.

In addition to playing sports, Freddy read library books avidly, but that did not make him a diligent student. In 1958 he was the only Black student in his eighth-grade class at St. Stephen School in Hazelwood.[52] There, as at St. Richard, he amassed a dismal attendance record, missing thirty-eight days and failing all of his courses.[53] Despite Freddy's dismal academic record, in the fall of 1959, he earned a score on an IQ test high enough to place him in the top quarter of the nation. Similarly, his score on the Stanford Achievement Test placed him at the tenth-, eleventh-, and twelfth-grade level in most subjects.[54] Those test results won Freddy a scholarship to Central Catholic, the city's premier Catholic high school for boys. Freddy was excited about attending Central Catholic and full of dreams of "really making it."[55] Located in Oakland near the University of Pittsburgh and Carnegie Institute of Technology (now Carnegie Mellon University), Central Catholic excelled both in athletics and in academics. It demanded much from its students, many of whom came from blue-collar immigrant backgrounds.

Despite high hopes, Freddy's career at Central Catholic was as bad as at St. Stephen. On many days, he arrived late or was absent. He got failing, or near-failing, marks in all his freshman classes—English, Latin, Art, Pennsylvania History, Health, and Physical Education.[56] In kindergarten at Letsche, Freddy had suffered racial harassment from Black students. At Central Catholic, he suffered harassment from white students. Almost every day, he would find a note on his desk saying, "Go home, nigger." He would pick it up and throw it away. At recess, someone might throw a potato chip bag at his back or run up and deliberately step on the back of his shoe and say, mockingly, "Excuse me." He had many fights. On one occasion, about forty students were waiting for him after school. The principal sent Freddy home in a taxi.[57]

Finally, one day in the spring of 1960, Freddy exploded. It happened when students were lining up to say the Pledge of Allegiance and he overheard someone refer to "the Nigger in the row behind him." At the words *liberty and justice for all*, he punched the offender in the face. When the school decided that Freddy should go home for the rest of day, he replied testily, "Hey, why don't we just do this permanently? I do not want to go to school here anymore."[58] The administration tried to talk him out of quitting, but Freddy was adamant.[59] The year was 1960. He was in the ninth grade.

Freddy's warrior temperament and his growing racial consciousness caused him to view much of life through a racial prism. Sometimes, this caused him to misinterpret a situation. For example, Freddy says he was the only Black student at Central Catholic.[60] The yearbook, however, shows he was the only Black student in his homeroom, but that there were at least five other Black students in his ninth-grade class. Freddy says racism kept him off the football team, but yearbook photographs show that Peter Hairston, another Black student, played that year on both the football and basketball teams. Photographs also show Black students participating in a range of student activities. Several were members of the color guard and orchestra. Walter Little, who went on to have a distinguished legal career, was a member of the school's marching band.[61]

Of course, this does not mean that Freddy's claims of harassment were without merit. Sala Udin endured similar harassment at Central Catholic. Two grades ahead of Freddy, Udin recalls the time a white student put a note on a lunch table frequented by Black students. The note read, "This is Negro History Week. Invite a nigger to dinner tonight." A fight ensued, and shortly afterward, Sala and several other Black students were asked to withdraw from the school.[62] Gene Keil, one of Freddy's white classmates, does not dispute accounts of racial harassment but doubts it was as open and widespread as Freddy says. Keil says student behavior was strictly monitored at Central Catholic, and students who openly engaged in fighting were subject to severe repercussions. Keil recalls that the word on Freddy was that he "did not take crap from anybody [and] was willing to fight if he was pushed.[63] The reputation may have inspired white students to amuse themselves by provoking Freddy.

Years later, as Freddy gained perspective on his time at Central Catholic, he conceded that he may have rushed to judgment. The Negro Shelf at the Hazelwood library, he says, had opened his eyes to racial discrimination. "I was just beginning to discover racism," he says, "and I think I was looking for something."[64] Central Catholic's faculty and staff, Freddy acknowledges, had been supportive. Brother Dominic, who taught English, recognized Freddy's talent as a poet and assured him he could be an author. Freddy appreciated the support but felt that Brother Dominic did not understand his search for racial identity because Dominic also encouraged him to avoid racial themes and write about nature.[65] One thing is clear: Freddy was developing a strong racial consciousness. That he also felt like an outsider is evident in the photograph of his homeroom class, which shows him looking down, with a sorrowful expression both on his face and in his body language.[66]

Daisy was beside herself when her "genius son" dropped out of Central Catholic.[67] One wonders why, given her own feistiness, she did not march to the school and protest. Perhaps she feared she might not control her anger; perhaps she suspected that the full story was more complicated than Freddy's version. In the end, Daisy enrolled Freddy at Connelley Vocational School, telling him that if he didn't want to study and become a lawyer, he could become an auto mechanic like his uncle John D.[68] Enrolling at Connelley Vocational created another disaster. The auto mechanic classes were full, so Freddy ended up taking a course in sheet metal. Utterly bored, he spent the fall term making tin cups.[69] Teachers complained that Freddy was careless with tools; Freddy complained that he was doing fifth-grade work.[70] A confrontation ensued when Freddy's shop teacher saw him driving a thumbtack with his T-square and knocked him off his chair. Freddy responded by bouncing the teacher off the blackboard, asking for a pink slip, and withdrawing from school.[71]

That was the fall of 1960, a memorable time in Pittsburgh. Freddy had ended many a day at Connelly in detention, but one day the teacher in charge let all the students out early: at Forbes Field in nearby Oakland, the Pirates's Bill Mazeroski had just hit a home run in the ninth inning of game seven to beat the New York Yankees and win the World Series. Freddy went downtown to watch all the wild celebration, while the police watched happily—very different from their reactions in the 1960s, when anyone so much as stepped into the street for antiwar or civil rights protests. Even before Central Catholic and Connelley, Freddy's rebelliousness was visible in his hygiene—or lack thereof. At St. Richard, his friend Tony was perplexed by Freddy's discolored teeth. In Hazelwood, Freddy went long periods without washing, making his neighbor Marva wonder whether his mother "had to fuss to make him take a bath." Freddy let his hair grow out, unruly and "real woolly like," according to Earl. When the family moved onto Sylvan Avenue, Earl says Freddy dressed in a white shirt and tie, as mandated by Catholic schools. After dropping out of Central Catholic and Connelley Vocational, he went around in disheveled clothing and an old military jacket. Earl wondered whether Freddy's parents had quit buying him clothes. And he absolutely shocked people by going barefoot—even in the winter. "It could be snow outside," Earl says in wonderment, "and he would wash [the] car, and a lot of times he would be out there barefooted. I couldn't believe what I was seeing. No shoes and no gloves. In the winter! In the snow!"[72]

Greg Montgomery, who moved onto Sylvan Avenue in 1959, became another friend of Freddy. Greg remembers the unforgettable sight of Freddy playing basketball in his bare feet, as well as other peculiarities that set him apart. These included a disagreeably runny nose, a "large mop" of hair, and a tendency to mumble like he had a "mouth full of marbles." Greg and other neighborhood kids were puzzled both by Freddy's behavior and by the range of skin tones in his family. They especially noticed the family's social isolation. Daisy and the others seldom left the apartment, Greg says, and were even less sociable than Freddy, who at least came out to play basketball.[73] Perhaps Freddy had simply become a nonconformist, determined "to go against the grain." Or perhaps his "wild" look was to make himself appear so fearsome that no one would "mess" with him. Freddy was never in a fight, Earl says, which was unusual because Black people in Hazelwood could be attacked simply for walking down the wrong street. Earl, however, thinks Freddy's looks signaled a growing sense of racial consciousness. His "wild, woolly" hair was his way of making sure people "knew who he was" racially.[74] Freddy's dress and behavior made him different, ever more an outsider. Neighborhood kids began referring to him as "Nature Boy," the title of a popular song by Nat King Cole.[75]

Despite all Freddy's peculiarities, Greg admired his intelligence and breadth of knowledge.[76] Greg was impressed that even in the ninth grade Freddy knew about William Shakespeare and other topics they had not yet studied. Greg wrote poetry himself, and one day while the two were sitting in front of Greg's house, Freddy asked him to read one of his poems. Greg can't remember the poem but says that for sure it was better than "roses are red, violets are blue." When Greg finished reading, Freddy casually reached into his own back pocket and pulled out a crumpled paper, written in pencil, words completely filling the page. Most surprisingly, the poem did not rhyme. In shock that the poem was more sophisticated than anything they had studied in school, Greg asked Freddy in disbelief: "You wrote that?"[77]

Now a successful attorney in New Jersey, Greg laughs when asked about August Wilson. "I did not know August Wilson," he says. "I knew Freddy Kittel." Greg only realized they were one and the same when he attended a play in Philadelphia. His sister leaned over and asked, "Greg, did you know Freddy Kittel is August Wilson?" Taking another look at a photograph in the program, Greg exclaimed, "Oh my goodness. It *is* Freddy!"[78] Like others, Greg remembers Freddy as quiet, a "loner" who kept to himself. However, Greg noticed that, when approached, Freddy could be likable and friendly.[79] Greg excelled in sports, but also was a straight-A student, whose placement in advanced classes set him apart from the others. Greg considered Freddy a kindred spirit, a fellow outsider, and one of the few people he could really talk to.[80]

In December 1960, Freddy was fifteen years old and had dropped out of his last two schools. Things did not improve when Daisy enrolled him that December in Gladstone High School, just across the street from their home. Given Freddy's poor record, Gladstone insisted that he repeat the ninth grade, in effect setting him back a year. Unhappy with the demotion, Freddy focused on irritating the teachers, partly with his slovenly dress. The school's basketball coach, Albert Zellman, was especially upset over Freddy's appearance. Zellman criticized nearly everything about the way Freddy dressed, Earl says. "His clothes, his shoes . . . hair, you name it."[81]

Predictably, Freddy exploded once again. Unfortunately, the explosion came at the expense of his well-meaning history and social studies teacher, Charles Biggs. Freddy had been underperforming in Biggs's class. "I was bored," he admitted later. "I was confused, I was disappointed in myself, and I didn't do any work." Biggs was African American, but Freddy was convinced that he favored the white students. He says Biggs would ask the class who did their homework. If a Black student raised their hand, Biggs would make him produce the homework.[82] However, Greg Montgomery recalls Biggs as a good teacher who was strict but showed no favoritism. He simply demanded excellence from his students. "In a lot of classes," Greg says, "they would be fooling around, but none of that kind of stuff would be going on in Mr. Biggs's class."[83] Biggs's widow Shirley recalls her husband's concerns about a certain Freddy Kittel, whom he considered bright but underperforming. Convinced that something outside school was making Freddy angry and withdrawn, Biggs and his wife often discussed possible ways to turn him around.[84]

When Biggs assigned students to write a research paper on a historical figure, Freddy decided to put in a real effort, having suddenly realized that not performing and not graduating would keep him from attending college.[85] Freddy wrote about Napoleon Bonaparte, the historical figure he had long idolized as a self-made man who had grown up impoverished and was teased for his provincial way of speaking. Freddy put his heart and soul into the paper. He titled the paper "Napoleon's Will to Power," a suggestive title given Freddy's own admiration of the warrior spirit. Hoping to impress Mr. Biggs even further, Freddy used money he had earned cutting grass and shoveling snow to rent a typewriter and paid his sister Linda Jean to type the paper.[86]

The paper was so good that, given Freddy's long indifference to school, Biggs wondered whether he really was the author. Biggs marked the paper with two grades—an A+ and an E. He told Freddy he would assign one of the two grades depending on whether Freddy could demonstrate that he had written the paper. Once again in full warrior mode, Freddy refused to prove anything. "I thought that . . . because I said I wrote it, and I put my name on it, that he should accept my word for it. Otherwise, I would not have put my name on it."[87] Biggs drew a circle around the failing grade and handed back the paper. Freddy tore up the paper, threw it in the wastebasket, and walked out. Freddy had dropped out of school twice before, but this time was different. For the next two weeks, he pretended to go to school. However, he did not enter the building but stayed outdoors on the basketball court, shooting baskets and waiting for someone to come out and ask why he was not in class. When no one came, Freddy quietly dropped out of school, permanently.[88] It was May 1, 1961, less than a week after Freddy's sixteenth birthday. He was still in the ninth grade.[89]

Knowing that his mother would be furious if she found out what had happened, Freddy left the house every morning and pretended to go to school. But on the way, he would detour and walk instead to Oakland, some two miles away, where he would spend the day reading at the Carnegie Library of Pittsburgh's Main branch. In a way, Freddy was repeating his past behavior pattern at St. Richard. Ever the loner, Freddy preferred studying on his own.[90] He devoured works by such African American luminaries as W. E. B. Du Bois, Arna Bontemps, Booker T. Washington, Jean Toomer, Richard Wright, James Baldwin, and Langston Hughes. He followed intellectual threads wherever his curiosity took him—from anthropologists like Claude Lévi-Strauss, to culinary arts, to agricultural techniques, to cattle and sheep ranchers in the Old West, to the settling of the West, to George Armstrong Custer, to Catholicism, to the pope—and beyond.[91] "For the first time in my life," Wilson says, "I felt free. I could read whole books on subjects that interested me."[92] Several years later, when Wilson's friend Lee Kiburi was introducing him to a group of students at CAPA, Pittsburgh's Creative and Performing Arts Academy, Kiburi turned to Wilson and said, "You dropped out of school, but you didn't drop out of life."[93] Wilson liked the phrase; in later years, he repeated it often.[94]

Throughout his warrior years in Hazelwood, Freddy retained much of the positive mindset he had acquired on Bedford Avenue. "Looking back on [my years in Hazelwood]," he said later, "those very important years from 12 to 18 were spent in a place that had little league teams and middle-class experiences. You could sleep with your windows open, and a friend could come stick his head in your window to wake you up."[95] Years later, he called white residents of Hazelwood "good, honest, hard-working people," and says that signs of their racism need to be put in perspective. "That was America at the time. . . . That's the way the world was. I don't fault them. To me, they were good people."[96]

Shortly after Freddy quit school, the family—for reasons unknown— moved again. They settled in a duplex at 617 North Murtland Avenue, a quiet, pleasant street in the middle-class neighborhood of Homewood, a few blocks from Westinghouse High School. In Homewood, Freddy's mood brightened. He contacted old friends and, for the first time, invited people over to his house. Earl Horsley could not figure out why there was such a change in Freddy's mood.[97] But as they say in *Guys and Dolls*, "When you see a guy / Reach for stars in the sky / You can bet that he's doin' it for some doll." The "doll" was Helen Lorraine Jackson, three years younger than Freddy and living a few blocks up Murtland. Helen was a sophomore at Westinghouse High School, where she was known as "Butch." She planned to attend beauty school and become a hairdresser.[98] Earl remembers Helen as one of the prettiest girls he ever saw.[99] John Brewer, a longtime Homewood resident, agrees, saying Helen "turned a lot of heads" during her time at Westinghouse.[100] Freddy was smitten. He recounted to Earl how on Sundays he and Helen would purchase a bus pass and spend the day riding around the city.

Happy times did not last. Before the end of May, about a month after Freddy dropped out of Gladstone, he told his mother what had happened at school. Daisy had suspected something, because Freddy had begun getting up later and later to go to school.[101] But when her fears were confirmed, she was furious, nonetheless. Daisy upbraided Freddy without mercy. "She told him he was no good," recounts his sister Linda Jean, "that he would amount to nothing. . . . She would take the food out of the refrigerator, put it in her bedroom, lock the door, and then go out. He was made to live in the basement for a while. She said he was dirty. She didn't want him in the house upstairs."[102] Trying to redeem himself, Freddy took a series of part-time jobs that would help him support himself while giving him time to write poems and stories that would show his mother he was working hard to succeed.[103]

Freddy did all that, but a seventeen-year-old boy would inevitably be interested in more than poetry. Curious about the larger world, Freddy began going over to the Northside, where he hung out at Group One art gallery, run by sculptor Thaddeus Mosley and serving as the city's main gathering place for Black artists and writers. But Freddy explored more than art. He and several others would meet up with Lacy McCoy, a friend from Homewood, and explore life up and down Centre Avenue. Despite being underage—or perhaps because of it—they were particularly interested in bars, the more disreputable the better. Their favorites included such notorious spots as "Bucket of Blood," located on Roberts Street near Centre Avenue.[104] Daisy was not amused. Fed up with what she saw as a waste of talent and promise, she kicked Freddy out of the house. "Go on, you're grown," she told him. "It's time for you to be out on your own."[105] Freddy knew he had disappointed his mother. "She saw a lot of potential that I'd squandered," he lamented.[106] Poems he wrote later likened his expulsion from home to Adam's expulsion from the Garden of Eden. Freddy felt like an outsider more than ever.

On May 25, 1962—a year after dropping out of school—Freddy joined the US Army. He completed his basic training at Fort Benning, Georgia, and was accepted into the elite Army Airborne School.[107] Misfortune, however, soon struck. Home on leave and smartly dressed in his paratrooper outfit, Freddy greeted three old Hazelwood friends who came over to visit—Earl Horsley, Ronnie Culpepper, and Vernon Saunders. They all admired his family's car—a 1961 Cadillac with black leather seats and fishtails—and talked Freddy into taking it out for a joyride. Ronnie was chosen as the driver because he was the only one with a license. License or not, Ronnie's driving skills were woefully inadequate. He had a head-on collision on Browns Hill Road, totaling the car and knocking the boys unconscious. When they came to their senses, the boys took off running. Scared and uncertain what to do, they called Marva for advice. She told them to go home right away because the police were already at Freddy's house.[108]

Understandably furious, Daisy pressed charges against the boys, who didn't know what to do. Some even considered leaving town.[109] Although Daisy relented and dropped the charges, Earl said the accident totally derailed Freddy's relations with his mother.[110] "We thought they were gonna kill Freddy," Earl says. "That was their precious Cadillac."[111] The tension was such that Earl stopped visiting. "I didn't go anywhere near that house after that."[112]

Freddy's military career ended prematurely, just like his time at various schools. He had wanted to be an officer, and scored high on the exam, but on May 28, 1963, he was let go with a general rather than an honorable discharge. The army said that officers had to be at least nineteen years old, and Freddy was just eighteen. Freddy said he was not interested in serving if he couldn't be an officer.[113] He left the service as a Private Second Class. An award as sharpshooter was about all he had to show for his time.[114] After washing out of the army, Freddy decided not to return home. Instead, he teamed up with Denny Hollis, one of his former basketball buddies and next-door neighbor in Hazelwood. The two traveled to Los Angeles, where they worked for a while in a drug store. Hollis, who had attended the University of Pittsburgh, chose to stay in Los Angeles. Freddy, after working at a series of odd jobs, such as short-order cook and soda jerk, came to hate Los Angeles, largely because of pervasive police violence. He seems to have run afoul of the California juvenile system, because in May 1964, the Reception Guidance Center in Tracy, near Stockton, requested Freddy's high school records, as did the Youth Training Center in Ontario, about thirty miles east of Los Angeles.

While Freddy was in California, his family in Pittsburgh was undergoing major changes. On January 6, 1964, Fred's wife Jennie died. Four months later, on May 1, Fred and Daisy were married in a civil ceremony in Butler, a small town some thirty miles north of Pittsburgh.[115] Daisy kept the marriage a secret—not even her best friend, Julia, knew about it. When I informed her, Julia was incredulous.

At the time of the marriage, Daisy was living on North Murtland Avenue with Dave and several of the children. Freddy was still in California, Freda was attending Fordham University in New York, and Linda Jean had married and left home. Sometime later, Daisy, Fred, Donna, Edwin, and Richie moved into a house that Dave owned at 1621 Bedford Avenue, just a block from Daisy's old residence. The house was formerly the home of Charlie Solomon, Dave's old friend and political sponsor.[116] Dave let Daisy, Fred, and the children live there, another example of his generous, considerate nature.[117]

Daisy's marriage to Fred did not terminate her relationship with Dave, a man for whom she retained great affection. By then Dave was suffering from diabetes and his health was deteriorating. This became evident in the spring of 1964, when Daisy drove to New York to visit her sister Faye and daughter Barbara Jean. Dave came along but was confined to a wheelchair and could not go with Daisy and the others to see the World's Fair. Several months later, in November 1964, Dave completed his ten-year probation, having made himself an asset to the community by serving as ward committeeman in the Hill, where he earned the respect of both residents and merchants.[118]

One can assume that money was involved in Daisy's decision to marry Fred. In all their years together, Fred never contributed significantly to the family's finances. Although he was an alcoholic, he was not a wastrel. Fred's estate included a life insurance policy, two savings accounts, four pieces of property, and an attractive home in Overbrook. On July 30, 1964, he and

Daisy sold the Overbrook home for $30,000 (equivalent to about $300,000 today).[119]

Marriage can be a blessing, but it also can ruin a relationship. In this case, marriage ruined a relationship that had lasted for almost a quarter century. Three months after Fred and Daisy married, a series of legal quarrels erupted over the disposition of Fred's assets. Fred filed for divorce but, because of his rapidly declining health, the proceedings were never concluded.[120] Toward the end of March 1965, Fred was admitted to Saint Joseph's Hospital on the South Side.

Freddy rushed home from California to be with his dying father, a sign of the affection Freddy still harbored for him. Freddy and Linda Jean visited their father regularly in the hospital. During one of those visits, Fred told them of his service during World War I, which he said included the bloody Meuse-Argonne Offensive.[121] Fred may have been confused, or he may have been trying to impress. At any rate, the US Army has no record that he served in either World War I or World War II.[122] In their hospital meetings, Fred referred to Freddy affectionately as "Fritz"—Fred's own nickname. Whatever transpired during their bedside meeting, Freddy and Linda Jean had a great time visiting with their father. Freddy later wrote a poem in his memory, the title of which—"Poem for the Old Man"—suggests ambivalence as well as bonding.[123]

Fred languished for thirty-eight days, during which time—and despite the divorce filing—Daisy visited him regularly. On April 5, 1965, at the age of seventy, Fred passed away from cirrhosis of the liver. A Requiem Mass was held in Holy Trinity Church (now St. Benedict the Moor), the Hill District parish where Freddy had attended elementary school.[124] Funeral services were held at Frederick's, a Black funeral home in Homewood. Daisy attended the service, along with her Bedford Avenue neighbor Pearl McClanahan and all the children except Barbara and Freda, who were in New York. Rudolph and Emil, Fred's two brothers, also attended. Fred was buried in St. Stanislaus Cemetery in Millvale, just outside Pittsburgh and affiliated with the historic St. Stanislaus Polish church where he and Jennie had been married. Fred was buried one plot away from Jennie in a grave that, like hers, is unmarked.[125] Following the burial, Daisy and the children went straight home, upset that Fred's relatives had not invited them to the wake.[126]

In his will, Fred left everything to his children. He left nothing to Daisy, something not permitted under Pennsylvania law. After considerable legal wrangling, Daisy received $10,000 from the settlement (equivalent to about

$100,000 today). Each of the children, except Freda and Barbara, received $659 (equivalent to about $6,000 today).[127] A poignant surprise was a $1,438 bill for the care of Fred's wife Jennie at Mayview State Hospital, a state-run mental facility. No dates are given for Jennie's stay there, but her disheveled appearance in the 1930s suggests that she may have long suffered from mental illness—perhaps another reason that Fred never sought a divorce.[128]

His father's death marked the end of a major stage in Freddy's life. His return to Pittsburgh marked the beginning of a new one, in which he would seek to find his way as a Black man, a poet, and a playwright.

4

Centre Avenue Poet

In Freddy's eyes, 1965 marked the year that he fully entered manhood.
At the age of twenty, he said, "I left my mother's house, I went out into the
world, into that community, to learn what it meant to be a man, to learn
whatever it is that the community had to teach me."[1] Those were not empty
words. Freddy immersed himself in the Black life of his city—observing, listening, learning.

That said, Freddy's assertion that he "left his mother's house" and "went
out into the world" is a bit misleading. He didn't go far from people and places
he already was at least somewhat familiar with. He moved into a rooming
house at 85 Crawford Street, about six blocks away from his mother's residence and only a few doors up from Holy Trinity Church, where he had
attended elementary school. For fifty dollars a month, Freddy rented a small
garden apartment partly below street level. The rent was no bargain for a
couple of rooms in a dismal building that lacked cooking facilities. But the
money he inherited from his father easily covered the rent. And he was only
a few minutes away from his mother's home-cooked meals—he and Daisy
by this point having at least partly reconciled.[2] A visitor described Freddy's
rooming house as an oddball place "tenanted by melancholics, retired coun-
terfeiters, and a suicidal singer who aspired to be Billy Eckstine and who asked
Freddy to type his final message to the world."[3] Freddy found the place ideal

for someone with his bohemian tendencies, a place, as he said, "befitting a 20-year-old poet."[4]

Freddy liked being a poet partly because the craft required so little in the way of expensive supplies. But he knew that a professional poet needed a typewriter in order to send work to a publisher. Freddy couldn't afford a typewriter, but Freda, who was studying at Fordham University in New York, needed a term paper. She offered Freddy twenty dollars to write a paper for her quickly.[5] Freddy obliged by dashing off "Two Violent Poets—Robert Frost and Carl Sandburg." He took the twenty bucks and went promptly to McFarren's Stationery downtown, where he bought a used Royal typewriter that he had had his eye on for some time.[6]

The typewriter changed Freddy's image of himself, giving him the identity of poet. "The exact day I became a poet," he says, "was April 1, 1965, the day I bought my first typewriter." It was Freddy's statement to the world that he was not going be a bus driver or a lawyer. He was going to be a writer.[7] More than that, he would be famous. Years later, when Wilson read at New York's prestigious 92nd Street Y, he told the audience about the day in October 1965 when he stood on the corner of Centre Avenue and Crawford Street as a twenty-year-old staring at the lights of downtown Pittsburgh and telling himself, "If you work hard for the next twenty years, you might possibly one day be invited to read at the 92nd Street Y." He regarded it as his "life ambition."[8]

To be a successful writer, Freddy felt, required more than a typewriter. He needed a name, one with more sonority and gravitas than Freddy Kittel. "So now I'm a poet," he told himself, "and I'm going to pick a pen name."[9] In Hazelwood, Freddy had told his friend Earl Horsley that he hated his birth name and one day would change it to August. Now, at the age of twenty, he decided to call himself August Wilson, August being his father's first name and Wilson his mother's family name. Sandra Shannon, a leading interpreter of Wilson's works, sees Freddy's new name as his determination "to formalize the rejection of his European heritage."[10] But this was not necessarily the case. Freddy did not change his name legally. For many years, he signed official papers as "Frederick August Kittel."[11] As he describes the choosing of a pen name, it had to do as much with esthetics as racial identity. "I typed F.A. Kittel. Fred A. Kittel. . . . Fred Wilson, Fred A. Wilson, Frederick Wilson." Finally, he liked the way August Wilson sounded and the way it looked. He said to himself, "that's it."[12]

The newly minted August Wilson typed up several poems, a slow, laborious process because he didn't know how to type. The effect, however, was galvanizing. "I'm really a writer now," he told himself. The newly minted writer sent off his first efforts to *Harper's Magazine*, a publication he had chosen because it paid three times the rate of other magazines.[13] As he soon learned, *Harper's* also had very high standards and summarily rejected his poems. As a warrior, Wilson knew he had to persist in the face of setbacks. "Oh, I see," he said to himself, "This is serious. I'm gonna have to learn how to write a poem."[14]

In learning how to write poetry, Wilson benefited from the support of a group of talented and nurturing friends. "We all knew each other," he said later, "and we all worked and supported each other in what we were doing. And it was very, very important that you do not have a sense that you are working in a vacuum, that you can say, 'Hey man, look at this, what do you think?'"[15] These friends helped August develop professionally and made him feel—perhaps for the first time in his life—that he belonged, that he was more than a perennial outsider. One of those friends, Sala Udin, says the group fully accepted Wilson and made him "a certified member of the fraternity."[16]

Rob Penny was one of the most important of those friends. Rob had grown up on Arcena Street, a few blocks from Wilson's childhood home.[17] Rob's brother J. D. was one of the tough guys whom Wilson had tried to befriend at Saint Richard's Parish school. Unlike J. D., Rob was quiet and shy, someone who became so embarrassed when classmates made fun of his Alabama accent that he would stutter. But Rob could also be assertive. When someone would ask where he was from, he would proudly answer, "Opelika, Alabama," adding emphatically, "That's my home."[18] It was almost like Daisy insisting that she was African American. Rob's father had traveled to Pittsburgh shortly after World War II. Once settled, he sent for the rest of his family.[19] Rob attended many of the same schools as August—Holy Trinity, St. Richard, and Central Catholic. But because he was a few years older, the two were never classmates.[20]

Rob was short and thin, but he held his own, even when confronted by gangs from the nearby Bedford Dwellings housing project. "Rob was no punk," says former neighbor Amos Lawson. "I'm telling you, don't let the size fool you. . . . He was a tough little guy."[21] Although Rob was tough, he didn't hang out with toughs, partly because his mother kept him focused on education.[22] Smart as well as athletic, Rob majored in science, Central Catholic's most rigorous academic track.[23] Whereas Freddy had a miserable time at Central Catholic, Rob—known then as Bob—enjoyed popularity as one of the greatest track stars in the school's history. Rob was liked for his affability as well as his athleticism. Albert Zangrilli, a friend and fellow member of the track team, remembers Rob as quiet, courteous, and friendly.[24] Rob's interest in writing began sometime in the early 1960s. One day after track practice, he stopped by to see his friend, Jerry Rhodes, who liked to write horror stories. Jerry read Rob one of his stories, and a few weeks later, Rob came by to tell Jerry that he had started writing detective stories. The two began reading and critiquing each other's work; not long afterward, Rob began writing poetry.[25]

Nick Flournoy was another of August's new friends. A poet and someone August relied on for critical feedback, Nick had grown up in the Smithfield neighborhood of Birmingham, Alabama. Nick's father had little formal education but was an avid reader. He had fought in World War II and died from wounds received during the Battle of the Bulge. Nick's mother stressed that, in memory of their father's sacrifice, the boys had a responsibility to fight for civil rights. The accomplishments and activism of Smithfield's residents made the neighborhood a target of racially motivated bombings. Worried that things in Birmingham were going to get "rough," Nick's mother moved the family to Pittsburgh, where they had relatives.[26]

In Pittsburgh, Nick attended Langley High School, where he excelled both in academics and sports. Slender, handsome, and stylish, Nick dressed in ascots and scarves—"like a British aristocrat," according to his brother Mike. Nick sported a mustache and hair with a premature streak of gray that appealed to women. He walked with a swagger and wore his trench coat over his shoulders, European style. To this day, Sala calls Nick "Mr. Cool." Nick was funny, lighthearted, and extroverted, someone who enjoyed telling jokes. But, like August, he gravitated toward serious works of literature. Before the age of ten, Nick was reading the Bible as literature. Later, he began poring over works by William Shakespeare, Martin Heidegger, Erich Fromm, and Jean Toomer. He loved classical music and played it on the car radio. He also loved golf and, like Roosevelt Hicks in Wilson's play *Radio Golf*, carried a putter in the trunk of his car. Nick also was politically active, in 1965 becoming chairman of the Pittsburgh chapter of the Congress of Racial Equality. With that, Nick stopped writing poetry and, as his mother had long wished, devoted himself to the struggle for civil rights. August considered Nick not just a fine poet but also "one of the finest people" he had ever known.[27]

Sala Udin was not a poet and was two years older than August. But the two had been friends ever since they attended elementary school at Holy Trinity. Born Samuel Howze, Sala grew up on Fullerton Street, a legendary corridor that, at its intersection with Wylie Avenue, had long been the center of Black life in the Hill.[28] Sala's mother hailed from Georgia and worked as a house cleaner; his father was from Mississippi and worked in a laundry. In the late 1950s, when Fullerton and Wylie succumbed to urban redevelopment, Sala and his parents relocated to the Bedford Dwellings public housing project.[29] Sala, like August, attended Central Catholic High School and, like his friend, left because of racial harassment. But his transfer to racially integrated Schenley High School did not improve matters. There, he endured the snobbery of middle-class Black students from Sugar Top.

Unhappy, and not doing well in school, Sala went to live with relatives in New York, where he found his calling in the civil rights movement, joining the National Association for the Advancement of Colored People (NAACP) and attending the 1963 March on Washington.[30] Inspired by Martin Luther King Jr., Sala spent four years in Mississippi organizing for the Student Nonviolent Coordinating Committee (SNCC). Frustrated by the racial violence of the South, in 1967 he followed SNCC when it renounced integration and turned toward Black Power. He joined the Nation of Islam, and in 1968, following King's assassination, returned to Pittsburgh, convinced that nonviolence and racial integration had become outdated as liberation strategies. Like Stokely Carmichael and Amiri Baraka, Sala shifted from fighting segregation in the South to fighting racism in the North.[31] He Africanized his name in 1969. A few years later, he founded Ile Elegba, a residential substance abuse treatment program.[32]

Charlie P. Williams, called "Chawley" by friends, was another poet and important friend of August's. Ten years August's senior, Chawley wrote powerful poetry that won him the informal title "Poet Laureate of the Hill." Born in Homestead, a mill town just outside Pittsburgh, Chawley grew up in the city's East Liberty neighborhood under trying circumstances. His father died when he was four years old, and he didn't get along with his mother, a singer who suffered a succession of brutal men and made it clear to Chawley and his brother that they were burdens.[33] Chawley dropped out of Westinghouse High School and enlisted in the Air Force. At some point—probably in the late 1950s—he became addicted to drugs, which led to desperate years of hustling and struggling to survive. Despite a hard life, Chawley had a winning smile and happy demeanor. He cut a dapper figure in jeans, sport jacket, and cap. "Everybody loved Chawley," says his wife Darzetta. Chawley loved to laugh and joke but was serious about poetry. His rich, baritone voice captivated audiences. Sala says that whenever someone asked Chawley to read, "he had the stuff in his back pocket, and he would pull it out." Chawley's poetry had what one commentator describes as "a pulsating beat; . . . a kind of a melody of the blues, jazz; references that flowed like music."[34]

Chawley came to know August through Dingbat—the nickname of Carl R. Smith, one of the Hill's most storied, idiosyncratic artists. "Bat," as he was usually called, told Chawley he needed to meet this "new, young poet," August Wilson. The two met one day while standing on Centre Avenue. Chawley took an immediate liking to August, feeling that his poems had a profundity that many did not understand. August, in turn, admired Chawley for writing poetry that captured the grittiness of street life. Others felt the same way. "Chawley came from the street academy," says Sala, adding that Chawley's poetry was "pungent, no-nonsense, self-critical but also critical of the environment that he was describing." It was said that Chawley's poems had an honesty, simplicity, accessibility, and pathos that captured the mind and mood of Centre Avenue, the heartbreaks and tragedies of residents trying to make their way.[35]

August was influenced as much by the places where he hung out as by the friends he made. Looking south from his rooming house, he could see the intersection of Crawford Street and Centre Avenue. Known as "Freedom Corner," that was where civil rights marchers often gathered before heading downtown to protest job discrimination and racial injustice.[36] Looking to the west, August was confronted by an enormous parking lot and domed arena that eight years earlier had been the commercial heart of the Hill District. In 1956 urban renewal razed much of the Lower Hill District's rich variety of stores, night clubs, churches, and institutions. Behind this wasteland rose the imposing skyline of the city's downtown business district.[37] Years later, August would make residents' fear of urban renewal the subject of several plays.

To the north and east, Wilson could see the baneful consequences of deindustrialization. In the 1960s, Pittsburgh's fabled steel industry began declining rapidly. Manufacturers trimmed their labor force and almost stopped hiring workers who had not completed high school.[38] The consequences were devastating, especially for Black workers, who were always the last hired and first fired. Lyndon Johnson's 1964 War on Poverty was an attempt to mitigate the consequences, but the loss of jobs inexorably brought on the devastating scourges of drug addiction and crime. Gary Robinson, now serving a life sentence for mistakes made during those times, bewails the changes he witnessed. In the 1950s and early 1960s, he says, "We loved to get clean, have our little smoke parties and everyone was peaceful with one another. Things changed when the heroin came to town in the mid-60's. We changed 180 degrees from who and what we were. The whole Hill became a different place. We became thieves (no guns) or sold drugs."[39]

Wilson felt a poet needed to be out and about, observing, listening, and learning. "You cannot sit at home as a twenty-year-old poet," he said. "You don't know anything about life."[40] He was not alone in this belief: in the 1950s, a new generation of white poets like Robert Creeley embraced personal experience rather than history and tradition as the source of their poetry.[41] Like other poets of his generation, Wilson walked the streets of the Hill, exploring life along Centre Avenue and the section of Wylie that urban renewal had not razed. With what he called an "anthropologist's eye," he treated the avenue like a virtual library whose volumes he could study and learn from.[42]

As a longtime outsider, both physically and socially, Wilson had years of practice standing back and observing. He did not have a car and did not drive—a benefit, because being on foot let him see and overhear things he would have missed riding by in a car.[43] When he was out walking, he carried a pen and yellow notepad on which he jotted down ideas for poems, snatches of poetry, things he saw, and bits of conversation he overheard. He did most of his writing while drinking coffee and smoking cigarettes in neighborhood diners, bars, and restaurants. In order to have as much time as possible to do this, he avoided looking for a "regular" job that would have filled his days. Instead, he worked a series of temporary, low-paying jobs with flexible hours.

Whether or not he was aware of it, Wilson was part of a long tradition that in France was known as *flanerie*. In nineteenth-century Paris, flaneurs— often young men of well-to-do backgrounds—would saunter along the city's back streets, observing life, especially in marginalized, working-class neighborhoods. They were thought by many to be idlers, wasting their time and avoiding work. But the noted poet Baudelaire said that the flaneur is "at his busiest when he seems to be at his laziest," because he is observing things overlooked by others and is transforming his observations into art, literature, and poetry.[44]

Wilson differed from most flaneurs in that he had grown up in economic conditions similar to those of the people he was observing.[45] On the other hand, he had not grown up immersed in Black street life. His mother had shielded her children from street life. In Wilson's case, this made him all the more eager to learn about that life. And so, as he says, he left his mother's house and set out "to learn whatever it is that the community had to teach me."[46] Wilson's semi-autobiographical play, *How I Learned What I Learned*, furnishes examples of how his forays along the streets of the Hill, particularly

Centre Avenue, taught him about Black street life. The play portrays Wilson as an outsider, an inexperienced newcomer unfamiliar with the ways of Black folk. Through a series of mishaps—sometimes amusing, sometimes exaggerated for dramatic effect—the play shows how Wilson acquired the sort of insider knowledge that later informed his plays.

Chawley proved essential in helping August with this. Chawley had "street cred," knowledge of and acceptance by those struggling to get by. Hanging with Chawley gave August entrée into places that otherwise would have been off limits.[47] Chawley recognized August's insecurities and knew the dangers inherent in his desire to be accepted. As Chawley told theater critic John Lahr, "I was in the drug world. Here come August. He's sensitive, he's articulate, he has talent, he's trying to write. And the hustlers of the streets is at him. They could get him to do things, 'cause he wanted to belong. He would allow them to come to wherever he stayed at to eat, to get high and shoot their dope, to lie up with different women. They were trying to get him to get high. I put a halt to that."[48]

Chawley knew that August's complexion contributed to his insecurities and sense of being an outsider. "August wasn't really black," Chawley says. "He was half-and-half. He was too dark to be white, and he was too white to be dark. He was in no man's land. . . . He was lost."[49] Chawley protected his friend. Once, when Chawley was shooting up at August's apartment, another man asked August if he wanted to try some. Chawley threw the man against the wall. "'That's August! Man don't you never give him no shit.'" With that, August says he realized Chawley was a true friend.[50] August occasionally smoked marijuana, but he never did hard drugs and never sold drugs when he needed money. For that, and more, he valued Chawley's guidance. "Chawley saw something in me," he says. "In all this time, I've been trying to reward that thing that Chawley seen in me."[51]

During Wilson's years on Centre—the mid-1960s to the mid-1970s—the avenue was the Hill District's main retail corridor and the heart of its vitality. The twelve blocks between Crawford and Soho streets boasted some 130 establishments. These included twenty-four groceries and confectioneries, seventeen restaurants, twelve bars, eleven variety stores, seven drug stores, seven dry cleaners, six barber shops, six beauticians, five churches, four clothing stores, four billiard parlors, three dentists, three shoe repair shops, three shoe stores, two funeral parlors, two theaters, two hotels, a tailor, a physician, a gas station, a hardware store, an untold number of jitney stations, plus a mixture of nonprofits and government agencies. Walking along Centre Avenue,

August noticed excitedly how it "would just shimmer with activity." Urban renewal destroyed the Hill's former business corridor, but the activity simply shifted to Centre Avenue. Hundreds of people on its sidewalks made for an unforgettable sight. Wilson says that on one occasion he didn't go to bed for three days because he feared he might miss something.[52]

Frank Hightower, a freelance photographer and friend of August's, felt the same way about Centre. In those days, he says, "It seemed like I just slept and ate and consumed that whole process . . . from the time I got up until the time I went to bed."[53] Tony Fountain, son of a leading funeral director, remembers Centre Avenue and the Hill District as having the same level of energy as Harlem.[54] Drugs and crime, he says, were present, but were not the problem they became after the riots of 1968.[55] Amos Lawson, a longtime resident, remembers the good times. "They'd start partying . . . at the Ringside, Hurricane, Hartzberg's, Marie's, The Avenue Bar, and places like that. You know how they used to do back in the day."[56] Centre's vitality also attracted white people. Jeff Folino, former director of alumni relations at Central Catholic High School, says that when his grandfather would talk about the Hill, "we all wanted to go to this magical place. We thought it was like Oz."[57]

Wilson was intrigued by any number of establishments on Centre. His play *Seven Guitars* mentions The Hurricane, a popular jazz club run by Birdie Dunlap, the cousin of Tony Kirven, Freddy's former classmate at St. Richard. A short distance farther up was Douglas King's B&M, a classy restaurant that was one of Wilson's favorite places to eat.[58] The stretch that was most important to him began at the intersection of Centre and Devilliers. On the corner sat Architecture 2001, a community outreach office established by Troy West and Jay Greenfield, two professors from Carnegie Mellon University who admired the Hill's dynamism and wanted to protect it from further redevelopment.[59] Wilson approved of West's efforts, and the two often lunched at Eddie's Restaurant nearby to discuss such concerns.[60] Just up from Architecture 2001 stood the New Granada Theatre, with its large auditorium where, in 1968, Wilson would deliver a moving address at a Malcolm X commemoration. A bit farther up was Irv's, a bar that attracted a rough crowd of drinkers and drug users. Neither Wilson nor his friends drank much, and only Chawley used hard drugs, but they liked to sit at Irv's front window and watch the passing scene.[61]

Two doors up from Irv's, Wilson spent many days drinking coffee, flirting with the waitress, and writing in Pope's Restaurant.[62] In homage to the time he spent there, Wilson made Pope's the setting for his first play, *Recycled*.

Pope's was one of Wilson's favorite places on Centre Avenue, partly because an attractive waitress named Willa Mae Montague worked there. Willa's nickname was "Snook," and the waitress character in Wilson's play *How I Learned What I Learned* is called Snookie.[63] In the play, August arranges to meet Snookie at the 88 Bar. When he arrives, he finds her already there with her husband, Billy. Billy places a gun on the bar and tells August he had planned to shoot him, but Snookie talked him out of it. August freezes with fear until the bartender walks up and tells Billy to put the gun back in his pocket. To August's surprise and relief, Billy buys him a beer and asks him to take good care of Snookie. Then, to his alarm, Billy starts crying. In the play, August says that "a distraught nigger with a gun" is a frightening sight when you have been sleeping with his wife. Slipping out of the bar, August runs as far and as fast as he can. And he breaks up with Snookie.

The reality was different. Willa says she was separated from her husband when she and August started dating. Billy never brandished a gun or said he had planned to kill August. In fact, she says, Billy and August got along well and would come by together to see her. Ultimately, Willa decided she was too young and didn't want to marry either one of them. As for her husband crying and telling August to take care of her, she only laughs. "That didn't happen. That's theater versus real life."[64]

August may have annoyed the owner of Pope's by spending so little money and taking up so much of his waitress's time, but he won Willa's affection.[65] She thought he had a nice personality and could be funny, even though she found him "very serious" and "a bit bookish." Willa sometimes accompanied August to the library, where he would check out poetry by Langston Hughes and someone Willa recalls as "a white English poet."[66] The poet no doubt was Dylan Thomas, the model for Wilson and the inspiration for his early poetry recitals. Willa also recalls that August was passionate about the blues, which she regarded as old-fashioned and of little interest.[67] Nonetheless, she says, the relationship meant a lot to both of them. "I was in love with him, and he was in love with me. He really loved me, and I really loved him."[68]

A bit farther up from Pope's, the Halfway Art Gallery functioned as one of the most important sites for Wilson's development as a poet. The gallery held art exhibitions and ministered to people recovering from drug addiction. On weekends, it held poetry readings and jazz performances. It was also the site of the dénouement of a lesson about the informal codes of the street that Wilson learned the hard way. One night, a white motorcyclist asked August where Chawley lived, and August volunteered to take him. When the two got there, Chawley's wife Jeanine told them he was not home. They left, but August found out later that Chawley had cheated the man in a drug deal, and now the man knew where Chawley and his wife lived. "I done fucked up big time," Wilson said. "I let my friend down." The next day at the Halfway Art Gallery, a furious Jeanine came at August with a knife—fortunately, gallery patrons restrained her. Chawley forgave him, but August had learned an important lesson.[69]

The Mainway Supermarket, located at Centre and Erin, was the Hill's principal grocery store. The Mainway's torching in the riots of 1968 and a photograph of Wilson casually smoking a cigarette in its ruins are iconic reminders of those times.[70] At the corner of Centre and Elmore was Lutz's Meat Market, memorialized in Wilson's play *Two Trains Running*. Just past Kirkpatrick was West's Funeral Home, one of the Hill District's leading businesses. Finally, at the corner of Centre and Soho Street, stands A. Leo Weil Elementary School, whose auditorium became the location for Black Horizons Theatre, where Wilson gained his first significant exposure to theater. When someone once asked August where he got his knowledge about the Hill, his friend Nick jumped in and said, only partly in jest, "Standing outside Pat's cigar store."[71] Indeed, Wilson spent many hours and many days at Pat's Place, a combination newsstand, billiards parlor, and cigar store near the intersection of Wylie Avenue and Elmore Street. Wilson found the old men and the stories they told there so intriguing that he began dressing like them, wearing corduroy pants, jackets, and hats. "While we were trying to be modern and flashy," his friend Sala said, August "would dress like the old men."[72]

Wilson first realized the importance of Pat's Place while reading *Home to Harlem*, Claude McKay's famous novel from the days of the Harlem Renaissance. In one of the chapters, "Snowstorm in Pittsburgh," McKay describes two porters who spend the night in a neighborhood they call "Soot Hill." The two patronize a Wiley (as it is spelled in the novel) Avenue pool room that sold tobacco, stationery, and odds and ends. In the back, patrons could write (or have an amanuensis write) letters to family and friends back home.[73] Immediately recognizing what place McKay was writing about, Wilson ran over to Pat's.[74]

He was not disappointed. Many of the patrons had come to Pittsburgh in the 1920s, bringing with them stories of the South and of their difficult adjustment to life in the North.[75] Wilson spent hours listening to their accounts, soaking up stories and conversations that later informed his plays.[76] Wilson says his listening strategy at Pat's consisted of keeping quiet and listening to all kinds of philosophy, ideas, and attitudes.[77] Pat's Place exposed him to people's philosophy of life, notions of what a man is, and sense of duties and responsibilities.[78] "A lot of what I know of the history of blacks," Wilson said later, "I picked up standing there in Pat's Place."[79] Pat's Place taught Wilson how the past shapes people's perceptions and behavior. A conversation he heard there appeared later in the play *Ma Rainey's Black Bottom*: "Someone said, 'I came to Pittsburgh in '42 on the B & O,' and another guy said, 'Oh no, you ain't come to Pittsburgh in '42 . . . the B & O Railroad didn't stop in Pittsburgh in '42!' And the first guy would say, 'You gonna tell me what railroad I came in on?' 'Hell yeah I'm gonna tell you the truth!'"[80]

Over time, Wilson eventually became one of the regulars at Pat's, part of the joking relationships that flourished there. The regulars nicknamed him "Youngblood," a joking reference to Youngblood Priest, the stylish cocaine dealer in the Blaxploitation film *Superfly*. "Hey, Youngblood," someone once asked, "how far the moon?" Wilson replied, "150,000 miles." Someone commented, "That boy don't know nothing! The moon's a million miles!" Pat's was just what Wilson had been looking for—a place where he could be accepted as an insider but remain enough of an outsider to listen and learn.[81] Wilson had read anthropology in the library, but at Pat's Place he actually operated like an anthropologist. As he said, "I had to look at black life with an anthropological eye."[82]

Wilson learned other important lessons through observation. Once, while sitting in a bar, he saw a man named Filmore come in with a white woman. A patron said casually, "I see you got your white ho' with you." Those were the man's last words. Pulling out a knife, Filmore yelled, "That's my wife, motherfucker!" and proceeded to cut the man to pieces. When the police arrived, no one had seen anything. The victim had broken a code of the street not to gratuitously insult somebody's wife. Wilson says that had the man simply tried to rob Filmore, people would have immediately pointed him out.[83]

Another place that was crucial to Wilson's education was Eddie's Restaurant, just a few doors up Wylie from Pat's and the place where Wilson did much of his writing.[84] Edward T. Owens and his brother Donald opened Eddie's in 1964, a year or so before Wilson came to Centre Avenue.[85] Eddie's stayed open most of the night, and the sidewalk out front was filled with late-night crowds looking for someplace to eat and socialize after other clubs had closed.[86] Eddie was known for letting down-on-their-luck patrons eat for free, sometimes lending them money, and sometimes even bringing them food when they took ill. "He didn't care if you were a minister, a judge, a drug addict or a prostitute," Eddie's sister said. "It was in his nature to treat everybody with the utmost respect."[87]

Sala, Rob, and August liked to gather at Eddie's, where they used a rear booth as an informal office.[88] After the others left, August would stay there all day—sometimes late into the night—listening in on patrons' conversations, nursing cups of coffee, and writing furiously. He also was known for smoking nonstop. People said Wilson needed only one match because he'd light the next cigarette with the embers of the previous one.[89] Thelma Smalls, the restaurant's waitress, knew August's habits and had a soft spot for him. "August would come in and sit at the counter," she says. "He'd sit there all day. He'd always have the same meal: two eggs over easy, home fries and biscuits with butter and jelly on wheat toast. He drank his coffee black, and he asked that I keep it coming."[90] Thelma may have been the waitress who gave Wilson a valuable insight that he treasured. Noticing him writing on a paper napkin, she asked if he wrote on napkins because that way "it doesn't count." Wilson was pleased. Writing on napkins did make him less self-conscious because in a way it was "not really writing."[91] Later, Wilson incorporated the atmosphere at Eddie's into some of his plays. When a visiting theater critic once visited Eddie's, he noticed how the restaurant's atmosphere—including its booth seating and jukebox playing soul music—had become the prototype for Memphis Lee's restaurant in *Two Trains Running*. "If there's a significant difference between Eddie's and Lee's," the critic wrote, "it's invisible from this booth."[92]

Eddie was a generous proprietor but became annoyed by the hours August spent there writing and asking for free refills of coffee. "That son of a bitch August is going to be here taking up space in a god damn booth and not buying shit. One cup of coffee a day, or some shit like that," Eddie would grouse.[93] Eddie once offered Wilson a job washing dishes, but fired him on day one when he found him sitting in a booth, writing.[94] "Man, I ain't got no job for you," Eddie scolded. "Now you take the book, and you go ahead on."[95]

How I Learned portrays Wilson not just as an outsider but also as a warrior, willing to fight for a principle and to walk off a job at the slightest affront. On Wilson's first day restocking items in a toy store, the owner warns him, "If I catch you stealing anything, I'm going to shoot you." He replies, quietly, "I quit, motherfucker." Hired to cut grass in the South Hills, he overhears a customer tell his boss to get him off her lawn. Assuming the objection was racial, Wilson quits when his boss orders him to move and cut another lawn. Working as a dishwasher at Klein's Restaurant downtown, Wilson brings books to work. When the kitchen manager asks what the books are for, he replies sarcastically, "They're for reading." Not long afterward, he quits—so he's unemployed once again.[96]

When he overstayed his welcome at Eddie's, Wilson often went next door to My Brother's Place, owned by Eddie's brother Donald. My Brother's Place attracted people who liked to come in after work to drink, rub shoulders, and chat. On one occasion, Kenneth Owens-El was in the restaurant with Wilson's friend Nick. Owens-El noticed someone in the corner writing on a yellow legal pad and said to Nick, "I keep seeing this guy around in some of the spots, some of the clubs, and some of the bars, but he looks like he's got issues." Nick asked, "What kind of issues are you talking about?" Owens-El replied, "Well, he's always writing on that yellow legal pad, but more importantly, he just looks different." Nick explained, "That's because he IS different. He's a genius. . . . that's August Wilson. . . . He's a poet and a writer." Nick told Owens-El that one day he "would hear about" Wilson because "he was no joke. He was a genuine genius." Bewildered, Owens-El said, "I'm glad to know, because I thought he was insane." After that, whenever Owens-El saw Wilson, he would smile at him in recognition of what he came to regard as "a beautiful spirit."[97]

Across the street from Eddie's and My Brother's Place was the Crawford Grill, Pittsburgh's leading jazz club. That was saying something, because the Hill had many fine jazz spots. Nelson Harrison, a leading figure in the local jazz scene, says that in the 1950s and 1960s the Hill boasted thirty or forty active clubs, not counting the many after-hours joints.[98] The first Crawford Grill had been located on lower Wylie Avenue. It opened in 1933 and closed in 1951, following a fire. The second grill, often referred to as Crawford Grill No. 2, opened in 1943, and during its heyday in the 1950s and 1960s, it brought in famous jazz artists, national as well as local, and attracted a diverse set of patrons—Black people, white people, professionals, blue-collar workers, artists, athletes, and students.[99]

Crowds flocked to hear jazz at the Grill. One night in 1963, Wilson saw an especially large crowd standing outside. Wondering if someone had been killed, he rushed over and began asking questions, only to be shushed because everyone was quietly listening to the music of John Coltrane as it wafted out into the night.[100] The scene made an indelible impression on Wilson. Until then, he had not appreciated the ability of jazz to captivate an audience in ways that words alone could not. He considered the scene one of the most remarkable in his life.[101]

Wilson became a regular at the Grill, usually arriving in the afternoon when no one was playing and he and friends could talk without being distracted by the music. Chawley says they discussed all manner of things: "Our history, our lives, our traditions, connecting with the [Harlem] Renaissance, the Black Power movement, self-defense, self-determination, self-respect, and how that [related to] our community and affected us as artists in our society."[102] Wilson contributed to those conversations but, always the outsider, his degree of engagement varied considerably. One moment he could be discussing why poetry should reflect commitment to social issues, and the next he might be standing off in a corner, writing.[103] Harrison remembers Wilson as something of a recluse at those gatherings. "He was just there. He was sitting there taking notes. Nobody knew what he was doing."[104]

Fifth Avenue had only one place that engaged Wilson, but that one forever changed him. Saint Vincent de Paul, a Catholic-operated retail outlet in the Hill, was located near the intersection of Wyandotte and Fifth Avenue. The store featured used clothing and other highly discounted items, including used records, which it sold for a pittance. Wilson loved music, and over the years acquired a large collection of 78 rpms. But his collection consisted mainly of mainstream white musicians such as Hoagy Carmichael and Patti Page.[105] At one point, he tried acquainting himself with jazz by listening to the artists in alphabetical order. Understandably, that sort of academic approach caused his enthusiasm to flag by the time he got to Jelly Roll Morton, only halfway through the alphabet.[106]

One day while looking through his collection, Wilson noticed a record with a label that was typewritten rather than printed. It was Bessie Smith's "Nobody in Town Can Bake a Sweet Jellyroll Like Mine." Wilson had discovered the blues and could scarcely control his emotions. He listened to the record twenty-two straight times, finding it something he "instantly emotionally understood" and making other music seem like something that "did not concern me, was not a part of me."[107] Wilson elaborated on his feelings:

> It is difficult to describe what happened to me. . . . For the first time some one was speaking directly to me about myself and the cultural environment of my life. I was stunned. by its beauty. by its honesty, and most important by the fact that it was mine. An affirmation of my presence in the world that would hold me up and give me ground to stand on. I began to look at the occupants of my [rooming] house in a different light. I saw behind the seeming despair and emptiness of their lives a force of life, and an

indomitable will that linked to their historical precedents became noble in a place where nobility wasn't supposed to exist.[108]

Wilson's discovery was quite fortuitous. Pittsburgh had little of a blues tradition and few clubs where one could hear the blues. Only one existing blues recording explicitly references Pittsburgh: "Wylie Avenue Blues," recorded in 1927 by Martha Copeland. However, it is possible that Wilson's discovery of the blues was not as accidental as he says. Just two years prior, in 1963, LeRoi Jones/Amiri Baraka had published *Blues People*, a powerful, widely read history of the blues. Given Wilson's voracious reading habits, he may well have read Baraka's history. Regardless of how he came to the blues, doing so changed the way he regarded Black people and Black culture. As Joan Herrington writes, "This awakening to Bessie Smith and the blues had a profound effect on Wilson who began writing to explore, in his own words, the nobility of those lives, first in poetry and later in plays."[109]

After discovering the blues, Wilson said, "I began to look at people in the rooming house differently. I had seen them as beaten. I was twenty, and these were old people. I didn't see the value to their lives. You could never have told me there was a richness and a fullness to their lives."[110] The blues changed the way Wilson saw them. "I discovered a beauty and a nobility in their struggle to survive. . . . The major fact that they were still able to make this music was a testament to the resiliency of their spirit."[111]

Wilson had gone out onto Centre Avenue to acquire material for his poetry. Ironically, his poems did not focus on the avenue so much as on the personal demons that confronted him as an outsider, especially his troubled relationship with his mother. Only years later, in his plays, did his anthropological forays pay off in the form of realistic dialogue and compelling characters. Before that, his writing was influenced more by what he read than by what he observed.

5

Early Poetry

Sometime in 1965 or early 1966, Rob Penny burst into the apartment of his friend Jerry Rhodes. "Man!" Rob exclaimed, "You got to hear this new poet. . . . He's reading Dylan Thomas. . . . [He] has everybody's head turned."[1] Rhodes rushed down to see this "head-turner." He immediately recognized that the new talent, August Wilson, was Freddy Kittel, his childhood friend and neighbor. Rhodes could see immediately why the listeners were so excited. Unlike most poets, Wilson did not read his poems. He recited them from memory, with a dramatic delivery that enthralled audiences even when they could not understand Dylan Thomas's Welsh dialect. "He was very theatrical," Rhodes says.[2]

Reciting poetry before a live audience at the Halfway Art Gallery helped Wilson develop his skills as a poet. At a lecture in 1988, he said that after leaving home he spent the next thirteen years "standing on the corner of Centre Avenue and Kirkpatrick." He added that "standing on a corner was actually being at the Halfway Art Gallery."[3] Halfway Art Gallery sponsored an affiliated group, Pittsburgh Organizers, which offered classes for the general community in drawing, drama, guitar, dance, and poetry.[4] On Sundays, the gallery was especially active. After church, it held poetry readings and live jazz that brought in addicts and the general public. Rhodes, the gallery's assistant director, convinced artists that exhibiting there was both socially

responsible and good for their careers.[5] Through his efforts, the gallery became a magnet that brought in an interracial collection of socially conscious
lovers of the arts.

It is remarkable that a city best known for steel mills and poor air quality
also had a lively cultural scene. Pittsburgh had a world-renowned symphony,
a major art museum, and generous patrons of the arts such as the Heinzes,
Fricks, Hillmans, Hunts, and Mellons. Over the years, the city had boasted
such luminaries of the arts as Mary Cassatt, Gertrude Stein, Gene Kelly, and
Andy Warhol. Pittsburgh's African American community also had a tradition
in the arts. In the early 1900s, it supported several literary societies and concert orchestras. In the 1920s, it became a center for jazz, spawning such greats
as Billy Strayhorn, Kenny Clarke, Earl "Fatha" Hines, Roy Eldridge, Mary
Lou Williams, and Lena Horne. Later, its jazz scene featured such Pittsburgh
stalwarts as Art Blakey, Louise Mann, Billy Eckstine, Maxine Sullivan, Stanley Turrentine, Erroll Garner, Ahmad Jamal, and George Benson.

Thad Mosley—a sculptor, photographer, and gallery owner—was a major figure in the local art scene. In the early 1950s, Mosley helped found
the Writers and Photographers Guild of Pittsburgh, which brought together
African American devotees of painting, sculpture, photography, and writing.
In 1955 the guild showcased many of the community's best artists and writers
in a landmark publication, *Compositions in Black & White*, which contained
over forty pages of photographs, essays, poetry, and short stories. A few years
later, Mosley expanded his leadership in the arts by opening Group One
Gallery. Located in his home on the North Side, the gallery offered poetry
readings, jazz concerts, and art exhibitions.[6] August Wilson and Rob Penny
were among its patrons.

Group One Gallery closed in 1964 and was quickly succeeded by the
Hill Art & Music Society. The brainchild of Hill District businessman and
politician Tony Upshur, the society held a significant place in Wilson's development; he says that when he went out on Centre Avenue, he "fell into the
clutches" of its talented poets and painters.[7] Operating out of a storefront on
Centre Avenue, the society exhibited works by the city's leading Black artists,
such as Sy Moraco and Jerry Rhodes, who did paintings and line art; Ed
Ellis and Barbara Peterson, who did portraits; Harold Ellis, who worked in
watercolors; Edward Upshur, who did murals; James Clemons, who painted
and sculpted; and Carl Smith, known as "Dingbat," who fashioned highly
original nail sculptures.[8] Although the gallery focused on the graphic and
plastic arts, it welcomed poets such as August, Rob, and Chawley. It also

featured jazz concerts by groups such as Kenny Fisher and his jazz ensemble, The Iconoclasts.

The Hill Art & Music Society faced financial difficulties that brought it to the brink of closure. It found a way to continue by joining forces with an organization founded by Rick Martin, a minister at St. Stephen's Anglican Church in the tony suburb of Sewickley. As part of his training to become a missionary, Martin wanted to work with people in the inner city suffering from drug addiction. He came up with the idea of a combination mission and art gallery, the idea being that an art gallery could provide addicts a nonstigmatized place where they could come in for treatment and counseling. Martin opened a storefront a few doors from the Hill Art & Music Society and recruited two other ministers from St. Stephen's, Bob Hetherington and Ted Weatherley, to run the day-to-day operations.

The combination of an art gallery and drug addiction treatment center may have been a fine idea, but as an operation run by a white outsider it faced difficulties. The principal difficulty was attracting people to enroll. Recognizing that they needed a local Black organization to partner with, the founders turned to the Hill Art & Music Society, which they knew was struggling financially. The two groups merged in April 1966, and the Art & Music Society moved into the storefront already occupied by St. Stephen's.[9] Chawley Williams suggested they call the new endeavor Halfway Art Gallery because it was "halfway along the road to understanding between the Negro and white community . . . and a 'halfway area' where the street people who need some direction can find understanding, a shoulder to lean on, a helpful word or a guiding hand."[10]

The gallery was supported by leading figures in the city's white and Black communities. White sponsors included George and David B. Oliver, descendants of the founders of Oliver Iron and Steel Company, and Roy Hunt Jr., vice president of Mellon Bank and grandson of Alfred Hunt, the founder of Alcoa Aluminum.[11] African American sponsors included Byrd Brown, a Yale-educated attorney and son of Pittsburgh's first Black judge; Wendell Freeland, a leading attorney and former Tuskegee Airmen; and Robert Lavelle, a real estate agent and founder of the city's only Black-owned bank.

Patrons of the gallery's exhibitions were interested both in the arts and in breaking down racial and class barriers.[12] Indeed, a substantial part of Halfway Art Gallery's patrons were white. Although sometimes viewed with suspicion, they generally were well accepted and sometimes considered "cool."[13] The gallery even attracted sex workers operating out of the nearby

Ellis Hotel. They would come into the gallery with their pimps, who might survey the art on display and, to impress their ladies, say something like, "Hey baby, pick any one you want." The presence of such atypical patrons helped protect the gallery. No one ever broke in and there was never any violence. Rhodes says the gallery had "a very good vibe."[14]

Wilson and his fellow poets supported the gallery's goals of interracial collaboration. In 1967 he and Nick Flournoy served as editors of the catalog to the gallery's first exhibition.[15] Ed Ellis and Chawley contributed essays to the catalog praising the gallery as a place where Black and white, city and suburb, elite and addicts could come together in harmony and goodwill.[16] A catalog photograph, titled "Sunday Night at the Gallery," features a group of Black and white musicians performing together. Other photographs spotlight works by white artists on exhibition, which included Virginia Allen, a local painter; Troy West, a professor of architecture at Carnegie Mellon University; and Virgil Cantini, one of the city's most prominent sculptors and an art professor at the University of Pittsburgh.[17]

From the time of its opening, Halfway Art Gallery enjoyed success in attracting artists, writers, musicians, and recovering addicts. Ellis, a well-known painter who had exhibited both locally and nationally, was chosen as the gallery's director. A former addict himself, Ellis had the sort of street cred that made him liked and trusted. In addition, the former storefront that housed the gallery had been remodeled into a modern, attractive space. Gail Austin, a student and community activist, considered Halfway Art Gallery one of the most attractive meeting places on Centre Avenue.[18]

At the gallery, Wilson could spend time with fellow artists and writers whose company he found inspiring. One of these was Sy Moraco. Born Sylvester Moraco Jones, Sy was a noted painter, sculptor, and musician. Wilson fondly called him "the original homeless man" because he "would show up out of nowhere and disappear as quickly as he came."[19] Sy had many idiosyncrasies, some quite endearing. He once walked down the street with heavy chains around his neck and a sign proclaiming him "The Bound Man." When asked what that meant, he replied, "I'm making a protest. I feel like I'm in shackles." Other stunts were less endearing. Once, someone came running up to Rhodes, imploring breathlessly, "You got to come down to the Gallery. . . . Sy has all your paintings out in the street. Talking about Sale!" Hurrying down, Rhodes spotted Sy standing next to his paintings with a sign proclaiming, "Liquidation Sale!" When asked what he was doing, Sy replied innocently, "Drumming up business."[20]

Poetry readings at the gallery took place on Sunday evenings, typically preceded by conga and bongo drumming and followed by a jazz performance. Sometimes the poets put on "free-for-alls" in which they improvised in free association with the music.[21] Wilson paid attention to audience priorities, noticing that most people came for the jazz, and that the poets were allowed to read only while the musicians were setting up. Nevertheless, Wilson relished that the audience included recovering addicts and "grassroots" residents. "That was part of our worldview," Sala Udin says. "We embraced the poor and the working class, and not the middle class."[22]

At these readings, Wilson enjoyed reciting poems by Dylan Thomas, an internationally famous Welsh poet. Thomas was very popular in the United States, becoming the public's image of the tortured and long-suffering poet. Notorious for his hard drinking, carousing, and womanizing, Thomas was not technically part of the Beat movement, but he influenced the Beats. Wilson never clarified whether he considered himself part of the Beat movement, but the way he dressed gave that impression. Local photographer Frank Hightower says the first time he met Rob and August, they were reading poetry at the Carnegie Lecture Hall dressed in tennis shoes and wearing "a beatnik type thing." Local followers of the arts, including William Strickland and Gail Austin, felt that Wilson was at least a follower of the Beats if not a full-fledged Beat himself.[23] Regardless of his actual affiliation, Wilson identified with Thomas, no doubt partly because Thomas was considered an outsider by the British poetry establishment.

Brilliant and hard driving, Thomas's poems, recorded on several albums, were rooted in his Welsh homeland. Wilson borrowed Thomas's recordings from Thad Mosley and learned to recite them in near-perfect Welsh dialect.[24] He even began dressing like Thomas, in a white shirt, tie, woolen tweed jacket, and British-style driving cap.[25] He also imitated Thomas's dramatic style of delivery. Reciting in full Welsh dialect kept most listeners clueless as to what Wilson was saying, but that did not seem to matter. Rhodes says, "Black people like theater, something with a sense of style. They may not understand it, but [August's] style of presentation and his confidence in it was enough for them."[26] Chawley and Nick also were fans of Thomas. At the end of a day, when they and August would part company, the three would recite the opening stanza of one of Thomas's best-known poems: "Do not go gentle into that good night, / Old age should burn and rave at close of day; / Rage, rage against the dying of the light."[27] But Chawley warned his friend not to imitate others. "Write your own material," he advised August.

Wilson liked reciting Thomas because of the positive feedback he got from audiences, but over time he recited the Welshman less and less as Thomas's reputation declined among other poets.[28] Wilson also stopped dressing like Thomas, switching to a military-style canvas jacket and cap.[29] However, August did not heed Chawley's advice to focus on his own poetry and his own voice. After abandoning Thomas, Wilson began writing and reciting in the manner of John Berryman, the new star of the poetry world. Berryman was a leading figure of the so-called Confessional School of poetry that depicted intense psychological traumas. In 1965, the year Wilson declared himself a poet, Berryman's collection *77 Dream Songs* won the Pulitzer Prize, and Berryman was featured in *Life* magazine. Berryman was someone an ambitious young poet might want to emulate.[30] He wrote tragic poems that take the reader to the darker places of life. Because these are "dream songs," they are unconstrained by logic and reality. Opaque and difficult to understand, Berryman famously said sarcastically that his poems "were not meant to be understood. You understand?"[31] Wilson's poems, like Berryman's, were dense and often inscrutable.[32]

One poet's practice Wilson never stopped imitating was Chawley's trademark habit of writing anywhere and on anything handy—scraps of paper, napkins, yellow pads, and the like. "I always had a napkin and a pencil," Wilson said. "That's one of the things [I like] about writing—the tools are so simple."[33] He did Chawley one better by writing and reciting even while walking down the street. Doing so puzzled onlookers and made some wonder whether he was writing "numbers."[34] Reggie Howze, Sala's brother, says that on a warm summer day, Wilson might be seen walking down the street in a long winter coat, apparently talking to himself. Some people did not realize he was reciting poetry and thought he had lost his mind. They were especially baffled when occasionally he would stop at a telephone pole and appear to be talking to it. They did not realize that he was reciting a poem. "Fortunately," Howze says, "that phase went away."[35]

Wilson worked diligently at his craft, jotting down over a hundred ideas for poems, both new and partially finished.[36] During his years in Pittsburgh, twenty were published—three in national outlets and seventeen in mimeographed publications that circulated among friends.[37] His earliest set of published poems appeared in in *Signal Magazine*, issued by Halfway Art Gallery.[38] Wilson has four entries in the magazine's 1966 issue. Written in the Confessional style of Berryman, the poems focus on the pain and suffering of the outsider. These tortured, highly personal poems are filled with lonely figures who exist beyond the pale of family and community. Like Adam and

Eve, they reside in a purgatory of past sins that will never be forgiven. They are victims of emotional—and sometimes physical—violence.

The poems are opaque but much of their meaning becomes apparent when one is acquainted with Wilson's life, particularly his strained relationship with his mother. "The Visit," for example, depicts the narrator alone in his room one stormy night when he is startled by the silent entrance of a woman. At first, he is unsure whether she is a stranger entering unannounced or someone returning home, but the familiar sound of her footsteps and the fact that she entered "as usual" indicates the latter. Their relationship has clearly soured. The speaker invites the visitor to stay, which she does, raising hopes that she has come "to end the war." This is not the case. An ominous silence pervades the room, and then lightning and claps of thunder signal that "the execution" has begun.

A second poem, "For D.Y.M. (After Dylan Thomas)," pays homage to Wilson's favorite poet while describing the painful existence of two people who share a common living space and are condemned to unending conflict. Theirs is a place of foreboding, of tension and past fights, where unspecified things lie "buried deep in the blood." The woman—"Adam's Eve"—enjoys tormenting the narrator and will not forgive his sins. He rebukes her, saying that she "Grieves the heaven-sent bread," likely a reference to the rolls young Freddy's father brought the family from work. Despite everything, the narrator weeps and pays loving tribute to her: "Where tears-groove shakes this throne / And my glory to your heaven's head." The poem is a meditation on the unforgiving response of Wilson's mother to his dropping out of school.

"To Whom It May Concern" explores the pain of the outsider. Its very title suggests alienation and emotional distance. The narrator wants to be pardoned for past mistakes and likens himself to Adam after his expulsion from the Garden of Eden. Seeking readmission to the "town," he claims he was "quite innocent" when he discarded his clothes and chose to "somersault" off the chariot's path that leads to community and respectability, symbolized in the poem as the church and the church bell. The narrator explains that he was enticed to his sins (casting off his clothes, carnal romps) by good times (the town's "fair Weather"). But he still desires membership in the accepted "arrangement" of the town, a sign that he wants to come home, even though—as suggested by the title "To Whom It May Concern"—no one knows him and no one will be there to welcome him back.

"Romona," Wilson's fourth and final poem in the magazine, describes the pain of an outsider condemned to emotional and physical exile. An overweight girl sits alone in a diner, eating a hamburger. Like the biblical Eve, she has been deceived in the "orchard with thin serpent" and now lives, tragically, "with garden lost." She is emotionally isolated and alone; her shouts of desperation make "no sound." When she listens for her own voice or that of Adam, she hears only "curses of bitch and dumb."

"Poet," a highly significant and revealing poem published the following year, 1967, in the catalog of an exhibition at Halfway Art Gallery, is written in a simple, straightforward style, quite different from Wilson's other poems of that period.

Poet

As though to stay the moment,
He straightened his tie and watched
The rain at the window. Always
As with the rain the resolved
Distance meant the startled meeting
Of shadow and actual entourage,
The visiting union, a more trivial
Or accident,

                              So he had to go,

Out from his mother's table. Bags and fright
out to the rush and ruin, drama
Of the frowning and flashing city.
And with indecency too. His mother
Towering behind him, the halo round
His head, set to rage and make
Her tongue stick out to taunt—
Like all the others

                        "Even the monsignor said . . ."
"Yes, mother."
A sheet of rain made a sound
At the window, and he straightened his tie.

                            His mother,

Her hard looks manifest by shame,
Unsheathed a flaming sword, . . .
And he had to go,
As two in a garden had to go,
The distance bright, and there

Where it was to set foot,

Bleak as a discarded crown.

His father, his purple head, laid grave-rest,

Turned to see him, go, and he set

Out against exquisite terror,

The streets a cobble-stone wreath.[39]

"Poet" is painful, personal, and accusatory. The poem's narrator is the victim of his mother's fury, and the beneficiary of his dead father's sympathy, as he quietly and obediently accepts expulsion and life in exile. More than anything that Wilson had written, or would write in the future, it shows the pain of his mother having expelled him from home, turning him into an outsider rejected even by his mother.

August clearly was not following Chawley's recommendation that he write his own work and not imitate others. However, neither was he writing in the manner of his circle of poet friends. While Wilson's early poems focus on the inner pain of an outsider, Chawley's poetry captures the texture of life in the Hill. Chawley was a gentle, caring man, but a man of the streets. A recovering addict himself, he wrote of the pain and hard times experienced by others, not himself. Wilson's poems also differ from those of his friend Nick Flournoy, which are characterized by erudite allusions to such cultural icons as Paul Klee, Modigliani, and Ezra Pound. Rob Penny's style differed starkly from those of August, Chawley, and Nick. His entry in the 1967 exhibition catalog of the Halfway Art Gallery, "The Doodle Bug Poem," displays not inner turmoil and suffering but anger and racial protest.

"Doodle-Bug" was a very important poem. The title is based on the sort of nickname likely belonging to someone from the street, someone Rob would refer to years later as a "stomp-down blood."[40] The poem mocks the white "diaphanous God, gulping down His / Pie in the sky" and warns ominously of Black muscles growing "taut." It addresses what it means to be part of "america's [sic] conflict." In that conflict, Doodle-Bug has died a noble death, similar to that of such historic race liberators as Harriet Tubman and Toussaint L'Ouverture. Doodle-Bug's death stands as a rebuke to "stupid niggers" unwilling to die for racial liberation—employing the taboo epithet that was increasingly used by Black nationalists to mock self-deceiving African Americans who have not freed their minds and embraced their Blackness. The poem ends with a question that amounts to a call to arms: "Can you back doodle-bug?"

The "Doodle-Bug Poem" made Rob the first major poet in Pittsburgh to call for Black power and Black resistance—including violence—to racial oppression. The poem signaled the arrival in Pittsburgh of the Black Arts Movement. As begun and led by New Jersey poet Amiri Baraka, the Black Arts Movement rejected Martin Luther King Jr.'s goal of racial integration in favor of Malcolm X's emphasis on racial protest, racial separatism, and Black power. Baraka called on Black artists, writers, and musicians to synchronize their artistic expressions with Malcolm X and Black Power. The "Doodle Bug Poem" was the sort of poem that made Rob the leading figure of Pittsburgh's Black Arts movement.[41]

A few months later, the *Pittsburgh Point,* a magazine of the arts, dedicated a section of its May 1967 issue to the state of local Black poetry. Wilson may have inspired this coverage when, curiously, he wrote a letter to the editor complaining that the city's most recent International Poetry Forum included no examples of contemporary, racially militant poetry.[42] Whatever the impetus, *Pittsburgh Point* took note of the poetry readings at Halfway Art Gallery and invited August, Rob, Nick, and Chawley to put together a feature article that would include examples of new trends in local Black poetry.[43] Titled "4 in the Centre Avenue Tradition," the group's submission brought citywide attention and provided the name by which they would subsequently refer to themselves: Poets in the Centre Avenue Tradition.

The poem that Rob submitted, "Crawling the Long Run Up Centre Avenue," has a Baraka-like, nationalist message similar to that of his "Doodle-Bug Poem." Poems by Nick, Chawley, and August, however, did not follow Rob's lead. Nick wrote the introduction to the collection, implicitly rebuking Rob by positing that "Centre Avenue does not generate poetry of protest" because on Centre "the very existence of poetry is a protest." Rather, Nick said, Centre Avenue poets "seek simply to capture the voice of the Avenue and the language of its residents."[44] August's submission, despite his previous criticism of the International Poetry Forum, had none of the anger and nationalist undertones of Baraka and Baraka's acolyte Rob Penny. August's poem in the collection, "Wakening and Walking Out" focuses on the intimate and personal rather than the political. A narrator lies alone in his room, dreaming of Honey Girl, a prostitute who winks and beckons to him. As he awakens, Honey Girl "walks with [her] fingers" over his body and awakens his "parcel." Following a masturbatory climax, "The burning comes down." Chawley's poem, "Center Avenue I," describes desperate times on the avenue and the desperate lives of those who inhabit the streets, places of "Cold and lighted love; / Concrete and glass lights; / Black poles and ancient walls; / Gutters and green streets after rain."

Although Rob, August, Nick, and Chawley claimed a group identity as Poets in the Centre Avenue Tradition, Rob saw himself as "different." Years later, he told friend and interviewer Lee Kiburi that others in the group "saw me as being different too. . . . I just never thought they recognized me as being a poet." Rob criticized the poetry of Chawley, August, and Nick as overly intellectual and European. "I wasn't interested in Dylan Thomas like August was," Rob said. "I wasn't interested in all those white poets . . . that Nick was interested in, and Chawley." Rob especially disliked a game the other three played in which someone would give the opening line of a poem and the others would recite the rest of the poem. "I couldn't do anything like that," he said dismissively, "because I wasn't interested in white poets."[45] Rather, Rob said he read and drew inspiration from African poets, Caribbean poets, and such militant African American poets as Ted Joans, The Last Poets, Marvin X, and Askia Muhammad Touré.[46] He said he especially liked Baraka, and carried around a copy of Baraka's "Black Dada Nihilismus," which made chillingly defiant calls to racial violence, urging Black revolutionaries to "Rape the white girls. Rape / their fathers. Cut the mothers' throats." Rob said he liked the poem because it said things he hadn't heard before in poetry.[47] And he was dismayed that August and the others wouldn't even read the poem. "They weren't interested in that," Rob lamented.[48]

Nick, Chawley, and August were influenced mainly by white poets. Nick liked Ezra Pound and Chawley favored Lawrence Ferlinghetti.[49] August read a large number of poets, including Wallace Stevens, John Cohen, the Black Mountain poets, Robert Creeley, and George Barker, but in a 1999 interview with Kiburi—a staunch local adherent of Malcolm X—he acknowledged that all the poets he read were white. He added, defensively and defiantly, "and, yeah, that's cool." Wilson told Kiburi that he did not read Baraka, and he did not read other Black poets because "they were all in essence following behind Baraka."[50]

Nonetheless, the nationalist outlook of Baraka and Rob were growing in popularity, especially among college students. Locally, the growth can be traced to a 1967 lecture delivered at the University of Pittsburgh by Stokely Carmichael, firebrand chairman of the Student Nonviolent Coordinating Committee (SNCC). Carmichael traveled to campus just a year after he had popularized the concept of Black Power during a nationally famous march to Jackson, Mississippi. Before an overflowing, racially mixed audience in the Student Union at the University of Pittsburgh, Carmichael maintained that Black Power, not racial integration, was the only way Black people could achieve liberation.[51] After his well-received address, Carmichael held a private meeting with Black students at which he told them the only way to achieve Black Power was through organizing. Inspired by Carmichael, students left the meeting resolved to organize.[52]

Carmichael's address coincided with the arrival of a new type of student at the University of Pittsburgh. In 1966 the university had suffered a financial crisis, and was rescued in a bailout organized by K. Leroy Irvis, Pittsburgh's influential Black state legislator. The terms of the bailout converted Pitt from an expensive, overwhelmingly white, private school into a state-related institution with tuition charges lowered to match those of other state universities. Reduced tuition fostered the enrollment of students of modest means, white as well as Black.

One of these new students was Curtiss Porter, who had served in the US Air Force and, upon returning home, used his government benefits to enroll at Penn State University's branch campus in McKeesport. In 1966, during his junior year, Porter transferred to Pitt, majoring in writing.[53] Carmichael's speech in the Student Union deeply affected Porter, even though at the time he dismissed it as superficial, another version of "Bang Bang Umgawa black powa." But when Porter saw how Carmichael inspired students to organize, he changed his mind. As he recalls, he was in awe of how Carmichael changed the atmosphere: "The chant [of Black Power] rose in the William Pitt Student Union Building," Porter says, "and everybody got involved."[54]

Acting on their pledge to Carmichael, Pitt students founded the Afro-American Cultural Society (AACS), and elected Porter as chairman.[55] At AACS meetings, students avidly discussed the Quran, Carter G. Woodson's *The Mis-Education of the Negro*, and writings by Black intellectuals such as Frantz Fanon, W. E. B. Du Bois, and Amiri Baraka, then still known as LeRoi Jones.[56] Activism at Pitt inspired students elsewhere in the city. Natalie Bazzell, a student at Chatham College, recalls how she and her husband Creamer were exhilarated by the rapid growth in Black consciousness at Pitt, which they felt exceeded anything they had known in Philadelphia.[57] "Everybody was trying to do something," Bazzell says. "We were young. We wanted to express ourselves. Some people did it in theater, some in dance, some in poetry, and some in jazz."[58]

As interest in Black Power spread beyond the university and into the larger Black community, the question arose whether AACS should admit nonstudents. Halfway Art Gallery was one of the AACS's favorite meeting places, and Ed Ellis, the gallery's director, insisted that nonstudents be allowed to join.[59] There was some resistance, but Ellis eventually won the argument. The Afro-American Cultural Society changed its name to the Afro-American Institute (AAI) and began accepting nonstudents. Among the leaders of the AAI, Porter and Phil McKain represented the university, while August, Sala, Ewari Ellis, and Rob represented "the street."[60]

Wilson joined the AAI, attended a few meetings, and occasionally read poetry at AAI events, but stayed largely on the sidelines. His lack of full engagement irritated Rob, who complained to Kiburi, "Well, you know how August was. He never was really a joiner of organizations."[61] Chawley and Nick were unmoved by Rob's urging that they take a more nationalist stance, and his argument that Poets in the Centre Avenue Tradition should follow Baraka's urging and migrate from poetry to theater. Baraka called for Black writers to prepare the masses for the coming race war. He had initially done so through poems like "Black Dada Nihilismus" and "Black Art," which called for "poems that kill," that annihilate the "enemies" of Black people—white liberals, Jews, and "assimilated Negroes." A year later, Baraka urged Black poets to switch to theater, believing the latter was more accessible to the masses. His play, *A Black Mass* (1966), provided a race-centered creation myth to contradict that of "white" Christianity. Baraka's book *Arm Yourself or Harm Yourself* (1967) urged Black people to take up arms.

Over the summer of 1967, Rob brought together Curtiss Porter, Jerry Rhodes, and members of Poets in the Centre Avenue Tradition for what turned out to be a series of long, difficult discussions about following Baraka's call. Ultimately, in what Rob describes as "a smoky, beer tainted room," the men agreed to make the switch and change their name from "Poets in the Centre Avenue Tradition" to the "Centre Avenue Poets Theatre Workshop."[62] The change marked a turning point for Wilson, who moved—a bit reluctantly—into theater. As he said later, "We talked about doing theater because theater was part of our name."[63]

In January 1968, the Centre Avenue Poets Theatre Workshop made its public debut with the publication of a new journal, *Connection*. The thirty-two-page inaugural issue was mimeographed and assembled by Porter. Rob served as the magazine's chairman, while August, Chawley, Porter, Rhodes, and Nick made up the board of directors. Rob wrote the introduction to the issue explaining the new group's origins. He noted that the shift to theater had been difficult, but that their "Afro-American Consciousness" eased conflicts and made the new organization possible.[64] Despite these claims, the inaugural issue of *Connection* contains poems and a short story, but no plays and not even any articles about theater. Rob submitted four poems to *Connection*, all written in the style of Baraka. One praised "Brutal revolutionaries / who cry out for the crackers [*sic*] death."[65] Wilson's poems employed a few nationalist tropes but focused mainly on the travails of the outsider.

One poem, "For Malcolm X and Others," went on to become nationally known when *Negro Digest* reprinted it in 1969.[66] The poem's title prepares the reader for a political, nationalist message, but the focus is on "Others" rather than Malcolm. In the poem, an emotionally detached narrator stands at a window, high above the street, observing and reflecting on the human condition. He regards Malcolm's assassination as just another sad example of brother killing brother. The narrator is lonely and alienated, having never known "love enough to stroke a cat," and stands above the fray, looking down and watching as "The sport of Cain" plays out below. He refuses to be constricted by the bloodshed and simply goes on with his life, moving stubbornly "from place to place, / Always forward, never behind." Although the poem's tone is apolitical, one passage carries a presumably race-based urge for revenge. Ghostlike figures crash the gates and spill blood as the narrator moves about, trying to put the act behind him. But the anger he carries within threatens violence, even though until now he has been disengaged. The poem makes a modest gesture to cultural nationalism but falls well short of Baraka's call for works that prepare the masses for revolution and a race war.

Wilson's second poem in the issue, "A Poem for Two Wars, Vietnam and America," also treats a topic that carries only a modest nationalist message. In his address at Pitt, Carmichael had urged Black people to resist serving in Vietnam because it amounted to fighting a "white man's war." Wilson's "Poem for Two Wars" is less about overtly refusing to fight than about war's meaninglessness. The narrator is a pilot who flies so high that he cannot see the people below. A detached outsider, he becomes merely an observer, his distance producing neither peace nor anger, only a sense of dread because he is committing an overwhelming wrong. He cannot be sure of anything, not even hope or love. Another submission by Wilson, "The Dark Christmas," is a bizarre poem that employs one nationalist trope—mocking Christianity. Strangely, it also employs egregious racial stereotypes such as being set in an African jungle where monkeys screech overhead while witch doctors boil and de-bone Christ. "Christmas and Cassandra," Wilson's fourth poem, takes as its subject the prophetess of Greek mythology whose predictions of misfortune were not believed until it was too late. "Circles and Sex," Wilson's fifth and final poem in the issue, is about a man who spends a lonely night masturbating.

Years later, Wilson looked back on his early poems with a degree of embarrassment that bordered on contempt. He criticized them for being unnecessarily obscure and not reflecting his own voice. When asked about the message of his most recognized poem, "For Malcolm X and Others," he said dismissively, "I have no idea what it means."[67] Indeed, it is difficult to tease out the poem's meaning, as can be seen in the opening stanza that easily matches Berryman in its obscurity:

> The hour rocks a clog,
> The midnight term,
> In bones no shape before
> Has warmed in such
> That loves these cold as dead,
> As stone; a flock of saints
> Run ground as thieves.

When August Wilson declared himself a poet, he did not become a flower trying to survive in an artistic desert. He was nurtured by a dynamic, vibrant, and thriving arts community. The Halfway Art Gallery provided a place where he could recite poetry on a regular basis and do so before a large and appreciative audience. Poets in the Centre Avenue Tradition constituted a brotherhood, a talented group of writers who welcomed him and critiqued his work. Sala Udin says the group welcomed Wilson and made him "a certified member of the fraternity."[68] Their support made Wilson feel—for the first time in his life—that he belonged, that he was more than a perennial outsider. He knew the importance of belonging, of not being alone when writing. As he said: "We all knew each other, and we all worked and supported each other in what we were doing. And it was very, very important that you do not have a sense that you are working in a vacuum, that you can say, 'Hey man, look at this, what do you think?'"[69] That Black Pittsburgh furnished Wilson such institutional support as well as a set of colleagues constitutes a powerful example of the power of place.

6

Race Man

In February 1968, three years after the assassination of Malcolm X, Pittsburgh's Afro-American Institute (AAI) held a commemoration of his life. During his lifetime, Malcolm's message of Black Power and racial separation resonated among a fairly narrow slice of the Black community. Following his assassination, however, Malcolm's appeal grew substantially, especially among college students, musicians, poets, and writers. On the third anniversary of his death, the AAI wanted to stage a commemoration of Malcom that would expand his message to a broader spectrum of the Black community. As Pittsburgh's leading Black nationalist organization, the AAI also wanted the commemoration to spread awareness of its presence in the larger community.

The AAI's "coming out" had been slow, partly because, as Curtiss Porter joked, it was known for "lots of meetings, lots of conversations, lots of dissension, lots of fallout, not a lot of progress, and many, many fights."[1] As the commemoration's theme, the AAI chose Black unity, the coming together of all segments of the community: middle class and working class, the church and the street, students and nonstudents, militants and moderates.

As a member of the AAI, August Wilson threw himself into helping prepare for the event. His assignment was to secure extra seating and distribute publicity flyers around the Hill. Surprisingly, the latter proved more challenging than the former. While handing out leaflets in a bar on Wylie Avenue, a patron told Wilson contemptuously, "I remember when Malcolm didn't have but twelve followers." Wilson replied sarcastically, "Well, why weren't you number thirteen?" This provoked an argument that ended with the patron saying angrily, "He ain't coming to nothing, and black folks ain't going to do this, Malcolm that." Next, Wilson approached three Marines. That didn't go well either. The Marines became incensed when Wilson criticized Black soldiers fighting in Vietnam on behalf of a "white racist" government. "The next thing I knew," Wilson says, "these three Marines had my back against the wall of this bar, and they took my flyers and they knocked them out of my hand." Fearing he was about to get an "ass-whipping," Wilson prepared to go down fighting. But that was not necessary. An elderly patron picked up the flyers, handed them to him, and said angrily, "Take this shit and get out of here!" As Wilson left the bar, patrons shouted, "And don't come back no more!" Walking down Wylie, Wilson began crying so hard he couldn't see where he was going.[2]

Despite such worrisome preliminaries, the commemoration went well. It ran for three days, from Friday, February 23, to Sunday, February 25. Each day's event took place in a different neighborhood as a way of symbolizing citywide unity. The Friday commemoration was held at Bidwell Street Presbyterian Church, a prominent congregation in Manchester with a sizable middle-class congregation. Curtiss Porter, who chronicled the proceedings for the *Pittsburgh Courier*, rejoiced at the diversity of the audience, saying it showed that the theme of racial unity was being fulfilled. "Natural hair and natural soul was [sic] everywhere," Porter exulted.[3] The second day's proceedings were held in Homewood. These also drew a diverse, enthusiastic audience.

The climax took place on Sunday at the New Granada Theater on Centre Avenue. An especially large crowd turned out because the New Granada commemoration featured Amiri Baraka and his Spirit House Movers, a dynamic and widely popular music-theater-dance group. Baraka was a huge attraction partly because of his racially militant writings. In addition, he had garnered widespread sympathy for the severe beating he suffered at the hands of the Newark police during the city's 1967 riots.[4]

Baraka's personal journey into Black Power and cultural nationalism began in 1965 when, distraught over the assassination of Malcolm X, he renounced his interracial lifestyle, divorced his white wife, moved from Greenwich Village to Harlem, and dedicated himself to promoting Malcolm X and his message of Black Power. Baraka established the Black Arts Repertory Theatre (BART) and almost single-handedly launched the Black Arts

Movement. In 1966, when the plays he staged at BART proved too racially controversial for the city's political figures, Baraka moved back to his hometown of Newark, New Jersey. There he founded Spirit House, which quickly became the national center for nationalist, revolutionary theater. His Spirit House Movers achieved great popularity through their high-energy, creative fusion of music, theater, and poetry.

Largely because of Baraka's presence, attendance at Sunday's commemoration far exceeded expectations. The Granada Theater's Savoy Ballroom was meant to hold 1,500, but about twice that number showed up. Wilson was overjoyed that the extra chairs he had secured were not nearly enough to seat everyone.[5] "People [were] standing in the halls," he rejoiced, "like jam packed."[6] As in Manchester and Homewood, the event attracted a socially and economically diverse audience, described by Porter as "young and old, poor and kinda' rich, high class and low down, militant and middle class, straight hair and straighten-ed hair, wigs and natural naps."[7] African-styled clothing had recently become popular, and local vendors like Juanita Miller did a big business selling dashikis and African jewelry.[8] Homewood's Avocados Drill Team, the Shondells singing group, and Kenny Fisher's jazz ensemble the Iconoclasts all gave memorable performances.[9]

The speeches and exhortations also were well received. Sala Udin's challenge: "There ain't but ONE thing going on—all you have to do is dig it!" drew enthusiastic applause.[10] Sababa Akili, a Cleveland-based poet and racial activist, drew applause when he told attendees they needed to "get Black, get Black, get Black." Rob Penny drew cheers when he urged those in the audience to "wash yo' hair, cleanse yo' mind, dig yo' self, an' come on home." Unfortunately, Chawley Williams's poetry proved too abstruse for the audience, which never quieted down enough to hear him.[11]

As a representative of the AAI, Wilson delivered welcoming remarks. His doing so was a bit surprising since he was not regarded as one of the community's leading Black nationalists. He secured the spot because at one of the planning meetings, he simply nominated himself to deliver the welcoming remarks. In the meeting, he had suggested that someone from the AAI should speak at the event so that Baraka could return to Newark with some words from Pittsburgh. When no one volunteered, Wilson said he felt comfortable giving the welcome because he had listened to Malcolm's speeches and had an idea of what to say.[12] No one objected, partly because people recognized Wilson's obvious speaking skills from hearing his poetry recitals at the Halfway Art Gallery.[13]

Wilson's remarks proved galvanizing. He started by comparing the plight of Black people in white America with that of Jews in Nazi Germany. The latter, he said, made the mistake of considering themselves Germans, but "ultimately—as Adolf Hitler told them—they were Jews."[14] Toward the end of his remarks, Wilson brought the crowd to its feet by thundering, "When you see a revolution going on and it's your revolution—you don't get out of the way—you join it!" The audience erupted with clapping, cheering, and clenched fists.[15] That speech marked the first occasion when, publicly and forcefully, Wilson declared his allegiance to the cause of Black Power and Black nationalism.[16]

As expected, Amiri Baraka was the main attraction. From the time of his arrival, Baraka was treated like visiting royalty. AAI representatives met him at the airport. Bodyguards made sure no one "messed" with him. He was given lodging at the Ellis Hotel, a Black-owned inn not far from the New Granada venue. And, before his appearance at the commemoration, he was taken to meet Sala Udin and other prominent nationalists for a discussion of how to advance the cause.[17]

The program listed Baraka as LeRoi Jones because many were not aware that he had recently Africanized his name. Nor did they know what he looked like. Every time somebody walked into the ballroom, people asked anxiously, "Is that him? Is that him?" Finally, people figured out that Baraka was "the little dude" in the midst of the Spirit House Movers.[18]

Belying his reputation as a firebrand, Baraka delivered a quiet, thoughtful address.[19] He chastised Black people, calling them brainwashed and obsessed with being around white people. He said they celebrated Malcolm X after he was assassinated but did not support him when he was alive.[20] Without referencing his own interracial marriage, he told the men to get rid of their "white bitches." That statement offended Moses Carper, a member of the welcoming committee, who was married to a white woman.[21] Carper says Baraka hypocritically "jumped on [us] militants very hard. Hey man," Carper said to himself, "You had your experience, and you want to deny these [to others]."[22]

Porter praised the success of the commemoration's theme of unity. "Black Unity," Porter wrote, "danced its black dance to the rhythms of a people who understood. It was crowded and it was hot, and the program was 'too long,' but nonetheless they stayed to hear the message of 'Black Unity and Culture.'"[23] Sala Udin praised the Spirit House Movers: "We had not seen a performance like that," he said. "It was bold, it was black, it was creative."[24] Wilson, like Udin, found the Spirit House Movers exhilarating. Years later, he used Black vernacular to describe their impact: "Them dudes walked out on the stage and started doing their poetry. I hadn't never heard nothing like it. I don't think anybody else in the area had either. . . . It was fiery. . . . It overwhelmed me."[25]

Wilson was especially impressed that Baraka brought a new type of poetry to Pittsburgh. "The whole poetry thing changed from the poetry readings we used to do in 1965, '66, '67," he said. "Now they were like Black power poems and [had] a certain delivery style that was pioneered by Baraka." However, Wilson also criticized Baraka. Years later, in referring to the commemoration, he said that afterward, "Everybody wanted to be like Baraka, do his style of poetry and stuff." But Wilson added that Baraka's style didn't suit him personally. "I was appreciative of it," he said, "but I felt I can't go out there and be like Baraka. I continued to write the same poems that I was writing before."[26]

In fact, the two men's compatibility was strained. The program listed August Wilson as delivering welcoming remarks. Baraka looked at the program and asked, "Who's August Wilson?" When people pointed Wilson out, Baraka looked over and simply said, "Hi." According to Wilson, that was all he said.[27] Baraka, however, disagrees. He insists that the two talked, and that Wilson asked him accusingly why he had "ditched . . . the Beat thing." Years later, apparently still annoyed by the question—which implied that Baraka was more of a Beat than a nationalist—he accused Wilson of being the one who had been into "the Beat thing." Years later, Baraka told Lee Kiburi, "I don't think [Wilson] ever got fully involved in the cultural nationalist thing, although ultimately he did get into the Nation of Islam."[28]

The commemoration was attended by two charming young women, Franki Williams and Melvena Lowery, who brought something special to the commemoration that they had made. This was one of Pittsburgh's first Black nationalist flags, featuring red, black, and green stripes. Sala and Rob liked the flags and introduced Franki to Wilson. "It was awful!" Franki recalls. "I blushed, and he did too. With all these people looking and having expectations—and a program going on—there was no opportunity for any conversation other than, 'Hi! It's good to meet you!'" When the event was over, Wilson beat a hasty retreat from the theater, prompting Franki to laughingly ask her friend Melvena, "Who was that masked man?"

A week or so afterward, Franki invited Wilson to her home to plan a follow-up that would build on the momentum the rally had created. After dinner, they talked about how to do that. Afterward, August offered to help clear away the dishes. More importantly, Franki says, "He liked my library.

He liked my grandmother (who did the cooking). He liked my mom. . . . He liked me! We excused ourselves . . . to take a walk."[29]

That walk was the first of many. "We walked everywhere," Franki says, "the Hill, Downtown, Oakland."[30] Franki was struck by the way Wilson used walking to observe passersby and listen in on their conversations. Over time, she came to realize how much he was interested in the way people talk. "He taught me how to listen," she says. "He taught me that each neighborhood, each place, each era has a voice." In the morning, the two might stop at Eddie's Restaurant where, over coffee and cigarettes, they would listen to the men getting breakfast and planning the day on their way to work. At lunchtime, they heard families passing on gossip and sometimes making funeral arrangements. At night, they overheard "hookups" and single people exchanging jokes and innuendo.[31] Occasionally they even walked to the Carnegie Library of Pittsburgh's Main branch in Oakland, which Wilson liked because it attracted all kinds of patrons. The two would camp out near the reference desk and listen in on requests for information and the ensuing conversation.[32] "It was about the conversations around us," Franki says.[33] "Wherever August was, he would write, and do so with whatever was handy—a napkin, a receipt, or the back of an envelope. Sometimes he would stop while walking down the street and write on a yellow pad. He would listen to conversations and memorize them, but he did not write them down. Instead, he was writing down ideas for a poem.[34]

In the mid-1960s, racial violence increasingly became part of the nation's urban landscape. Wilson never said much about those days, but they marked a turning point in his life. The violence began in 1963 in Birmingham, Alabama, and Cambridge, Maryland. It spread the next year to New York, Philadelphia, Chicago, Rochester, and Jersey City. In 1965 the Watts neighborhood of Los Angeles exploded in what became the largest riot in US history, leaving thirty-four dead and a thousand injured. The next year, Cleveland, Chicago, and San Francisco saw major outbreaks. And in 1967 sixteen riots erupted in such places as Newark, Detroit, Harlem, Rochester, and Toledo.

During all of this unrest—often referred to as "long hot summers"—Pittsburgh remained calm. The National Opinion Research Center cited the city as one of the nation's few places making solid progress in race relations.[35] The Ford Foundation funded a study examining what Pittsburgh could teach the nation about race.[36] Pittsburghers, too, proudly felt there was "something special" about their city. Charles Owen Rice, an Irish-born priest as well as a civil rights and labor activist, predicted that Pittsburgh would be spared the sort of racial turmoil afflicting much of the country.[37]

However, beginning in 1967, Pittsburgh experienced increasing racial tensions. Racial fights broke out at Oliver High School on the city's North Side.[38] In Homewood, four white-owned businesses were firebombed and thirty-five had their windows broken.[39] In the Hill, police officers and fire-fighters doused a firebomb on the roof of Mainway Supermarket. In addition, there were rumors that some on the North Side were preparing for a riot. Despite these worrisome signs, the *Pittsburgh Courier* reported that, with the exception of a few extremists, Black Pittsburghers were ignoring the call to violence.[40] However, in early April 1968, the paper spoke ominously of rumors circulating on the North Side about an upcoming "B-Day," or "Burn Day."[41]

"Burn Day" came to Pittsburgh in 1968, several days after the assassination of Martin Luther King Jr. on Thursday, April 4. People remembered where they were and what they were doing when they learned of the assassination. Moses Carper recalls: "I remember an announcement that Martin Luther King had been shot. At that point, everybody, at least the young people, ran out . . . They were angry and they started to go up the street messing with all the white-owned stores. And that was the beginning of the revolution in the Hill. I can remember we just roamed the streets for three days playing games with the cops. They go up one street and we go down another street."[42] Harvey Adams, a Black police sergeant, kept things relatively quiet by herding young rioters behind the New Granada Theatre and then releasing them with the warning, "Guys, you can't do this. Can't let you do this."[43]

Because of Adams and a few other Black leaders, notably state legislator K. Leroy Irvis, the Hill District stayed relatively calm for two days. However, on Saturday night, Centre Avenue erupted in looting and burning that torched many, if not most, of the avenue's businesses. Amos Lawson, who was attending a Delfonics concert at the Savoy Ballroom, says the group sang only two songs before they announced, "Well, due to what's going on, we're going to have to cancel the show." Rioters stoned firefighters all night. Looters had their way, even taking over the Hill's Number 2 police station and holding it until the arrival of riot trucks.[44] But there was no saving the businesses. "I saw all the businesses on fire," Lawson says sadly. "The cleaners, the hat store, shoe shops, everything was on fire."[45]

Mainway Supermarket, the Hill's principal grocery store, went up in flames that night. Several days later, Rob Penny organized a poetry reading at the site. An iconic photograph taken at that reading shows Wilson casually smoking a cigarette amid the rubble. Years later, the photograph generated controversy when it was shown, greatly enlarged, at the 1994 Pittsburgh staging of Wilson's play *Two Trains Running*. In *How I Learned What I Learned*, Wilson uses humor and sarcasm to play down the significance of the photograph. "I want everybody to know," he intones, "I did not burn down the Mainway Supermarket during the riots. "There's a lot of people think I did, but I did not. It's true that I did have my picture taken standing triumphantly in the smoldering ruins, but I did not burn it down. I'm just a man that recognized a good photo opportunity. I'm not an arsonist."[46]

Wilson never seriously addressed the riots themselves—where he was, what he did, what he did not do, and how he felt about the destruction of Centre Avenue, the Hill's retail corridor. Years later, when asked about it, Wilson replied evasively, "Actually, I don't remember. Everyone was affected by his assassination—here's the good guy, not like Malcolm X. He was the lamb."[47] Nor did Wilson comment publicly on how the riots destroyed the Hill's social and economic vibrancy. The riots were followed by attacks on white residents, sometimes on racial grounds, sometimes on the assumption that they had something worth stealing. Louis Butera, August's former next-door neighbor, was assaulted and ordered to leave the Hill because, he was told, it was "for black people only." Louis moved out of the city and settled in the nearby suburb of Penn Hills. But his brothers Johnny and Frank continued residing in their family home next door to the Wilson's old residence. Doing so had tragic consequences. In 1969 Frank was killed in an attempted robbery, and in 2002 Johnny suffered the same fate. Julia Burley says neighbors were devastated by the attacks, for the neighborhood had historically been safe and racially amicable.[48]

The riots matched, or exceeded, urban renewal in destroying the Hill. Many blame urban renewal for undercutting the Hill's vitality.[49] Urban renewal of the 1950s certainly destroyed much of the old Lower Hill. However, property owners (but not roomers and residents) were compensated for their loss. Many took that compensation and relocated to Centre Avenue. However, when Centre Avenue burned in 1968, property owners were not compensated. Moreover, they did not reopen elsewhere in the Hill because insurance companies stopped issuing policies in the Hill. As a result, abandoned businesses and empty houses gradually turned into empty, weed-filled lots. The 130 retail shops that were operating in 1965 when Wilson went out on Centre Avenue were reduced to only sixty-six after the riots, and many of those were struggling to survive.[50] After Mainway Market was torched, the Hill District went forty-five years without a supermarket. Increasingly, thefts harmed the few merchants who managed to stay open. Douglas King, African American owner of the B&M Restaurant, complained that looting during the riots made people think stealing from "the establishment" was acceptable.[51] Chawley Williams confirms the new ethos. "I used to call Centre Avenue the Centre Avenue Mall," he says. "We didn't steal from our homes. Refrigerators were stolen from stores on Centre Avenue and Uptown, and there was even this guy who stole a chair, sofa and more to furnish my home."[52]

Even during times of unrest and tragedy, daily life goes on. For Wilson, it went on in the person of Brenda Burton. Known today as Brenda Shakur, she is dark, attractive, vivacious, and passionate about the arts. Brenda grew up on Landleiss Place in the Upper Hill. Her father owned Burton's Pool Hall on Centre Avenue, and her mother was a devout member of Pentecostal churches. Like her mother, Brenda did not smoke, drink, or eat pork.

While still in high school, Brenda met August at the Halfway Art Gallery, where she took guitar lessons. Brenda was fascinated by August's ability to recite from memory almost every poem Dylan Thomas had ever written. She was especially impressed that he could do so "with the [Welsh] accent and everything."[53]

The two soon fell madly in love and became well-known for walking around hand-in-hand. Moses Carper says Brenda's outgoing personality helped bring August out of his shell. "He was a loner," Carper says, and "all of a sudden now, he had this black woman in his life [who] just made him blossom out."[54] The two would go to the Oyster House Restaurant downtown on Market Square. After dinner, they would sit outside and engage in long conversations.[55] Brenda found August intelligent, interesting, and easy to talk to, someone who could be serious one moment and laugh and display a good sense of humor the next. She appreciated that, like herself, he was something of an outsider, not a "mainstream" person.[56]

In the spring of 1968, Brenda graduated from Schenley High School and enrolled at New York University. August accompanied her to New York and helped her settle in. While there, he made a surprise visit to his Aunt Faye and his sister Barbara. Barbara had been raised apart from the other Wilson children because, shortly after her birth, Daisy asked her sister Faye to raise the child at her place in New York. Barbara had little contact with the rest of the family, and so August's coming to see her made for a very meaningful encounter, one that Barbara remembers well.[57] She was in the kitchen when August suddenly rounded the corner, extended his hand, and said, simply and emphatically, "After twenty-one years!"[58] He then took out the photograph of a man Barbara didn't recognize. "I don't know if that was my dad," she says. "He was not dark, yet he was somehow African American."[59] The two did not discuss the photograph, but Barbara was pleased that he had cared enough to bring it and show it to her.

Growing up, Barbara had found it painful being separated from her siblings. However, she did well, thanks largely to a supportive group of African American nuns from Georgia who taught school and belonged to the Franciscan Handmaids of the Most Pure Heart of Mary. "Because of them," Barbara says, "I had very positive role models in my life." Barbara and her children have done well. Michael, the oldest, has an influential position in government. Adair, the middle child, is a computer specialist with New York's Metropolitan Transportation Authority. And Emmanuel, the youngest, went on to have a successful career in theater.

Barbara was pleased at her brother's visit. His words, his handshake, and the photograph all showed her that he accepted her as his sister. The bonds formed in that first meeting persisted over the years.[60] August embraced Barbara's children, and they embraced him. Michael was about seventeen when *Ma Rainey's Black Bottom* was in rehearsal for its Broadway opening. August invited Michael to rehearsals, got him free tickets to the play, introduced him to the play's director, Lloyd Richards, and occasionally ate with him at his favorite hotel, the Edison. Years later, when Michael entered public service, he would call August and ask if he could meet with some students to inspire them. When he was in town, he always tried to honor those requests.[61]

August had an especially strong influence on Emmanuel, who fondly recalls the time he and his mother attended the opening night of *Joe Turner's Come and Gone*. Emmanuel describes that evening as "a very emotional experience, a magical moment. I went with my mother ... to the opening party. . . . It was my first Broadway show. . . . It was at that moment that I decided to become a playwright. I said to myself theater is something I want to do. But specifically, I want to do what August did and it's really been that way ever since."[62]

At school the next day, Emmanuel began writing a play and recruiting classmates to help put it on. He embraced the world of theater, later becoming director of the Dramatists Guild of America, a national nonprofit association of playwrights, librettists, composers, and lyricists.[63]

August's brief visit to New York was impactful. But back in Pittsburgh, things were changing rapidly. As the local Black Power movement gathered momentum, its center of gravity shifted from the Hill to the University of

Pittsburgh. The shift began in 1967 when Stokely Carmichael gave a powerful, well-received lecture there. The shift accelerated after King's assassination, when student activists in the AAI—Tony Fountain, Joe McCormick, Gail Austin, Luddy Haden, Bobby Williams, and others—determined to make the University a center for Black studies and nationalist activities. Toward that end, they founded a student group, the Black Action Society (BAS).[64] They liked that the university served as neutral turf where Black people from different neighborhoods could come together.[65]

As an officially recognized student group, the BAS had access to programming funds. Curtiss Porter, chair of the BAS, used those funds to bring in nationally known artists and performers, including Amiri Baraka, Don L. Lee, Ron Karenga, Cassius Clay (Muhammad Ali), Dick Gregory, Julian Bond, and Roy Innis.[66] Most importantly, following a BAS sit-in at the computer center, the university agreed to create a Black studies program and recruit Black students and faculty. Named the Department of Black Community Education, Research, and Development (DBCERD), the resulting infusion of Afrocentric programing and hires reinforced the university as the city's center of Black nationalist activity. Not surprisingly, August and Rob spent many hours on the fourth floor of the Student Union, where the BAS was located.[67]

The increasing prominence of Black cultural nationalism became evident in the spring 1968 issue of *Connection Magazine*. Wilson served as the issue's poetry editor and Rob as its contributing editor. Curtiss Porter, the general editor, ran off mimeographed copies of the magazine in his apartment, under the imprint Oduduwa Publications. The issue contains ninety pages of book reviews, drawings, woodcuts, poems, and a play by Rob Penny. It also includes a short story and four poems by Wilson, and the famous photograph of him standing in the burned-out ruins of Mainway Supermarket. The issue bristles with passages of racial anger and calls for armed resistance. Sala Udin (still known as Samuel Howze at the time), wrote a fiery introduction, calling on Black people to acquire weapons, "however possible, wherever possible, as soon as possible."[68]

Most of the poems were written in the angry, nationalist style popularized by Baraka. A poem by Reggie Howze, Sala Udin's brother, gives an idea of the new tone. It urges Black women to fight alongside their men: "Sister, Sister! Our roles are the same. / Die cracker die! is the name of the game." The poem includes one possibly antisemitic allusion: "Come on Aunt Fannie, come on Sister Sue / Kill a cracker, kill a cracker / DON'T forget the Jew / Cause he's a cracker too."

In sharp contrast, Wilson's submissions carry no message of racial protest or Black nationalism. "Night Never Comes," his first (and perhaps only) short story, focuses on two men, Jake and Graham, whose values, ethics, and friendship have been lost to heroin addiction. In the end, Jake overdoses and dies in Graham's apartment. Graham has little sympathy for Jake, and is concerned only about his own fate. "Come on, Jake," he yells at his dead companion, "don't do this to me." Fearing the consequences of the police finding a man in his apartment dead from a drug overdose, Graham waits until night and quietly throws Jake's body into tall weeds, saying that, for his friend, "night will never come." The story continues Wilson's earlier biblical themes of Cain murdering his brother as well as that of the exile's pain and isolation. The protagonists are far from being proud race men. They complain about the white police, but their lives are so constrained by drug use that neither friendship nor race is of much importance to them.

Two of Wilson's poems carry a political message, though more implicit than explicit. "A Cluster of Lions" depicts sadness rather than anger over the assassination of Martin Luther King Jr. The poem opens with the plea, "Turn, gunman, back," referring apparently to James Earl Ray as he trained his rifle on King. The last stanza reflects King's statement the night before that he has "been to the mountain top and seen the Promised Land." Wilson's poem sadly mentions "One more mountain, one more, / And the world is a damaged sunset / Bleeding us all into darkness." The poem makes a nod toward racial militancy by ending with a warning that, in the morning, the raven of death will be buried and replaced by a lion.

A second Wilson poem, "In Defense of the Serpent's Head," comes closer to embracing militant nationalism through references to angry rioters who carry a desire for vengeance. But esoteric language mutes much of the political message. A typical example: "The heavy hand lashes back, / Lashes out" in a "rack of terror." The perpetrators "dance" and then proceed "in rage / Torn from the hissing cause" and continue, "in fever," until morning. Both poems are told from the perspective of the outsider, an observer rather than someone directly immersed in the racial struggle.

Wilson's two other poems in the journal show that he continued to be more interested in the personal than the political. "Poem for the New Year" bewails life's quick passage. The narrator, a "sad and aging man," seeks to "force the clocks" at midnight. He remains "The King of Fools at this carnival," but realizes too late that the hero's task is "To die unwilling in the arms / Of Dance." The other poem, "For Her Reading Creeley," pays homage to one of the nation's leading avant-garde poets. The poem continues Wilson's exploration of the plight of the outsider. In this case, it is a woman inspired by two lines from Robert Creeley, "Dances of the surface / Of my skin." In the second stanza, a man stands alone facing a window, suggesting that he and the woman have spent an unsatisfying night together. With the sexual act having proven disappointing, things return to reality. That only two of Wilson's five entries even modestly incorporate nationalist tropes shows that his efforts to shore up his image as a nationalist remained tentative and inconclusive.

August's early efforts to embrace Black nationalism reflect the influence of his friend Rob Penny. Local nationalists like Curtiss Porter recognized this and considered August as someone who, under Rob's guidance, had undergone only an incomplete, tentative turn toward nationalism.[69] August always acknowledged that he first discovered himself as a Black man while sitting in Rob's living room and listening to his collection of Malcolm X's speeches.[70]

However, despite seeking to be part of the Black Power and Black consciousness movements, Wilson did not adopt the movement's most commonly used indicators of racial identity. One example is his so-called free name. The Nation of Islam urged its followers to replace their "slave" name with the letter X, which was stood for their lost African name. Black nationalists who were not part of the Nation of Islam often adopted names of Arabic, Swahili, or Yoruba origin. Sam Howze, for example, changed his name to Sala Udin. His brother Reggie changed his name to Abdullah. Frank Hightower became Omodi, and John Reynolds became Temujin Ekunfeo. Wilson did the same, but apparently never used his "free" name.

Chip Brown of *Esquire* magazine was present during an amusing exchange at the Crawford Grill about names. During a discussion of "free" names, Wilson refused to answer when Brown asked him about his name. Rob volunteered that it was Mbulu, provoking laughter among the others. They told Brown that Mbulu means "crazy person" in Swahili.[71] In fact, the word means "trouble," but whatever the name's possible meanings, Wilson was not offended when Rob continued to address him as "Mbulu."

To a remarkable extent, Wilson remained true to his own conception of what it means to be African American. He willingly remained an outsider, a warrior, a race man, and a poet, but he did so on his own terms. He did not wear a dashiki, he did not use his Africanized "free name," and he barely changed the way he wrote and what he wrote about.

This created problems because, following the riots of 1968, the growing surge of Black nationalism caused audiences to demand poems with a much stronger racial message than what Wilson was interested in delivering. Jerry Rhodes, codirector of the Halfway Art Gallery, says that Wilson had simply gave his poetry a veneer of nationalism in order to maintain a claim to membership in the nationalist fraternity. "He just threw some things in there about blackness and white folks," Rhodes says, "and he was over."[72] In the mid-1960s, audiences enjoyed Wilson's recitals of Dylan Thomas even though they could not understand his Welsh dialect. They simply liked his dramatic way of reciting. By the late 1960s, however, audiences were less forgiving as Wilson recited his own poems, which, in the manner of John Berryman, were both obscure and lacking a racial theme.[73] Curtiss Porter remembers that, after the riots of 1968, he saw Wilson "rejected, dejected, and almost ejected" while reciting at the Halfway Art Gallery. "People would ask themselves," Porter says, 'where is he coming from?' Like he wasn't doing Black poetry."[74]

In a city that was becoming ever more racially divided, the sort of racial inclusiveness championed by the Halfway Art Gallery fell increasingly out of favor. In 1969 or 1970, director Ed Ellis let his hair grow into a large Afro and replaced his sport coats and turtlenecks with dashikis. Ellis severed ties with his white sponsors, adopted the African name Ewari, and became active in militantly nationalist organizations such as the Black Panther Party and the United Black Front.[75] Already physically large and imposing, the stylistic changes made Ellis even more intimidating. Ralph Proctor, then an administrator at the University of Pittsburgh, describes him as "a big, hulking dude" who frightened people, especially white people.[76]

To the distress of many, Ellis made it clear that white people were no longer welcome at the Halfway Art Gallery. Troy West, a professor of architecture at Carnegie Mellon University and a longtime white supporter of the gallery, was depressed by the change. "Ed became really militant," West says sadly, "really racist in a sense. He changed. He really changed."[77] On the other hand, Ellis's nationalism sometimes came with a bit of posturing. To everyone's surprise, he married a white artist who worked at the gallery. Rhodes says his boss "was a dashiki-wearing guy, and when he came in with this white wife, everyone said 'Whoa!'"[78]

The gallery's new stance provoked criticism from Black patrons. Sculptor Thad Mosley cut his ties when Ellis told him he had to stop showing his works in "white" venues.[79] William Strickland, a talented potter, says the city's Black art scene was unified until the Halfway Art Gallery adopted a Black Power stance. When that happened, Strickland says, he and others "went [one] way and the Afrocentric guys went [another] way." He adds, bitterly and emphatically, "We never did connect. . . . Never!"[80]

The gallery's clientele changed markedly. Drug addicts—not all of whom were recovering—became a more prominent presence, making art patrons uncomfortable and creating suspicions about what was going on.[81] Temujin Ekunfeo, a local Yoruba priest active in the Black Arts Movement, says that the gallery became "a hang-out for drug users, ex-convicts, a fair amount of bad art, and quite a few thugs and unsavory characters."[82] Strickland rolls his eyes at the mention of the post-riot gallery. "The Halfway Art Gallery was not producing quality art," he says. "It was a political front. . . . It wasn't based on art. It was based on protest."[83]

Sometime in 1970 or 1971, the gallery relocated across the street next to "House of the Crossroads," a treatment center for drug addicts founded by Sala Udin. Shortly afterward, the gallery closed, ending an extraordinary chapter in August Wilson's life and in the cultural history of the Hill.[84]

7

Black Horizons Theatre

The riots of 1968 left Black people—both nationally and locally—
wondering how to move forward. This was complicated by differing interpretations of the significance of the riots. Integrationists regarded the riots with
dismay while militant nationalists saw them as an encouraging sign of the
coming racial war. At the Afro-American Institute (AAI), Rob Penny and others urged artists and writers to produce works that would advance the Black
Power agenda and prepare people psychologically for an inevitable racial war.
Accordingly, Rob persuaded the Poets in the Centre Avenue Tradition to shift
their focus from poetry to theater, following Amiri Baraka in the belief that
theater was more accessible to the masses. The AAI now charged Rob with
establishing a nationalist theater in Pittsburgh.[1]

Rob knew little about theater. His only exposure had come in elementary
school when the nuns took his class to see a Passion play. It was a transformative experience. "I was young," Rob says, "just a little kid. I was overwhelmed
by the action that took place on stage. I remember when Jesus Christ died,
there was this thunder and lightning. . . . That scared me, but it was fascinating that they could do that. . . . It must've had some kind of subconscious
impact on me."[2] Sala Udin also had no exposure to theater, but nonetheless
was excited by the idea of a nationalist theater company, which he regarded as "cheap and live and relevant and risqué and dangerous and radical."

Sala firmly believed that theater had great potential for developing the racial consciousness of the masses.[3] August Wilson was not a fan of theater. He had seen only parts of two plays—Bertolt Brecht's *A Man's a Man* and Eugène Ionesco's *The Rhinoceros*—and had not liked either, walking out of both early.[4] Nonetheless, he agreed that theater was more accessible to the masses than poetry.[5] During his early poetry recitals at the Halfway Art Gallery, he had noticed that audiences were drawn to his poetry more for the dramatic style of his delivery than for the content.

The members of the Centre Avenue Poets Theatre Workshop were unaware of it, but Black Pittsburgh had a robust theatrical tradition. In the 1930s, the Negro Drama League supported a dozen or so companies and gave classes in stagecraft and acting.[6] In the 1940s, the Curtaineers, an innovative theatrical group at the Irene Kaufmann Settlement House, drew large audiences to see Black actors cast in colorblind roles, something almost unheard of nationally. August regretted that he and his friends did not know of these early efforts. "It never occurred to us," he lamented in an interview in 1999, that "there had been [Black] people doing theater before us. Every day we walked by Walter Worthington's record store, never knowing that 20 years before he'd had a theater, the Pittsburgh Negro Theater. Had we known, we could have tapped into that. No institution had developed out of that for us to fit into. It was our failure to access our history, and a failure on their part not to hand it on, to preserve cultural values."[7]

Rob asked August to help him cofound this new, nationalist theater. August was not an obvious choice. He had delivered a well-received keynote address at the Malcolm X commemoration earlier that year, but his credentials as a nationalist were modest, his poetry only nodding toward the style advocated by Baraka. On the other hand, Rob knew that August was a hard worker, someone who would throw himself into whatever task he undertook. As Lee Kiburi said, once August got excited about something, he worked on it diligently with "professionalism and enthusiasm."[8] In addition, Rob may well have shared Chawley Williams's belief that August would work hard on a joint project because he "wanted to belong."[9]

Indeed, August was a good choice. Over the summer, he, Rob, Sala, and Curtiss Porter met regularly with a few others—notably Jake Milliones, Creamer Bazzell, and Phil McKain—to lay plans for the new theater. They gathered at Mahon Street House, an outreach satellite of the Hill House, which itself was a descendant of the old Irene Kaufmann Settlement House, a Jewish community center. The IKS, as it was often called, had been established in the late nineteenth century to serve the Hill District's rapidly growing Jewish population. By the 1960s most Jews had left the Hill and the IKS, a large, impressive structure with a swimming pool and a theater, was donated to the Black community and renamed the Hill House. The main building was razed and, while a replacement was under construction, the Hill House moved its programs to some ten neighborhood development houses, one of which was located on Mahon Street near the intersection of Centre and Kirkpatrick.[10]

Moses Carper, the manager of Mahon House, actively and enthusiastically arranged to make the building available.[11] Quite early, the men decided to call the new endeavor Black Horizon Theatre. The word *Black* reflected the popularity of the phrase *Black is Beautiful*, and *Horizon* was meant to convey that the theater was like "a new beginning, something rising."[12] However, before Black Horizon put on its first play, the name morphed into "Black Horizons Theatre," the result of the popularity of *Black Horizons*, a highly popular new show hosted by Ralph Proctor on the local PBS television station, WQED.[13]

The group's first challenge was acquiring plays to perform. Rob and August were thrilled when the summer 1968 issue of *The Drama Review* came out, dedicated to new trends in Black theater, which provided the scripts of some twenty plays that they could choose from.[14] Ed Bullins, the issue editor, grouped these new plays in two categories. One, which he labeled "Black Revolutionary Theatre," sought to portray a victorious Black revolution, on the assumption that letting Black audiences participate vicariously in an uprising would prepare them psychologically for the coming racial Armageddon. These plays were written by followers of Baraka's Black Arts Movement, notably Baraka himself, Ben Caldwell, Herbert Stokes, Jimmy Garrett, John O'Neal, Sonia Sanchez, Marvin X, and Ronald Milner. A second group of plays, which Bullins labeled "Theatre of the Black Experience," aimed to raise the self-esteem of Black people by dramatizing their lives and language in realistic, yet sympathetic, detail. Plays of this type were written by such figures as Bill Gunn, Dorothy Ahmad, Adam David Miller, Joseph White, Henrietta Harris, and Bullins himself.[15]

August no doubt would have favored plays about the Black experience while Rob would have favored those of the "Black Revolutionary Theatre." Apparently, the two men compromised by not siding exclusively with either. As August described the selection process, "We looked for work that was in those days what we called 'revolutionary and progressive.' . . . Plays that were most positive in terms of the Black experience and also plays that taught a lesson for the masses of the people."[16] It took several months to evaluate the plays because Rob and August both had summer jobs—August as a recreational aide and youth counselor at the Hill House, Rob as an employee at Opportunities Industrialization Centers (OIC).[17] In the end, they disliked almost all of the plays, and felt unprepared to stage the few they did like.

To solve the impasse, Rob went home and, overnight, wrote two one-act plays, *Deeds of Blackness* and *Dance of the Blues Dead*.[18] *Deeds of Blackness* dramatizes a future war of Black liberation, and asks whether Black people in the military would shoot their own people.[19] The play was inspired by the riots, when Rob saw racially integrated national guard companies lined up along Centre Avenue with their rifles drawn and wondered whether they would indeed open fire on their fellow Black people.[20] August liked both plays, and told Rob enthusiastically, "Let's do it!"[21] Rob asked, "How?" and August replied, "I don't know. Let's do it."[22] This informality set the pattern for how Black Horizons would operate going forward, a process that August described as "Hey man, let's do this," followed by "Yeah, okay, that's cool" or "Naw, I don't want to do that . . . let's do this one."[23]

Somebody asked, "Who's going to direct it?" and Wilson volunteered, confident he could learn how to direct. "I knew my way to the library," he says.[24] The next day, Wilson went to the Carnegie Library of Pittsburgh's Main branch in Oakland, looking for a book with a title like "How to Do Excellent Plays." He soon found what he needed, Alexander Dean and Lawrence Carra's *Fundamentals of Play Directing*. Especially helpful was Appendix A, "What to Do in Rehearsal." The key advice boiled down to "Read the play." Wilson said to himself, "That's all I need to know."[25] At the first rehearsal, he told the actors, with feigned confidence, "Okay, this is what we're going to do. We're going to read the play." They finished reading it, and asked "Now what?" Thinking quickly because he had not read Appendix B, Wilson said, "Let's read the play again." That night, he went back to the book and "sort of figured out what to do from that point on."[26]

Wilson quickly learned how to move characters around the stage, how to get the best out of the actors, and how a play would look onstage.[27] He also learned how to match actors and characters. For example, in Ed Bullins's play *In New England Winter*, Lee Kiburi wanted to play the part of the bank robber, but Wilson emphatically told him "No, no, no! Oscar!" Kiburi later realized that Oscar was in fact the more fitting character for him to play.[28]

Wilson embraced "method acting," in which the actor immerses himself in his character. Kiburi says Wilson insisted that actors know "what time [their] character woke up, what he ate, why he ate it, how he slept, what his past was . . . everything about [the] character. . . . He wanted you to know that person better than you knew yourself."[29] Wilson also liked to bring out complexities in a character. At first, Kiburi played Oscar as aggressive and abusive, but Wilson saw additional dimensions to the character, and insisted that Kiburi sometimes portray Oscar gently, even playfully.[30] Wilson also would take actors aside and talk to them individually, something rarely done in those days.[31]

Wilson did much more than direct. He handled lighting, costumes, publicity, programs, set design and construction. He even handled the money and controlled day-to-day operations. His involvement in virtually all aspects of the theater earned him the nickname "Mister Everything Else." Wilson became, in fact, the de facto head of the theater. "It was my signature on the bank account," he says proudly. "I made the decisions about what to do, when to do it."[32] Rob confirms this: "Everything went through August. Everything came from him, and everything went through him."[33]

Wilson's involvement in Black Horizons gave him a crash course in nearly all facets of theater. It even inspired him to try his hand at writing a play, an effort that ended disastrously. He had one character say to the other, "Hey, man, what's happening." The other answered, "Nothing." Wilson says he sat there for twenty minutes and neither character would say anything. Finally, Wilson said to himself, "Well, that's all right. After all, I'm a poet. I don't have to be a playwright. To hell with writing plays. Let other people write plays."[34] It would be several years before he would again try his hand at playwriting.

Black Horizons opened with Rob's two plays, *Dance of the Blues Dead* and *Deeds of Blackness*.[35] Wilson was so busy putting the set together and getting everything ready that he skipped work on opening day. To his eternal chagrin, doing so cost him his job at the Hill House. Carper fired him for not being on the playground that day with the kids. Wilson was furious. "I went to help build the set," he says, so "rather than go to the playground with the kids, I'm running around getting props, going down to the theater trying to get everything situated, going to pick up the programs from the printer. You know, all that kind of stuff, man. And I get fired for that." Wilson says it taught him a lesson: "Everybody you think are in your corner, they ain't in your corner. It's as simple as that."[36] Years later, when asked about this, Carper laughed and replied innocently: "No recollection."[37] When pressed, he said a bit evasively that Wilson's position at Hill House was simply a summer program and that, at the end of summer, the funding ended, and they couldn't hire anybody.[38]

As a nationalist endeavor, Black Horizons' founders wanted their theater to be physically located in the Black community. They initially tried to rent space at the New Granada Theatre on Centre Avenue, but when that proved too expensive, they considered several other venues. They finally settled on A. Leo Weil Elementary School, farther up Centre Avenue at Soho Street.[39] For many years, the principal at Weil had let community groups use the school's auditorium for a variety of functions. Despite the controversial language and provocative themes of Black Horizons' plays, Principal Booker Reeves let them use the auditorium free of charge. They even could store their props behind the stage.[40] The theater seated 450, but the stage was small, designed for elementary students, and so could not accommodate a large cast.[41]

The company wanted to attract the "grassroots," and so charged only fifth cents for admission. Black Horizons' founders also felt the community should control the theater, and so they never sought outside grants. Sala served as the chief fundraiser and went out to neighborhood churches asking for support—a hard sell, because the churches were racially moderate and suspicious of Black nationalism.[42] It also was time-consuming, because donations came in small amounts. For example, August's old elementary school, St. Richard, donated twenty-five dollars. Most other church contributions also were small. Several businesses placed program ads for ten dollars and twenty-five dollars. WAMO, the local Black radio station, provided free public service announcements. August's friend Amir Rashidd did the same at community radio station WYEP.[43]

Being chronically short of money, Black Horizons learned to improvise. August and Rob borrowed costumes and props from wherever they could, sometimes getting them at discount places like the Salvation Army.[44] At other times, the actors were told to consider the clothes they wore as their costume. "You're playing in a role," August told them. "So, if you have a suit because you're dressed up, and you're out in the bar and you're looking good, you know. So don't come in with no blue jeans."[45]

Fortunately, Black Horizons' financial shortages were alleviated when the Black Action Society (BAS) at the University of Pittsburgh stepped in. Curtiss Porter, cochair of Black studies, knew the company had virtually no money, not even a telephone.[46] He also knew that the BAS, as an officially recognized student organization, had an annual budget of $25,000–$50,000.[47] And he knew that the BAS had a strong community orientation, which is why they omitted the word *student* from their name.[48] The BAS soon became the major funding source for Black Horizons. It was not enough to meet all the company's needs, but it was a big help.

Students from the university also became a key part of the Black Horizons family. Looking for potential actors, Rob and August visited the campus frequently, and were pleasantly surprised by what they found.[49] One of their first recruits, Cathy Simpson, called "Lufituaeb," ("Beautiful" spelled backward), had training as well as talent.[50] Others came with no training but had talent and energy. These included Porter himself, Frank Hightower (Omodi), Joyce Campbell (Adetutu, or Sakina A'la), Rocko Swain, Hasani Lillie, and two of Sala's brothers, Chaka (Tommy Howze) and Abdullah (Reggie Howze).

Sala Udin had no training in theater, but his natural ability immediately made him the company's lead actor. "He was a mean actor," August says, laughing. "He got the best roles in all the plays. That's the way that went."[51] Sala, like August, was involved in many aspects of Black Horizons. In addition to acting, he built sets, printed flyers, raised money, and put out public service announcements.[52] To the extent that there was a division of labor, Rob served as the playwright-in-residence, August as the director, and Sala as the lead actor.[53] However, most worked without titles and did whatever needed to be done. "People might work in the box office one performance," Sala says, "and then they may be on the . . . stage crew the next performance. And the next time they may be working lights. The next time they may be acting."[54] Hightower, a professional photographer affiliated with the company, often was there to take pictures.[55]

August took pride in the quality of the productions and claimed that they were of high quality because he "insisted that we do the best we could do."[56] Not everyone agrees. Betty Douglas, a local Black artist trained in the highly regarded drama program at Carnegie Mellon University, found Black Horizons' performances passionate but not especially accomplished. "You can really learn how to improvise on things if you know the basics," Douglas says, "but if you don't . . . you're sort of out there just flailing in the dark."[57]

Because the company wanted Black patrons to see only people who looked like themselves onstage, they did not use white actors.[58] When necessary, white characters were performed in whiteface. It is not clear whether the humor of this was appreciated at the time, but Rob performed in whiteface in his play *Centre Avenue; A Trip.*[59] Black Horizons did not encourage white people to attend their performances but, unlike Baraka's Spirit House, did not bar them.[60] In fact, some members of Black Horizons were mystified by the number of white people who came to see the performances. Sakina A'la, an actor, marveled: "I don't know if I could go anyplace and just be . . . insulted and sit there and applaud and clap and go right on. But they [whites] didn't have a problem with it."[61] Black Horizons also had little interest in attracting middle-class Black people, assuming that they would be there for an evening's entertainment rather than for the political message. Toward that end, Black Horizons performed at many community events, elementary and secondary schools, and virtually every college in Pittsburgh.[62]

Audiences at a Black Horizons performance got more than a play. The evening might begin with one or more short dramas. Following intermission there might be a performance by the Sounds of Ebony, a vocal group featuring Phyllis Hyman, a talented singer and actor who went on to fame in cinema and on Broadway.[63] Sometimes the audience would be treated to jazz by the Kenny Fisher Quintet[64] or African dance and drumming by Bob Johnson's Black Horizons Dance Ensemble. The evening might end with a poetry reading by August, Rob, or another member of the Centre Avenue Poets Theatre Workshop, or with a speech bearing a Black Power and Black consciousness message.[65] Black Horizons also included a post-performance discussion and interaction among audience, actors, and director. Porter introduced this practice, and it became a tradition in local Black theater.[66]

Despite efforts to appeal to the grassroots, audiences consisted primarily of college students already sympathetic to a nationalist message. A'la explained: "There was a certain cultural nationalist clique in Pittsburgh, and these people were always present because it was a chance to see theater. And, if nothing else, the drummers would be there, and it would be kind of a festive . . . atmosphere. So, it wasn't difficult to get a crowd."[67] Plays were held on the weekend, and typically ran for three weeks.[68] A hundred or so patrons might attend opening night, and twenty or thirty at subsequent performances. Numbers could be augmented by good publicity and by combining performances with such events as a festival or Negro History Month.[69] However, Black Horizons did not rely solely on its fan base. A half hour before the performance, Wilson and others would go into the street and cajole people into attending.[70] "Once they got in," Wilson says, "they really liked it: 'Hey, hey, you gonna do another play?' 'Next Thursday.' 'I'm gonna be there!'"[71]

The local white media never reviewed Black Horizons productions. Members of Black Horizons did not mind. They believed white critics' opinions of their productions did not matter because white people did not understand the Black experience.[72] As A'la says, "We weren't the type that would have read the reviews anyway. How could [white reviewers] possibly understand black art?"[73] But the Black media also failed to cover Black Horizons productions. The *New Pittsburgh Courier* sometimes published notices when a performance was part of a larger community event, but it never reviewed a performance.[74] "The white press . . . never come out," Wilson complained, "and the Black papers would send someone out "who was totally unqualified, but at least we get a write up.""[75]

Considering themselves part of the national Black Arts Movement, members of Black Horizons traveled to other cities, partly to stay abreast of national developments. Porter says that whenever there was "something new, something black, something that they needed to know about," folks would jump in the car and go to places like Newark or Philadelphia or Chicago.[76] In addition, Black Horizons performed outside Pittsburgh. They especially liked invitations from colleges because payments were more substantial. In its first year, Black Horizons performed at Oberlin College and Case Western Reserve University in Ohio as well as at several colleges in and around Philadelphia. In 1969 the company performed at Barbara Ann Teer's National Black Theatre in Harlem and the Lee Cultural Center in Philadelphia. They were especially proud when Baraka invited them to Newark to perform his play *Black Mass* at Spirit House.[77] In 1970 the company traveled as far away as Tougaloo College in Mississippi.[78] Also that year, it returned to Spirit House and staged a performance of Rob's plays *Deeds of Blackness* and *Dance of the Blues Dead*. Baraka liked the play, which further solidified Rob's reputation as Pittsburgh's leading Black playwright.[79]

Given Wilson's deep personal involvement in Black Horizons Theatre, people were shocked when, in the spring of 1969, less than a year after cofounding the company, he resigned.[80] Years later, Wilson tried to explain why he left. One fairly weak excuse was that he found the auditorium at A. Leo Weil Elementary School too large; he wanted a smaller, more intimate space like that at Harlem's National Black Theatre.[81] Another reason—also rather suspect—was a disagreement about whether the company should have a van. "The first thing for me," Wilson said, "was the damn van. We needed that. I just saw 'Black Horizons Theatre' on there and driving by Centre Avenue, and people saying, 'there's that theater van.'"[82] August had squirreled away $3,000 of Black Horizons' finances, of which he was in charge, to buy a van, and had gotten the actors to agree in principle to purchase one. Ultimately, however, members of the company preferred to divide up the money. They pointed out that they had been working for free and that people had bills to pay, rent to pay, and so forth.[83] Wilson gave in. "They wanted the money. So, I said 'Okay, I'll go to the bank tomorrow and I'll have the money here and we'll divide it up.' I was mad though. And I left. That was my last involvement with the theater."[84]

There is no question that Wilson was overworked. He painted sets, provided costumes, set up lighting boards, sold tickets, generated publicity, solicited funds, and did all manner of tasks, large and small. Rehearsals took up two hours a night and were held after people got off work. The staff were volunteers, meaning that the director could not be sure that actors would show up for rehearsal—or even for a performance. When that happened, Wilson scrambled to find a replacement, and sometimes played the part himself. "As the director," he says, "I knew all the lines and I took over more times than I wanted to."[85] Moreover, conditions were getting even more burdensome. By the time Wilson decided to leave, the enthusiasm of the first group of student volunteers was beginning to wane. Some felt the pressures of studying and final exams. Tony Fountain and Kenny Fisher fell away when the theater began traveling out of town.[86] Others were just ready to move on with their lives.

Rob has a more plausible explanation for why Wilson left: a power struggle. As Rob described it in an interview with Kiburi, without naming names or providing specifics, "There were some who came into the theater—perhaps a few were already there—who really wanted to control the direction and the impact that Black Horizons Theatre was having on the community. There were certain people that were involved in the theater [who] . . . always have to be in the leadership and [be the] controlling factor. . . . Somebody wanted to be in control and wanted . . . someone . . . they felt more comfortable with." Rob ended his explanation with the cryptic statement: "Strange things happened."[87]

A few years later, Rob expanded on his explanation, telling Elva Branson, an actress in the company and later its director, that August had objected to the direction Black Horizons was going, and this caused "some bad words and ill will" between him and Sala.[88] Rob said that August wanted Black Horizons to stage more character-driven plays, but Sala insisted on political, explicitly revolutionary plays. Elva thinks this interpretation makes sense. Sala, she said, was very militant, "always 'blacker' than anybody" and quick to challenge people about race: "Why'd you straighten your hair?"[89] Rob, of course, also was partial to revolutionary, nationalist theater, but had a soft-spoken, low-key manner that would have been less antagonizing.

Hightower, who succeeded Wilson as director of Black Horizons, echoes Rob's sense that personal reasons caused the departure. "August could be very moody sometimes," Hightower says. In addition, Wilson objected to Black Horizons doing plays that were mainly in the revolutionary, political mode of Baraka.[90] "The way I remember it," Hightower adds tactfully, "at a certain point August was going in another direction. August had a particular philosophy [and] . . . direction that he wanted to go in. There were some disagreements about direction. I think August got frustrated."[91]

Whatever the reason, or reasons, for his breakup with Black Horizons, it left Wilson angry for a long time. "I don't need this," he told himself, and vowed to return to his first love: poetry. 'Y'all do that. I'm going over here, write my poems, and do my thing.'"[92] August told Rob, 'I've gotten the money, I'm going to New York.'" He took his share of the proceeds and caught a Greyhound bus to New York.[93]

8

Return to Poetry

After his break with Black Horizons Theatre, August Wilson caught a bus to New York City.[1] His mother, Daisy, came along with him. When they got to New York, they stopped by to visit Faye and Barbara in the Bronx. What was meant to be a pleasant get-together turned into a painful confrontation when August asked his mother pointedly, "Why is it you always say you have six children when you have seven?" Enraged, Daisy gave him a severe tongue-lashing, following which August dropped his head and quietly walked away.[2]

The main purpose of August's trip was to spend time with his girlfriend Brenda.[3] She had had a fulfilling freshman year at New York University, both on campus and off. In Pittsburgh, she had been attracted to the Black Panther Party but had been put off by the aura of violence that surrounded it. In New York, she attended several rallies by the Black Muslim minister Louis Farrakhan. The Nation of Islam appealed to Brenda because of its advocacy of self-reliance and success in taking what she calls "outcast people" and "cleaning them up." At the time of August's visit in the spring of 1969, Brenda was two months pregnant, and the two of them were finalizing plans for their wedding.

On June 20, 1969, August and Brenda were married. The service was conducted by Dr. Isaac Green, pastor of Central Baptist Church in the Hill

District. The marriage license shows that August resided on Wooster Street and was still using his birth name, Frederick August Kittel. Brenda was eighteen and living with her father, her mother having died.[4] It was a small wedding, with Rob Penny the only non-family member present. The wedding came as a surprise to August's friends.[5] Nathan Oliver, a local poet and frequenter of Halfway Art Gallery, wondered whether Brenda's dark complexion was part of what August grappled with "in search of himself"—meaning in search of his own Black identity.[6]

After the ceremony, August and Brenda rented a small apartment on Milwaukee Street in the Upper Hill. Two months later, August suffered a jolt when David Bedford, his mother's longtime companion and helpmate, passed away. Dave had developed diabetes and used a wheelchair. Unquestionably, he had been good for Daisy and had won the affection of the children. He also had been an asset to the community, serving as ward organizer and treasurer of the Hill District Citizens' Committee on Economic Opportunity.[7] August had come to regard Dave as a good man who, because of racism, made a single, tragic mistake. As August understood it, Dave had been a football star who hoped to win a sports scholarship and go to medical school. But in those days, white colleges almost never gave scholarships to Black students. Dave tried to obtain the money by robbing the store where he worked, in the course of which, he accidentally killed the pharmacist.[8] The example of Dave's misfortune led August to generalize that many African Americans who are labeled "outlaws" should actually be viewed as "warriors" who, because of racial injustice, act in ways that often end tragically. That Dave ultimately became a community asset and a devoted partner of Daisy and her children led August to admire others who served time in prison. "For a long time," he says, "I thought the most valuable blacks were those in the penitentiary."[9]

Not long after losing his surrogate father, August became a father himself. On January 22, 1970, Brenda and August became the proud parents of a daughter, whom they named Sakina Ansari, meaning "tranquil helper" in Arabic. Brenda says that August was overjoyed that Sakina looked "just like him."[10]

Wilson had vowed to leave theater and return to poetry. But the return proved neither easy nor satisfying. After the riots, Wilson's adherence to John Berryman's confessional, apolitical poetry was out of sync with the times. To make matters worse, Wilson was not happy with his poetry. Chawley Williams also disliked it, saying it was imitative.[11]

To be sure, a few of Wilson's poems employ nationalist tropes. "Theme One: The Variations," which appeared in the journal *Connection* in 1970, uses

the collective *we*, preferred by nationalists as a sign of racial unity and community.[12] It also uses the term *nigger*, a designation seldom found in mainstream
Black writing. And it references such themes as Black victimization, the riots
of 1968, the beauty and strength of Black people, and the importance of Islam
as "the hands and voice of Allah."[13] But the poem's meaning is practically
impenetrable. It is inconceivable that "Theme One: The Variations" would
raise the consciousness of Black people and prepare them for revolution. The
poem's opening stanza reads:

> Life is ours like the real
> turning point the moon pointing
> the sun becoming the dance
> and life is ours and we breathe

A second poem, "To a Sister Who Can't Conceive of Her Beauty," celebrates Black women, but contains no overtly political messaging.[14] "Bessie,"
which appeared in 1971, is Wilson's first use of Black vernacular English. The
poem also features a rhythmic cadence that resembles the staccato sounds
of a jazz drummer. Overall, however, the poem reprises Wilson's favorite
trope, the outsider, portraying a woman who is ridiculed by others but who
has something important to say. Only Wilson's fifth poem in that 1970 issue
of *Connection*, "Muhammad Ali Is a Lion," contains even a moderately strong
expression of nationalist thought. Written in the form of an African praise
poem,[15] it exalts Ali and portrays him as the symbol of powerful "secrets of
the African bush," capable of driving a stake through the heart of vampire
Europe.[16]

Not surprisingly, Pittsburgh's cultural nationalists considered Wilson only
nominally one of them. Gail Austin, a local nationalist and activist, considers
him part of the Beat movement rather than the Black Arts Movement. "I don't
know August as a nationalist or a revolutionary," Austin says emphatically.
"No, no, no! August wasn't like that. At best," she says, "he was a *wanna-be*
black nationalist."[17]

While Wilson was struggling to find his footing as a poet, his friend Rob
Penny was moving ahead nicely. Widely regarded as Pittsburgh's leading
Black playwright, Rob held a faculty position in the University of Pittsburgh's
Black studies department, which had become the center of the city's Black
Arts Movement. The establishment of the department had been a key demand
of the Black Action Society (BAS). On Martin Luther King Jr.'s birthday

in January 1969, members of the BAS occupied the university's computer center. Following intense negotiations, the university agreed to open a Black studies program the following fall. It turned out to be a department rather than a program, and was cochaired by Curtiss Porter, a recent graduate of the university, and Jack Daniel, one of the school's newly minted African American doctorates.[18] The department had a strong nationalist orientation that reflected the goals laid out by Porter and Daniel in their manifesto, *Black Paper for Black Studies*.[19] The walls of the department offices, located on South Craig Street in Oakland, were painted in Garveyite red, green, and black. The department's official name—the Department of Black Community Education, Research and Development—signaled a commitment to serving the Black community. Rob was one of the first hires, brought in to teach courses in Black consciousness, Black theater, and Black poetry.[20]

The de facto shift of the city's Black nationalist movement from the Hill District to the university generated some resentment. Ralph Proctor, whose television show, *Black Horizons*, had been a major showplace for Black activities locally, now worked as assistant to the dean of Arts and Sciences. Proctor recalls the day that Ed Ellis, head of Halfway Art Gallery, terrified his secretaries by storming into the office and warning: "Mind you, just because you going to Pitt doesn't mean you still don't belong to us. Any time we want your ass, we're gonna reach out and snatch you and bring you back."[21]

Wilson was not offered a position in the new department. Porter said this was because he was not a leading figure in the Black Arts Movement. Porter felt that Wilson's allegiance to the cause was insincere and forced, and that his writing manifested an "incomplete conversion to cultural blackness." In particular, Porter felt that Wilson moved slyly, "chameleon-like," from Dylan Thomas to Rob Penny and Amiri Baraka.[22] He added sympathetically that Wilson's "black perspective was still developing."[23] In a later conversation, he added that Wilson's not even having graduated from high school may also have been a factor. Happily, August did not resent Rob's success. In fact, the two men got on famously. August could be found almost every day camped out in Rob's office, smoking cigarettes, writing, and talking. The two became almost inseparable, to the extent that, as one mutual friend said, "Where you saw one, you saw the other."[24]

Wilson might not have wanted a faculty position; he preferred part-time jobs that gave him plenty of free time for writing. Such temporary, low-paying jobs no doubt added to his mother's dismay, for they often consisted of washing dishes, busing tables, and sweeping up in fast-food restaurants. Vernell Lillie, who joined the Black studies department in 1973, long retained a mental image of Wilson standing in his white cap and apron in the doorway of Hemingway's Café on Forbes Avenue.[25] As Wilson said later, he was "still smarting from this Black Horizons Theatre thing," and so kept largely to himself.[26] His sole regret in distancing himself from the Black studies department is that he never met Sonia Sanchez, the well-known poet who briefly taught there.

Despite a preference for part-time jobs, in 1971 or 1972, Wilson accepted an offer by Porter to run Waumba World, also known as The Kraal, an Afrocentric cultural center in Homewood.[27] Shelly Stevenson, the only other staff employee at Waumba, recalls Wilson as being committed, at least superficially, to Black nationalism. "He *always* came to work in military fatigues," Stevenson says, and he *always* made her begin each day by reciting Maulana Karenga's Nguzo Saba, or Seven Principles of Kawaida.[28] These were Unity (Umoja), Self-Determination (Kujichagulia), Collective Work and Responsibility (Ujima), Cooperative Economics (Ujamaa), Purpose (Nia), Creativity (Kuumba), and Faith (Imani).

August seems to have found Karenga a bit more appealing than Baraka, even though the two men had more similarities than differences. Karenga, like Baraka, had been galvanized by the assassination of Malcolm X to create an organization dedicated to using culture in the service of Black Power. He founded US (as opposed to "THEM") in Los Angeles and urged writers to create works that would do three things: "Expose the enemy, praise the people, and support the revolution."[29] One of Karenga's most popular innovations was Kwanzaa, established in 1966 as an African-centered way to celebrate the coming of the New Year. Baraka adopted Karenga's philosophy of Kawaida as a guiding principle for Spirit House in 1967, and it was following Karenga's urging that he Africanized his name, changing it from LeRoi Jones to Imamu Ameer Baraka and finally to Amiri Baraka.[30]

Despite the fact that Wilson made Stevenson begin each day reciting the Nguzo Saba, she doubted the depth and sincerity of his commitment. She says he spent most of his time at Waumba World sitting in his office and writing poetry rather than working to make the center an effective Kawaida institution. After checking that she had recited the Nguzo Saba, he would spend the rest of the day secluded in his office, writing. "That's all he *ever* did," she said tartly. "Sat in there writing. All day. Every day."[31]

Wilson's neglect of Waumba World came to a head when the center was practically a no-show at a major cultural festival. The Program to Aid Citizen Enterprise, the center's funding organization, issued a scathing report on its shortcomings. Stung, August insisted that the public was unaware of how many Waumba-trained artists had exhibited because many of them had not worn tags indicating their affiliation. He also blamed Waumba's instructors for resisting advice on such things as how to run their classes, what to teach, and what age groups they should cater to. He fumed that the instructors "expected things to just blossom overnight" and seemed to believe that "if you sit around and talk about what you are going to do, it will happen."[32] Understandably, Wilson's tenure at Waumba was short.

Wilson says that Black Horizons Theatre "sort of like fell apart" when he quit.[33] But that was not the case. Rob's classes in the Black studies department provided a built-in student audience for the theater's productions. The department secretaries—Marcie Spidell, Carol Wise, B. J. Grier, and Angie Devine—did whatever was needed to make the theater's operations run smoothly.[34] Most importantly, following Wilson's tenure, Black Horizons attracted a string of talented and dedicated directors. The first was Frank Hightower. Modest, handsome, and soft-spoken, Hightower was a talented photographer who, according to one observer, "had Gordon Parks written all over him."[35] Active in the Black Power movement and sympathetic to the Nation of Islam, Hightower embraced Yoruba culture and went by the African name Omodi.[36] He had no prior experience in theater, but his background in photography gave him a good eye for how things would look onstage. Although quite modest by nature, Hightower feels that many of the plays he directed were convincing. Two of the most important were *We Own the Night* by Jimmy Garrison and *The Bronx Is Next* by Sonia Sanchez.[37]

Under Hightower, Black Horizons productions intrigued Wilson enough that he kept coming to rehearsals, quietly entering the auditorium after rehearsal had started and leaving before it was over. Clearly, he did not care to interact with the staff, but nonetheless he carefully observed rehearsals. On one occasion, Wilson noticed a young actress rehearsing Sanchez's one-woman play *Sister Sonji*. Troubled that no one was working with her, Wilson started giving her pointers, even though he had vowed never to work with Black Horizons. "I wasn't going to direct no plays for Black Horizons Theatre," he said angrily. "I was pissed off. If they had said, 'we're going to put you down as director,' I would've said 'No. I ain't working for you all no more.'"[38] Nevertheless, August came by so often that, according to Hightower, it was like he never really left. "He would still come to see what we were doing," Hightower says. "He might not've been there every night, but he was around. To me, he was always around."[39]

Hightower served a year as director, and then left to study photography in Philadelphia. For a while after his departure, Black Horizons productions were group directed. Then, in 1972, Elva Branson became the company's first female director.[40] More importantly, she was the company's first director with formal training in theater. She had majored in theater at Chatham, a local elite women's college, before transferring to the University of Pittsburgh, where she also majored in theater. Soon after arriving at Pitt, Elva joined Black Horizons Theatre, thrilled that the company's political orientation let her combine her passion for theater with her recent embrace of Black nationalism.[41]

Elva's credentials as a nationalist were weaker even than August's. She had belonged to a few nationalist groups but had not been active.[42] She had grown up in Elliott, a predominantly white neighborhood in the city's West End, and so had limited exposure to Black culture. Growing up in a predominantly white environment, one of Elva's first challenges was learning to "talk Black." Her early efforts were hilarious. While rehearsing Ed Bullins's play *In New England Winter*, she would pronounce the *t* in *winter*, causing cast members to laugh. "Say 'winner,'" they urged. Elva herself now laughs at how she "had to learn to drop my T's!"[43] Playful and lighthearted, Elva was warmly received. Staff recognized her talent and training, and quickly elevated her to a position of leadership.

During her first year with Black Horizons Theatre, Elva was chosen to direct Rob's play *Centre Avenue, A Trip*.[44] That same year, to Elva's surprise, Sala Udin and Curtiss Porter asked her to become the company's general director. The men explained that they could no longer serve because they were exhausted and preoccupied with other projects—Curtiss with the Black studies department and Sala with Ile Elegba, a drug treatment center he had established in the Hill. Elva accepted the offer, flattered that such an opportunity had been offered to a woman and a newcomer. Elva quickly became one of the company's most dynamic leaders. She maintained traditions when necessary and made changes when needed. She moved the theater from A. Leo Weil Elementary School to the Hill House, which had a larger stage. She increased the company's engagement with the community. This included cosponsoring a performance in 1972 to celebrate Sala Udin's release from Lewisburg federal penitentiary, where he had served a short sentence on trumped-up charges.[45] Elva continued the tradition of giving performances out of town, as well as almost anywhere they were invited to perform.[46] She experimented with "ritual theater," in which a loose structure and message allowed actors to improvise. Finally, in addition to her theatrical talents, Elva was a skilled administrator and fundraiser, crucial skills for an organization with limited financial support.

During Elva's time at the helm, Black Horizons Theatre saw the arrival of a new person on the scene, one of enormous talent and training in theater: Claude Purdy, with whom August quickly bonded. Born in 1940 in Lake Charles, Louisiana, Claude came from a combination working-class and privileged background. At Southern University in Baton Rouge, he majored in theater and studied under Joan Williams, who herself had studied under Thomas Poag, a legendary figure in the history of Black theater.[47] Under Williams's mentorship, Claude's natural gifts developed quickly and became obvious to others. At a theater competition in 1959, he captured the attention of Lloyd Richards, the Black director who in the 1950s had brought Lorraine Hansberry's *Raisin in the Sun* to Broadway.[48] Eager to get on with his acting career, Claude dropped out of Southern and moved to New York City, where he worked with the Negro Ensemble Company.[49]

In 1962 Claude traveled to Paris, planning to stay only a couple of weeks. What began as a brief interlude turned into six years, during which he worked at the American Theater in Paris with such leading figures as Philip Glass, Lee Breuer and JoAnne Akalaitis. He also traveled to Africa, where he worked with famed playwrights Wole Soyinka and John Pepper Clark. As one commentator said, Claude may not have graduated college, but his years abroad amounted to a form of graduate school.[50]

While in Paris, Claude met Gwendolyn Ormes, the woman ultimately responsible for bringing him to Pittsburgh. Gwen had won a prestigious Fulbright Award to conduct research with the Paris Theatre Workshop. Gwen decided to stage Baraka's play *The Slave*, and sent out a casting call to Paris's large expat community. Claude responded, and, after looking over his impressive résumé, Gwen cast him in the role of Walker. Gwen and Claude became an item and, in 1967, had a son, Akbar.[51] However, Claude was interested in someone who could support him financially, and so married the Paris-based daughter of a Washington, DC, realtor. Gwen and baby Akbar moved back to the United States, settling in Harlem. Claude, however, like any number of expats, sensed that the civil rights movement had shifted the center of Black social, political, and cultural energy to the United States. Inspired by developments back home, he left his wife and returned to the United States, where he reunited with Gwen and Akbar.

In 1968, Claude, Gwen, and Akbar motored cross-country on their way to Los Angeles. On the way, they stopped in Pittsburgh to visit Gwen's mother.

She was not impressed with Claude, but Claude was impressed with Pittsburgh—especially with Elva Branson and the people connected with Black Horizons Theatre.[52] Once they arrived in Los Angeles, Claude traveled around acting and directing. Feeling abandoned, Gwen and Akbar returned to Pittsburgh while Claude remained on the West Coast, performing in any number of cities. Claude liked Pittsburgh, and kept coming back, both to work with Black Horizons Theatre and to visit his son. He also took advantage of the opportunity to study with Jewel Walker, a noted professor of theater at Carnegie Tech.[53]

Elva was charmed by Claude, and quickly set up what she calls a "tender trap" for the newcomer. "I made him my assistant director and my man, in that order," Elva said. "And very short order at that. I'm no fool!"[54] Serving as Elva's assistant and codirector, Claude brought the company to a higher level of skill than it had ever known.[55] His talent and insights were widely recognized. "We had never been exposed to big time black directors here in Pittsburgh," Sala says, "but here was Claude, who had directed many plays."[56] Claude's presence made Black Horizons increasingly professional.

Like others, August was enthralled by Claude's talent and charisma. He especially was fascinated by the way Claude could infuse character and nuance into a performance. For example, when Claude directed Baraka's *Black Mass*, he did so in a way that converted what Curtiss Porter says was "pretty straightforward street propaganda" into a character-driven work.[57] August and Claude enjoyed each other's company, and constituted what Elva considers a "match made in Heaven."[58] When Claude was away—and he traveled frequently for acting opportunities—August occasionally would come by Black Horizons. But when Claude was in town, August came by every chance he could. After rehearsals had ended and everyone had left except Claude and Elva, the three would go out for drinks.[59] Sometimes Rob came along, but usually he went home because of teaching responsibilities and family obligations. The trio's go-to place was Irv's Bar on Centre Avenue. Long notorious for drugs and violence, Irv's had quieted down, providing Elva, Claude, and August an intimate, quiet place, suitable for serious discussions of poetry and theater.[60]

August would bring scripts to these sessions and ask Claude for feedback, something Claude was very good at.[61] Maisha Baton of Pitt's Black studies department says, "If [Claude] told you your stuff was good, it was good. If he told you it needed worked on, then your heart was hurting. . . . He knew his shit."[62] August loved critical feedback, but had not received much from Rob, who did not enjoy playing the role of critic. Vernell Lillie, later director of Kuntu Repertory Theatre in Pittsburgh, says, "Rob did not seem to read to

[August] and get feedback; [August] did not seem to read to Rob and get feedback."[63] As a result, Claude replaced Rob as August's closest colleague and mentor.[64] Claude especially enjoyed critiquing August because he recognized his enormous talent and promise.[65] Indeed, Claude was crucial to August's development. Hightower said that Claude helped August "find himself and rise to the next level."[66]

Elva thinks that Claude's appeal for August was that he too was "sort of an outsider . . . a little weird, not an inner-city person." Elva fit in well with both men because she considered herself as "something of an outsider."[67] Elva loved the men's companionship because they respected her as a person and a woman. "They didn't treat me like a rube," Elva says proudly.[68] However, respect for women was not part of the ethos at Black Horizons. In the Black Power movement, as in wider society at the time, men were expected to be dominant and women submissive. As Amiri Baraka said: "We do not believe in 'equality' of men and women . . . nature has not provided thus. . . . [men] have certain functions which are more natural to us, and [women] have certain graces that are yours alone."[69] Elva considered such attitudes chauvinistic and hypocritical. "The schizophrenic rhetoric," she says sharply, often went something like: "You beautiful black woman, you're a black queen, . . . but walk two steps behind me because I'm a black king . . . And kings can have as many women as they can take care of . . . but I'm a little short right now and don't actually have a home of my own, so could you let me live with you and your kids and loan me a few dollars 'til Tuesday?"[70]

Other women at Black Horizons felt the same. Sakina A'la, who had joined Black Horizons to gain experience for a possible career in Hollywood, says sarcastically, "Females had certain roles based upon their gender, and males had certain . . . privileges based upon the fact that they had penises."[71] Sala acknowledges that roles assigned to women in Black Power plays were secondary and supportive.[72] Rob Penny, however, was appreciated by the women for making a conscious effort at writing strong roles for them. Rob's play *Deeds of Blackness* features female soldiers who were no different from the men. They were not washing things or cleaning clothes, but doing the same things that the male soldiers were doing. "They were just as mean and dedicated to the struggle as the men," Rob says.[73]

Gender tensions came to a head following a meeting of the National Involvement of Africans (NIA), a militant group headed nationally by Amiri Baraka and locally by Sababa Akili and Kaimu Tukufu. The NIA's women members underwent training in weapons and the martial arts but were expected to assume traditionally feminine roles at rallies and demonstrations.[74] At one NIA meeting, Sakina overheard some of the men endorse polygamy, arguing that incarceration and the early death of so many Black men made it necessary that women share their men. Sakina was furious when she saw some male members of Black Horizons smile at the suggestion, for it reinforced an even larger grievance: that the men had been hitting on the women. This happened typically when a woman was driven home after rehearsal and the male driver would ask "a favor for a favor."[75] Thoroughly enraged, Sakina and Elva decided to teach the men a lesson. In consultation with the other women, they baked a two-layer Duncan Hines cake and put laxatives in the icing.[76] After rehearsal, they served the men cake and coffee. They then explained that they felt they were being taken advantage of during rides home. The men listened to the full presentation. They said they understood and would change. But by then it was too late. They had already eaten the cake. Some suffered bouts of diarrhea, and one required medical treatment.[77]

Today, the laxatives incident provokes more mirth than anger, but at the time, Sakina and Elva were accused of a "treacherous" scheme. One of Rob's sisters called it "a low thing" to do to Black men.[78] Sakina and the other culprits agreed that Rob was innocent. Elva told him not to eat the cake but, Rob says sheepishly, "Like a nut, I tasted a little bit of it."[79] Today, Sakina and Elva are all right with accepting blame. "To this day," Elva says laughing, "I will not apologize because I told them they were all full of shit."[80]

August was a loving father, who truly loved both Brenda and Sakina. "There was no doubt about that," Brenda says.[81] Praising him for the love he lavished on his daughter Sakina, Vernell Lillie gushed, "I wish you could see him with that little girl. He was a good father. Oh God yes!"[82] Religious differences, however, were straining his marriage. Brenda was a devout Black Muslim who had joined the Nation of Islam and worshipped at Mosque No. 22 in Homewood. August attended services with her but was not particularly engaged. Sandra Gould Ford, a mutual friend, says that almost anytime during the service, August might step out into the hallway. Brenda agreed. "When he gets that [distant] look in his eyes," she says, "he wants to put a sticker across his forehead [saying] 'back in five minutes.'"[83]

Brenda hoped August would convert, if only for the sake of their daughter. "Of course, I wanted him to be a good member and go to services," she says. "Sakina and I were going to the mosque and that would have been an ideal situation." Realizing that his casual attitude toward Islam was undermining the marriage, August formally joined the Nation of Islam, a move that surprised his friends. He even donned the Nation of Islam's traditional black suit and tie, and sold *Muhammad Speaks* outside Hillman Library at the University of Pittsburgh.[84] Some think August had some ulterior motives in joining the Nation of Islam, though. Temujin Ekunfeo recalls seeing August in his Muslim suit and tie and asking, in disbelief, "August?" August's reply was revealing: "Yeah, man," he said, "I'm planning a piece about charismatic leaders like Daddy Grace, Father Divine, Elijah Muhammad, and all that. How'm I going to find out about them if I don't learn it from the inside?"[85]

Wilson's inattention may have had a typical Pittsburgh cause. Christopher Rawson says that when he asked Wilson about his reaction to Sunday services, he jokingly replied that he'd rather have been watching a Steelers game—but it wasn't entirely a joke. Some years later when Rawson met Brenda, he told her what August had said, and she smiled broadly, laughed, and said, "He said that?"[86]

August's religious indifference cooled his relationship with his wife. Brenda says they just kind of "coexisted."[87] But while religious differences strained the marriage, economic issues shattered it. Brenda was a stay-at-home mother, and income from August's part-time jobs was not enough to support the family.[88] The result was a perpetually peripatetic existence that included changing residences often and brief stints living with friends like the Pennys. According to Rob's wife Betty, family finances caused so much tension that August and Brenda were "always mad about something."[89] When the Bazzells had the Wilsons for dinner, they knew August would eat heartily because he was hungry and didn't know where the money was coming from for food.[90] Women in the Black studies department asked in exasperation, "Why doesn't he get a job? Why did he spend so much time around the Department? How did he eat? How did he pay his rent?"[91]

Too often, in fact, August could not pay the rent. On October 7, 1972, the family was evicted from their public housing apartment in Saint Clair Village. Five days later, Brenda filed for divorce and moved out, taking Sakina with her. August came home to an empty apartment and to what his sister Linda Jean calls "unbearable" pain.[92] On April 5, 1973, their divorce was finalized, following which August and Brenda did not speak for fifteen years.[93]

Brenda says that *How I Learned What I Learned* helps explain how things looked to her at the time. In the play, whenever an employer showed any sign of racial prejudice or disrespect, August would quit. Chawley confirms the reality of this behavior, saying August would get a dishwashing job, and then just quit.[94] Such an attitude, Brenda says, was not compatible with having a family. "Once children come into the equation," she says, "you have to have more stability. I needed more stability than that situation offered."[95]

Today, Brenda is reconciled to what happened, recognizing that sporadic employment and low-paying jobs gave August the time he needed to write. "We have to follow our own rhythms and energy," she says. "He did what he had to do, and that's why we're talking about August Wilson now. . . . So I do not begrudge him that."[96] Brenda also recognizes that Islam was too constricting for August. "That was not the kind of venue he could function in," she says. "That just was not a good fit for him."[97] In Wilson's play *Ma Rainey's Black Bottom*, Toledo's marriage disintegrates on account of religious differences. Toledo says:

> She went out and joined the church. Soon she figured she got a heathen on her hands. She figures she couldn't live like that. Packed up one day and moved out. To this day I ain't never said another word to her. Come home one day and my house was empty! And I sat down and figured out that I was a fool not to see that she needed something that I wasn't giving her. . . . Yeah, so Toledo been a fool about a woman. That's part of making life. . . . But I ain't never been the same fool twice.

The divorce marked a low point in August's life, somewhat similar to what he felt when his mother expelled him from home. Now he had no home, no family, no regular job, and not even ties to Black Horizons Theatre. August had become more of an outsider than ever.

Added to his list of woes, Wilson's poetry was going nowhere. Some audiences loved hearing him recite because of his dramatic delivery style. "You have not heard August," Elva exclaims, "until you have heard August read August. Oh, my goodness, that is an experience! . . . If you just read them off the page, they would maybe make some sense, but if you listen to August read his scripts or his poems, it became music. Listening to him recite his poems was like listening to music, like listening to jazz."[98]

Wilson's poetry may have been opaque and imitative, but it made a lasting impact on Patricia Packard, a white freelance journalist from Connecticut. In the early 1960s, Packard had traveled to Pittsburgh with her husband Richard, a lawyer with Pittsburgh Plate Glass Corporation. A dedicated social activist, she started an innovative drug-treatment program called RAP (Recognize All Potential) that aimed to treat heroin addicts without removing them from the community or giving them medication. Packard was so dedicated to the idea that she even allowed drug users to stay in her home, along with the family's four children. We do not know how she met August, but around Christmas 1971 she sent a letter to a close friend, explaining that one time while working in the Hill and feeling "unwanted and unloved," she went to a poetry reading at which "a fine black poet named August Wilson" announced he would recite a poem titled "For Pat Packard." After the reading, and without comment, he handed Patricia the signed poem. She kept the poem as one of her "most treasured and profound possessions," before ultimately passing it on to a friend.[99]

The poem pays tribute to Packard for the affection she brought to the Hill, praising her for having "Made processions through / Full fields of wishes, forcing / The city open, spread like / A lover, anxious at the fruit." The poem ends sadly, with references to "Burning then, the cherish of motives / Flamed," an apparent reference to the riots of 1968. "The stars went out," it concludes, "white with death/ And fire and fear. . . ." The poem differs from most of Wilson's writing by focusing not on the inner pain of an outsider, but on the good deeds of someone who cared about the Hill and worked to help some of its most vulnerable residents.

Claude disliked Wilson's poems because they did not capture the way Black people talk. He often told Wilson that his poetry was beautiful, but people don't talk like that. Claude had the same complaints about many other Black poets. "If these young brothers," Claude grumbled, "would just write the vernacular and not be afraid of it and not be always trying to run to this jazz language" of people like Baraka, their poems would make more sense to people.[100] Claude urged Wilson to write in a simpler way that would appeal to the masses. He also suggested that he think of scripts that could be made into a musical or, even better, a movie.

Wilson was not interested in imitating Baraka, but he found it difficult to give up avant-garde poets like John Berryman. However, he worked on writing in a way that captured the way people actually talk.[101] The happy result was what Wilson considered his breakthrough poem, "Morning Statement." Written in 1973, it is the first poem Wilson felt was truly his. "It took me until 1973," he says, "before I could find my own voice as a poet, before I could write a poem that was MY poem, that was not influenced by John Berryman or Amiri Baraka or anyone else."[102] A short, free-verse, four-sentence poem, "Morning Statement" has no political referents and shuns the dense, obscure phrasing of Berryman. It does not employ Black vernacular, yet still captures a natural, conversational way of speaking. Wilson called the poem "a breath of fresh air," very different from his previous poetry, which he said was "a very obscure muddled way of saying things."[103] Given these qualities, it is remarkable that "Morning Statement" has appeared in print only once, in an article by John Lahr in *The New Yorker*.

Morning Statement

It is the middle of winter November 21 to be exact
I got up, buckled my shoes,
I caught a bus and went riding into town.
I just thought I'd tell you.[104]

In fact, shortly after his divorce, Wilson began traveling daily to write poetry in an Arby's restaurant on Liberty Avenue downtown. Barbara Evans, who worked there as assistant manager, recalls the first evening an odd-looking stranger in a Marine overcoat came in, ordered a cup of coffee, and asked if he could have a few paper bags. The stranger surprised her by taking the bags to his table and writing on them. His behavior made Barbara and the other staff nervous. But she said nothing as he sat quietly writing until about 11:00 p.m. and then left. The stranger came back the next night, again around 8:00 p.m. As before, he asked for coffee and some bags, and wrote until about 11:00 p.m. When he came in the third night, Barbara said to him, "Excuse me, I see you're doing a lot of writing," to which he replied, "Yes, I'm a writer. I like to write. That's why I like to come down here." The stranger told Barbara that he liked to watch people as he writes, and found Arby's had an interesting, mixed clientele. Then he went right back to work. "He was so focused," she says, "it was unreal."

For about two weeks, the stranger continued the same routine.[105] Then one evening, when he came to the counter to order coffee, he politely asked if he could speak with her. Barbara went back to his table, and he introduced himself as August Wilson and asked if she would like to go out with him. Taken aback, and a bit nervous, Barbara hesitantly said, "Well, okay." The stranger promised to come back tomorrow on her break, and take her to Richest Restaurant, which he said had the best corned beef sandwiches in town.[106] The next evening, as they ate at Richest, August did most of the talking. He said he had been married, that he loved his wife and daughter, but that they "just didn't make it." He finished his sandwich, stopped talking, and began checking out the surroundings. Then he walked Barbara back to Arby's.

135

This happened every night for a week or so. On one visit, he gave Barbara three poems he had written on the Arby's bags. Barbara showed them to her mother, who happened to be a fan of poetry, and told her not to get rid of the poems. "This man is going to go somewhere," her mother said.

One night, August told Barbara he wanted something more "serious," and asked whether she would be interested in dating. Barbara nervously told him that her parents would not approve of her being in a relationship with a divorcé. Up to that point, he had been very polite, never trying to kiss Barbara or even ask for her telephone number. Now, she says, he got very angry and, for several nights, did not come to the restaurant. When he did, he brusquely asked her to return the poems. When she asked why, he said, "You did not want to have anything to do with me. . . . I want my bags back with the poetry." When Barbara protested that she really liked the poems, August made her an offer. "I'll tell you what, if you give me my poems back, I will make sure that you get two." He kept his word, returning a few days later with two poems, typed on regular paper and dedicated to "B. E.," her initials. Today, Barbara is still surprised that the stranger went on to become a playwright, for she assumed he was going to win fame as a poet.

The poems that August gave Barbara feature the simple, straightforward language of "Morning Statement." One of the poems, "NEW WORLD (Christopher Columbus), for B. E." closes almost conversationally:

> We are following a course Due East
> though the compass has, of late,
> been acting up.
> Tonight the moon is unusually bright.
> I will try to sleep now.
> God Bless the Queen.
> In the morning I will climb the lookout.

The second poem, "VISION & PRAYER (for B. E.)," seems to refer directly to Barbara, dressed in the Arby's uniform of gold and black. The opening lines read:

> The silence parades around this room
> like a peacock
> flouncing it's [sic] golden colors, a skirt
> around it's [sic] black legs.[107]

Wilson's new style of writing may reflect more than Claude's influence. Wilson could have also been embracing, directly or indirectly, the so-called plain style of poets like William Carlos Williams, who was becoming increasingly popular among a new generation of poets. Beat poets like Williams and Allen Ginsberg rejected the ornate, obscure, aesthetic-driven poetry of Berryman, Wallace Stevens, and the Black Mountain poets, and stressed the importance of writing plainly and simply in a direct, accessible way about the writer's own life. The aim was to stress truthful communication over poetic beauty.[108]

Wilson's poetry in the late 1960s and early 1970s seemed behind the times, incompatible with the message of Black cultural nationalism. Later, however, it became increasingly in sync with emerging trends in Black writing, largely because by then the Black Arts Movement was fragmenting and losing adherents. This process can be seen in the ideological evolution of Baraka, its founder and guiding spirit. In 1970 Baraka established the Congress of Afrikan People (CAP), with chapters across the country—including one in Pittsburgh under Sala Udin—meant to spread the message of advancing Black Power through the political process rather than through violence. However, Baraka soon grew dissatisfied with the "revolutionary commitment" of many elected Black leaders. Searching for what he hoped would be a "truly revolutionary" politics, he began shifting leftward, culminating in 1974 with a surprising, full-throated rejection of Black nationalism and embrace of revolutionary socialism. Having argued in the 1960s that racism is the problem and nationalism the answer, Baraka now argued the opposite—that capitalism is the problem and socialism the answer. Denouncing Black nationalism as a form of reverse racism, he declared himself a follower of "Marxist-Leninist-Maoist" thought and changed the name of his Congress of Afrikan People to the Revolutionary Communist League.[109]

As might be imagined, Baraka's shift caused confusion and consternation in nationalist circles. In Chicago, Haki Madhubuti of Third World Press, the leading outlet for nationalist writing, resigned from the CAP. The reaction in Pittsburgh was more complex. Rob Penny remained faithful to Baraka's earlier nationalist stance,[110] while Sala Udin followed him down this new path. Udin changed the title of his column in the *Pittsburgh Courier* from "Afrikan View" to "Serve the People," and criticized what he called "reactionary petit bourgeoisie [*sic*] defenders of capitalism."

The waning of cultural nationalism sucked much of the energy out of Black Horizons Theatre. So did economic and social changes. Two of Black

Horizons' founding fathers, Rob Penny and Curtiss Porter, took academic positions at the University of Pittsburgh. They remained committed nationalists but had a growing list of other concerns and responsibilities. Sala Udin became increasingly engaged with his new operation, House of the Crossroads, dedicated to helping recovering drug addicts. Nick Flournoy quit writing poetry and established the Pittsburgh chapter of the Congress of Racial Equality (CORE). Chawley Williams was arrested and spent time in prison for robberies to support his drug addiction.[111] Kiburi left in 1974 when the CAP turned from nationalism to Marxism, Leninism, and Maoist thought. Even more damaging, newly admitted students lacked the commitment to Black nationalism that had characterized the theater's founders.

By 1974, Elva and Claude were ready to move on, having concluded that they wanted more than what Pittsburgh had to offer.[112] Elva wanted to go to New York, but agreed to accompany Claude to Los Angeles, where he had relatives and hoped to break into the film industry.[113] As they left, Claude and Elva asked August to take over as director of Black Horizons. Given his long estrangement from the theater, August was not a likely choice. But Claude and Elva thought his return to Black Horizons would be a positive and natural progression.[114] In addition, August had just written his first play, *Recycled*, which was under rehearsal at Black Horizons Theatre.[115] So, just as he was finding his voice in poetry, fate was moving August Wilson back to theater.

9

Leaving Pittsburgh

One evening in the spring of 1977, Ron Pitts was sitting in his car outside Oakland's Original Hot Dog Shop. He was waiting for August Wilson to come out of rehearsals of Ed Bullins's play *In New England Winter*. Vernell Lillie, the head of Kuntu Repertory Theatre at the University of Pittsburgh, had asked August if he wanted to direct the play. Ron knew there had been tension between the two, but was not aware of how bad things had gotten. Suddenly, August opened the door and climbed into the car. He told Ron that he and Vernell had gotten into an argument, and she had cursed him out. With tears in his eyes, August told Ron that he was leaving. "I can't take it!" he shouted. "I can't do this!" Ron thought August meant he was leaving Kuntu Theatre. Not so, Ron quickly learned. August was leaving Pittsburgh. "He was getting out of there," he told Ron.[1]

Four years earlier, just as Claude Purdy and Elva Branson were thinking of leaving Pittsburgh, August had reengaged with theater. His friend Rob Penny had invited him once again to cofound a theater—in this case seven theaters, each to be in a different neighborhood and each to be based on one of the seven principles of Ron Karenga's philosophy of Nguzo Saba, or Seven Principles of Kawaida.[2] August found Rob's idea ambitious and exciting, but he quickly found that putting it into practice proved difficult. The men opened the first Kawaida theater in Northview Heights, a troubled housing project on the city's North Side. The effort quickly failed. The young people would miss rehearsal and apologize, but at the next rehearsal, August says, "only two dudes would show up out of the six who said they were coming." August thought the problem might be that because he and Rob were from the Hill District, they were regarded as outsiders.[3] More likely, the problem was that the kids had not been asked what kind of plays they wanted to perform, and they lost interest in the sort of plays that Rob and August had in mind.

Nevertheless, the men's efforts bore fruit. Sarah Dixon, a community activist from August's old neighborhood of Hazelwood, learned of their project and asked Rob to consider opening a theater there. The neighborhood's youth, she said, had too little to occupy their time, so she and her husband thought getting them engaged in theater might keep them out of trouble and also develop their reading and social skills.[4] Rob and August jumped at the offer. The two went with Sarah, who arranged for them to meet with the children and their parents, along with the staff at the Glen Hazel Recreation Center. Perhaps learning from their failure to engage the young people in Northview Heights, Rob and August asked what sort of plays they wanted to put on. The enthusiastic response was *Superfly*, a Blaxploitation film that had come out the year before. The wildly popular film features Youngblood Priest, a cocaine dealer trying to stage one final, triumphant deal before quitting the business.[5] The film's glorification of the drug world appalled August, who laughed at the idea. Ron Pitts and Mary Bradley, staff members at Glen Hazel, also scoffed.[6] Rob, however, took the suggestion seriously. He went home and, the next day, returned with a script he had written overnight. Rob threw the script on the table and told the kids they could do *Superfly* if afterward they would do the plays that he and August wanted to stage. The kids readily agreed.[7]

During rehearsals, Mary detected tension between August and Rob.[8] She never figured out the reason for it, but says that Rob distanced himself from the production and left most decisions to August and Ron.[9] August took up the challenge and did the staging without Rob, working with Ron, who proved willing to do whatever would make the play a success—even chauffeuring August to and from Hazelwood. This was necessary because August held only temporary, low-paying jobs and often did not have money for bus fare.[10] August threw himself into the production. He sketched a model of the lighting board and got the electrical shop at Connelley Vocational School to build it.[11] The Hazelwood community enthusiastically supported the project. A sewing club made costumes, and Sarah Dixon's daughter worked on artwork and announcements.[12] The women were disturbed by the movie's glorification of drug culture, but were won over when August promised that, before each performance, a disclaimer would be handed out stating that attendees did not approve of drugs or violence.[13]

Virtually all the kids wanted to be in the play, so casting was no problem. August quickly recognized that Ron had acting talent and encouraged him to think about a career in theater. Ron declined, saying he was focused on completing high school and going to college. But, he said, he would act in *Superfly* if August would do the same.[14] At first, August resisted, but ultimately agreed, choosing to play the role of the movie's white photographer, while Ron took the part of the bar owner. In rehearsals, Ron recognized that August had acting ability. "He was believable!" Ron says. "He did it well!"[15]

Happily, the play exceeded expectations. At every performance, overflow audiences packed the two-hundred-seat theater.[16] "Everybody wanted to come," Ron says. "They just kept coming. It was a beautiful sight. . . . just a good feeling."[17] Ron was gratified that the play gave people something to think about besides the riots.[18] The production bolstered residents' sense of pride and self-confidence. "We did it!" Ron says "It was all homemade, but it was ours. We . . . could look around and be very proud."[19] Parents thanked Rob and August for making a positive impact on their children.[20] The mother of Gilbert, who played the lead role, said the experience had transformed her son. "When he got involved in this theater," she said, Gilbert "became a whole different person. He got confidence in his self . . . and turned his life around. I can't thank you enough for what you've done to my son."[21] The young actors loved the experience, although one gave August mixed reviews, describing him as "a great guy" but "stand-offish . . . didn't laugh that much . . . looked like he always had things on his mind . . . real serious."[22]

Although August and Rob felt good about the play's appeal to the youth and the Hazelwood community, staging proved so exhausting that they dropped the idea of founding a string of theaters.[23] However, in deference to their original idea, they christened the Hazelwood initiative Ujima Theatre—*Ujima* being the Swahili term for collective work and responsibility. After the success of *Superfly*, the young people kept their promise to act in whatever plays August and Rob wanted to stage next. August and Rob chose three classics from the Black Arts repertory: Amiri Baraka's *Black Mass*, Ed Bullins's *The Corner*, and Benjamin Caldwell's *Prayer Meeting*. They also decided to stage August's play *Recycled*, his first effort at playwriting, which had been in rehearsal at Black Horizons Theatre when Elva and Claude left for California.

Staging *Recycled*, a one-act play that Rob directed and August acted in, proved challenging. Some of the play's dialogue retains the flowery, enigmatic language of Wilson's early poetry, but some of it captures the cadence and flow of everyday Black speech. Like his breakthrough poem, "Morning Statement," the play shows that Wilson continued to work on capturing the way Black people actually talk. The plot was inspired by a gruesome scene Wilson had witnessed earlier that year. A bartender got into an argument with a patron, chased the patron onto Centre Avenue, and shot him. A nurse who happened to be nearby tried to revive the victim until someone said, "No need you beating on the man's chest. That man dead. His brain laying right there on the car." The nurse crossed Centre Avenue and went into Pope's Restaurant. Wilson followed and heard her tell Pope, "The niggers are killing one another these days." Pope replied matter-of-factly, "Yeah. Is he dead?"

"Yeah," the nurse said. "I beat on his chest. He's dead."[24]

That true-to-life exchange became the background for the play's opening scene, in which a shot is heard offstage and a man enters the bar. A woman says to no one in particular, "The niggers are killing each other." Later, toward the end of the play, the woman says something that informs the audience that the man who was shot at the play's opening has been "recycled" into this bar.[25] In the opening scene, when the man comes into the bar, the woman looks at him and asks, "Where did you come from?" He replies: "Down the street, lady, and did you forget?" She asks, "Forget about what?" He replies, "Forget about everything. Long dancing one afternoon. . . . All the mean shit we gotten together." Coldly and dismissively, she retorts, "Nigger, I don't know you from a lump of coal. You got a woman? Why don't you go home to her."[26] The woman's dismissive words turn the man into an unloved stranger, a trope that had long intrigued Wilson.

Some of the male-female tensions in *Recycled* harken back to Wilson's recent divorce. He called the play "a way to get [the anger] out of me, kind of find a way to purge that, to write about that in poetry and whatnot."[27] At times, however, his anger came out in dangerous ways. At one point, Wilson got carried away and physically struck Maisha Baton, who was playing the female antagonist. Years later, Maisha could laugh about the incident, but clearly had not found it funny at the time. "We only did it that one time," she says sharply. "I wasn't going to let him hit me again!"[28]

Despite realistic dialogue, *Recycled* was a failure. The plot's complexity left audiences baffled. "What's it about?" they asked. "Where is he going with this?"[29] The first night's performance had a large turnout because people thought it was going to be like *Superfly*. But Ron needed only one word to describe audience reaction to *Recycled*: "Phew!"[30] Beside himself with frustration, August asked Ron to tell him what was wrong. Fearing that August was "going to explode," Ron stayed silent.[31]

Not long afterward, Wilson did explode. During rehearsals for Ujima's next play, *The Corner*,[32] several kids were not taking their parts seriously, resisting directions and arguing over minor points. "I'm not going to do this part. I'm not going to do that part."[33] The most troublesome was Rodney, who always had a story to tell while actors were trying to rehearse. Finally, Wilson lost his patience and said, "Hey man, we're rehearsing," to which Rodney replied flippantly, "Oh man, we can do it later." Enraged, Wilson picked up a chair and hurled it through a window.[34] Ron was shocked. "I have never seen August get that mad," he says. "I could see the frustration building up in him. I could see it, but I did not know what he would do. And when he walked over to the chair and picked it up and threw it through the window, everybody stopped." People worried August might do the same to Rodney, but after fuming and cursing for a while, he told Rodney, "Get the hell out of here!" Ron thought, "This guy's crazy!"[35]

In 1976 Wilson wrote *The Coldest Day of the Year*, patterned after Samuel Beckett's *Waiting for Godot*. The play is set on a cold winter's day and features an elderly man who engages in conversation with a woman waiting at a bus stop.[36] The theme is intriguing, but the dialogue, with such tortured lines as "Our lives are frozen in the deepest hate and spiritual turbulence," shows that Wilson still had not freed himself from stilted, overblown language. *The Coldest Day of the Year* closed after only one performance.[37] Disappointed again, Wilson shelved a third play he was working on, "Rite of Passage," which to this day remains undated, unpublished, and unperformed.[38]

While Wilson was busy working with Ujima, Black theater in Pittsburgh was advancing through talented new arrivals to the University of Pittsburgh's Black studies department. One of these was Bob Johnson, called BJ, who had arrived in Pittsburgh in 1970 with an interest in combining music, dance, and theater. Born in New York City in 1938, BJ had worked with the Alvin Ailey Studio, the Katherine Dunham School, the June Taylor Dance Studio, and the New Lafayette Theatre Workshop. He also had performed in the original New York Shakespeare Festival production of *Hair* and in Ed Bullins's *Goin' a Buffalo* at the American Place Theatre.[39]

Recruited by the Black studies department, BJ and his productions quickly became leading features of the local arts scene.[40] His student-based Black

Horizons Dance Ensemble performed around town, as well as at Black Horizons Theatre. The Bob Johnson Dancers and the Harambee Dancers also were popular.[41] BJ's most important group, the Black Theater Dance Ensemble, founded in 1972, boasted two instructors from the highly acclaimed Alvin Ailey Studio.[42]

In addition to talent and energy, BJ had one particular personality trait that Wilson greatly admired: warrior. BJ demonstrated that trait during an unforgettable outing to Western State Penitentiary, where he, August, and Rob performed for the inmates. BJ had not brought along the women members of his company, and the inmates vociferously expressed their unhappiness.[43] When August and Rob came out to read poetry, the inmates made it clear they didn't want to hear any poetry. When BJ started dancing, they let it be known they didn't want to see him dance. They wanted to see the women. Finally, in a move that stunned August, BJ went back out and, in front of several hundred very unhappy men, danced a tribute to baseball legend Roberto Clemente and did so with such power and feeling that, at the end, the inmates applauded vigorously and called for more.[44]

Having witnessed that incredible performance, Wilson was overjoyed when in 1975 BJ established Theatre Urge and asked him to direct its production of Phillip Hayes Dean's 1976 play *Owl Killer*. Wilson considered working with BJ a great opportunity and was sorely disappointed that BJ apparently did not feel the same, and never asked him to direct again. "I thought that BJ would ask me to do other stuff," Wilson lamented. "I used to go home and think about plays I would direct. And then the next play he did, he had some group from Philadelphia come in and direct it. And I was wounded by that."[45]

Meanwhile, a new company at Pitt's Black studies department, Kuntu Repertory Theatre, was becoming the city's leading center for Black theater. The director of Kuntu, Professor Vernell Lillie, was hailed as the city's leading Black director. Born and raised in the Brazos Bottom region of Texas, Lillie traveled to Pittsburgh in 1969 to pursue graduate studies in theater at Carnegie Mellon University.[46] In 1973, just as she was completing her doctoral program, she was recruited to teach in Pitt's Black studies department.[47] Lillie agreed to do so but had no intention of starting a theater. She simply wanted to finish her dissertation and return home to Houston.[48] Nonetheless, despite misgivings, in 1974 Lillie founded Kuntu Repertory Theatre at the University of Pittsburgh.[49]

Lillie's appointment in the Black studies department brought her in close contact with Rob Penny, whom she admired for writing plays that focus on the lives of the marginalized and for urging Black men to think about their responsibilities.[50] She also liked Rob's portrayal of women, saying that he "can create women with such beauty, even better than most . . . female writers."[51] In 1975, during Kuntu's first year of operation, Lillie staged four of Penny's works—*Little Willie Armstrong Jones, Just Rob Penny* (a collage), *The Depths of Her Star,* and *Slow Lives on the Humdrum.* The plays were staged at the University of Pittsburgh in the Stephen Foster Memorial Theater as well as in several community locations.

Being in the Black studies department and working with Rob also brought Lillie in contact with August, who spent lots of time in Rob's office, smoking and talking with his friend for hours. August came by even when Rob was not there, so much so that Brenda Berrian, a new faculty member, at first confused the two. "He lived there!" Berrian exclaims.[52] August also palled around with BJ and Maisha, two of the department's other theatrically inclined members. August, Rob, BJ, and Maisha formed what Berrian calls a "little clique . . . really tight . . . like brothers and sisters."[53] Lillie says laughingly that the group often spent the lunch hour "solving the world's problems" at Pace's Restaurant nearby.[54]

In the evening, Wilson would stop by rehearsals at Kuntu Repertory Theatre, working with the actors informally and helping them learn their lines. Lillie says that, as usual, Wilson stayed in the back of the theater, quietly observing and not saying much or asking many questions.[55] Lillie was intrigued when Rob told her that his friend August Wilson had experience as a director. Lillie asked Wilson to direct two plays for her, *The Corner* by Ed Bullins and *Prayer Meeting* by Ben Caldwell. Wilson jumped at the chance, and impressed Lillie with his directing skills, especially what she considered his "sophisticated approaches to blocking, character development, plot nuances, social purposes of the author, and the capabilities of each actor."[56] When Lillie learned that Wilson also had written plays, she asked if he had anything that Kuntu might stage. Wilson replied that he had three plays, two of which—*Recycled* and *The Coldest Day of the Year*—were still being revised. However, a third play, *The Homecoming,* was complete.

The Homecoming is a fictionalized account of two men's reactions to the death of their friend, blues singer Blind Lemon Jefferson. Called Blind Willie Johnson in the play (there also was an actual blues singer by that name), Jefferson in reality was a Texas-born guitarist who sang for a pittance on street corners and at social gatherings. Considered by many as the "Father of Texas blues," he was recruited sometime in the late 1920s by Paramount

Records to travel to Chicago and make some recordings. While there, Jefferson complained of exploitation by the company.[57] Legend has it that following a recording session he was found dead one cold, wintry morning on a Chicago street.[58] In the play, Obadiah and Leroy sit in an abandoned train station in rural Alabama awaiting the arrival of Blind Willie's coffin. Two white agents from a Northern record company happen to be in the station and tell Obadiah and Leroy that they are looking for "any coon with a guitar" to come North and record. Angry about what happened to their friend, Obadiah and Leroy kill the agents.[59]

Featuring Black men settling racial scores through violent retribution, *The Homecoming* would have pleased Baraka. Usually, Wilson was not comfortable with overtly political messages and racial conflict. He recognized as much when he said that in his early one-act play—presumably, *The Homecoming*—he tried to imitate Baraka, but realized he "wasn't [Baraka] and that wasn't going to work."[60] The play was not well received for reasons that went beyond its political messaging. The dialogue is not opaque but is burdened with awkward lines, such as: "Well, I'll tell you, it's cold up North, all right. That's what I hear anyway. Froze to death! . . . Don't make much sense. . . . Yessir, that's something the way they treated Blind Willie."[61]

In 1976 Lillie presented *The Homecoming* at Pittsburgh's Schenley High School and at Ujima Theatre in Hazelwood.[62] After seeing the play performed, Lillie concluded in disappointment that Wilson had a future as a director but not as a playwright.[63] "I had no idea," she said years later, "that he was going to emerge as the great, great playwright. I really thought he was going to emerge . . . as a tremendous director."[64] "It was not that I was denying August," Lillie adds. "You must keep in mind that, at this point, August Wilson was not at all involved in playwriting. He had only written one play"—which, she adds proudly, she was the first to stage.[65] Lillie was not alone in feeling that Wilson did not measure up to Rob Penny, who was widely regarded as Pittsburgh's premiere Black playwright.[66] Mary Bradley, who had worked with Rob and August at Ujima, says Rob was the one who was always getting the recognition. "Never August," she says. Years later, Bradley was surprised that it was August, not Rob, who became nationally famous.[67] In addition to having doubts about Wilson's ability as a playwright, Lillie did not warm to him personally. Similarly, Wilson had ambivalent feelings about Lillie. He said, "I didn't really have a relationship with Lillie, other than the fact that . . . she discovered that I wrote this one-act play that she wanted to do . . . and I said Okay."[68]

Overall, Wilson was unhappy with theater in Pittsburgh. He was still smarting from the lack of public interest in Hazelwood for the plays he presented at Ujima Theatre. Deeply disappointed, Wilson lost interest in Ujima. In his words, the theater "just like faded out" and closed sometime that year.[69] Ujima was not the only theater that "faded out." Something similar happened to Black Horizons. Curtiss Porter thinks it closed around 1972. Rob Penny says it was functioning, "off and on," as late as 1973. In 1976 Elva asked Wilson what happened to Black Horizons' demise, and he replied in vague generalities. Elva got the impression that the theater quietly died—with no formal death notice—shortly after Wilson became director.[70]

In 1976 August's friend Rob launched a new Black studies initiative, the Kuntu Writers Workshop. The workshop was meant to be a place where aspiring playwrights could come together, support one another, and get feedback. However, once the workshop started up, many potential participants expressed an interest in poetry rather than theater. Rob advocated for theater but did not denigrate poetry. Like August, he considered himself a poet. According to Lillie, Rob and August both thought that "the highest honor was to be called a poet, and they would correct you on not calling them a poet."[71] Accordingly, Rob willingly opened the workshop to poets.[72]

Wilson was one of three coleaders, tasked with giving feedback on participants' poetry. Wilson walked from his home at the Penn-Negley apartment in East Liberty, some two miles away. Ever the bohemian, he did not mind walking. "I walked and I said that's okay because when I get there, I can get fifty cents from Rob and . . . get me some cigarettes. And Rob will give me a ride home, and I'm cool man. That's all I needed, that's all I wanted. To get . . . cigarettes and then talk about poetry."[73]

August and Maisha both regularly attended the Kuntu Writers Workshop, which met every other Saturday in the Black studies department. August and Maisha began dating on and off. As Maisha recalls, "What happened was he was obsessed with writing and I was interested, [but] not as obsessed as he was. But [I was] still in love with the writer and the writing and the potential . . . so we hung out together a lot."[74] August and his friends appreciated that Maisha had a car. "That was another reason they liked me," she says, laughing. "If somebody needed to go somewhere, if there was a theater thing . . . I would drive."[75]

Maisha (née Shirley) was born in 1939 in Harrisburg, Pennsylvania, and moved to New York City at the age of seventeen, planning to become a nurse. When she realized she did not like nursing, she took a variety of jobs and lived in the East Village.[76] Maisha never met Baraka, but attended poetry readings by such leaders of the Beat movement as Allen Ginsberg and Gregory Corso.[77] Their writing appealed to her because, she says, "It had a rhythm, it had a beat that was more like the old poets, John Donne and Baudelaire. . . . [They] were saying, 'Bam! Bam! Bam!, I saw the best minds of my generation,' you know, Ginsberg, 'destroyed by madness, starving, naked, dragging themselves.'"[78] In 1969 or 1970, she moved to Pittsburgh, where a cousin lived, and settled in the Hill District. She liked that Pittsburgh had a strong sense of community and a number of places where writers, artists, and actors gathered regularly and supported one another. In short order, Maisha joined Black Horizons Theatre and hung out at Eddie's Restaurant with August and others.[79] In the 1970s, she followed August's lead and wrote a play while sitting in Eddie's Restaurant, *Tears for the Living Children*, which BJ later staged.[80]

At the workshop, August and Maisha bonded even further. They had misgivings about the way Rob ran things and faulted him especially for two things: His reluctance to critique others' work, and not insisting that participants come with original work.[81] They also objected to the political nature of the writing Rob favored, which was much more political and Afrocentric than August's. Natalie Bazzell says, "A lot of the poetry at that time was very rhetorical, very black black power, nigger nigger nigger. It was more than that, but it had a lot of that in it." She adds that Rob's poetry was like that, while August's was very different.[82]

The Homecoming, Wilson's one effort at an overtly political, nationalist play, had not impressed Lillie. He began casting about for a new approach that would appeal both to Black nationalists and the general public. He did not have to look far. Years previously, Wilson had begun composing "Black Bart and the Sacred Hills," a long poem about the exploits of a Black bandit in the Old West. Knowing little of the Old West presented difficulties, of course. Uncertain about whether to develop the poem, at one point he gave it as a present to Barbara Evans, the assistant manager at the Arby's where he wrote poetry on paper bags. Fortunately, not long afterward, he asked Barbara to return the draft he had given her and decided to continue working on the poem.[83] At some point, Wilson decided to turn his poem into a musical.

National interest in the Black cowboy likely inspired Wilson to compose "Black Bart and the Sacred Hills." In the 1960s, Black cowboys had become all the rage. It began in 1965 when Philip Durham and Everett Jones published *The Negro Cowboys*, a groundbreaking study of Black people in the Old West. George Schuyler, prominent columnist for the *Pittsburgh Courier*, brought the book to the attention of the Black public. In a long, ecstatic review, he praised the book for bringing to light the heroic, nontraditional roles enjoyed by Black settlers, who worked as cowboys, mountain men, "Indian fighters," cattle drivers, horse wranglers, bronco busters, and even bandits. Two years later, interest in Black cowboys increased even more when Arno Press republished the gripping autobiography of one of those cowboys, Nat Love, also known as "Deadwood Dick."[84] *The Life and Adventures of Nat Love*, which originally appeared in 1907, recounts the adventures of a young Black man, born enslaved in Tennessee, who in 1870, at the age of sixteen, left home and headed West. There he lived a derring-do life of freedom and adventure. An expert marksman, he fought cattle rustlers, won prizes in rodeos, and even came to know such famed outlaws as Billy the Kid. Love treasured the cowboy life. "Mounted on my favorite horse," he writes, "lariat near my hand, and my rusty guns in my belt . . . I felt I could defy the world." A photograph portrays Love as a handsome young man with curly locks, sporting a large, flamboyant hat and a dramatic scarf. At his side is a large rifle and around his waist are his gun belt, revolver, and holster. In the 1960s and 1970s, intense years of the Black freedom struggle, Nat Love's saga captured the imagination of both white and Black America. His dramatic life called for a movie, or at least a play. In 1976 New York's Black Theatre Alliance announced plans to do a play about him; in 1979 Penumbra Theatre in Saint Paul, Minnesota, staged *Deadwood Dick: Legend of the West*.[85]

Although "Black Bart and the Sacred Hills" may have been inspired by the romance of Black cowboys, the poem itself was a humorous, satirical reinterpretation of the life and exploits of Charles E. Boles, a white stagecoach robber, prospector, and soldier. Known far and wide as "Black Bart," Boles had a reputation for style and sophistication. His place in the folklore of the American West ranks just behind Jesse James and Billy the Kid. Boles had a flair for the dramatic, a wicked sense of humor, and disdain for the elite. After a robbery, he sometimes left behind a poem that had the sort of impudent, sardonic humor that Wilson would have loved. One reads:

Black Bart, 1877

I've labored long and hard for bread,
For honor, and for riches,
But on my corns too long you've tread,
You fine-haired sons of bitches.[86]

The central character of Wilson's poem is a Black cattleman who, angry that the government has built a railroad through his ranch, turns to rustling. He gets caught but, after taking a course in magic, escapes from jail. Once free, he settles in a retreat he calls the Sacred Hills. There he begins making gold out of water with the intention of flooding the world with so much of the precious metal that it would lose its value. Bart hangs out with a zany, interracial cast of characters whose wickedly funny names reinforce a sense of absurd fantasy. Master Divine—a spoof of Father Divine, the founder of a Black religious cult in the 1920s—is a preacher and self-admitted "fake prophet." Pharaoh Goldstein, the Jewish mayor of Little Egypt, is a member of the Culturally Independent Adults (CIA) and financial overseer of the Nile Valley Pyramid Construction Company. Horsefeathers, the all-knowing Indigenous narrator, can be found sitting atop a barrel in front of the "Hoe-down in the John" saloon, owned by Chauncey Riff Raff III. Mother Principle is the saloon's madam who oversees the women who work at the Hoedown saloon, also known as the "Ain't No Ho' Down in the John" saloon.[87]

While Wilson was working on "Black Bart and the Sacred Hills," his old friend Claude Purdy returned to Pittsburgh, having given up on his dream of breaking into the movies. Claude and Elva took a position with the Pittsburgh City Players, an experimental, integrated theater on the North Side.[88] Happy to reestablish ties with August, Claude and Elva went to the Crawford Grill one night to hear him read "Black Bart and the Sacred Hills." Claude loved the poem, and felt it had commercial possibilities. "Hey man," he told August excitedly, "we could make this into a film!"[89] Making a movie was not realistic at the time, but Claude's reaction inspired Wilson to give it a try. Working furiously, he sat down and, in a week of intense effort, converted "Black Bart and the Sacred Hills" into a 137-page, single-spaced script for a musical.[90]

Musicals require collaboration, and so August called up Maisha and BJ. The four held brainstorming sessions, usually at Maisha's apartment and occasionally at Kuntu Writers Workshop.[91] Maisha tape recorded some of the collaboration. On one tape, Claude can be heard encouraging August: "Come on, let's do it . . . I know you can work that up. Have Bart saying blah blah blah." August replies, "Let me try it this way." Others join in with their own suggestions.[92]

The dialogue in *Black Bart and the Sacred Hills* shows that August was following Claude's suggestion to write in a way that reflects how people actually talk. Maisha approved of the result.[93] *Recycled* and *The Coldest Day of the Year*, she says, had been written in August's "James Joyce voice," in which the characters speak "classic" English. But in *Black Bart*, the characters talk, and they "talk shit." Later, Maisha says, the Bart voice takes over and "becomes *Ma Rainey*, becomes *Two Trains [Running]*."[94]

The dialogue captures the cadence and lilt of Black speech, as in this interchange between Horsefeathers and Sweet Delight, one of the saloon's "fancy ladies."

H F: Just call me stranger.

S D: Okay. Stranger.

H F: I put your key on the dresser

S D: Okay stranger. You sound kind of different

H F: You do too. You sure I'm in the right room?

S D: Sure, daddy. You write [*sic*] where you belong.[95]

Wilson remained committed, at least formally, to cultural nationalism. However, *Black Bart* distanced him even further from the nationalist movement. The play has elements of racial protest, but satire does not lend itself to politicizing the masses and raising their racial consciousness. As a musical version of the Greek classic *Lysistrata*,[96] *Black Bart* illustrates Sandra Shannon's contention that Wilson embraced the politics of empowerment and cultural affirmation, but his writing "was not to be the belligerent, vindictive voice of Baraka or Bullins but the subtly provocative . . . voice of a playwright with some thoughts of his own."[97]

Wilson's decision to write about Black cowboys may have been inspired by Nat Love, but the manner in which he chose to write about it reflects the influence of someone else. In the years that Wilson was working on *Black Bart*, two anthologies by the renowned Argentine writer Jorge Luis Borges, *Labyrinths* and *A Universal History of Infamy*, were enjoying international acclaim and his short stories were featured in *The New Yorker* and *The Atlantic*. Like Wilson, Borges had a fondness for the outsider, the outlaw, the renegade. One of his most acclaimed stories, "The Disinterested Killer," is a fictional account of Bill Harrigan, an impoverished Irish American youth who, born in the "cellar room of a New York City tenement" and "brought up among Negroes," went West. As described by Borges, Bill Harrigan became Billy the Kid, a "hard rider firm on his horse, [with] relentless six-shooters" capable of "sending out invisible bullets which (like magic) kill at a distance."

Borges intermixed magic, fantasy, and the supernatural in compelling short stories set in the "real world." His literary style, known as magical realism, influenced a generation of Latin American writers, including Gabriel García Márquez and Isabel Allende. In the tradition of Borges, the story of Black Bart is framed by a combination of magic and the mundane.[98] Indeed, examples of magical realism would be present in many of Wilson's subsequent writings.

To write the score for *Black Bart*, Wilson recruited Nelson Harrison, a talented local musician who had played in the Pittsburgh Youth Symphony and also accompanied such musical figures as Dionne Warwick, Nancy Wilson, and James Brown when they came through Pittsburgh. Harrison also had composed a number of musical scores, most notably "Isis au Noir," a reinterpretation of the Egyptian legend of Isis and Osiris.[99] Harrison had also previously been recruited, along with Wilson, by BJ, to work on a musical. In 1975 BJ planned to have Theatre Urge stage a musical about Stagger Lee, the mythical renegade whose adventures were celebrated in song and Black folklore. Wilson recruited Harrison to compose the music while he worked on the script. In the end, nothing came of the idea,[100] but working on the Stagger Lee project may have given Wilson the idea of adapting his poem "Black Bart and the Sacred Hills" into a musical. For *Black Bart and the Sacred Hills*, Harrison composed a string of musical gems with titles such as "The Last Stop Camel Feed and Water Company," "The Hoedown in the Gambling Hall," and "The Nile Valley Pyramid Construction Company."

Claude Purdy was to direct the musical and Ron was to play the lead role of Bart.[101] Given this enthusiasm, one can understand Wilson's disappointment when, at the last minute, he had to report that the performance was cancelled because he had been unable to get financing.[102] The failed opening of *Black Bart* was one more in a long string of disappointments. To make matters worse, the musical's collapse was followed by a heated confrontation with Lillie. This came while rehearsing Bullins's play *In New England Winter*, scheduled to open in late June at the University of Pittsburgh's Studio Theatre. Wilson considered it the biggest project he had ever undertaken.[103] Unfortunately, the chemistry between him and Lillie had never been very good. Unhappy with Wilson's directing, Lillie clashed sharply with Wilson on the night Ron Pitts was waiting outside the Original Hot Dog Shop to drive him home.

August got in the car and announced loudly that he was leaving Pittsburgh.[104] Ron said he found the announcement "surreal, almost like a play." When August confirmed that he was serious, Ron pleaded for him to reconsider: "Man, you got to finish what you started." This was not the first time August had threatened to leave Pittsburgh. "But this time," Ron said, "you could see it in his face. . . . He was going to be with Claude Purdy somewhere in Minnesota. He was through with everything—Ujima, Kuntu—anything that had to do with theater in Pittsburgh."[105]

By this time Claude had returned to Saint Paul and was directing plays for Penumbra, an up-and-coming new Black theater company. Claude missed August and wanted to work with him again. So, just before Christmas 1977, he sent August a plane ticket to Saint Paul, inviting him to come out and work with him on revising *Black Bart*.[106] August found the invitation too good to resist. "A free trip to St. Paul?" he said to himself. "What the hell."[107]

The following January, August stopped by to tell his friend Thad Mosley of his plans. Thad was stunned by the reason August gave him for leaving. "I'm stopping writing poetry. You don't get anything back from poetry." It was an astonishing statement from someone who had always considered himself first and foremost a poet.[108] It was also a sign that, after so many disappointments, Wilson hoped that musical theater might bring the sort of success he had sought for so long.

Most people think Wilson went to Saint Paul in order to work with Penumbra, but "I can remember as plain as day," Mosley says, "[August] told me he was going to Minneapolis to go to the Tyrone Guthrie drama school."[109] Indeed, the Guthrie Theater would have been attractive to someone with Wilson's ambitions. Founded in 1963 and located just across the Mississippi River from Saint Paul, it staged high-quality plays while avoiding the cutthroat commercial environment of Broadway.[110] Elva confirmed that August's goal was the Guthrie, saying that he wound up at Penumbra because Claude was there. "But he always had his eye on the Guthrie," Elva said. "I know that."[111]

Early in January 1978, August caught a plane to Saint Paul.[112] On his way to the airport, he stopped by Maisha's for some Valium to ease his anxieties about flying.[113] As August left, he implored Ron to keep Kuntu going. "Man," he implored, "you got to do it, you're what's going to keep theater going in Pittsburgh."[114]

August's departure left his friends despondent. Sala Udin acknowledges that it was time for August to move on, although his departure would be a great loss for Pittsburgh.[115] August Wilson may have occupied space only on the periphery of the city's Black Arts Movement, but his enthusiasm, energy, and talent meant that his departure contributed to the decline of the overall movement in Pittsburgh. "It was a thriving scene for a while," Ralph Proctor says, "but when the movement died, it all died. Everybody just scattered and went their own way."[116]

Figure 1 (*left*). Friel Vance of Avery County (Plumtree), North Carolina, possibly Daisy Wilson's father, 1922.

Figure 2 (*below*). Looking east on rear yards of dwellings facing Bedford Avenue, Fullerton Street, and Gilmore Way.

Figure 3. Wylie Avenue near Fullerton Street looking west on Wylie toward downtown Pittsburgh. The view includes the storefronts of "Ma" Pitts, the Crawford Grill jazz club, and Crampton's Drugs.

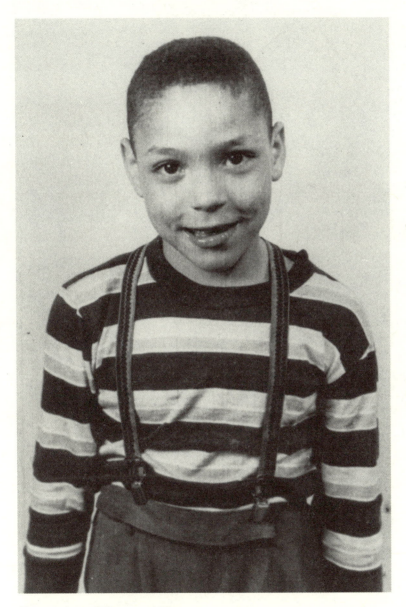

Figure 4. August Wilson as a child.

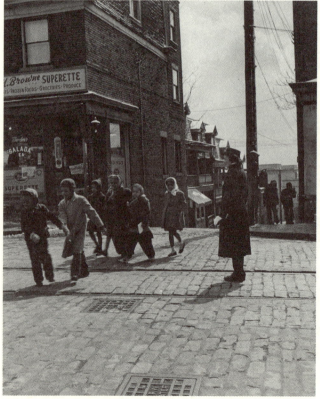

Figure 5 (*above*).
Probable image of
Freddy at St. Brigid
Church. As is
typical, he is seated
alone and reading
(*row 4, center aisle*).

Figure 6 (*left*).
A policewoman
directs traffic for
school children at
Watt Street and
Bedford Avenue in
the Hill District,
ca. 1951.

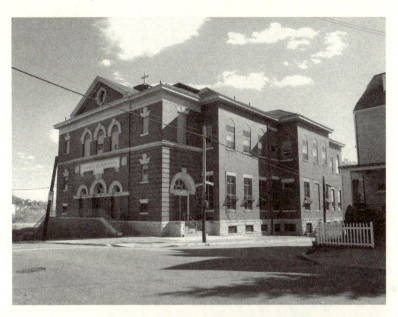

Figure 7 (*above*). St. Richard (now St. Benedict the Moor) School. August attended elementary school at St. Richard.

Figure 8 (*right*). Tony Kirven, Freddy's friend and classmate at St. Richard School.

Figure 9. Charley Burley. The prominent prizefighter was August's much admired neighbor and substitute father figure.

Figure 10. Lou and Bella Siger. The Sigers operated Bella's Market at 1727 Bedford, directly in front of the Wilsons.

Figure 11. The Wilson family's first home in Hazelwood, located at 2015 Flowers Avenue. The Wilsons were harassed while living there.

Figure 12 (*above*). Historic Hazelwood Branch of the Carnegie Library, at 4748 Monongahela Street. Reading at the Hazelwood public library, located just behind the Wilsons' house, gave August his first taste of Black literature, and awakened his interest in being a writer.

Figure 13 (*right*). Charles Biggs. As the social studies teacher at Gladstone High School, Charles Biggs insisted that Freddy prove he was author of a suspiciously good term paper, prompting Freddy to drop out of school in the ninth grade.

Figure 14. Freddy Wilson on the Hazelwood basketball team, seated forlornly on the first row at the far left. Freddy's nemesis Coach Zellman is standing at the far right. Gladstone High School yearbook, 1961.

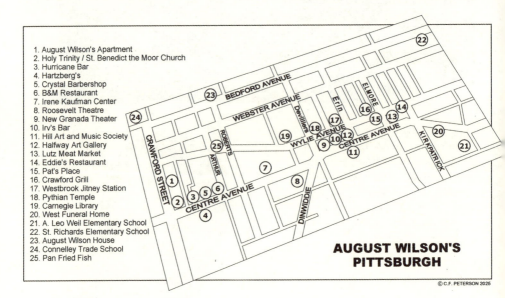

1. August Wilson's Apartment
2. Holy Trinity / St. Benedict the Moor Church
3. Hurricane Bar
4. Hartzberg's
5. Crystal Barbershop
6. B&M Restaurant
7. Irene Kaufman Center
8. Roosevelt Theatre
9. New Granada Theater
10. Irv's Bar
11. Hill Art and Music Society
12. Halfway Art Gallery
13. Lutz Meat Market
14. Eddie's Restaurant
15. Pat's Place
16. Crawford Grill
17. Westbrook Jitney Station
18. Pythian Temple
19. Carnegie Library
20. West Funeral Home
21. A. Leo Weil Elementary School
22. St. Richards Elementary School
23. August Wilson House
24. Connelley Trade School
25. Pan Fried Fish

AUGUST WILSON'S PITTSBURGH

© C.F. PETERSON 2025

Figure 15. Key places in August Wilson's years in Pittsburgh's Hill District.

Figure 16. Eddie's Restaurant on Wylie Avenue was one of Wilson's favorite spots for drinking coffee and writing.

Figure 17. Men playing checkers on Centre Avenue, ca. 1949.

Figure 18 (*left*).
Savoy Theater/
New Granada
Theater and
Irv's Bar. Pop-
ular spots on
Centre Avenue
frequented by
August Wilson
and friends.

Figure 19 (*below*).
Mainway
Market, leading
grocery of the
Hill District.

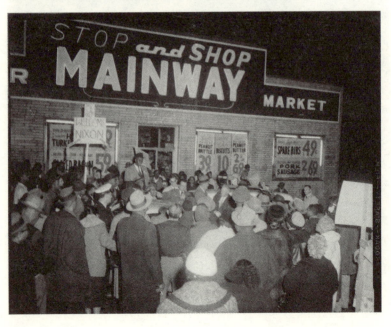

Figure 20. Lutz Meat Market. Lutz training Calvin Cunningham to be a butcher. Ultimately Lutz sold the business to Cunningham. In the play *Two Trains Running*, Wilson unfairly portrays Lutz as a racist exploiter.

Figure 21. Crawford Grill, a popular restaurant, bar, and jazz spot in the Hill. Interior view of the grill on a busy night.

Figure 22 (*left*). Carl "Dingbat" Smith, the Hill's most highly popular and influential artist, displaying one of his famous pieces of nail sculpture.

Figure 23 (*below*). The Halfway Art Gallery, on Centre Avenue, where Wilson and friends recited poetry before a live audience.

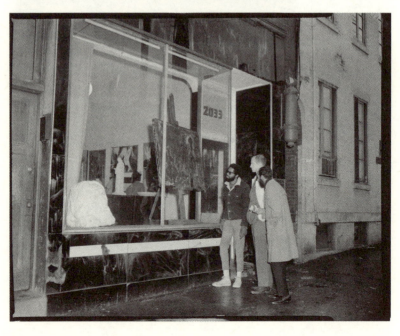

Figure 24 (*above*). Ed (Ewari) Ellis, director of Halfway Art Gallery.

Figure 25 (*right*). Sala Udin, leading Black nationalist and good friend of August.

Figure 26. August Wilson contemplating the ruins of the Mainway Supermarket, the leading grocery in the Hill. The Mainway was torched during the riots that followed the assassination of Martin Luther King Jr. in 1968.

Greater Pittsburgh's Complete Entertainment Magazine

Dateline: Pittsburgh

September 1-15, Vol. 2, No. 1

The Ghetto Kids: New Day for Young Talent

Figure 27. Elva Branson, a talented actor and friend of Wilson as well as the sometime director of Black Horizons Theatre.

Figure 28. August Wilson and Brenda Burton's wedding day, June 1969. *From left to right*: unknown young woman, Brenda, August, Rob Penny.

Figure 29. Maisha Baton, poet and sometime girlfriend of August Wilson.

Figure 30. Claude Purdy and Jacqui Shoholm, Wilson's close friends in Saint Paul.

Figure 31. August Wilson and Judy Oliver at their Grand Avenue apartment, Saint Paul, 1980.

Figure 32. August Wilson (*far right*) with Saint Paul friends Randi Yoder, Daniel Gabriel, Judith Gabriel, and Judy Oliver, August 1981.

Figure 33. August, his mother Daisy, and daughter Sakina at August's wedding to Judy Oliver, Saint Paul, 1981.

Figure 34. Family gathering to celebrate one of Wilson's early Broadway successes. *From left to right*: (*front row*): Daisy, Linda Jean, Faye (*next two rows*): Paul, Freda, August, Kim, Donna, Richard, and George.

Figure 35. Daisy Wilson's headstone, Greenwood Cemetery, O'Hara Township.

Figure 36. Zonia Wilson's headstone, Greenwood Cemetery, O'Hara Township.

Figure 37. Julia Burley and August Wilson. Julia and Charley Burley lived across the street from the Wilsons. Julia was Daisy's closest friend; Charley was August's much-needed father figure.

Figure 38. August Wilson with friend and fellow poet Nick Flournoy.

Figure 39. August with friends Rob Penny and Ed Ellis, director of Halfway Art Gallery, ca. 1990.

Figure 40. Prizewinning drawing for Two Trains Running by Dennis Biggs, cousin of Charles Biggs, the teacher at Gladstone High School who gave August an F on a term paper.

Figure 41. Christopher Rawson and August Wilson.

Figure 42. August Wilson and Constanza Romero.

Figure 43 (*right*). August Wilson's headstone, Greenwood Cemetery, O'Hara Township.

Figure 44 (*below*). The Oyster House, a historic and beloved bar/restaurant in downtown Pittsburgh. On Saturdays, Fred Kittel took his sons August and Edwin for lunch at Oyster House. The restaurant remained one of Wilson's most treasured places.

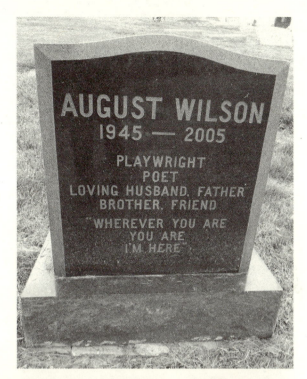

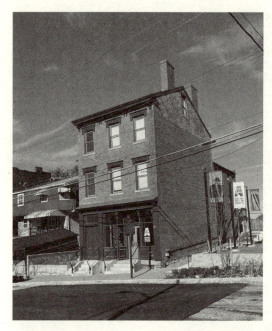

Figure 45 (*left*). Wilson's home at 1727 Bedford Avenue, as restored in 2023 by Robert Pfaffman, architects.

Figure 46 (*below*). Wilson Cultural Center. The August Wilson African American Cultural Center was established in 2006 at the corner of 10th and Liberty Avenues downtown. Though named for August Wilson, the center features a wide range of artistic and cultural events.

10

Discovering Bearden, Finding His Way

Discouraged by his lack of full acceptance in his hometown, August Wilson left Pittsburgh with mixed feelings. Years later, he confided how he felt to his friend and local theater critic Christopher Rawson. Pittsburgh, he said, "is my home and at times I miss it and find it tremendously exciting. But at other times I want to catch the first thing out that has wheels."[1] In the end, Wilson left on something that had wings rather than wheels.

On a cold day in January 1978, Wilson's plane touched down at the Minneapolis–Saint Paul International Airport. Meeting him there was his friend Claude Purdy, who arrived with his girlfriend, Jacqui Shoholm. Claude and Jacqui had met just a few months earlier at the opening of *Eden*, a play he was directing for Saint Paul's Penumbra Theatre. Jacqui had been at the opening because she was the compliance officer for the city's Comprehensive Employment and Training Act (CETA), which oversaw the funding of Penumbra and other arts organizations.[2] Claude had told Jacqui little about August, and so she had no particular expectations of what he was like. However, she was taken aback by August's disheveled appearance, which included a very large, unkempt head of hair and a bulky, ill-fitting overcoat that reached down to mid-calf.[3]

After dropping off August's bags at the Commodore Hotel, the three went out for a bite.[4] While the men were catching up on each other's lives, Jacqui happened to notice the script of a short play that Claude was carrying with him. It was Wilson's *The Coldest Day of the Year*, which he had written a couple of years previously. Jacqui found the play touching and poetic, so much so that, by the time she finished, she found herself quietly crying.[5] Jacqui immediately realized that, despite appearances, Claude's friend was a writer of considerable talent.

After dropping off Jacqui at her apartment, Claude asked to borrow her car. August had told Claude he wanted to visit the Washington Avenue Bridge, which spanned the Mississippi River not far from the University of Minnesota. Wilson's idol, the award-winning poet John Berryman, had once taught near that bridge. Six years previously, Berryman died by suicide by jumping off the bridge. Wilson wanted to pay homage to the man whose poetry had been such a major influence.

Wilson spent two weeks in Saint Paul busily revising *Black Bart and the Sacred Hills* with Claude, who had arranged for a stage reading of the play in Los Angeles.[6] When he got back to Pittsburgh after the two weeks were up, Wilson gave out clear signals that he intended to return to Saint Paul, perhaps permanently. Partly this was because he liked the city. But especially it was because he had been smitten by someone he met there: an independent young woman named Judy Oliver, a friend of Jacqui and a social worker at a local youth services organization. Inspired by the civil rights movement, Judy's passion for racial justice had led to a career in social work. At their very first meeting, the two had been captivated by each other. August showed Judy one of his scripts; Judy made him dinner. Judy told Jacqui how much she admired August's honesty and the sense that he spoke with a "true heart."[7] Judy soon became the first non–African American woman August dated.

After returning to Pittsburgh, August gave clear signs of his infatuation with Judy. He telephoned her almost daily. He dropped by Rob Penny's office less often, and when he did, he worked on persuading Rob to come back with him to Saint Paul. He told Rob that to "make it big," they needed to leave Pittsburgh. Rob declined—understandably, since he had a family in Pittsburgh and a secure faculty position as playwright-in-residence in Black Studies at the University of Pittsburgh. "Okay, I'll go," August finally told him, "and hopefully you'll come."[8]

On March 5, 1978, shortly before his thirty-third birthday, August returned to Saint Paul, this time with the intention of relocating permanently.[9] He moved into Judy's apartment in the Ramsey Hill neighborhood at the edge of Saint Paul's small Black community.[10] Through Jacqui, August secured a position at the Science Museum of Minnesota, tasked with creating fictional vignettes of Minnesota Native American life in the 1800s.[11] August was thrilled at the job's flexibility. "It was the kind of job," August said, "where you could announce at 10 o'clock, 'I'm going to the library,' and disappear for the rest of the day."[12] Happily, this gave him plenty of time to work on *Black Bart*.

Spring passed quickly and pleasantly. So did summer. After work, August and Judy often went over to Jacqui's for dinner. Sometimes, they were joined by others because Claude—who by then had moved in with Jacqui—liked inviting friends over. August often did the cooking at these gatherings, usually preparing roasts and steaks. His specialties were Southern dishes he had learned from his mother. Years later, at the time of his death, he left behind his personal, handwritten recipe for making his mother's sweet potato pie.[13] On holidays and special occasions, August's daughter Sakina and Jacqui's son Damon might be present. In addition, Sakina came to live with August and Judy for a year of junior high school. Maisha Baton, August's collaborator and former girlfriend, also came for a visit, staying with Claude and Jacqui.[14]

Through much of 1978, Claude and August spent many afternoons and evenings together, working to get *Black Bart* ready for its stage reading the following spring in Los Angeles. Discussions about the script often began before dinner and lasted until late in the evening. From those discussions, August became so familiar with the musical that he could recite much of it from memory.[15] In addition to working on *Black Bart*, the two men liked to discuss interesting things they had read.[16] One evening, Claude brought out a book he had borrowed from a friend, *The Art of Romare Bearden: The Prevalence of Ritual*. The book opened with a long essay on Bearden followed by some ninety of his paintings and collages. It made an immediate, profound impact. August says that, "after dinner and much talk," Claude

laid it open on the table before me. "Look at this," he said. "Look at this." The book lay open on the table. I looked. What for me had been so difficult, Bearden made seem so simple, so easy. What I saw was black life presented on its own terms, on a grand and epic scale, with all its richness and fullness, in a language that was vibrant and which, made attendant to everyday life, ennobled it, affirmed its value, and exalted its presence. It was the art of a large and generous spirit that defined not only the character of black American life, but also its conscience. I don't recall what I said as I looked at it. My response was visceral. I was looking at myself in ways I hadn't thought of before and have never ceased to think of since.[17]

Widely regarded as the nation's foremost visual interpreter of the Black experience, Bearden changed the way Wilson would write about Black life henceforth. It was a turning point in Wilson's professional development, more profound even than his discovery in 1966 of Bessie Smith and the blues. Wilson admits that the blues provided him a framework for interpreting Black life and remained the wellspring of his art. But now he realized that Bearden provided him something that the blues did not: "A narrative that encompasses all the elements of [Black] culture and tradition."[18] In asking the blues for such an all-encompassing narrative, Wilson had been asking too much of an art form that excels at recounting the feelings of an individual. Others may identify with those feelings, but at bottom the blues is a monologue. Theater, however, features multiple characters and multiple voices. Bearden's paintings feature multiple characters and multiple voices positioned on the canvas like characters on a stage.[19] No wonder Wilson responded so viscerally.

Born in 1911, Bearden belonged to one of the most prominent Black families in Charlotte, North Carolina. In 1915 the family fled Charlotte after a group of white men sharply questioned Romare's darker-skinned father about why he was in the company of a "white" boy—the light-complexioned Romare.[20] After leaving Charlotte, Romare lived with a succession of relatives, including his maternal grandparents, who ran a boardinghouse in Pittsburgh.[21] There, at 3142 Penn Avenue in the city's Strip District, he lived among Black ironworkers who toiled at the Clark, Black Diamond, and Crucible mills located just across the street. The sight of men returning from a day's work with bodies blistered from the heat of the furnaces left an indelible impression on the future artist.[22]

Romare's family finally settled in Harlem, where his father found work as a civil servant for the city and his mother found work as New York editor for the African American newspaper *The Chicago Defender*. The Bearden family quickly became part of Harlem's African American elite. At their residence on 131st Street, young Romare met such leading figures of the Harlem Renaissance as W. E. B. Du Bois, Paul Robeson, Langston Hughes, A'Lelia Walker, and Marcus Garvey.

During the Great Depression, Bearden's parents had the means to finance his studies at New York University, from which he graduated with a degree in mathematics. He also pursued an interest in art, studying under the noted German caricaturist George Grosz and painting scenes of Black life in the social realism style popular at the time. After serving in the US Army, Bearden switched from realistic depictions of Black life to the sort of abstract style popular in the

1940s. His highly regarded, nonracial paintings of the time were exhibited throughout the United States as well as in Europe and South America. In 1950 Bearden traveled to Paris, where he studied the works of the great masters, met such prominent artists as Constantin Brâncuşi and Georges Braque, and became friends with Black expats James Baldwin and Albert Murray.[23]

In the 1960s, as the civil rights movement heated up, Bearden produced realistic paintings of Black life that he hoped would advance the cause of racial justice. This was a risky career move at a time when abstract art reigned supreme. Bearden persevered and began painting scenes based on life as he had observed it in Harlem, Pittsburgh, and Mecklenburg County, North Carolina. Seeking a distinctive way of portraying Black life, Bearden turned to collage, a style popularized early in the twentieth century by modernist painters Pablo Picasso and Braque, but which had fallen out of favor. Expanding the technique, Bearden mastered an extraordinary number of materials, gluing pieces of cloth, paper, and magazine pages to his canvases.[24] To give his collages a sense of immediacy, he inserted bits of photographs, a technique known as photomontage.[25] Considering himself a painter as well as a collagist, he painted over those objects, sometimes adding cubist-style images of African masks.

In 1964, the year that Bearden returned to figurative renderings, Harlem erupted in a race riot, an upheaval that gave his art social as well as aesthetic significance. His collages were featured in major museums and galleries, and even graced the covers of *Time* magazine and *Fortune*.[26] In 1971 Bearden's rising trajectory was enhanced with the opening of *The Prevalence of Ritual*, a retrospective of fifty-six works at New York's Museum of Modern Art. Two years later, MoMA followed up with *The Art of Romare Bearden: The Prevalence of Ritual*, a large, imposing volume that featured ninety or so images, along with an introduction by famed novelist John A. Williams and text by visual artist M. Bunch Washington.[27]

Like a visual anthropologist, Bearden depicted patterns of behavior that carry social and cultural significance, rituals of daily life that promote group identity and social cohesion. *Baptism*, *The Funeral*, and *Fish Fry* explore three such ritualized activities. Similarly, *Conjur Woman* depicts an iconic figure whose ties to Africa and contact with the spirit world enable her to foresee the future, heal the sick, punish miscreants, and maintain group norms and solidarity. Such a woman lived behind the Pittsburgh boardinghouse of Bearden's grandmother. Sarah Degree, a sort of conjure woman herself, introduced Wilson to Catholicism and intrigued him with her ritual-based sprinkling of salt over the threshold of her house.[28]

Bearden painted only occasional scenes of rural life; it is the city that looms largest in his work.[29] *The Street* is an example of this, and a good example of how he influenced Wilson. The painting depicts Black urban life presented in a dense collection of buildings, steps, a crowded sidewalk, and a bridge. Some twenty figures—male and female, young and old, middle class, working class, and of indeterminate status—cluster on stoops outside a tenement. As Bearden's biographer says: "The figures are pictured in sharp detail, their eyes locking with the viewers' eyes, their hand enlarged, their expression bold; they physically engage with each other and with the viewer."[30] The painting displays the energy, diversity, and humanity of street life, enticing the viewer to visually engage with a collection of intriguing, enigmatic figures.

Figures in *The Street* cluster around the tenement as though on the set of a play, close enough that they almost engulf the viewer.[31] Williams's introduction captures the energy created by their closeness to themselves and to the viewer. They "burst upon you," he writes, "people, faces, eyes, going in every direction, tenement windows not quite concealing still other faces." They are people, Williams says, who have survived in spite of everything.[32] Bearden's figures, in all their diversity, constitute a community. Their crowded, chaotic, peaceful gathering strikes the viewer as taking place regularly, amounting to a ritual in and of itself. *The Street* is the sort of scene that prompted Wilson to praise Bearden for creating art that "ennobled" Black life, affirming its value and exalting its presence.[33]

Bearden did not seek to romanticize Black life. Rather, he sought to depict the rituals of daily life as honestly, passionately, and dispassionately as Pieter Bruegel depicted Flemish peasants in sixteenth-century Belgium.[34] As Bearden said: "I did not need to go looking for . . . the absurd or the surreal, because I have seen these things out of my studio window on 125th Street."[35] Lively, crowded streets existed throughout urban Black America. Bearden's painting *The Street* depicts life in Harlem in the early 1960s, but in many ways life there resembled Centre Avenue in Pittsburgh's Hill District. Wilson had long been entranced by the way Centre would "shimmer with activity" from the hundreds of people who gathered there regularly.[36] One time he didn't go to bed for three days because he worried he might miss something.[37]

If the depiction of daily life constitutes one aspect of Bearden's art, the other was his technique of collage. The latter incorporates a variety of objects, such as photographs and pages torn from magazines.[38] Wilson had long been fascinated by objects, feeling that they amounted to relics and souvenirs. He loved to rummage through secondhand stores, looking for things that had been saved because they provide insights into the sorts of things their owners held dear.[39] His own writing style possessed such collage-like qualities as jotting down thoughts on anything handy—napkins, envelopes, notepads—and later reconfiguring them into a poem or play. "I often use the image of a stewing pot," Wilson says, "in which I toss various things that I'm going to make use of—a black cat, a garden, a bicycle, a man with a scar on his face, a pregnant woman, a man with a gun. Then I assemble the pieces into a cohesive whole."[40]

Thanks to Bearden, Pittsburgh's Hill District became what Christopher Rawson calls "the deep well of memory into which [Wilson] kept dipping the ladle of his art."[41] Inspired by Bearden's example, Wilson henceforth would set his plays in a place he knew well, filled with the sort of people he knew well. Wilson's future plays would not be as crowded as Bearden's *The Street*, but they would take place in such public settings as a backyard, a boardinghouse, a recording studio, a living room, a restaurant, or an office.

The first poetry group Wilson belonged to, Poets in the Centre Avenue Tradition, had resolved to depict life on and around Centre Avenue. Chawley Williams excelled in doing that, but Wilson's poems long focused on his own inner demons and insecurities rather than on life along the avenue. Wilson was deeply familiar with life on and around Centre Avenue, but after his encounter with Bearden he systematically made it the basis of his plays. Bearden gave Wilson a new way of visualizing the Black experience, one that proved to be a turning point in his career. His paintings taught Wilson that success depended on depicting daily life simply and honestly, focusing on people he knew well, writing about places he was familiar with, and using the sort of language people actually use when they talk. There was no need to write complicated dialogue in the obscure manner of a John Berryman or in the strident political discourse of an Amiri Baraka. There was no need for complicated plots of zany characters like Black Bart residing in such improbable places as "The Sacred Hills." Bearden showed Wilson that depicting everyday life among ordinary people could provide what he most needed: "A narrative that would encompass all the elements of [Black] culture and tradition."

Wilson wrote a two-page foreword to Myron Schwartzman's *Romare Bearden: His Life and Art* (1990). In a 1991 *New York Times* op-ed, Wilson declared Bearden one of his "Four B's," one of the key influences on his work, along with Baraka, the blues, and Jorge Luis Borges, the Argentine writer of magical realism.[42] Bearden provided Wilson with a way forward, a way out of the trap that his previous approaches had created. He "showed me a doorway," Wilson exulted, "a road marked with signposts, with sharp and sure direction." Wilson vowed to do with words what Bearden had done with images: "To make my plays the equal of his canvases."[43]

It is a shame the two never met. Wilson once walked by Bearden's New York studio but could not summon the courage to knock. He stood there, he says, "in silent homage." Years later, he wondered what he might have said had he knocked and Bearden answered. "I probably would just have looked at him," he says. "I would have looked, and if I were wearing a hat, I would have taken it off in tribute."[44]

Making good use of the free time afforded by his job at the Science Museum, Wilson finished revisions to *Black Bart* long before the onstage reading, which was scheduled for six months later, in April or May 1979, at Los Angeles' Inner City Cultural Center.[45] Claude and August flew to Los Angeles for the reading, joined there by Bob Johnson, the play's choreographer, and Maisha Baton, the lyricist. Despite all their hard work, the audience gave *Black Bart* a tepid response, largely because they were baffled by its complex storyline and numerous characters.[46] As so many times before, August was sorely disappointed. Maisha took it all in stride. "The play wasn't very good," she says laughing, and "the lyrics aren't that good either, but they're mine!"[47]

The stage reading in Los Angeles had been disappointing, but Wilson was inspired by seeing his own work onstage. For the first time, he thought of himself as a playwright.[48] Judy worked at keeping his spirits up after the play's poor reception in Los Angeles. At one social gathering, as the evening was getting late and people were quietly swilling their brandy, wondering whether it was time to leave, Judy blurted out, "Hey, tell Bart stories!" The naturally shy August immediately began reciting one of his *Black Bart* pieces.[49]

Claude never lost faith in the musical, a reaction that was to be expected since, as Jacqui says, Claude loved "almost every word" that August ever wrote.[50] Touting his friend as a genius, Claude carried a copy of *Black Bart* in his briefcase, prepared to show it to anyone who cared to look.[51] Claude campaigned to persuade Penumbra to give *Black Bart* a full performance. Finally, after much prodding, the Penumbra Theatre agreed to give *Black Bart* a stage reading in late 1979. Once again, August and Claude threw themselves into revising the script. Friends were eager to help. Judy and Jacqui introduced August to Saint Paul's writing and arts community by organizing a poetry reading at a local pub.[52] Unfortunately, audience reaction to the stage reading was as underwhelming as it had been in Los Angeles.

While still deflated by the fate of *Black Bart*, Wilson's spirits were raised in the fall of 1979 when two new people entered his orbit, Dan Gabriel and his wife Judith. Judith and Jacqui worked at the same community center. When they realized that the men in their lives were aspiring writers, they arranged for them to meet. Before long, the two men were gathering regularly to discuss their craft.[53] Dan and August both liked to write in public places, Dan during the day and August beginning later in the day and continuing late into the night. They began meeting regularly at a series of greasy spoons in Saint Paul, especially Sweeney's and another diner near August's workplace at Little Brothers of the Poor. They would move to a new café whenever the owner grew tired of two men occupying a table for hours, drinking endless rounds of coffee and passing piles of paper between them. August's heavy smoking enveloped the room in a gray cloud. Dan worried about the health consequences but found the meetings so productive that he put up with it.

August and Dan talked at length about their current projects, often coming with partially completed manuscripts and asking the other for feedback. August still considered himself as much a poet as a playwright, and so he often brought poems to these meetings, as well as short stories and other plays he was either thinking about or working on. Dan had written short stories and travel articles. His recent trip up the Nile became the basis for a book titled *Twice a False Messiah*.[54] At first, Dan was skeptical about how much he would get out of regular meetings with another writer, but his doubts quickly gave way to enthusiasm.[55] "I learned so much so fast," Dan says, "that I couldn't get enough of it. I would be coming in and trying to do a short story or starting a novel or something, and August would say, 'Well here's something that relates to what you had before, so try this and that.'"[56] Dan in turn would give August historical background for plays he was thinking about writing as well as feedback on *Black Bart*.

Dan noticed that August liked to socialize, but also that he operated as an outsider, which made him a keen observer of people and situations. "There were many social situations," Dan says, "where August would slide along, and Judy would do the niceties. He would play his role, but you could . . . see he's thinking about something else."[57] At social gatherings, he would position himself at the edge of a group, apparently lost in thought but actually paying close attention to what was being said and how it was said, "where they put the emphasis and how they used a particular phrase." Later, August might tell Dan about some minor things that had been said or had happened across the room. And he remembered seemingly trivial information in astonishing detail.[58] Dan also noticed that August avoided confrontations, inclined to withdraw rather than face down an uncomfortable situation. But there was a bit of aggression behind the withdrawal. "He's not going to tell so-and-so off," Dan says, "but they're done getting anything out of him. He'll move away and never deal with these people again."[59]

Dan and Jacqui noticed that August came to Saint Paul as something of a "race man," but that over time the openness of the local arts community made him less and less invested in his racial identity.[60] He still referred to himself as a Black nationalist, but he became increasingly at ease around white people, accepting them as individuals rather than assuming they were prejudiced. Early in their friendship, Dan wondered how August was going to respond to him. He found that his new friend "might rant and rail about a white man doing this and that, but I never felt that he was looking at me and pointing at me." Dan was relieved that August's interactions with white people conveyed the message, "Hey, I'm treating you like an individual. As long as you're straight with me, I'll be straight with you."[61]

August would have agreed with Dan's assessments. He was aware of his skills as an observer. On one occasion, he described a group of Japanese Americans he had seen eating breakfast at a Saint Paul bus station. They chatted quietly among themselves and, when the check came, went their own way. August says a group of African Americans would have behaved differently:

> The first thing they'd notice is the jukebox. This is very important: it never entered the mind of those Japanese guys to play the jukebox. Six black guys walk in, somebody's going to the jukebox. He's gonna drop a quarter. Another guy's gonna say, "Hey Rodney, play this:' And he's gonna say, "Man, get out of here, play your own record." . . . Another thing I notice, none of the Japanese guys said anything to the waitress. But a black guy would say: "Hey, mama, don't talk to him. Look, baby, where ya from? Why don't you give me your phone number?"[62]

While in Saint Paul, August played shortstop on a softball team operated by Little Brothers of the Poor. Years of heavy smoking meant he didn't have much breath for running bases.[63] But he was still a threat at the plate, always swinging for the fence. "He swung a mean bat," Dan says. "He let it go every single time. He was all out."[64] August's warrior identity also showed up in his love of boxing. He made friends with some boxers in a club called Knuckleheads, and so impressed them with his knowledge of boxing that they gifted him a jacket and enrolled him in the club. August was deeply moved by the gesture.[65]

During August's meetings with Dan, the two men talked about a broad range of topics, including baseball, theology, symbolism, and such technical matters as sound equipment and concert stages.[66] At their early meetings, they focused on the sorts of things each other had read and liked. From these exchanges, Dan learned that not only was August knowledgeable about the blues, he regarded the music as a source for future plays. Dan was intrigued when August talked about possibly setting a play in a Southern turpentine camp because the camps figure in so many blues songs.[67] August also talked about Romare Bearden, from which Dan quickly concluded that Bearden was another of August's major inspirations. At one of their first meetings, August termed himself to Dan as being a Black nationalist and an admirer of Baraka. However, Dan noticed that in subsequent meetings August never circled back to discuss Baraka further. Dan also could sense the influence of Borges, whose *A Universal History of Infamy* had ushered in the genre known as "magical realism." Impressively, August knew the book's short stories almost by heart, especially "Hakima Merve" and "The Dread Redeemer Lazarus Morrell."

Dan also realized that, more than Bearden, Borges, Baraka, or the blues, Pittsburgh was what most excited August. Pittsburgh was what he most enjoyed talking about, and what he spoke about at the greatest length. He regaled Dan with stories about the Hill District, about Rob Penny, about Pat's Place, about his mother (but not his father), and about his sister Freda, whom he looked to for guidance.[68] August talked about how he exchanged letters with his old friend Rob, who came to visit on several occasions, and of how he invited his mother Daisy and his sister Freda to visit. During a later conversation, in 1980, August spoke of how he had invited his two brothers, Edwin and Richard, to move to Saint Paul, and helped them find jobs.[69]

Pittsburgh remained August's Wilson's principal point of reference. "Everything he saw was through that prism," Dan recalls. "This is how it was in Pittsburgh, and these are the things that are different here. Why is that?"[70] Dan felt that sometimes August's Pittsburgh seemed suspiciously idyllic—"this wonderful place where you just wander out into the street and you would have all these great encounters and there were people hanging out here, and some old characters sitting up on a [bar] stool there." August told Dan of the hours he had spent listening to migrants talk about coming up from the South and the difficulties they faced adjusting to life in Pittsburgh. He spoke of how he admired those men for trying to maintain their Southern ways. Connected to that, he spoke of how he had haunted secondhand stores because he saw significance in the things transplanted people hang on to, something that mattered enough that they kept it for many years. Maybe it was the only thing they had kept from the South, or from a previous relationship.[71] Dan realized that in Saint Paul, August had become something of a migrant himself, and was trying to hang onto his own roots.

11

Breakthroughs

Inspired by Romare Bearden's paintings and collages, August Wilson began thinking about ways of writing characters and scenes he was already familiar with, of ordinary folks engaged in everyday activities. For years, Wilson had walked the Hill District, observing residents on its streets and in its bars, in tobacco shops, rooming houses, backyards, and diners. In 1979, shortly after his exposure to Bearden's art, Wilson visited Pittsburgh so he could once again walk those streets of the Hill District. This time, however, he did so with the intention of finding material that he could make into a play.

First, he took Judy to meet his mother, then walked past some of his old haunts on Centre Avenue.[1] At Pat's Place, one of the regulars called him over and, referring to him by his old nickname, "Youngblood," asked how often he got back to Pittsburgh. Wilson said once or twice a year, which elicited some fatherly advice. "I ain't going to be here when you come back," the elderly gentleman said, "but I want to tell you, I've been watching you for about six or seven years now and you are going through life carrying a 10-gallon bucket. If you go through life carrying a 10-gallon bucket, you're going to always be disappointed because it ain't never going to get filled. Don't you go through life carrying no 10-gallon bucket. Get you a little cup. Carry that through life. That way if somebody put a little something in, you got something."[2]

At the time of Wilson's return home, jitneys were very much in the news. Silas Knox, a local Black businessman, was engaged in a spirited battle to force the Public Utilities Commission to let him start a licensed taxi company with vehicles driven by former jitney drivers. Knox argued that his new operation would fill a need because many white taxi drivers were still resistant to serving Black neighborhoods.[3] Throughout much of Black America, jitneys had a long and cherished history. Known as "gypsy cabs" in New York, "hacks" in Philadelphia, and "bandits" in the West, they constituted an important part of urban Black America's transportation system. Although technically illegal, they were tolerated by the authorities. In Pittsburgh they were especially popular, so much so that in 1941 Pittsburgh jazz great Earl "Fatha" Hines recorded "The Jitney Man," featuring vocals by renowned Pittsburgh balladeer Billy Eckstine.[4] In 1985 a national magazine, *Reason*, celebrated jitneys' importance to the city. "Pittsburgh is to jitneys," it declared, "as San Francisco is to cable cars." The magazine estimated that Pittsburgh's Black neighborhoods had twice as many jitneys as taxicabs.[5]

Numbers operators often worked out of a jitney station because "numbers" were as much a part of Black life as jitneys. For financial help, many Hill residents turned to this illegal lottery that involved guessing the last three digits of the stock market transactions for a particular day. Wagers could be as low as a penny and the payoff as high as 600–1, making it popular with everyday folks. Numbers operators had a good reputation. During the Great Depression many businesses survived by operating as an informal numbers station. Because banks would not make loans to Black people, the Hill's leading "numbers" men—Gus Greenlee and "Woogie" Harris—became the community's informal bankers and philanthropists. Jitney stations, moreover, were more than a business. They provided a space where drivers could sit around gossiping and bantering while waiting for the next call.

In addition, jitneys are examples of small-scale, independent enterprise.[6] Wilson admired the entrepreneurial attitude of station owners and drivers. "These guys," he said, "would just get an abandoned storefront and put a pay phone in there and disseminate the number throughout the community and go into business, thereby creating something out of nothing. These were guys who sent their kids to college driving jitneys." As he described it: "There was a head of the station. All of these guys pay their dues; they pay $15 a month. That gives you the right to use that phone. People know that number, and they call up to order a cab. There were certain rules and things. One of the rules is that you can't drink. Otherwise . . . they'll call somebody else. . . . There's a certain [phone number]—COURT-1-9802—which has been a jitney number for about 45 years. If you go to Pittsburgh now and call 'COURT-1-9802' you'll get a jitney."[7]

For years, August and his friend Sala Udin liked to meet for lunch at Pan Fried Fish, a diner at 1707 Wylie Avenue, near Arthur Street. August typically arrived early and, while waiting for Sala, would step inside a nearby jitney station. After lunch, August would go back to the station accompanied by his friend. As a result of those visits, August became familiar with the station and the people who worked there and others who just hung out there. The station consisted of a one-room storefront sparsely furnished with a sofa and chairs, a telephone on the wall, a blackboard that served as a sign-in sheet and also gave the day's winning "numbers."[8] While at the station, August loved listening to the drivers chitchat with one another as they played checkers.[9]

Sala says he spent almost as much time at the station as August, but "never saw anything there worthy of theater."[10] August, however, was an especially keen observer. He immediately recognized the station as just what he was looking for—a place where men gathered on a daily basis and engaged in all sorts of banter and conversations, rituals of daily life. As he told an interviewer years later, "I thought it would be great to capture a Black tradition, the setting where Black males congregate, like barbershops and restaurants."[11] Inspired by what he saw at the station, August rushed back to Saint Paul and, in ten days of feverish writing, produced the draft of a new play. He titled it *Jitney!*, with an exclamation point perhaps signaling someone calling out for a ride, and dated the script 1979.[12]

The visit home gave Wilson an idea for a second play. He titled it *Fullerton Street*, after a legendary thoroughfare in the Hill where, back in the thirties, forties, and fifties, one could enjoy superb dining while being entertained by the likes of Pittsburgh's own Lena Horne or Billy Eckstine. Fullerton had it all. The Loendi Club catered to the city's Black elite. The Ritz Café (later named the Bambola), featured hot bands and hot dancing, and Hartzberg's bar attracted an interracial clientele of drag queens, respectables, and less-than-respectables.[13] Locals referred to the intersection of Fullerton and Wylie as "Crossroads of the World" because, it was said, if you hung out there long enough, anyone you might want to see was sure to pass by.[14] Fullerton Street succumbed to urban renewal when August was only twelve years old, but he often had heard his mother speak excitedly of the street. Daisy's family had settled near Fullerton when they arrived in Pittsburgh. Years later, she and Julia often went there to shop and see a movie.

Wilson set *Fullerton Street* on June 18, 1941, the anxiety-filled night when Joe Louis almost lost the heavyweight championship to Billy Conn, known locally as "The Pittsburgh Kid." The play's storyline focuses not on the fight but on how life in a Northern city undermines the traditional values and mores of migrants.[15] The play has autobiographical features, such as a father who suffers from alcoholism and a mother who gets by on public assistance. Unfortunately, like *Black Bart and the Sacred Hills*, the play is burdened by a large, overly complicated plot.[16]

While writing *Jitney!* and *Fullerton Street*, Wilson received a letter from his friend Rob Penny, urging him to submit a play to the Eugene O'Neill Theater's National Playwrights Conference in Connecticut. Acceptance, Rob told him, would bring prestige and the chance to get feedback from prominent writers, directors, and critics in attendance. Taking Rob's advice, Wilson submitted *Fullerton Street* and *Jitney!* for the 1980 competition.

To Wilson's disappointment, the O'Neill rejected both plays. However, convinced that *Jitney!* had real possibilities, Wilson applied for, and won, a grant from Minneapolis's Playwrights Center to revise the play.[17] The award did wonders for Wilson self-confidence. "Wow," he said to himself, "I must be a playwright."[18] Wilson quit his job at the Science Museum and took a part-time position at Little Brothers of the Poor, a Catholic charity for men. The new job gave him even more free time to write. And so, for the next three years, Wilson spent part of his mornings and afternoons writing, and his evenings typing up drafts at home. He often worked late into the night, sometimes until three or four in the morning. From her bedroom, Judy could hear him pounding the keys. "It sounds like a lullaby," she said.[19]

Judy assured August that his talent would eventually be recognized. She urged him to revise and resubmit his plays. "Send that play out. Okay, so the O'Neill turned you down once. Don't let them stop you. Send them another thing."[20] Perhaps Judy overdid the encouragement. Wilson became convinced of the plays' quality, so much so that he assumed people at the O'Neill simply had not read them. The next year, he resubmitted the same plays, with few if any changes.[21] When the O'Neill rejected them again, he finally admitted to himself that they simply were not good enough.

Judy was tremendously supportive. Their relationship was so compatible that August decided once again to risk marriage. This was no small matter, for August was still distressed by the failure of his first marriage and he was not the type to marry casually. In fact, Dan Gabriel says, August "was not the sort of person who would do anything casually." On April 25, 1981, two days shy of his thirty-sixth birthday, August and Judy married. The two continued living in Judy's apartment, but a few years later they purchased an attractive, old Victorian house nearby.[22] The marriage certificate identifies the groom as "August Wilson," the first known indication that Wilson had finally begun using his pen name as his legal name.[23]

The wedding was held at the home of one of Judy's friends. Claude and Jacqui served as best man and maid of honor, respectively. Other Saint Paul attendees included the Gabriels, Jacqui's son Damon, and Judy's mother and sisters. Those attending from Pittsburgh included Daisy, August's brothers Edwin and Richard, and two of his sisters, Freda and Linda Jean. Also in attendance was August's eleven-year-old daughter, Sakina Ansari. The reception was held at Little Brothers.[24] Daisy's delight at the marriage can be seen in a photograph of her at the reception, beaming with joy. The couple's happiness proved contagious, for the following year, Claude and Jacqui exchanged wedding vows.[25]

At the time of the wedding, Wilson was busily revising *Black Bart*, for the Penumbra Theatre had finally acceded to Claude's urgings and scheduled a full production of the musical for July 1981. Working with Penumbra to prepare for the staging marked a turning point in Wilson's relationship with the company. He had attended many performances at Penumbra, learning much by paying close attention to what worked and what did not. However, it took time for Wilson to overcome his natural shyness and feel comfortable around Penumbra's actors and staff.[26] Similarly, it took members of the company time to warm to Wilson, whom some had dismissed as "just a scruffy-looking guy from Pittsburgh with a bad temper."[27] As attitudes changed, Wilson was invited after rehearsals to join Claude and other staff at Esteban's Restaurant, where they engaged in lively conversations until closing time. Wilson also joined cast parties and got comfortable participating in the banter that took place backstage.[28]

Despite all this, Penumbra's staging of *Black Bart* proved one more disappointment. Dialogue was the play's strong suit, leading the Saint Paul *Pioneer Press* to praise Wilson's gift for "powerful language." But lively dialogue and Claude's directing skills could not make up for a storyline that was burdened with fourteen songs, a cast of twenty-six, and a complicated plot that left audiences bewildered.[29] The paper complained that *Black Bart* tried to do so much that it became "a little bit of everything, . . . a Western spoof, a Marvel comic book . . . a sleaze-bag cabaret show."[30] Lou Bellamy, Penumbra's artistic director, called the plot "rough"; another member described it as "way out there."[31] Ultimately, Wilson decided enough was enough. He permanently shelved *Black Bart and the Sacred Hills*. To this day, it has never undergone another production.[32]

Audiences' rejection of *Black Bart* came on top of the O'Neill's dismaying rejection of both *Jitney!* and *The Homecoming*. However, Wilson's spirits got a boost when Bob Johnson, or BJ as he was commonly known, submitted *Jitney!* to Pittsburgh's Allegheny Repertory Theatre (ART), a new company dedicated to performing experimental plays.[33] The ART liked the play and agreed to stage it in 1982 at the Fine Line Cultural Center.[34] Codirected by BJ and Beryl Berry, the production ran ninety minutes and featured University of Pittsburgh undergraduate Montae Russell, who went on with Wilson's active encouragement to a successful television career and a stage career in which he has acted in all Pittsburgh Cycle plays. The cast included Curtiss Porter of the University of Pittsburgh, Ron Pitts of the former Ujima Theatre, and Milt Thompson. Sala Udin turned in an especially powerful performance as station owner Becker. Afterward, Sala modestly credited his success to August, saying that his friend wrote the part of Becker expressly with him in mind.[35]

Adding to Wilson's continuing string of disappointments, the play garnered mixed reviews.[36] Jim Davidson of the *Pittsburgh Press* applauded the directing and dialogue but complained that the plot was static and left too many themes fuzzy and unresolved.[37] Donald Miller of the *Pittsburgh Post-Gazette* praised the directing and acting but complained that Becker's denouncing of his son seemed too strong to be completely believable, and that his sudden death seemed unrelated to the play's overall structure.[38]

However, whatever the critics' misgivings, *Jitney!* was a huge success with the Black public, who turned out in droves. Jitney drivers attended the performances, fascinated but a little anxious at having their technically illegal livelihood portrayed on stage. Some asked Wilson, "What you doing writing a story about us?" To Wilson's eternal satisfaction, the play sold out for the entire run.[39] After so many failures and disappointments, he had found success. "They were having 300 people a night showing up and milling around," he rejoiced. "Black people who weren't used to going to the theater." August took his mother to see it—appropriately in a jitney. He was proud to show her that he was moving forward. He was especially pleased when the driver of the jitney they took to the play asked them if they wanted him to pick them up when the play was over, but with a warning. "People be coming out of there crying," he said. "Don't you be doing all that crying and stuff."[40] The play's initial run was so successful that the following year, 1983, it was repeated, this time at the Famous Rider Cultural Center, also located in Oakland. Again, BJ and Berry codirected, with other local figures acting, including Claude Purdy as Becker and Ron Pitts as Fielding.[41]

Jitney! provided the blueprint for Wilson's subsequent works. Like all but one of the plays that later became known as the American Century Cycle, it is set in Pittsburgh and portrays the rituals of daily life among everyday Black residents. In portraying life in a jitney station, the play deals with one of Black Pittsburghers' most important and beloved institutions. The play dramatizes the well-founded fears of jitney drivers, and indeed of most Black Pittsburghers, of urban renewal. When Wilson was in his early twenties and living on Crawford Street, his apartment had looked out on the wasteland left by urban renewal's razing of the social, cultural, and institutional heart of the Lower Hill. Residents were traumatized by the loss and feared that the city might use urban renewal to tear down more of the Hill. In 1976, just a couple of years before Wilson wrote *Jitney!*, the *Pittsburgh Courier* warned readers that white business owners still owned much of the property in the Hill and were plotting to come back when the time was ripe.[42] In fact, a decade or so after the play's premiere, the city razed the jitney station that August and Sala had loved to frequent. To the consternation of many, the city operated once again in the name of urban renewal. Station owner Herman Westbrook relocated his station, the one that August and Sala had frequented, several blocks up Wylie Avenue, continuing with the same phone number that Wilson used in the play. Years later, unfortunately, that station burned down, and Westbrook has now relocated to Centre Avenue.[43]

Jitney! opens in a dilapidated station where the drivers are going about their daily routines of gossip, banter, and checkers while waiting for a call from someone in need of a ride. Jim Becker, the station's owner, has fatalistically accepted that, in the name of urban renewal, the city will soon raze the entire block on which the station stands. Becker's dispirited drivers feel the same way, a mood that reflects the era. In 1973, five years after the Martin Luther King riots, the *Pittsburgh Courier* found Hill residents exhausted and resigned to their fate. The paper concluded that there would be no riots, not because people were satisfied but because they felt powerless to do anything about their plight.[44] The men in Becker's station, like their real-life counterparts, felt it was hopeless to fight city hall.

The station's quiet daily life is disrupted by the sudden, unexpected appearance of Booster, station master Becker's wayward son. Booster has been newly released from prison after serving twenty years for the murder of his white girlfriend, who had claimed Booster had raped her when in fact they had been discovered by her father while having consensual sex in the back of a car. In a pattern that would characterize all of Wilson's subsequent plays, Booster, as the play's leading character, bears Wilson's own identity traits. He is an outsider. He is alienated from his father, who despises him for having killed his girlfriend and shaming the family. Booster is also a warrior, albeit a foolish, mistaken one, and a "race man," albeit an impetuous, unthinking one. Booster resents that his girlfriend's lie made him feel small, and his response was to do something that would tell the world he wasn't "just another nigger." He condemns his father for having quietly accepted tongue-lashings from the family's white landlord when they were behind in the rent. Like Wilson, he struggles to become a race man and find his racial identity. Finally, Booster is a poet, who speaks with a cadence and rhythm that amounts to free-verse poetry. Wilson was deeply aware that Booster and his plays' main characters bear his identity traits. As he said, his characters "are all made up of myself, every character plays some aspect of my personality, my beliefs, my whatevers."[45]

Jitney! has two notable details that reference Wilson's personal history. First, Booster's twenty-year prison sentence for murder echoes David Bedford's twenty-three-year sentence for the same crime. Second, and even more significant, at the play's conclusion, following Becker's death, Booster reconciles with his deceased father by following in his dad's footsteps and taking over ownership of his jitney station. "He had his ways," Booster says. "But he was a good man inside where it counts. . . . I'm proud of my old man. . . . I'm proud to be Becker's boy."[46] Booster's reconciliation with his father is reminiscent of Wilson's reconciliation with his own. In 1980, one year after writing *Jitney!*, Wilson composed a poem whose narrator is a son who returned from California to be with his dying father, a baker by trade. Titled "My Father," the poem reads in part:

> I came home from California
> What do you say to a dying man?
> Brace up? Better weather ahead?
>
> . . .
>
> Where do I go from here
> My own person? Do I have to drag you around with me, a sack of bones?
> The day my father died (he called me Fritz)
> I took off my apron, wiped the flour

Out of my beard and set out for El Dorado . . . ·
15 years later I put the apron back on
I bake bread
My oven's [*sic*] sing
The loaves are golden.[47]

Like all of Wilson's subsequent plays, and unlike his John Berryman–influenced poems, *Jitney!* features simple, compelling dialogue that converts the rhythmic cadence of Black speech into poetry. His success in doing so is evident in Becker's advice in the play about marriage. (Stressed words and syllables are in boldface):

Come No**vem**ber it'll be seven**teen** years me and Lu**cille** been to**geth**er. **Seventeen years**. I told her, say **work** with me. She say **OK**. I wasn't **sure** what that meant my**self**. I thought it meant **pull** or **push** to**geth**er, but she showed me one can **push** and the other can **pull** as long as it's in the same di**rec**tion. Know what I **mean**? It ain't **all** gonna flow to**geth**er all the **time**. **That's** life. As **long** as it **don't** break a**part**. When you look a**round**, you'll **see** all you got is each **other**. There ain't much **more**.[48]

The authentic yet poetic nature of Wilson's dialogue was not just the result of years of listening to the way Black Pittsburghers spoke. Wilson was blessed with the ability to reproduce the syntax and intonation of anyone—Black, white, male, female, educated, uneducated. At Halfway Art Gallery, Wilson had famously recited Dylan Thomas from memory in full Welsh dialect. In Saint Paul, he impressed Dan Gabriel with his ability to recite all the parts of a play, from an uneducated laborer to a middle-aged woman to some elder. Wilson "had all those voices inside him," Gabriel says in awe.[49]

Wilson says that *Jitney!* was the first play in which he "listened to" the characters, rather than "trying to force words into their mouths."[50] He once had asked Rob how he could make his characters talk. Rob answered, "You don't make them talk. You listen to them."[51] For a long time August had not heeded Rob's advice, feeling that unvarnished Black voices were too simple and unsophisticated to form the basis of poetry or theater. "I couldn't write dialogue," he said, "because I didn't respect the way blacks talked. I didn't see a value in it. I was always trying to alter the language into something else."[52] Rob understood. "It's hard to see the art in the things you walk through life with every day," he says.[53]

Ironically, it was only after Wilson left Pittsburgh that he succeeded in creating dialogue that captured the voices of Black Pittsburgh. In Saint Paul, he had grown homesick and, as an outsider, a migrant, had sought to recall and hold onto old memories. "I missed Pittsburgh," he says, "It was the removal from that that allowed me to for the first time to begin to hear the voices of the people that I had grown up with all my life.[54] In addition, Wilson recognized that poetry was an inherent part of the way Black people talk.[55] In discovering Bearden, he turned his attention to capturing the voice of the people. In doing so, he found his own voice.

Although *Jitney!* was Wilson's first play to win popular approval, it contained the sort of structural problems that had long plagued his writing. Wilson scholar Joan Herrington describes these problems as "the insecurities of an inexperienced writer—repetition, glaring emotional signposts for the audience, inconsistent dialogue, and an obscure central conflict."[56] Uncertain how to fix those problems and stung by the O'Neill's rejection, Wilson responded like a warrior, vowing to write something so good that it could not be rejected.[57] He set aside *Jitney!* and *Fullerton Street* and began reworking an earlier play, *The Homecoming*.

In 1976 Pittsburgh's Kuntu Repertory Theatre had performed *The Homecoming*, but director Vernell Lillie considered it stiff and uninteresting. Wilson himself had been dissatisfied with the play. Now he returned to it with renewed optimism and confidence. He quit his job at Little Brothers of the Poor and set to work correcting problems with the play, especially its length.[58] He wanted to make the play longer than *Jitney!* but shorter and less complex than *Fullerton Street*.[59] He changed the setting from Alabama to Chicago and shifted the focus from Blind Willie Johnson, a relatively obscure blues singer, to Ma Rainey, one of the leading blues singers of her time. For the new play, which he titled *Ma Rainey's Black Bottom*, Wilson stitched together two scripts: the original story of the band members as portrayed in *The Homecoming*, and a new script about Ma.

For *Ma Rainey's Black Bottom*, Wilson immersed himself in the history of her music. He long been aware of Ma because Pope, owner of one of his favorite restaurants, had told him of the excitement generated by Ma's performance in 1924 at Lincoln Theatre in the Hill.[60] Her remarkable career clearly merited theatrical treatment. Born around 1882 in either Alabama or Georgia, Gertrude "Ma" Pridgett toured the South with her husband William Rainey as part of the Rabbit Foot Minstrels. Ma had no formal training, but was a bold innovator, the first woman to incorporate the blues into minstrel and tent shows.[61] She learned much by hanging out in New Orleans with such musical pioneers as King Oliver, Louis Armstrong, and Sidney Bechet. She became nationally known when, in the 1920s, she recorded with Paramount Records, including the 1927 Chicago recording of one of her best-known numbers, "Ma Rainey's Black Bottom."

Known as "Mother of the Blues," Ma became the nation's first commercially successful blues singer, respected by musicians and beloved by the public. A flashy dresser, she had a flair for the dramatic: a big smile, a large wig, a set of gold-capped teeth, and lots of jewelry. Her fans loved her countrified ways.[62] However, by the late 1920s, just as she was recording "Ma Rainey's Black Bottom," her style of slow "country" blues, originally brought north by early migrants, was losing favor to up-tempo "city blues," also known as "urban" blues.[63] In presenting this conflict, *Ma Rainey's Black Bottom* was historically accurate even though, when writing a play, Wilson normally did not conduct historical research because he worried doing so would stifle his imagination. However, by themselves, the lyrics would not have informed Wilson that Ma's country blues was going out of style as migrants became more "citified." He may have become aware of that from the album's detailed liner notes, written by the renowned music critic Dan Morgenstern. Or, he could have learned about it from *Blues People*, a widely read monograph by Amiri Baraka that chronicled the history of the blues. At any rate, Wilson made stylistic competition a key theme of the play.[64]

Wilson finished the script just in time to meet the O'Neill's December deadline. As always, the competition was stiff, with some 1,500 scripts battling for sixteen slots.[65] This time, the O'Neill accepted Wilson's submission. He had indeed written a play that caught the attention of Lloyd Richards, artistic director of the Playwrights Conference and dean of the Yale School of Drama. Richards was famous as the Black director who in 1959 made Lorraine Hansberry's *A Raisin in the Sun* the first play by a Black woman writer and the first directed by a Black person to reach Broadway. Richards had rejected Wilson's previous submissions, and he almost rejected this one because of its structural problems. Ultimately, however, he felt those problems could be fixed. Most importantly, Richards loved the dialogue, which made the characters come alive in a way that reminded him of the Saturday-morning banter he was familiar with in Black barbershops.[66]

Playwrights accepted for summer workshops at the O'Neill had a preconference gathering in the winter to read their scripts to each other. That was Wilson's job in 1982. As was so often the case, he was something of an outsider.

Richards assumed that the playwright was African American because of the play's title and the dialogue's authenticity. Surveying the room, however, he had difficulty identifying Wilson. "I didn't immediately find him," Richards said. "It was not obvious."[67]

When the workshop began in July, the cast assembled by Richards was led by Charles Dutton. A graduate student at Yale, Dutton intended to spend the summer earning money, but Richards told him to come to the O'Neill. "I'd rather be earning money," Dutton said. "No, you'd better come to the O'Neill," Richards insisted, knowing Levee was the role that could make Dutton's career. Dutton had the same initial response as Richards had. He pictured the author as "a big, black guy with a scar on his face, that was a street fighter, that had been in the penitentiary, played crap in the alleys, was a hard nigger." When someone pointed Wilson out, Dutton said to himself, "That ain't the guy that wrote this play. That guy looks like an insurance salesman!"[68]

Happy to show his mother that he was moving forward in his career, August had brought her to the staged reading at the Eugene O'Neill Theater in Connecticut.[69] Doing so was important, for the rift between the two had never fully healed. Daisy still saw August as something of a failure, holding up the example of Sidney McClanahan, one of their Bedford Avenue neighbors. "Look at Sidney," she would say. "He's making $11 an hour" working in an auto plant. The implication, August says, was that "Sidney had a house, a car, he was a success. I had nothing."[70] Daisy had every reason to be pleased with the success of her son's play, for it had caught the attention of prominent critics, including at *The New York Times*.

On the way back to Pittsburgh, August and Daisy stopped to briefly visit her sister Faye and her daughter Barbara. It was fortunate they did because shortly afterward, Daisy took ill. Less than a year later, on March 15, 1983, she passed away, the victim of lung cancer, brought on no doubt by years of heavy smoking.[71] Faye went to Pittsburgh to be with her dying sister. August, distraught at her passing, telephoned Barbara and told her tearfully, "Mommy just died."[72] Barbara had known of Daisy's approaching death because, toward the end, she had called Barbara and apologetically told her, "I have always loved you."[73]

Daisy died as "Daisy Kittel," having assumed Fred's last name after their marriage in 1964. Services were held at Sheffield Funeral Home on the North Side, possibly because Daisy's brothers, John and George, lived there. It was a small funeral, with only family members present, and was followed by a

Requiem Mass at St. Benedict the Moor Church.[74] Barbara did not attend. Despite Daisy's deathbed apologies, there was no bond between the two, which pained Barbara.

Daisy was buried in Greenwood Cemetery, not far from the grave of her mother Zonia. Having reconciled with his mother, August made it a point to return home annually on the anniversary of her death and place flowers on her grave. His visits inspired other family members and soon became an annual family reunion. Those coming from out of town stayed with Freda, sleeping on sofas, homemade cots, and pallets. Conversations lasted late into the night, along with board games, card-playing, storytelling, laughter, and the sharing of memories.[75] Barbara was not a part of these gatherings. "They grew up with their mother," she says quietly. "I did not."[76]

August regretted that Daisy died before he had fully arrived on the national scene. "It would have meant a lot to her," he said, "if she could have lived . . . long enough to see me with a play on Broadway."[77] In reviewing *Ma Rainey* at the O'Neill's staged reading, Frank Rich of *The New York Times* had given the dialogue unstinting praise, saying that Wilson operated "in the same poetic tradition as [Eugene O'Neill], the man . . . who gave American theater its past." However, Rich faulted the play's structure, complaining that it had "virtually no story."[78] But director Lloyd Richards was thrilled by the compelling nature of the characters and dialogue, and worked with Wilson on blending the two scripts.[79] He considered the results stunning, "one in a thousand."[80]

But there were a number of steps to take first. Rich's praise of the workshop in *The New York Times* brought Wilson and *Ma Rainey* to the attention of a horde of theater people and agents. Some besieged Wilson to turn it into a musical, a movie, or pair up with an experienced playwright. Wilson held firm. But it needed a professional production, probably at Richards's professional Yale Repertory Theatre, and it took him a while to set that up.

Finally in 1984 it had its professional premiere at Yale Repertory Theatre, and then on October 11, 1984, *Ma Rainey's Black Bottom* opened on Broadway. No play by an African American had garnered such acclaim since Lorraine Hansberry's *A Raisin in the Sun*, which coincidentally had been directed by Richards. Rich felt similarly. He had praised the earlier version of *Ma Rainey* but liked the Broadway version even more.[81] The trade publication *Variety* was a bit more cautious, mentioning what it called shortcomings typical of a newcomer: overreliance on reminiscences of past events in addition to plot contrivances that "challenge credibility." The magazine added, however, that the play signaled that "a new writer with passion and imaginative flair has emerged."[82] *Ma Rainey* went on to win the New York Drama Critics Award and was nominated for a Tony Award.

To a remarkable degree, the play captures both the time and the place. Ma battles white record producers who, interested only in profits, want her to jettison her traditional rural blues and adopt the new urban style. Set in 1927, however, the play's focus is not on the music or on Ma. Rather, it is on interactions among the four band members: Cutler, Slow Drag, Toledo, and Levee. Like the characters in *Jitney!*, the musicians are a colorful group, who sit in the recording studio—much like in a Bearden painting—teasing, grousing, and waiting for the session to begin. Cutler, the trombonist, is the group's leader and the most sensible.[83]

As in *Jitney!*, the lead character in *Ma Rainey* has the same identity traits as Wilson. Levee is an outsider, disliked by the others because of his openly expressed disdain for Ma's country style of blues. Hoping to win favor with Paramount and possibly get his own songs recorded, he joins the studio in calling on Ma to adapt to the times. Levee's self-serving harping makes him an outsider who is rejected by others in the band, who consider him a toady of the white recording officers. The criticism stings, triggering flashbacks of the time when, as a child in Mississippi, he could not prevent his mother from being sexually assaulted by a group of white men. The trauma made Levee a walking powder keg, an explosive combination of warrior and race man. However, rather than directing his anger at the white managers, who have offered him an oppressive pittance for his compositions, he turns it on his fellow musicians, fatally stabbing Toledo, the band's pianist, who accidentally steps on Levee's expensive new shoes.

An outsider, a warrior, and a race man, Levee is also a poet, with lilting monologues that drew praise from Rich, the theater critic, as akin to the blues.[84] Wilson had always regarded himself first and foremost a poet. Now he was using poetry to create blues-inflected dialogue. Richards was aware of this. He praised Wilson as a "wonderful poet turning into a playwright." The actor Eugene Lee loves the poetic quality of Wilson's dialogue, which he says makes it a pleasure to recite. However, Lee adds, the lines must be delivered exactly as written because even slight improvisation risks losing the poetry.[85] Some actors joke about Wilson's dialogue, saying that Black people do not actually speak as elegantly and poetically as in a Wilson play. Dutton, who starred as Levee in *Ma Rainey*'s Broadway opening, said jokingly, "I've never heard anything in my life like that, have you?"[86]

The dialogue may have been a bit too poetic for Dutton, but its authenticity is undeniable. Wilson was blessed with a photographic memory, which let him accurately re-create dialogue that he had heard years before. It is the sort of talk he had heard at Pat's Place, the news station and tobacco outlet where Wilson spent hours listening to old timers banter, grouse, and discuss the day's events.

The success of *Ma Rainey's Black Bottom* put Wilson in the position of being a promising newcomer. Like Charley Burley years earlier, Richards became something of a surrogate father, someone whose advice Wilson followed implicitly. In particular, Richards furnished Wilson with a strategy for future success: touring plays in regional theaters so that he could observe them in production and polish the script before their Broadway opening. This strategy raised the ire of theater critic Robert Brustein, who saw it as great for Broadway but risked turning nonprofit, regional theaters into nothing more than proving grounds for Broadway productions.[87] Brustein's argument had merit, but Richards's strategy paid off handsomely as a successful strategy for polishing subsequent plays and preparing them for their Broadway debut. Wilson loved traveling with the plays, observing and revising. It was hard work, but it reminded him of the book he read as a child that referred proudly to the "Negro's power of hard work."[88]

Although Wilson usually wrote with Broadway in mind, on at least one occasion he composed something that had no chance of appearing on the Great White Way. This was *The Janitor*, a four-minute play he wrote a year after the opening of *Ma Rainey's Black Bottom*. A janitor is diligently sweeping the room where a conference on youth is about to begin. A sign announcing the conference's topic prompts him to walk up to the lectern and deliver an extemporaneous speech. Midway through, the janitor's white supervisor comes in, sees him at the podium, and tells him to get back to work. The janitor meekly and silently resumes sweeping.[89] As Wilson says, the janitor may well have a valuable contribution to make, "and yet society has relegated him, and others like him, to a position where they sweep the floor."[90] He had a similar response to complaints about the long speeches in his plays: "He has a lot to say" in a culture that hasn't allowed him to say it.

The janitor never got to deliver his speech, but *Ma Rainey's Black Bottom* brought Wilson many speaking opportunities, most of which he turned down. But in 1986 he accepted an invitation to something he had looked forward to ever since he had left home and declared himself a poet—a chance to read poetry at New York's prestigious 92nd Street Y. Wilson opened by telling the audience about the time in Pittsburgh twenty years previously when he began writing poems. "I thought at that time," he said, "that if I wrote long enough, hard enough, and serious enough that one day I might be invited to read at the 92nd St. Y."[91]

The opaqueness of Wilson's first poem that night, "Let," showed he retained an interest in avant-garde poetry. However, his second poem, "The Founding of the Republic," has a direct, albeit muted, nationalist message that attests to Wilson's yearning for a family tree that places him squarely within the Black experience and makes him unequivocally African American. The poem identifies Bynum Cutler as Wilson's grandfather, portraying him as an archetypal race man, the founding father of the "Black republic," a cultivator of cane and cotton, and the virile, symbolic progenitor of much of Black America. Bynum Cutler is a warrior, whose rage was released upon his death in the form of a raven. And he has left a legacy in the person of his grandson August, who walks in his shoes. The opening verse of this tribute to an imagined grandfather reads:

> Bynum Cutler farmer,
> mule trainer,
> singer and shaper of wood and iron,
> grandfather,
> poet.
> Bynum Cutler,
> who spread his seed over the nine counties of North Carolina . . .
> leaving behind the manners and makings of his heart,
> the language and fruits of his penis,
> and the grandson who is walking toward you in his shoes.

Bynum Cutler may be August's symbolic grandfather, but in reality he is not his biological grandfather. In August's dream poem, Cutler becomes a poetic fiction who draws his name and occupation from Zonia Cutler, August's grandmother, and Bynum Wilson, Zonia's husband and a farm laborer from North Carolina. Whether or not August was aware, Daisy's marriage certificate lists her father as Friel Vance, the wealthiest resident of Avery County, North Carolina. The poem implies that, despite what the audience might assume from August's light appearance, he is a full-blooded Black American, a proud physical and historical representative of the African American experience.[92]

On his way back from his reading at the 92nd Street Y, Wilson passed through Pittsburgh, where he was honored by fellow members of the Poets in the Centre Avenue Tradition—Rob Penny, Chawley Williams, and Nick Flournoy. The evening brought back memories of old times as well as hopes for the future.[93] "Between the four of us," Wilson told those assembled, "it's still very much there," even though he worried that the energy of those earlier times had dissipated.

Upon his return to Saint Paul, Wilson resumed his feverish pace of writing. After the workshop success of *Ma Rainey* at the O'Neill in 1982, he had no further problem being accepted. *Fences* was workshopped in 1983; *Joe Turner's Come and Gone* in 1984. Then came professional premieres at Yale Repertory Theatre. So it was in 1987, three years after the Broadway premiere of *Ma Rainey*, he had a new play, *Fences*, ready to open. Despite critics' assumption that "last year's triumph . . . is this year's hard act to follow,"[94] *Fences* opened at Broadway's 46th Street Theatre. The play went on to become Wilson's most profitable and highly regarded work, grossing $11 million in its first year and winning a Pulitzer Prize and a Tony Award.[95]

Fences is a study of how racial injustice can eat away at a person and destroy family relationships. The play's message is based on the historical travails of Negro League players in the 1940s and 1950s. Set in the backyard of Troy Maxson, *Fences* opens with the characters engaged in a Bearden-like scene, what the program notes call "a ritual of talk and drink" by Troy and his friend Bono. Some of the talk is serious, such as Troy's battle to become the first Black man to drive the garbage truck. Some is humorous, such as bantering between the two about women's anatomy and even about Troy's courtship of Rose, the woman he married and who comes out of the house to join in the good-natured teasing.

Not all of the repartee is good-natured. A former star of the Negro Leagues now working as a garbage collector, Troy has long been bitter that racial integration of the major leagues came too late to benefit him. With little in the way of formal education, Troy had little chance of advancing in some other endeavor. However, things are different for his son Cory. Opportunities for Black people in the military began opening in the years following World War II. Also, white universities had begun adding Black athletes to their roster. In 1947, for example, Jimmy Joe Robinson became the first Black man ever to play on the University of Pittsburgh's football team. Cory was young enough to take advantage of such changes, but his father Troy was not. Bitterness at not getting a chance to try out for the majors sours Troy's relationship with

Cory, who has been offered an athletic scholarship to a white university. On the pretext of sparing Cory the sort of disappointment he himself has suffered, Troy insists the boy reject the scholarship and take a job at the local A&P. Cory objects, ultimately leaving home and joining the Marines, reminiscent of the time Wilson left home and joined the army.

Dan Gabriel, August's friend in Saint Paul, had long expected that one day he would write a play like *Fences*. Almost from the time the two met, August had regaled Dan with stories about the Pittsburgh Crawfords and the Homestead Grays, two of the finest teams in the Negro Leagues.[96] August told Dan how Jackie Robinson's breakthrough in the late 1940s created opportunities for young Black players but left older players like Josh Gibson frustrated at never getting the chance to prove themselves. Wilson decided against making Gibson the play's central character because people knew the details of Gibson's life and would have objected to any deviation. Rather, he based the play on a fictional character like Troy, someone not as good as Gibson but good enough that he deserved the chance to play in the majors.[97]

The play speaks to the plight of more than baseball players. Set in 1957, it reflects several of the decade's major historical developments. The 1940s had been a decade of full employment and occupational gains for both the Black working class and the middle class. Once the war was over, however, the combination of returning servicemen and declining number of war-related jobs undercut Black occupational gains.[98] By the 1950s, many would have considered Troy fortunate for having a steady, decent-paying job, even though it consisted of hauling garbage.[99] Julia Burley, for example, insists that her husband Charley's position as a city garbage collector was "a darn good job," meaning "good" for a Black man at the time. Regarding Troy's struggles to drive the truck, Julia says Charley never drove the truck, but other Black men on his route did.[100]

Charley Burley, August's childhood neighbor, was likely the prototype for Troy. Although a legendary prize fighter whom the light-heavyweight champion Archie Moore once called the best fighter he had ever faced, Burley never got a chance to fight for the title. Like Troy, Charley spent his later years working as a city garbage collector.[101] Unlike Troy, however, Charley accepted his fate with grace and composure. When residents asked, "Hey Champ, could you have beat Sugar Ray?" Charley would just shrug and reply, "Hey, I wish I had my chance, but those things happen."[102]

Elements of *Fences* parallel Wilson's own life. Troy's determination that his sons take "practical" jobs recalls Daisy's worry that August was wasting his time writing poetry when he could be making good money working at an auto plant. The bitter argument between Troy and Cory, in which the boy asks "how come you ain't never liked me" was inspired by an actual exchange August and his girlfriend Franki Williams overheard while walking past an apartment on Centre Avenue.[103] Cory's battles with his father result in his leaving home and joining the Marines, not unlike August's leaving home and joining the army after falling out with his mother. Troy's pontificating about how people should lead their lives while hiding the fact that he has fathered a child out of wedlock may reflect Wilson's impatience with his own mother, which came out when he asked her pointedly, "Why is it you always say you have six children when you have seven?" Troy's conviction for an unintended murder during a robbery, followed by a quiet, respectable life, echoes the path of David Bedford, who became a model citizen and surrogate father after being released from prison. And in the play, Troy is building a fence around his house, presumably to protect himself and his family from the outside world. That fence recalls the gate that closed off the long narrow walk that cut off Wilson's childhood home from the street.

Like Booster in *Jitney!* and Levee in *Ma Rainey's Black Bottom*, Troy is the bearer of Wilson's four key identities: outsider, warrior, race man, and poet. Troy is a former convict at odds with his wife, his sons, and much of the outside world, and he is building a fence around his home to insulate himself from that world. Troy fights for the right to drive the garbage truck, and rails against the historical racial injustice of Major League Baseball. And, of course, the beauty of his spoken dialogue makes him, in effect, a poet. *Fences'* compelling dialogue and plot made both theater critics and the theatergoing public curious about the Hill District, depicted by Wilson as a vibrant place full of fascinating residents. Critics wanted to see the Hill, and Wilson loved showing them around. He especially loved when passersby recognized him, calling out, "Freddy Kittel! Hey, how you doing, man? We proud of you."[104] Samuel Freedman of *The New York Times* was struck by the affection residents bestowed on their neighborhood bard. "Wilson gives words to trumpeters and trash men, cabbies and conjurers, boarders and landladies, all joined by a heritage of slavery," Freedman enthused. "Their patois is his poetry, their dreams are his dramas."[105]

Freedman, however, was dismayed by the Hill itself, finding it devoid of the vibrancy depicted in the play. Many notable sites were either gone or unrecognizable. "The Hill looks godforsaken indeed," he groused. "Gone are Lutz's Meat Market, the Hilltop Club and Pope's Bar. The New Granada

Theater is closed. An abandoned truck rusts in a weeded lot and a junkie lurches up the street."[106] Freedman was caught unaware of the neighborhood's history. *Fences* is set in 1957, the year in which urban renewal tore down much of the Hill's commercial corridor along Wylie Avenue. Most of the residents who had been evicted by urban renewal did not return. However, many merchants took the compensation they received for their property and relocated to Centre Avenue, making Centre the Hill's new commercial corridor. The sort of massive devastation that shocked Freedman came in 1968, when riots sparked by the assassination of Martin Luther King Jr. torched much of Centre Avenue. Those businesses could not reopen because the city did not compensate them, and they could not get new insurance policies. At the time of Freedman's visit in 1987, the Hill was a shadow of its former self.

Wilson did not sugarcoat the neighborhood's deterioration. He told Freedman the Hill was not like the friendly, vibrant, and safe neighborhood he had grown up in. He gave Freedman an example of how things had deteriorated. He says that on one occasion he saw a man drive off calmly with his white wife after furiously slashing a man who had casually referred to her as his "white 'ho."[107] Despite such terrible violence, Wilson stressed how he empathized with Black people who broke the law, whom he considered people with the warrior spirit. One might fault them for the way they choose to fight, he said, but "you need people who will battle."[108]

Impressed by the success of *Fences* nationally, local Black people began to shower their native son with adulation. In the fall of 1987, the Kuntu Repertory Theatre staged a celebratory production of *Ma Rainey's Black Bottom.* The program featured a musical score by Nelson Harrison, who had worked with Wilson on *Black Bart and the Sacred Hills.* Local critics heaped praise on the staging, especially the performance of Don Marshall as Levee.[109] One critic likened the enthusiasm of the standing-room-only crowd to a church meeting.[110]

Wilson attended the play's Pittsburgh opening and was touched by the warmth with which he was welcomed home. He was particularly pleased when Lillie, whose criticism had been one of the things that prompted his leaving Pittsburgh ten years earlier, asked him to come onstage and accept a plaque in his honor. Wilson cried as he accepted the award, something he had not done earlier that year when he accepted a Tony.[111] Overlooking old quarrels, he called it a special thrill to have Kuntu stage his play.[112]

While in town, August visited St. Benedict the Moor Church, site of his former elementary school. When he was introduced, the congregation rose in rhythmic clapping that Sister Kathleen Healy thought it might go on forever. August spoke to parishioners about his mother, who had passed away four years previously. He told them that she devoted herself to being a mother and teaching her children how to live. August then stepped outside for a cigarette and Sister Healy followed. The two had a long conversation about August's years at St. Richard Elementary School. Sister Healy was especially pleased that August could recall the names of all the nuns who had taught him there.[113]

In follow-up interviews on radio and television, Wilson stressed how much Pittsburgh meant to him. When WQED, the local PBS affiliate, asked about Negro League baseball, he explained that *Fences* had been inspired by the Homestead Grays, the Pittsburgh Crawfords, and Josh Gibson.[114] Elaine Effort of KQV radio asked Wilson why he left, and he replied, "I never really left. I don't know if one can do that because you carry your home with you wherever you go. I carry [Pittsburgh] around in my heart with me."[115] Lynne Hayes-Freeland of WAMO, the local Black radio station, asked Wilson what he missed most about Pittsburgh, and he replied, "The people."[116] The visit to Pittsburgh showed Wilson that he had been accepted, that in his hometown he was no longer a stranger, an outsider.

Because of *Fences*' unprecedented success, Wilson received proposals to turn the play into a movie. He found the idea intriguing, a realization of the dream that he and Claude had had for *Black Bart and the Sacred Hills*. However, a problem quickly emerged when Wilson insisted that the movie have a Black director, arguing that white people do not have the necessary cultural background to accurately depict the Black experience. He was criticized for this stance, including by Black people in the film industry, who had long argued that race should not be a factor in choosing a director.[117] Ultimately, Denzel Washington made the movie in 2016, a decade after Wilson's death.

Despite all the acclaim, Wilson said that *Fences* was not his favorite play, just what he had written to show doubters that he was capable of writing "a more commercial, conventional play" that had a "protagonist and supporting characters." Having made his point, Wilson said he planned to return to writing ensemble plays in which the focus is on the group.[118]

As Wilson worked on *Fences*, he made a crucial decision based on the fact that, inadvertently, he had set each of his first three plays in different decades of the twentieth century—*Jitney!* in the 1970s, *Ma Rainey's Black Bottom* in the 1920s, and *Fences* in the 1950s.[119] "I have written plays set in three different decades," he told an interviewer, "I thought to myself, Why don't I continue to do that. It gave me an agenda, a focus, something to hone in on, so that I never had to worry about what the next play would be about. I could always pick a decade and work on that."[120] Ever after, Wilson set each play in a different decade. However, after *Ma Rainey's Black Bottom*, he never deviated from his early decision to follow the lessons he took from Bearden and set his plays in Pittsburgh, the place he knew best. He says he set *Ma Rainey* in Chicago because it was his first play aimed at a national audience and so he thought it needed a "more important" setting.[121] Setting his plays in Pittsburgh might have seemed provincial, but Rob Penny convinced August Wilson that Pittsburgh had national significance. "Everything that is America," Rob assured him, "exists here, from the artistic beauty to the ugliness."[122]

12

Grappling with Black Nationalism

While August Wilson basked in the glow of national and local acclaim, he faced doubts, or at least questions, about whether he was a true Black nationalist. He had long claimed he was a nationalist, and that Amiri Baraka was one of his greatest influencers. However, local nationalists had long questioned his commitment to the cause, one calling him, at best, a "wannabe" nationalist.[1] By 1987, theater critics had begun asking similar questions. One noted that white audiences left Wilson's plays "feeling comfortable, not threatened."[2] Another noted that the plays were free of the racial stridency found in the works of "true" cultural nationalists like Baraka.[3] Samuel Freedman of the *New York Times* suggested that Wilson's sympathies resided with Black nationalism, but as a writer "he could not produce convincing agitprop."[4]

Wilson's first two Broadway plays treated racial issues, but unlike works by Baraka, they feature no white characters who exhibit explicit racial animus. The white recording managers in *Ma Rainey's Black Bottom* show little interest in Ma's music, but only because they have a single-minded focus on what kind of recordings they think Black people would purchase. In *Fences*, Troy denounces the racism of Major League Baseball because it came too late to benefit him personally. Notably, Troy's battle to drive the truck takes place offstage.

Whether Wilson should be considered a nationalist depends partly on definition. He certainly did not write what Ed Bullins called "Black Revolutionary Theatre"—works meant to prepare Black people psychologically for a coming race war. Wilson told his friend Lee Kiburi that he was incapable of writing that type of play.[5] It is fair to say that Wilson wrote in the spirit of what Bullins called "Theatre of the Black Experience"—plays intended to raise Black people's self-esteem by seeing themselves portrayed accurately yet sympathetically onstage. That Wilson's plays fall into the latter category can be gauged by his admiration of Romare Bearden, who captures the nuances of Black life while simultaneously illustrating transracial cultural commonalities. As Wilson told *The New York Times'* Mervyn Rothstein, Black people and white people "all do the same things, they just do them differently."[6]

Wilson appreciated the uniqueness of the Black experience but wanted his plays to show that universal themes such as love, honor, duty, beauty, betrayal, and the human condition apply also to the Black experience. And he wanted to do so in a way that would foster Black pride.[7] He wanted his writing to benefit "ordinary" Black people, who he believed had lost touch with their cultural roots. At least in this respect, Wilson was faithful to the goals of Black nationalism and the Black Arts Movement. As his friend Sala Udin says, the movement was interested in works that uplift the poor and the working class.[8]

Wilson seemed conflicted. At times, he agreed that his plays were not angry and threatening, telling a reporter that he considered himself "an artist first, a playwright second and a black third." For good measure, he added that he did not write "message" plays.[9] However, in his public lectures, he often sounded like a committed nationalist, a follower of Malcolm X and Baraka. In March 1988, at Pittsburgh's Carnegie Music Hall, Wilson delivered an angry lecture he titled "Blacks, Blues and Cultural Imperialism." The talk featured exactly the sort of racial "agitprop" that Freedman and other theater critics said he avoided, delivered to a predominantly white audience who likely had come to the talk expecting a heartwarming story of how Pittsburgh had laid the foundation for his later success.[10] Many were left squirming in stunned silence.

Throughout the talk, Wilson denounced "white cultural imperialism," describing it as a centuries-old conspiracy to control the behavior of Black people by controlling their culture. During slavery, he insisted, "cultural imperialists" stripped enslaved persons of their African culture. When they responded by creating a new, blues-based culture, the cultural imperialists worked to destroy that through a seemingly benign appropriation process that continues to the present. In a statement that caused an audible inhalation, Wilson condemned

George Gershwin, composer of *Porgy and Bess*, as one of the "cultural imperialists."[11] He then went on to dismiss newly opened avenues for Black advancement as simply a scheme to maintain white supremacy by opening opportunity's doors only to Black people willing to assimilate and "deny their black name." The lecture ended with the warning that his eighteen-year-old daughter would not enter American society under those conditions. "Someday," Wilson said ominously, "somebody is going to . . . tear down the door. . . . . They will either tear down the door or tear down the house."

A bewildered audience gave the talk only tepid applause.[12] The question-and-answer period ended abruptly when an audience member said, "Your argument helps to perpetuate the problem you're complaining about." Wilson responded by gathering up his papers and exiting. As he did, he asked sarcastically: "I am the cause of the problem?"[13]

Some approved of Wilson's message. Murmurs of "That's right. Tell it," could be heard coming from some Black audience members. However, the lecture left other Black people uncomfortable. Ron Davenport, African American dean of Duquesne University's Law School and owner of WAMO, the local Black radio station, told Wilson afterward that the speech was simply "wrong."[14] Some of Wilson's family members were upset, voicing their displeasure in a way that prompted Lee Kiburi to conclude that they were fine with Wilson being a famous playwright but did not approve of his views on Black art, Black theater, or anything like that.[15] The neighbors also were upset. Julia Burley said that August's mother would not have approved of the speech because Daisy "wanted nothing to do with that Black power mess. *Nothing.*"[16]

The lecture was Wilson's first public expression of nationalist leanings in twenty years, the first since his 1968 address at a local Malcolm X commemoration. It is not clear what prompted him to deliver this particular speech at this particular time. However, there likely was an indirect relationship between Wilson's "Cultural Imperialism" speech and his plays. In 1988, the same year as the speech, *Joe Turner's Come and Gone* opened on Broadway. Regarded by Wilson and others as his most nationalist play, it is set in 1911 and is based on the depravity of an actual historical figure: Joe Turney, brother of the governor of Tennessee, who made a fortune out of luring Black men into illegal activities like gambling, then having them arrested and fined. Unable to pay the fine, the men would be sentenced to work for years as convict labor on one of Turney's Mississippi River plantations. Famed musician W. C. Handy memorialized Turney's exploitive practices in the blues song "Joe Turner's Come and Gone."[17]

In addition to having an historical background, the play also owes much to Wilson's inspiration, Romare Bearden. While browsing an issue of *National Geographic*, Wilson noticed a painting based on a scene Bearden had observed during his childhood summers at his grandparents' boardinghouse, in Pittsburgh's Strip District. Titled *The Mill Hand's Lunch Bucket*, the painting features a laborer who exudes strength and quiet dignity as he comes down the stairs holding a lunch bucket in his massively large hand.[18] Wilson decided to make that large, muscular worker the subject of a short story, "The Matter of the Mill Hand's Lunch Bucket." But after writing a few pages, he became intrigued by another figure in the painting, a diminutive man hunched over in what Wilson saw as "a posture of defeat." Deeply affected by the figure, Wilson reinterpreted the painting as about a man who was going to be left alone "just when what he needed most was human contact."[19] The figure—an outsider like Wilson himself—became Herald Loomis. The story became Wilson's play *Joe Turner's Come and Gone*.[20]

In the play, after seven years laboring on Joe Turner's chain gang, Loomis has traveled to Pittsburgh in search of his wife. While he had been away, she gave their daughter to relatives and reportedly moved to Pittsburgh. Looking for her, Loomis arrives at a Hill District boardinghouse. The residents are leisurely going about the rituals of their daily lives when they are joined by the arrival this unheralded stranger. Loomis has brought his daughter with him and is determined to reconnect with his wife. When the two finally meet, however, she tells him she moved on with her life because she couldn't wait for him any longer. Heartbroken, Loomis angrily sets out to find his "song," his true racial identity. Formerly a minister, he rejects Christianity and immerses himself in a series of African religious and cultural ceremonies. Residents at the boardinghouse join him in performing the rituals, including juba, an African-based circle dance that survived in the United States. The climax comes when Loomis slashes his chest and bathes in his own blood. Doing so symbolizes his having found and embraced his African identity.[21] Outsider, warrior, and now race man, Loomis has found his "song," his identity, and inner peace.[22]

Wilson's biracial background made Loomis's story deeply personal. Years later, Wilson said that Loomis's search for his identity made *Joe Turner's Come and Gone* his favorite work, the play that "best crystallized" what he wanted to say. As Wilson described the personal meaning of the play: "I found a way to crystallize that [search for Loomis's African and racial identities] by having him slashing his chest. He was willing to bleed to redeem himself, because redemption does not come outside yourself. 'You want blood? Blood make you clean? You clean with blood?' That one moment in which he becomes luminous, there's certainly not a moment like it in any of the other plays. So I think for all those reasons it's my favorite."[23]

Joe Turner's Come and Gone opened on Broadway in 1988, garnering positive reviews from critics and winning the New York Drama Critics' Circle Award for Best Play. It also won praise from August's old friend Rob Penny. Ever the devoted nationalist, Rob reviewed the play for *Shooting Star Review*, a local Black magazine of the arts. He praised the play's focus on finding one's African roots and its depictions of such African cultural elements as juba. He also praised August for his embrace of "revolutionary change and spiritual liberation."[24] But while the play appealed to nationalists like Rob, it appealed less to the general public, drawing much smaller audiences than *Fences* and *Ma Rainey's Black Bottom*.[25]

Wilson wanted his plays to be historically accurate enough that if our world was ever destroyed, a future anthropologist could use them to create a reliable account of the twentieth-century urban Black experience.[26] For all its imaginative truth, *Joe Turner's Come and Gone* does not provide a reliable historical account of Pittsburgh Black life. Loomis hailed from the plantation area of the Deep South. But in 1911, the year of the play's setting, very few Black Pittsburghers hailed from that part of the country. Rather, they were largely Northern-born descendants of migrants who for a century had trickled in from Maryland and the Shenandoah Valley of Virginia. These early Black settlers stressed their identity as Christians. In their daily lives, they stressed gentility, respectability, and high culture. In the early 1800s, a local newspaper praised local Black people for their religiosity and their "orderly conduct, sobriety, and [respect for] the civilities of life."[27] "Afro-American Notes," a weekly column that ran in the *Pittsburgh Press* in the late nineteenth and early twentieth century, shows that those qualities long remained of important to Black Pittsburghers. In the early twentieth century, they supported several literary societies and some six concert orchestras that specialized in European classical music. As devout Christians, they would have been scandalized at Loomis rejecting Christianity, slashing himself and bathing in his own blood.[28]

The world depicted in *Joe Turner's Come and Gone* existed factually only in 1917 and subsequent years. The year 1917 marked the beginning of the Great Migration, a massive movement of Black people northward from the plantation areas of the Deep South. Between 1917 and 1940, some 1.5 million Black people left the South, settling in places like New York City, Pittsburgh,

Detroit, and Chicago. Those who settled in Pittsburgh worked mainly in the region's mines and mills. Before that, only a few migrants, like Loomis and his wife, migrated in from the Mississippi Delta region of western Tennessee.

The Great Migration has spawned an enormous literature, and so Wilson's imaginative re-creation of the history of that era stems partly from the fact that, although a voracious reader, he refused to do research for his plays. "I don't do historical research," he said defiantly. "I believe if you do research, you're limited by it. . . . It's like putting on a straitjacket."[29] As a result, Wilson had only rudimentary notions of life in 1911. As he says, "When I wrote *Joe Turner's Come and Gone*, I certainly did not think about anything that happened in 1911, but I had a sense that they didn't have cars but had horses. And I envisioned people coming into the cities, and there were boarding houses and people setting down roots."[30] Wilson aimed to create a literary rather than a document-based history. As he said: "This is stuff that beats in my heart."[31]

Despite Wilson's success on Broadway, his hometown was slow to embrace him. At the theatrical heart of this was William T. Gardner, producing director of the city's leading professional company, the Pittsburgh Public Theater. Gardner didn't much like *Ma Rainey's Black Bottom* and passed on a chance for an early production, which Wilson certainly noticed, so the Public Theater missed joining other national companies in doing pre-Broadway productions until *Jitney!* in 1996. It didn't do any August Wilson play until *Fences* in 1989. Five years after *Ma Rainey's Black Bottom* opened in New York, and two years after *Fences*, no major theater in Pittsburgh had performed a Wilson play. Christopher Rawson, theater critic at the *Pittsburgh Post-Gazette*, lamented this state of affairs and blamed it on a racial myopia that caused the city's theater establishment to offer "white plays performed by white casts for white audiences."[32] Perhaps spurred by Rawson's criticisms, Pittsburgh's theater scene opened rapidly to Wilson. In 1989 the Pittsburgh Public Theater closed its spring season with *Fences* and opened the next season with *Joe Turner's Come and Gone*, all the while enjoying record-breaking attendance. Local patrons, white as well as Black, proved eager to see nationally acclaimed plays by a local son. Standing-room-only audiences overflowed the Hazlett Theater on the North Side where, thirteen years earlier, Wilson had seen Athol Fugard's *Sizwe Bansi Is Dead*, the first professional play he had liked.[33]

Fences opened locally to rave reviews. Susan Harris Smith of the *Pittsburgh Press* considered the Hazlett staging more effective even than that in New York, partly because of Claude Purdy's superb directing and partly because the Hazlett provided a more intimate atmosphere than the larger Broadway theaters.[34] Three months later, enthusiastic crowds turned out to see *Joe Turner's Come and Gone*. Audience size was large but not the equal of *Fences*, but local critics were ecstatic. George Anderson of the *Post-Gazette* praised Purdy's directing and the acting of Roscoe Lee Browne and John Henry Redwood, saying they made the production stirring and magical.[35] Anderson added that if *Joe Turner* should prove less popular than *Fences*, the reason would not be its quality but because it is a more difficult play.[36]

Shortly after the closing of *Joe Turner's Come and Gone*, the Carnegie Library of Pittsburgh's Hill District branch presented Wilson with an honorary high school diploma in recognition of the "studies" he had made there after dropping out of school. Wilson was not present for the honor, but sent a message saying how much he cherished the gesture and that he considered himself a "graduate" of the Carnegie Library.[37] In December the local PBS station named Wilson "Pittsburgher of the Year" and featured his life story in its publication, *Pittsburgh Magazine*.[38] Mayor Sophie Masloff proclaimed January 22, 1990, "Pittsburgher of the Year Day" and honored Wilson with a public reception.[39]

A few months later, in April 1990, Wilson's fourth play, *The Piano Lesson*, opened on Broadway. The play was inspired by Bearden's painting of the same name. Bearing the subtitle *Homage to Mary Lou Williams*, the painting pays tribute to Pittsburgh's most noted female jazz pianist, showing her seated at the piano taking piano lessons from her mother.

Set in 1936, *The Piano Lesson* centers on a dispute between a brother and his sister over how to deal with history—specifically, what to do with a family piano that dates back to slavery times. Captivated by childhood memories of her late mother polishing the piano with her tears, Berniece has made the piano a sacred icon, to be preserved at her home in Pittsburgh but never again to be played. Berniece's brother Boy Willie has other ideas. He has driven up from Mississippi, determined to sell the piano and use his share of the inheritance to purchase the Sutter plantation on which the family had toiled when enslaved. The plantation is for sale because Sutter has mysteriously died by falling down one of the property's wells.

Boy Willie's boisterous, unexpected arrival upends the tranquility of Berniece's quiet, well-maintained home. As such, he is treated like an outsider, causing him to grouse: "I been with strangers all day and they treated me like family. I come in here to family and you treat me like a stranger." Boy Willie is also a warrior and a race man, with contempt for the white man's law in the tradition of a Baraka-like nationalist. Despite having done hard time at Mississippi's notorious Parchman prison farm, Boy Willie declares defiantly, "It don't matter to me what the law say. I take and look at it for myself." His goal of gaining control of Sutter's plantation echoes the call of Black nationalists like Malcolm X and Elijah Muhammad for Black people to own property and become economically independent. Finally, Boy Willie is a versifier, whose manner of speaking amounts to free-verse poetry.

In the play's most riveting scene, Berniece becomes terrified when she sees the ghost of Sutter, whom she fears Boy Willie has killed by pushing him into the well. The scene harkens back to the time from Wilson's childhood when Zella, the sister of his neighbor Charley Burley, visited from California. While upstairs in the Burley's house, Zella saw a ghost. Terrified, she raced down the steps, falling and slightly injuring herself.[40] Zella's encounter with a ghost became part of neighborhood folklore, augmented by rumors that at one time the area had been a cemetery.[41] That Wilson made Sutter's ghost a palpable part of the story also reflects the influence of Jorge Luis Borges, the Argentine writer whose technique of magical realism had become internationally famous.

At first glance, *The Piano Lesson* seems oblivious to historical context. It is set in the 1930s, in the midst of the Great Depression, a time when some 60 percent of Black Pittsburghers were on relief and a federal study characterized the Hill District as "the worst that a fiercely industrial city . . . can do to human beings."[42] In those circumstances, it is hard to imagine a Black family arguing over whether to sell the family's prized piano in order to purchase a plantation. On the other hand, not all Black families were suffering. Black ministers continued serving their congregations. Black maids continued working for their wealthy employers. And Black elevator operators continued working in hotels, department stores, and downtown office buildings. Not coincidentally, Berniece cleans house for a "big shot" in the well-off Squirrel Hill neighborhood. Her boyfriend Avery is a pastor and also has "one of them good jobs" downtown as an elevator operator.[43] Meanwhile, Boy Willie has driven up with a truckload of watermelons that he peddles in town, earning enough to outfit himself with some sharp clothes so that he can go out looking for music, drinks, and women.

Theater critics and the theatergoing public were less interested in the play's historical accuracy than in the conflict over a cherished family icon. *The Piano Lesson* opened to rave reviews and went on to win the New York Drama Critics' Circle Award for Best Play. It garnered Wilson a second Pulitzer Prize and was performed abroad, attracting enthusiastic crowds in England, Germany, China, Japan, Uganda, and South Africa.[44]

The Piano Lesson's popularity made theater critics ask once again whether Wilson's work represented that of an avowed Black nationalist. Richard Bernstein of the *New York Times* concluded that Wilson was not a nationalist and praised him for avoiding "expressions of black rage."[45] Wilson seemed to accept Bernstein's assessment, telling a theater scholar that he tried not to write plays that were didactic or polemical, maintaining that theater does not have to be agitprop.[46]

People were especially curious about Wilson's biracial background and the influence of his white father—two topics that he disliked talking about. August may have looked down on Fred Kittel for being weak and unable to keep a job, but he loved his father and would have wanted to protect his image. In an era of rising Black consciousness, reticence would also have stemmed from being light-skinned and biracial. In 1988, when Bill Moyers of PBS asked Wilson about his father, he broke off the discussion by replying curtly, "He wasn't around very much."[47] In 1989, when Dennis Watlington of *Vanity Fair* asked August about his biracial background, he cut off further probing by replying curtly, "Yeah, my father was white, if that's what you mean."[48] August avoided the topic even among friends. Claude Purdy did not know his friend had a white father until he read it in a magazine. Sala Udin, a longtime close friend, never once heard August mention his father. "He just kept that in the background," Udin says.[49]

Invasive questions are the price of fame. While living in Saint Paul, Wilson achieved the sort of recognition that he and his mother had always dreamed of. Macelle Mahala's history of the Penumbra Theatre argues that Saint Paul was more important than Pittsburgh in making Wilson a successful playwright. Mahala acknowledges that Black Horizons marked the beginning of Wilson's work in theater, but says it was at Penumbra that he truly became a playwright.[50] Mahala has a point, but one can say with confidence that Wilson's success came from both cities. Pittsburgh bequeathed him a set of memories and identity traits that were crucial to his personal development; Saint Paul gave him the training and support he needed to develop professionally. Both were necessary, as was his discovery of Bearden, which of course took place in Saint Paul.

Wilson expressed gratefulness to the people of Saint Paul for all they had done to help him develop. In an address to city council in 1987, he thanked them for declaring August Wilson Day in the city.[51] From the time of his arrival, he said, Saint Paul had impressed him with its tranquility, its cleanliness, and its efficiency. But it was the people and institutions that most helped him realize his dream. He singled out his good friend Jacqui Shoholm for helping him find a job at the Science Museum. He thanked the Playwrights' Center, the Penumbra Theatre, and the city's other arts organizations that had supported him.[52]

By the end of the decade, Wilson's ties to Saint Paul had frayed. The time he spent on the road viewing and revising his plays exacted a toll on his marriage. Estimating that of late he had been away from home for an average of nine months a year, August blamed a punishing work schedule for weakening his marital ties. "I was never there for her," he said. "It simply came down to the fact that she doesn't want to live by herself."[53] He and Judy drifted apart.

Then, in 1987, while Wilson was preparing *The Piano Lesson* for Yale Repertory Theatre, a group of drama students helped in revising and staging the play. August became romantically involved with the costume designer, Constanza Romero. In addition to his busy schedule that kept him away from home and the breakdown of his marriage, he and Claude also were separated professionally, with Claude directing his plays in regional theaters and Lloyd Richards directing their openings on Broadway. Ultimately, August Wilson decided it was time to leave Saint Paul.

13

The Seattle Years

In 1990 August Wilson and Constanza Romero moved to Seattle.[1]
They had considered settling in California, where Constanza had relatives,
but August still harbored bad memories of his time there in the 1960s. They
decided against New York because August wanted a city where he was not
well-known and could find public spaces where he could write in peace.
Seattle met all those requirements. In 1992 August's divorce was finalized,
and shortly afterward he and Constanza moved into a large home in Seattle's
historic Capitol Hill neighborhood.

In addition to fine old homes, Capitol Hill had quiet cafés where Wilson
could write without being disturbed.[2] This became more difficult, however, after
the *Seattle Times* informed readers that he could often be found in any of three
coffeehouses—the B&O Espresso, The Mecca, and Victrola—"sipping coffee,
smoking, writing in longhand, [and] sometimes chatting with fans."[3] A greater
problem was that few of the coffeehouses allowed smoking. On any number of
occasions, August had tried to quit the habit, but never stayed off for long. To
make matters worse, when he finally found a place that allowed smoking, it
lacked the sort of everyman clientele he needed in order to write. As a reporter
put it humorously: "So there it is. The one place he can smoke is full of writers."[4]

Wilson seldom attended movies or plays because he worried that exposure
to others' dialogue might corrupt his own voice.[5] The one exception was

opera, which he regarded as poetry set to music.[6] In fact, Ben Brantley of *The New York Times* saw a resemblance between opera and the dialogue in Wilson's plays. "All great playwrights," Brantley said, "write dialogue that in one way or another is musical, but only Wilson has written plays that sound like grand opera, albeit opera rooted in the blues."[7]

By this time, Wilson had been the recipient of numerous awards and honors. In 1988 Carnegie Mellon University awarded him an honorary doctorate. In 1991 the University of Pittsburgh Press published a volume of his plays. In 1992 Pitt honored him with an honorary doctorate, appointment to the Board of Trustees, and an invitation to give the keynote address at the Honors Convocation.[8] Wilson generally accepted such honors and delivered the speeches requested and met with students and faculty. On one occasion, he was censorious of Bill Cosby, who arrived minutes before accepting an honor and left right after, without giving anything in return. But as he told an interviewer in 1989, "You hang it up on the wall. None of that shit helps you write."[9] Wilson was demanding of himself. "He could explode over small things," Constanza says in exasperation. "A misplaced telephone number could drive him absolutely bonkers and cause him to start speaking very strongly, cussing himself out. He really doesn't allow himself any mistakes, any leeway."[10]

Although acclaimed for his plays, Wilson still considered himself very much a poet. As a boy, he had written love poems to girlfriends; now, his poetry included love poems to Constanza. In 1991, when the 92nd Street Y invited him for another reading, he recited "Paloma," a poem dedicated to Constanza about the bird of peace that brings messages of love to sailors who are lost at sea. The narrator is an outsider, one whose words have "lost their way."

Paloma

I called her Paloma.
I called her many things.
Some were lost between us in the dark.
More than a lost vowel or a dropped consonant,
the things I called her were scouts that had lost their way
And still I called her many things.
I said "Paloma, tu eres mi Paloma."

Wilson continued spending a lot of time on the road, observing pre-Broadway stagings of his plays and revising them before they opened on Broadway. On his return from these trips, he would bring back a gift for Constanza, often an art book or jewelry.[11] They married in 1994.[12]

In 1992 *Two Trains Running* opened on Broadway. Set in 1969, a year after the riots precipitated by the assassination of the Reverend Martin Luther King Jr., the play accurately captures the mood of the times. The militant nationalism that had characterized the late 1960s was largely gone, as evidenced by a *Pittsburgh Courier* survey in 1973—five years after the riots—that found the prevailing mood to be one of pessimism and resignation rather than anger.[13]

It was a sad ending for a decade that had begun with great hopes. The 1960s had, in fact, seen positive racial change, but the benefits flowed mainly to the middle class, those with training and education. Blue-collar and "ordinary" Black people remained besieged by racism and the effects of automation and globalization. Nothing seemed to stem their downward spiral—not the civil rights movement, not the so-called war on poverty, not the Black Power movement, and certainly not the riots, which destroyed Black neighborhoods and ushered in Richard Nixon as president, a man with little interest in Black people or racial justice.

Two Trains Running examines Black people's uncertainty as to which train they should take into the future: integration, which promises material success at the cost of losing their racial identity, or separation, which promises the preservation of identity at the cost of economic privation. The play's answer comes from a Muddy Waters blues song, "Two Trains Running," whose refrain says despondently, "neither one going my way." Despite the play's subject matter, *Two Trains Running* is only moderately political. Sterling, a recently released prison inmate, urges patrons at Memphis Lee's diner to attend a forthcoming rally honoring Malcolm X. This sets off a vigorous debate over whether "black power niggers" are the cause of Black people's current plight. Looming in the background—and the immediate source of patrons' anxiety—is the threat of urban renewal tearing down the block where Memphis's diner is located.

The diner is a community institution where the waitress (Risa), the numbers runner (Wolf), and several patrons regularly sit around drinking coffee while discussing life's injustices and the inability to do anything about them. Wolf, who uses the restaurant as his informal office, answers the phone to write a "numbers" wager. Memphis complains about Wolf tying up his phone. A long discussion ensues on the pros and cons of the numbers. Memphis complains to one and all about his wife leaving him despite his having treated her like a "queen." A patron comes in to tell the customers about the long line

225

of people waiting outside West's funeral home to see the Prophet Samuel. This bit of news prompts a long conversation about the large amount of money and jewelry in Samuel's casket, and the likelihood that West, a prominent funeral director who wants to buy Memphis's diner on the cheap, will surreptitiously strip those off the body before it is buried. The conversation then turns to just when the city will tear down the block for urban renewal, and what Memphis and his patrons will do then. Memphis bewails the loss of so many businesses up and down the avenue. But he and his patrons have little appetite for heeding a call to arms—or even fighting city hall. Memphis simply wants the city to compensate him for the loss of his diner.

One of the play's two central figures comes in the restaurant: Hambone, who possesses two of Wilson's own character traits. He is an outsider, the butt of ridicule and jokes. He is also a warrior, who for nine years has insisted that Lutz, the neighborhood's white butcher, pay him the ham he is owed for painting Lutz's fence. Finally, Hambone is a race man, who embodies what Wilson terms Black Americans' tradition of peacefully insisting that "we want our ham," meaning payment for what they are owed.[14]

August wove some of his personal history into the play. When Sterling hands out flyers for the rally, one of the patrons says dismissively, "I remember when Malcolm didn't have but twelve followers," almost verbatim what bar patrons had told August back in 1968 when he was handing out leaflets for a Malcolm X commemoration. The rally prompts patrons' tirades about the foolishness of "black power niggers"—all variations on comments August had heard in 1968. Hambone's insistence on being paid what he was promised harkens back to August's childhood, when his mother insisted that she be awarded the new washing she had won in a radio contest rather than the used one the station offered when it learned she was African American. West advises Sterling to carry around a "little cup" of expectations rather than a "ten-gallon bucket," echoing the advice August was given years earlier by a patron at Pat's Place.

Other characters in the play are more loosely based on people August had met at assorted diners and bars. Risa, the restaurant's waitress, is based on Willa Mae Montague, August's girlfriend who waitressed at Pope's Restaurant, one of his favorite places to hang out. But while Risa has intentionally scarred her legs in an effort to define herself by more than her gender, Willa Mae's legs were scarred while roughhousing as a young girl with her brothers in a bramble-filled lot near her home.[15]

Wilson took imaginative and sometimes controversial liberties with some of the play's characters. The real Lutz, unlike the miserly figure in the play, was a beloved figure in the Hill District, praised by the *Pittsburgh Courier* for helping the NAACP force a local bakery to hire Black people.[16] The son of German immigrants, Lutz had several Black employees and taught the butchering trade to one of them, Calvin Cunningham. On weekends, Lutz and his wife would get together with the Cunninghams and play cards.[17] In addition, the real-life West was a respected member of the community as well as owner of one of the Hill's most prominent funeral homes. When West's family protested his portrayal in the play, Wilson replied disingenuously that the character just *happens* to have the same name as the funeral home director.[18]

Two Trains Running won critical acclaim on Broadway, but reviewers nonetheless expressed ambivalence about its political message. *The Christian Science Monitor* said that August "might as well have simply hung posters on the seat backs with the message 'No more accommodation with whites; no more scraping and bowing to whites; no more waiting for respect and rights.'"[19] On the other hand, *The New York Times* almost thankfully applauded the play's avoidance of aggressive racial militancy. "Mr. Wilson's play," the *Times* reviewer wrote, "recognizes that there weren't militants everywhere and that two blocks away from the big protest march life tends to its homely course, anyway."[20]

Pittsburgh theater companies, Black as well as white, remained slow in staging Wilson's plays. In 1987 Kuntu Repertory, the city's main Black theater, staged the Pittsburgh premiere of *Ma Rainey's Black Bottom*, but afterward staged no other play by Wilson. Some speculated that Kuntu's director, Vernell Lillie, felt the plays were not militant, or nationalist, enough. The city's "white" theaters also were slow in staging Wilson's plays, primarily because production rights were held back waiting for the Pittsburgh Public Theater to do each play first. But once they started, enthusiastic audience reception and favorable reviews inspired them to continue. In 1989 the Pittsburgh Public Theater staged two plays by Wilson, *Fences* and *Joe Turner's Come and Gone*. In 1992 the national tour of *The Piano Lesson* arrived, and the Public Theater staged *Ma Rainey's Black Bottom*. The Public Theater went all out in its promotion of *Ma Rainey* by holding a "Jazzbo Ball" set in a replica 1920s speakeasy, perhaps in apology for doing it so late.[21] In 1994 the Public Theater staged *Two Trains Running* and boosted attendance by way of a contest, "Drawn on Your Dramatic Imagination." For the contest, students were asked to create a piece of art that reflected their reaction to the play. Dennis Biggs Jr., a cousin of the Gladstone High School teacher in Hazelwood whose class August had stormed out of years earlier, submitted the winning entry.[22] August signed

Dennis's prize-winning poster, but gave no sign that he was aware of any ties to his former teacher.

Wilson continued turning out plays at a remarkable pace. In 1994, only two years after *Two Trains Running* opened on Broadway, Hallmark Cards offered to film *The Piano Lesson* for its popular television series, "The Hallmark Hall of Fame." The company promised to invest four to five million dollars in the project. Hallmark also agreed to Wilson's historic demand for a Black director. It agreed that Lloyd Richards could direct the film and that Wilson could serve as screenwriter and coproducer. Wilson quickly and eagerly accepted the offer.[23]

Wilson had no experience in film, save writing scripts for *Fences*, but quickly made himself knowledgeable of the differences between cinema and theater. "On the stage," he said, "you tell the story with your ears; on film, with your eyes." Wilson threw himself into the project, shortening the script, adding new scenes, casting extras, arranging rehearsals, and scouting filming locations. Filming concluded in only twenty-five hectic days, the last scene being shot at 4:00 a.m. Unfortunately, the film could not be shot in the Hill District because empty lots and abandoned houses had despoiled so much of the streetscape. Instead, a home in middle-class Shadyside was used for exterior shots of Berniece's home, and a set in Harmarville was used for the interior.[24] A number of minor roles went to locals. One went to Nate Smith, an old friend of Wilson and a prominent labor and civil rights leader. Another went to Teenie Harris, legendary photographer at the *Pittsburgh Courier*. Elva Branson, former director of Black Horizons Theatre, played Mama Berniece, a character that was added to the play's filmed version.[25]

The play drew widespread local interest and support. In February 1995, some 150 friends gathered at the Crawford Grill in the Hill to watch the film's television broadcast. Wilson was not present but sent a message stating how much it meant to him that the film was shot in Pittsburgh. "Wherever I am or wherever I travel," he said, "I carry Pittsburgh, and the vibrant life and experiences of the Hill, with me."[26] The film drew mixed reviews. *DVD Verdict* praised its "excellent writing [that] leaps off the screen," but *TV Guide* felt it belabored its points.[27] *TV Guide* found especially problematic the climactic scene when Sutter's ghost makes its appearance. Magical realism works well in theater, where audiences are accustomed to suspending disbelief, but not in a highly realistic medium like cinema.

As Pittsburgh increasingly embraced Wilson's works, it is no surprise that he increasingly embraced his hometown. In 1996 he told an interviewer, "I have fond memories of [Pittsburgh]. It's where I came of age. It formed and shaped me. It's the place I know best, which is probably why I keep returning to it."[28] He came back every December to be with family, and again every spring to lay flowers on his mother's grave. In 1994 he declared Pittsburgh "fertile ground" and even did some writing there.[29] The film inspired journalists and theater critics once again to come to Pittsburgh and survey the neighborhood. Ben Brantley of the *New York Times* compared what Wilson had done for Pittsburgh to what James Joyce had done for Dublin and William Faulkner for Mississippi.[30]

Wilson enjoyed giving tours to out-of-town theater critics who wanted to see his beloved Hill District. But as usual, visitors who came expecting to see the vibrant, magical Hill portrayed in Wilson's writing were disappointed. Brantley found that the 1968 riots had left a depressing streetscape of empty lots and scattered houses that, he said, stood like "the last teeth in an old man's smile."[31] Wilson told Brantley that when he was young, the Hill had twice as many houses and that sometimes one would see two or three hundred people standing on the sidewalk. Brantley noted sadly: "On that piercingly clear day, you couldn't see a soul."[32]

Wilson next wrote *Seven Guitars*, set in the 1940s, the decade of his childhood. The play had its origins as *Fullerton Street*. Over the years, it underwent several revisions, at one time being set in a Southern turpentine camp and called "Moon Going Down."[33] As the script evolved, the setting returned to Pittsburgh. The play had its Broadway opening in 1996 and won enthusiastic reviews. Vincent Canby of *The New York Times* called it a "big, invigorating" work whose "epic proportions and abundant spirit remind us of what the American theater once was."[34]

Set in 1948, *Seven Guitars* is a flashback in the manner of Jorge Luis Borges, whose storytelling techniques often involve beginning the story at the end, and showing the reader how the ending came to be.[35] The play opens with a group of friends sitting around recounting the life of Floyd "Schoolboy" Barton, the husband of Vera and a recently deceased blues guitarist. Six neighbors (including Floyd) have gathered in a backyard—as they are wont to do—to play cards, talk, and eat. Later, they are joined by Ruby, Louise's niece, who has just come in from Alabama. Through the friends' conversation, we learn of Floyd's excitement when a music company writes, asking him to come back to Chicago and make another recording. Floyd's previous recording had been regarded as a flop, but later became a hit. Convinced that he is on the verge of fame and fortune if only he can get back to Chicago, Floyd is faced with the need to raise money to get his guitar out of the pawnshop. To do that, he and Poochie, a neighbor's boy, rob a store, in the course of which Poochie is killed. Fearing arrest, Floyd quickly buries the money in the backyard.

Hedley, the play's most engaging character, is a slightly demented West Indian who speaks with an accent, walks with a limp, and coughs in a way that causes people to worry he has tuberculosis. Hedley embodies Wilson's four identity traits. An outsider and race man, he does not play cards with the others. Rather, he sells them chicken sandwiches and pontificates on the racial glories of Ethiopia and Marcus Garvey. Hedley also is a warrior, whose anger at an incessantly crowing rooster prompts him to slit the bird's throat, an omen of bad things to come. Indeed, when Hedley later sees Floyd digging up the stolen money, he believes it is money that had long been promised him by someone else. He slits Floyd's throat when Floyd refuses to hand over the money.

As with *Two Trains Running*, *Seven Guitars* uses details loosely inspired by people and places Wilson knew growing up, which make *Seven Guitars*, along with *Jitney!*, one of his most "Pittsburgh" plays. In the yard outside August's childhood home on Bedford Avenue, his mother would set up a table and invite neighbors over to play cards in the afternoon. Those invited typically included Daisy's upstairs neighbors, Louise and Hedley. The latter spoke with a strong accent, either Jamaican or, in the opinion of Julia, Geechee, from the South Carolina or Georgia seacoast.[36] The sanitarium that Hedley is advised to see for his tuberculosis was located several blocks up Bedford Avenue from the Wilson's home.[37] Poochie, another character in the play, was one of August's childhood playmates and the son of his neighbor Florence Tucker.[38] The Workingmen's Club, where Floyd plays guitar, was a popular Hill District nightclub, albeit one that featured jazz rather than blues.

Wilson was aware that the 1940s marked a special time, one he called "the last time we had jobs."[39] Nearly everyone, including musicians and businesses, prospered as never before—or since. *Seven Guitars* captures the optimism of the forties, when Pittsburgh served as the "Arsenal of Democracy" and its factories turned out much of the steel that helped the Allies win World War II. In doing so, the plants ran seven days a week, jobs were plentiful, and spirits were high. It was the sort of positive atmosphere that would have stoked Floyd's hope of making it big in Chicago.

Seven Guitars also captures the drama of the famous rematch between Joe Louis and Billy Conn. Known as "The Pittsburgh Kid," Conn almost defeated Louis in their first match. As in the play, there was widespread hope among Black people over the rematch. *The Pittsburgh Courier* reported that just before the opening bell, "on Wylie not an automobile moved, and fewer than five people were seen traversing the streets." Black people listened raptly as the fight was broadcast on the radio in Wilson's backyard. When Louis scored a knockout in the eighth round, fans rushed from their homes. "Every tavern was filled," the *Courier* exulted, "and automobiles seemed to be doing stunts in their haste to reach their destination so that occupants could celebrate."[40]

In 1996, the same year that *Seven Guitars* opened on Broadway, the Pittsburgh Public Theater scheduled a staging of *Jitney* (August dropped the exclamation point) for early June, prompting Wilson to rush back to Pittsburgh for a final, feverish round of revisions. The play had premiered in Pittsburgh in 1982, garnering enthusiasm among local Black audiences. However, technical and structural problems, as well as mixed reviews from local theater critics, caused Wilson to set the play aside until later. Happily, the new production drew large audiences and also won praise from of local theater critics. Christopher Rawson, writing for the *Pittsburgh Post-Gazette*, described the dialogue as supple and heartfelt.[41] *Jitney* ran for fifty-six performances, making it and *Fences* two of the Public Theater's best-attended theatrical runs at the time.[42]

June 1996 was especially busy for Wilson. Toward the end of the month, he gave the keynote address at the annual conference of the Theater Communications Group. Titled "The Ground on Which I Stand," it became the most influential, controversial, and defining address of Wilson's career. It was an angry speech, one that to a considerable extent was a long-delayed response to attacks by Robert Brustein, theater critic for the neoliberal magazine *The New Republic*. Brustein was no fan of Wilson. He called *The Piano Lesson* a flawed play and demeaned Wilson's success as the "cultural equivalent of affirmative action."[43] Most grating, he portrayed Wilson as a cynical opportunist whose nationalist pretensions were belied by the widespread appeal of his plays to white audiences.[44] Wilson's long-anticipated response was delivered on June 26, 1996, at the McCarter Theatre near Princeton University.[45]

In his lecture, Wilson called himself one of the "warriors on the cultural battlefield," the inheritor of African American culture and values that his mother passed on to him and that date back to the first Africans who set foot in what would become the United States. He described the Black Power movement as the "kiln" in which his identity had been fired. He termed himself an old-fashioned "race man" in the tradition of Marcus Garvey, and believed that race is "the largest, most identifiable and most important part" of one's identity. For good measure, he insisted that Black Americans are Africans, with all that such an identity implies.

"The Ground on Which I Stand" expanded on themes Wilson had expressed eight years previously in his "Blacks, Blues and Cultural Imperialism" lecture in Pittsburgh. In that lecture, Wilson had accused white people of trying to control Black culture as part of a scheme to control Black minds and Black bodies. He now accused the theater world of continuing that practice through such means as colorblind casting and the refusal to fund separate Black theaters.[46] He praised playwrights working in the tradition of the Black Arts Movement for developing a racially conscious Black theater. In a not-so-veiled reference to Brustein, he criticized those who cloak their prejudices with aesthetic criteria. "To suggest that funding agencies are rewarding inferior work by pursuing sociological criteria only serves to call into question the tremendous outpouring of plays by white playwrights who benefit from funding given to the 66 LORT theatres," Wilson declared, referring to the League of Resident Theatres, the major professional theater association in the United States. "Do we have 66 excellent theatres? Or do those theatres benefit from the sociological advantage that they are run by whites and cater to largely white audiences?"[47]

With Wilson having thrown down the gauntlet, Brustein was certain to pick it up. Two months later, he disparaged Wilson's call for separate funding of Black theaters as "subsidized separatism." "What next?" Brustein asked rhetorically. "Separate schools? Separate washrooms? Separate drinking fountains?"[48] The dustup agitated the theatrical community enough that, seven months later, a forum was arranged for the two men to debate their differences before a live audience in New York City's Town Hall. Margo Jefferson, African American theater critic for *The New York Times*, found the evening unenlightening and boring. Brustein, she said, retreated into being "the lofty ambassador to the court of great Western art," and refused to acknowledge "the possibility that any sort of human foible . . . could ever affect the artistic judgment of a cultivated man like himself." Wilson, she bemoaned, "cast himself as the warrior-king of all people of African descent living in the United States . . . as though all authentic . . . black art was being forged in the smithy of the slave ship of his soul." Jefferson concluded that it all amounted to "a long-winded drama about two men trapped and chained together in their own mulishness."[49]

However mulish the two men's nondebate had been, it brought a welcome truce to the war. Afterward, Brustein ceased his attacks on Wilson, and Wilson softened his rhetoric. At a poetry reading the following spring at the 92nd Street Y, Wilson went so far as to characterize his plays as apolitical and say they reflect his worldview. "Through my characters," he declared, "I can say my truths that I have uncovered."[50] Because with few exceptions the characters in Wilson's plays avoid obviously nationalist tropes, this admission implicitly undercut his declaration at Princeton that his plays were grounded in Black nationalism.

Wilson continued advocating for separate funding of Black theater. To advance the notion of such funding, he convened a five-day conference at Dartmouth College.[51] The conference offended Richard Hornby, theater critic at *The Hudson Review*, who chastised Wilson as "the most separatist major writer in America." To support the charge, Hornby trotted out presumed examples of Wilson's sins: his denunciation of George Gershwin's *Porgy and Bess*, his opposition to African American art being displayed in major "white" museums, his ridiculing of colorblind casting, his labeling as "tokenism" the annual staging of "one or two" Black plays by major theaters, and his insistence that only Black directors had the necessary racial sensibilities needed to interpret his plays.[52]

These skirmishes in the world of theater fascinated those inclined to follow such matters, but they had minimal impact on theater critics and audiences. Certainly, this was true in Pittsburgh, where in June 1997 Marion McClinton returned to direct *Seven Guitars* for the Pittsburgh Public Theater. The performance received rave reviews, with Rawson praising both McClinton's directorial touch and the performance of Leland Gantt, a McKeesport native well-known from his appearances in film and television.[53]

Wilson was so pleased with the reception his plays had enjoyed in Pittsburgh that in early 2000 he helped the Pittsburgh Public Theater celebrate the opening of its new venue, the O'Reilly Theater, by allowing it to premiere his new play, *King Hedley II*. The Public Theater went all out in promoting the play, including a special outreach to the Black community. The efforts paid off; a large attendance by Black people helped make *King Hedley II* the third best-attended play in the Public Theater's history.[54]

King Hedley II is set in the 1980s, a decade that witnessed both the collapse of the city's steel industry and the emergence of a devastating epidemic of crack cocaine, *King Hedley II* depicts the resultant unraveling of a community's social and moral fabric. The play is a sequel to *Seven Guitars*, but with striking differences. Where *Seven Guitars* is set in a neighborly backyard where friends gather to play cards and enjoy one another's company, *King Hedley II* is set in three joyless backyards filled with bickering and tension. Early in the play, the community's soothsayer Stool Pigeon announces to one and all that Aunt

Ester, the 366-year-old keeper of the community's memory and morals, has died. "Lock your doors!" he screams in alarm. "Close your windows! We in trouble now." Following Ester's death, God will bring death and destruction to the land, creating a dystopian world of guns, knives, and killings, a place where men do not know who their parents are, and women abort their fetuses rather than rear children in such a horrid environment.

As one might expect, the play's leading figure embodies Wilson's own identity traits. King is an outsider, so much so that he does not even know the identity of his true parents. He mistakenly believes they are Louise and Hedley, two characters from *Seven Guitars*, but later he learns that his father is Leroy Slater, who had been murdered by Elmore, the sometime boyfriend of his mother Ruby. King also is a warrior, marked with a long scar down his cheek that speaks of past violence and foreshadows more to come. Before the play opens, King lived up to the murderous reputation of his ersatz father by killing a man over disrespect and something as trivial as a nickname. King lives by his own violent code—made necessary, he insists, because society has given him no other choice. King's world is the closest Wilson came to a play in the nationalist tradition of Amiri Baraka. "I want everybody to know that King Hedley II is here," King proclaims, "and I want everybody to know, just like my daddy, that you can't fuck with me." King also is a race man, who rages against white dominance. "They got everything stacked up against you," he fumes. "They block you at every turn." King's sense of racial oppression borders on paranoia. When a store does not give him his photos because of a problem with the receipt, he complains that telling him his receipt doesn't count is telling him, in effect, that he doesn't count.

Wilson dedicated *King Hedley II* to the men he termed the "fallen oaks" of the Centre Avenue tradition—Rob Penny, Nick Flournoy, and especially Chawley Williams.[55] Chawley attended the play's premiere, sitting in the second row so he could savor the evening. Chawley says he smiled when he heard phrases he had whispered to August years before. "King Hedley," he says, "resonated so inside of me as the person I once was, that it was breathtaking."[56] Chawley says the only trait of King not based on his own persona is violence, for he was not a violent person.[57] Wilson says King was not based entirely on Chawley, but on several people he had known.[58] Stool Pigeon, another character in the play, is based at least partly on one of the Hill's more bizarre figures, a mentally struggling man who carried newspaper clippings in his hat and bore signs with messages like "History is the lifeblood of mankind." His appearance on the streets of the Hill struck fear in some, but fascinated Wilson, who believed that people who were different were valuable. They "carried the history," he says. Chawley regards this nameless outsider as "the epitome of the stranger," the sort of outsider who often appears in a Wilson play.[59]

Christopher Rawson, reviewing the play's Pittsburgh opening, knew that audiences would find *King Hedley II* a challenge. He called it Wilson's "darkest play," devoid of the humor and encouraging message of the others, a tragedy "without the final uplift of *Fences* or *Jitney*." Nonetheless, Rawson labeled the play a "masterpiece" in its own way, bolstered by outstanding performances and directing.[60] Rawson also used the occasion to brand Wilson's body of work as the "Pittsburgh Cycle," a label that soon became the accepted way of referring to his ten principal plays. Rawson wrote, "Now that August has completed the eighth of his projected cycle of plays set in each decade of the 20th century, it's time we gave it a name. Since all the plays but *Ma Rainey* take place in Pittsburgh (August says, 'If I knew then what I know now, I would have set it in Pittsburgh'), I propose we refer to them collectively as 'The Pittsburgh Cycle.' All in favor? . . . Good—motion passed."[61]

In Pittsburgh, *King Hedley II* was a major success, but in New York it became Wilson's first play not to draw large crowds, closing after only seventy-two performances. *King Hedley II* also became Wilson's first play to draw mixed reviews from New York's theater critics. *The New York Times* likened it to high opera. "You would need to look to a Verdi," Brantley wrote, "to find a more stirringly musical fusion of public crisis and private pain." However, Brantley complained that, as in opera, the plot is difficult to follow and at times hardly credible.[62] *King Hedley II* became Wilson's first play not to win the New York Drama Critics' Circle Award.[63]

One reviewer badly missed the mark. Charles Isherwood of *The New York Times* called the play "unmoored from the real currents of the era."[64] Unfortunately, Isherwood was terribly wrong. The 1980s actually *was* plagued by violence and ethical unraveling. Not coincidentally, it was the decade when Pittsburgh suffered the most wrenching economic collapse in its history, with dire consequences for blue-collar workers, especially African American. For years, there had been predictions that the "Wolf" actually was "at the door" and the era of steel was ending.[65] By the end of the decade, Pittsburghers acknowledged that this time the mill closings were permanent, and the consequences would be agonizing. It had been twenty years since Sala Udin, executive director of House of the Crossroads, warned that heroin addiction was on the rise. Crack cocaine wreaked even greater damage. As unprecedented levels of violence settled over the Hill, it is natural that Wilson would have King carrying a Glock, a second character embracing his Beretta, and a third bragging about his .38 Special.

John Edgar Wideman, the city's leading Black novelist, was worried about the deterioration of his beloved Homewood neighborhood. Wideman bewailed the fate of his brother Robby, who was serving a life sentence for being an accomplice to a 1975 robbery that had gone terribly wrong. Wideman's book on the tragedy, *Brothers and Keepers*, asked how the lives of two men who had shared the same family and played on the same streets could have diverged so terribly.[66] Prior to the 1968 riots, Wideman says, Homewood was one of the city's most pleasant places to live, a place of nice houses and tree-lined streets. But now, he lamented, "It's coming apart. It's coming apart now."[67]

In regular trips back home, Wilson had observed the Hill District's ever-mounting violence and decline in social values. Once while riding up Centre Avenue, he saw the bloodstained victim of a shooting ask someone for a ride to the hospital. The driver brusquely turned him down, in a way that might have come from *King Hedley II*: "You ain't gon' get all that blood in my car!"[68] In the play, Stool Pigeon is sent to the hospital after being beaten and robbed by a gang of Black toughs from the Bedford Dwellings housing project, located just a few blocks from Wilson's childhood home. Railing at the irony of being saved by a white physician, Stool Pigeon asks, "If it wasn't for the white man, what would I do? Nigger bust you up and the white man fix you up."[69] Wilson blamed the decline on Black people losing touch with their roots. "So much of the vibrancy and the life are no longer there," he told Rawson. "To me, it's simply because we don't know who we are."[70]

Indeed, things had declined so much that, on some of his return visits, Wilson occasionally went to diners and bars outside the Hill in order to write. Charlie McCollester, a Pittsburgh-area professor and labor historian, recalls sitting and writing one day in the Onyx, a predominantly African American bar on Pittsburgh's South Side. The waitress said to him, "You know, you're the second person today who sat in this bar with a pad and pen and wrote." McCollester asked the waitress, "Who was the first?" She replied, "August Wilson."[71]

Some of Wilson's visits home were to accept local honors. One of the recognitions that he found especially meaningful came in 1998, when old friends honored him at a special event at Carnegie Lecture Hall. Accompanied by Constanza and their daughter, Azula Carmen, born six months earlier, August was deeply touched when Rob Penny, Amir Rashidd, and

Chawley Williams recited poems in his honor.[72] Sala Udin, by then a city councilman, delivered a proclamation declaring March 16 "August Wilson Day" in Pittsburgh. To top off the evening, Thad Mosley presented him with one of his sculptures.[73] August used the opportunity to reflect on how Pittsburgh had shaped him and prepared him for life. He said he carried that message to other places, describing how, during his time at Dartmouth, he taught every class around the theme "When I lived in Pittsburgh." The idea, he said, was to show students "there are stories all around you."[74]

In 1999 August Wilson returned to Pittsburgh to help celebrate the centennial of the Carnegie Public Library of Pittsburgh's Hill District branch. That was the branch where, as a boy, August obtained his first library card and spent many days reading virtually everything he came across. It also was where, ten years previously, the library had awarded him an honorary diploma for the studies he did there after dropping out of high school.[75] At the ceremony, Wilson extolled the importance of reading, saying that it was a library book that had told him of the "the Negro's power of hard work," two things he had never before seen associated. He said that advice later attracted him to Malcolm X, who equated Black Power with self-determination, self-respect, and self-defense. Wilson closed by saying that he hoped his presentation would do for others what his discovery of the blues had done for him: affirm their value and worth.[76] Wilson's comments provided a fitting statement of the ways in which Pittsburgh had provided him the tools to understand life and appreciate his place in the larger scheme of things. Reading and knowledge, he said, had helped him make sense of the world around him. He wanted his own writings to do the same for future generations.

14

Completing the Cycle

In the year 2000, eighteen years after *Jitney!* premiered at Pittsburgh's Fine Line Cultural Center and four years after a revised version of the play opened at Pittsburgh Public Theater, August Wilson had a new version ready for its New York premiere.[1] *Jitney* opened off-Broadway, the first Wilson play not to have the prestige of a Broadway opening. *Jitney* also was Wilson's first play not directed by Lloyd Richards, whose health had been declining. One critic took Richards's departure as a sign that, after twenty years of tutelage, the "surrogate son" no longer required the guidance of his "surrogate father."[2] To direct, Wilson chose Marion McClinton, with whom he had worked at Penumbra.[3] New York critics gave the play positive but not enthusiastic reviews. John Lahr said the play's "authentic voices" showed that Wilson had learned "to listen to his characters and let them speak."[4] Ben Brantley of *The New York Times* acknowledged that *Jitney* holds its audience in "charmed captivity," but complained about it being "slim on plot."[5] In the end, *Jitney* won Off-Broadway Theater Awards for both the cast and director.[6]

Twelve years earlier, Wilson had given his controversial "Blacks, Blues and Cultural Imperialism" address at Carnegie Music Hall in Pittsburgh. On March 20, 2000, he returned to the same venue to deliver the Drue Heinz Lecture. The timing was most unfortunate. The event took place just three weeks after several New York police officers were acquitted in one of the nation's worst incidents of police brutality. The officers had killed Amadou Diallo, a twenty-three-year-old African immigrant, in a hail of forty-one bullets as he was standing, unarmed, in the doorway of his New York apartment. Both the incident and the acquittal prompted national outrage. Wilson was so distraught that he abandoned his prepared comments and delivered an extemporaneous, bitter denunciation of slavery, race, and racial violence in America, an outpouring of grief that the *Pittsburgh Post-Gazette* termed a "90-minute angry assault."[7] Still seething, Wilson published an essay that appeared that appeared in the April 23, 2000, edition of *The New York Times* in which he asserted: "Before I am anything, a man or a playwright, I am an African American," a reversal of what he had told *The Los Angeles Times* thirteen years previously, that he was "an artist first, a playwright second and a black third."[8]

August's next return to Pittsburgh, in March 2003, was another sad occasion: the funeral of his old friend Rob Penny.[9] August wept during the service, crying out to no one in particular, "What am I going to do?"[10] It was Rob who had introduced August to the speeches of Malcolm X, who had invited him to cofound Black Horizons and Ujima theaters, who had brought him into the Poets in the Centre Avenue Tradition, who had advised him how to get his characters to "talk," and who had urged him to submit his plays to the National Playwrights Conference at the Eugene O'Neill Theater. On more than one occasion, Rob and his wife Betty had taken August and his family in when they had no place to stay.

For reasons that are not clear, the relationship between the two men had deteriorated, something painfully obvious when August was not asked to give remarks or serve as a pallbearer. At the service, "Hop" Kendrick, a longtime acquaintance of both men, noticed August standing off to the side, alone and sad. Hop invited him to take his place as pallbearer. Rob's widow Betty objected, telling Hop, "You ain't got the right." Hop fired back, "It IS my right. You gave me the privilege of being the pallbearer, and I gave it to August. And that's the way Rob would want it."

Hop thinks the rift may have been the result of a perceived snub.[11] He says that the last time August had traveled to Pittsburgh, he didn't call Rob. "Don't ask me why. Until this day, nobody knows why. He never, never failed to call Rob." But this time he didn't. When Rob and Betty saw August on television, they were "absolutely, absolutely furious," and Betty never forgave him.[12]

Nathan Oliver, a poet and friend of Rob, thinks the estrangement stemmed from ideological differences. Nathan, Rob, and many others had been bothered by the mainstream direction August's plays had taken and the outsized role he was playing in theater.[13] In addition, Oliver says, Rob had a certain ideological intractability, wanting things to be in "a nice, tight little place, [a] box" that didn't allow for much flexibility. August was the opposite, always interested in complexity and the contradictions inherent in a person and a situation.[14]

Wilson had written many plays and, during his years in Pittsburgh, had directed several more. But he almost never had acted in one. However, two months after Rob's death, Wilson performed in a one-person autobiographical play, *How I Learned What I Learned*, which opened in Seattle.[15] Wilson wrote the play at the request of Sharon Ott, artistic director of the Seattle Repertory Theatre, who was looking for something to feature as part of its annual new plays series. An extended one-act play, *How I Learned What I Learned* alternates between seriousness and self-deprecatory humor. It focuses on the year 1965, when, at the age of twenty, Wilson left his mother's house and went out onto Centre Avenue "to learn whatever it is that the community had to teach."[16] To shape these teaching moments into a play, Wilson recruited Todd Kreidler, a white dramaturg with whom he had collaborated for the Pittsburgh premiere of *King Hedley II*.[17] Given his previous insistence on a Black director for the proposed film version of *Fences*, Wilson apparently felt the need to defend his choice, praising Kreidler's abilities in an interview for NPR.[18]

For the first time in his life, Wilson directly confronted the issue of his light complexion, albeit with humor. Wearing a T-shirt that reads THIS IS AN ACCIDENT on one side and I WAS MEANT TO BE WHITE on the other, the character (August) says that white people who think they are complimenting him when they tell him they don't see color are really saying they accept him only as long as his body projects the message "I am supposed to be white."[19] Ripping off the T-shirt, he uncovers another shirt that proudly exclaims, WE ARE AN AFRICAN PEOPLE! Theater critic Stephen Kinzer of *The New York Times* likened the play's dialogue to a meeting between Dylan Thomas and Malcolm X.[20] The comparison would have pleased Wilson, who proudly considered himself a poet as well as a playwright.

Five months after performing in *How I Learned What I Learned*, Wilson returned to New York's 92nd Street Y, for an evening of poetry. There he recited one of Troy's monologues from *Fences*. A recording of the reading reveals the dialogue's poetic cadence and rhythm, as seen in the following, with Wilson's emphases in boldface.

Look here Bono.

I looked **up** one day.

Death was marching straight **at** me.

Like **sól**diers on paráde!

The ármy of **death**

marching straight **at** me.

It was the **míd**dle of Julý,

níneteen forty-**one**.

It got **real cold**

just like it be **wín**ter.

And death **stánd**ing there **stár**ing at me.[21]

The audience easily accepted the monologue as poetry, but during the question-and-answer period they seemed more interested in whether Wilson was a nationalist. Over the years he had often insisted that he was, but that night at the Y, when asked what literary figures inspired him, he mentioned only white authors: Anton Chekhov, Henrik Ibsen, William Shakespeare, Eugene O'Neill, and Arthur Miller. When a follow-up questioner asked Wilson how the "Four B's"—the blues, Bearden, Borges, and Baraka—had influenced his writing. he talked about three of the B's but said nothing about Baraka. When the host pointed this out, Wilson joked that the omission showed he didn't know how to count. He then gave a short, perfunctory affirmation of Baraka's importance. "Amiri Baraka fathered the Black Arts Movement," he said. "I fell under the influence of Baraka in terms of his political ideas, which I embraced and still do, even though some of which he has abandoned now. But that's on him, you know. He taught me well." Wilson closed by adding simply, "And . . . that's well," pivoting abruptly, and closing the evening with a curt "Thank you."[22] Clearly, he did not want to discuss his relationship—or nonrelationship—with Baraka and Black nationalism.

Wilson ended the year on a high note: in December 2003 Teresa Heinz, widow of Senator John Heinz III, presented him the Heinz Award in the category of the Arts and Humanities. Teresa Heinz established the award in honor of her late husband, whose family had founded the Pittsburgh-based Heinz food-processing enterprise. The prize totals $250,000, making it one of the nation's largest such awards. In his acceptance speech, Wilson recalled his grade school trip to the Heinz plant, where he got his "little pickle."[23] He expressed appreciation for the award both "because it's Pittsburgh" and because "Pittsburgh is a big part of me." He credited family and friends for his success, particularly two of his sisters: Freda, who gave him the money to buy his first typewriter, and Linda Jean, who had typed his early poems and manuscripts. He thanked his youngest brother Richard, and he acknowledged Kim and Paul Ellis, his niece and nephew, as well as Nicky Porter, the woman he called his "adopted niece," and Julia Burley, his mother's best friend and someone who "can remember me when I was in diapers."[24]

Not long before Rob's death, August and Billy Jackson, a local filmmaker, went over to Rob's home. As they sat around the dining table, August pulled out a piece of folded paper resembling origami and asked people if they knew what it was. They said it looked like a ship. August said, "Yeah, this is the *Gem*," a ship that would be the centerpiece of his new play, which would premiere the following year.[25] In 2004 *Gem of the Ocean* opened on Broadway.

Set in 1904, the action takes place in an old Hill District mansion. The house's 285-year-old matriarch Aunt Ester Tyler has personally witnessed the entire history of African Americans. Her year of birth, 1619, marks the arrival of the first Africans in British North America. She had appeared in previous plays in the Pittsburgh Cycle, first as an offstage spirit in *Two Trains Running* and again offstage in *King Hedley II* as the unofficial keeper of the community's morals and history. Now, in *Gem of the Ocean*, she returns, only this time onstage. Wilson had come to regard Ester as what he termed "the most significant persona of the cycle," the ancestor of all the other characters, a woman whose wisdom and sense of tradition provide valuable tools for dealing with a hostile society.[26]

Almost everything about Aunt Ester is symbolic. If said rapidly, her name sounds like "ancestor." She also represents someone of deep personal significance. Back in the 1950s, Sarah Degree had recruited Freddy and other neighborhood kids to Catholicism. "Miss Sarah," as she was called, enrolled him and his sisters in Saint Brigid's Sunday school, which helped mitigate the color-based harassment they suffered at Letsche Elementary School. Miss Sarah passed away in 1986, at the age of eighty-four.

Wilson was saddened by her death and outraged that the church had never honored her life. "I've been threatening to write the bishop of the Diocese of Pittsburgh," he complained, "because we need to honor her in some way: Miss Sarah Degree Gymnasium, or Miss Sarah Degree House for Wayward Women. . . . There's no question: If she was white, they'd have a Miss Sarah Degree Child Care Center or something. . . . God, she probably didn't even have a decent burial. But that's the way it goes."[27] Wilson decided to honor Miss Sarah himself and did so in his plays. In 1990, four years after her death, he reincarnated her as Aunt Ester Tyler, her last name a variant of Taylor, Miss Sarah's maiden name.[28]

The spiritual power of Aunt Ester places her at the center of Wilson's Pittsburgh Cycle.[29] From the time August came to know Miss Sarah, he had been fascinated by her rituals, which included sprinkling salt over her house's doorstep and placing pennies across its threshold.[30] In *Gem of the Ocean*, Aunt Ester Tyler has magical powers, including the ability to cleanse souls and put people in touch with their past. In this way, Aunt Ester resembles a "conjure woman," a combination herbalist, diviner, and African priestess.

In the play, Ester Tyler resides at 1839 Wylie Avenue, a location that never actually housed a private residence. Wilson may have chosen 1839 because it is the year of the Amistad mutiny. However, while working on the play's Broadway premiere, he told Phylicia Rashad—who played the part of Aunt Ester—that 1839 refers to the earliest use of the term *Underground Railroad* to describe the informal network that helped enslaved persons escape to freedom. Solly Two Kings, one of the play's central characters, was a former conductor on the Underground Railroad.[31] 1839 Wylie also was the address of St. Brigid Church and Catholic School (now torn down), which August attended as a child.[32]

Gem of the Ocean opens as in a Romare Bearden painting, with house residents going about their daily affairs, what Bearden would call their "rituals of daily life." Eli and Black Mary are in the kitchen, having just finished breakfast. They are puzzled by the unexpected appearance of an outsider, a stranger in the person of Citizen Barlow, who is waiting patiently across the street to see Aunt Ester. Citizen has come because he had been told Ester can help him find emotional relief for having caused the death of an innocent man. Citizen hails from Alabama. He has come to Pittsburgh and found work in one of the city's mills. However, underpaid and hungry, he stole a bucket of nails and remained silent when another worker, Garrett Brown, was accused of the crime. He also remained silent when the detested Black sheriff, Caesar Wilks—considered a toady of the white man—pursued Brown relentlessly. Protesting his innocence, Brown finally jumped in the river and drowned.

Citizen, like Wilson, is a warrior as well as an outsider. In an era when Black people were being lynched and disfranchised for asserting their rights as citizens, his very name hints at struggle. As one of the house residents tells him: "It's hard to be a citizen. You gonna' have to fight to get that." Citizen has come to the right person. Ester sends him to find two pennies lying side by side on the ground—a reference to Miss Sarah's use of pennies for magical purposes. In a scene that reflects the influence of the magical realism of Jorge Luis Borges, Ester has Citizen board the slave ship *Gem of the Ocean* and go on a voyage to "City of Bones," the massive cemetery at the bottom of the ocean that houses the bones of his African ancestors who died in the Middle Passage. To gain entry, Citizen offers the gatekeeper the pennies he had collected at Ester's behest. The gatekeeper, it turns out, is Garrett Brown, the man who drowned after being falsely accused of theft. Citizen confesses to Brown and is forgiven. Citizen, like all the chief characters of Wilson's plays, has become a race man, spiritually reconnecting with both the victim and his African ancestors. In doing so, Citizen emerges at peace with himself and his people.

While Citizen was away, Black mill workers, furious at Brown's drowning and with Caesar for relentlessly pursuing him, go on strike and set the mill afire. Caesar believes Solly, a resident of Ester's house, to be the instigator of this strike and arson. Solly had been a conductor on the Underground Railroad, leading fellow enslaved Alabamans to freedom. Caesar impetuously kills Solly, prompting Citizen takes up Solly's former occupation of guiding Black people north to freedom, only now bringing them up for jobs in the mills.

Gem of the Ocean is compelling theater but, like *Joe Turner's Come and Gone*, mischaracterizes the city's early Black community. The play is set in 1904, but until 1917 mills in in the North hired Black people only as temporary strikebreakers. In Pittsburgh, one of the remarkable exceptions to this practice involved a few Black millworkers. Highly skilled iron puddlers, had been brought up as strikebreakers from the Tredegar Iron Works in Richmond, Virginia. Their exceptional job skills and work ethic impressed owners so much that they did something almost unthinkable: they kept the men on after the strike was broken and made them a permanent part of the labor force. The mills were in the Strip District, and so the men would have lived there—most likely in the boardinghouse run by Bearden's grandparents—rather than in Aunt Ester's Hill District battered mansion.[33]

These men were well paid, in some cases earning more than white workers, and sometimes even supervising white employees. Unlike Citizen, they would not have been driven by hunger to steal a bucket of nails. Moreover, they were grateful to the mill owners for having hired them over the objections of white unions. They would not have gone out on strike and most certainly would not have burned down the mill. As one puddler told a Black sociologist investigating their situation, "I stand by the man that stands by me, and that is the rich man every time."[34] Pillars of the community, these puddlers led lives of propriety and respectability. They drank little, had small families, often belonged to the Masons, and attended churches whose services featured "an entire absence of the emotional expressions." They dressed well and, after their shift, changed into clean clothes, leaving no sign of the dirty environment in which they had worked. Their modest homes often contained a piano and walls decorated with portraits and landscapes.[35]

The world Wilson describes came into being only with the Great Migration beginning in 1917. When the United States entered World War I on the side of the Allies, Germany closed transatlantic shipping lanes, cutting off European immigration and creating a labor shortage so severe that manufacturers quickly dropped their long-held policy of hiring Black people only as temporary strikebreakers. The resulting availability of mill jobs—in Pittsburgh and other Northern cities—set off the Great Migration, a massive movement of Black laborers, largely from the Deep South, to the North. In Pittsburgh, these migrants came mainly from Alabama and, to a lesser extent, Georgia and a few other Deep South states. *Gem of the Ocean*, populated in 1904 by Alabamans, would not have been part of this pre-1917 community.

Theater critics were not aware of, nor particularly interested in, problems of historical accuracy. However, even as theater, *Gem of the Ocean* did not quite rise to the level that some critics and audiences had come to expect.[36] Ben Brantley of *The New York Times* regarded the play as the first Wilson drama whose characters were not fully fleshed out, who resemble "pieces of parchment on which legends of the past and maps to the future have been drawn in swooping strokes of ink." Despite these caveats, in 2005 *Gem of the Ocean* was nominated for five Tony Awards. Audiences were not convinced, but they never had a chance to make up their mind, because the primary producer wanted the theater for another play and so closed *Gem of the Ocean* prematurely after only seventy-two performances. That it closed during Black History Month was particularly disheartening to the actors. And the fact that Wilson's previous play, *King Hedley II*, also had closed after only seventy-two performances caused some to wonder whether the playwright was losing his magic.[37]

While *Gem of the Ocean* was running on Broadway, Wilson devoted himself to finishing *Radio Golf*, the tenth and final play of the Pittsburgh Cycle. He wanted *Gem of the Ocean*, set in the first decade of the century, and *Radio Golf*, set in the final decade, to depict the long arc of the Black experience in twentieth-century Pittsburgh. Wilson referred to them as "bookend plays" because their settings mark them as the Pittsburgh Cycle's beginning and closing works. Certainly, the plays' overarching themes parallel one another. *Gem of the Ocean*, set in 1904, deals with Black people discovering their African roots; *Radio Golf*, set in 1997, depicts how, generations later, Black people can rediscover those roots.[38] Their characters are related, and Aunt Ester's house reappears in 1997 as a central offstage scene.

Radio Golf premiered at Yale Repertory Theatre on April 28, 2005, one day after Wilson's sixtieth birthday. In June 2005 the playwright was diagnosed with advanced liver cancer and was told he only had three to five months to live. He tried to keep the illness a secret, but rumors began spreading among actors and family. In early August he phoned critic and friend Christopher Rawson to tell him he was dying and that he wanted Rawson to do his final interview. He told him not to come to Seattle, where there was family circling around and he wasn't even living at home. They agreed to talk by phone.

Rawson didn't tell anyone about the call, which was clearly private. The interview never happened. Then in late August his newspaper told him there were rumors coming in about Wilson's heath, especially from the daughter of one of Wilson's friends, and they were going to print something. So rather than seeing misinformation in the paper, Rawson submitted a short story, printed on August 26, using what Wilson said to him several weeks earlier. Wilson told him that he accepted his fate with equanimity.[39] "It's not like poker," he said. "You can't throw your hand in. I've lived a blessed life. I'm ready."[40] Wilson refused chemotherapy and a liver transplant because the side effects would have prevented his work on *Radio Golf*. Fighting through the pain, Wilson revised the script, but was too weak to attend the play's opening in Los Angeles—the first time he had missed an opening in his career.[41]

Coincidentally, before Wilson's illness had been made public, *American Theater* magazine had asked Suzan-Lori Parks, a Pulitzer Prize–winning African American playwright, to interview him. Having just seen Rawson's story and sensitive to the difficult issue of health, Parks was uncertain how to proceed. To her considerable relief, Wilson remained focused, funny, and, she says, "brilliant as hell."[42] He was pleased that *Radio Golf* let him explore the Black middle class, a topic he had long avoided. He expressed optimism about the future, convinced that music would provide the strength necessary for Black people to keep up the struggle.[43] He maintained a sense of humor, expressing the desire to write a comedy with cameo appearances by Queen Victoria, Fidel Castro, and Benny Goodman.[44] To the end, he remained ambitious, confessing to his sister Freda that he regretted he would not be eligible for a Nobel Prize because they were not awarded posthumously.[45]

On Sunday, October 2, 2005, surrounded by friends, relatives, and family in Seattle's Swedish Medical Center, August Wilson passed away.[46] With his usual dogged determination, he had planned things down to the last detail. He wanted the funeral to be held in Pittsburgh, he wanted to be buried near his mother in Greenwood Cemetery, and he wanted his old friend Chawley Williams to organize the service.[47] Years of carefully tending his finances meant August left a substantial estate that included unpublished poems as well as short stories and ideas for future plays. Constanza asked Kreidler, who had lived in the home during August's last few months, to sort through his papers and decide what should be kept.[48] Perhaps remembering the drama around the settlement of his father's estate, August placed all literary rights in the August Wilson Literary and Dramatic Property Trust and made Constanza the trustee.[49]

Two years after Wilson's death, *Radio Golf* opened. As was true of *Gem of the Ocean*, it did so to mixed reviews. *Variety* magazine felt that because Wilson had not been able to observe and revise the play as it toured regional theaters, it lacked "much of the singing lyricism and quasi-mythic qualities" for which his other works were famous.[50] Others gave the play more positive reviews. In the end, it was nominated for three Tony Awards.

Set in 1997 in the office of the "Bedford Hills Redevelopment Company," *Radio Golf* chronicles the maneuverings of Harmond Wilks, Ivy League graduate, ambitious real estate developer, and hopeful politician, who wants to gentrify the Hill with high-rise apartments and such upscale stores as Starbucks and Whole Foods. The development would improve the Hill, benefit Harmond economically, and advance his plans to become the city's first Black mayor. Roosevelt Hicks, Harmond's partner, is a shameless affirmative action front man for Pittsburgh's white-owned radio station that serves the city's Black population. Hicks also is an avid golfer and keeps a set of clubs in the trunk of his car.

A complication arises when Harmond's redevelopment plan requires tearing down an old, abandoned house at 1839 Wylie Avenue. The two learn that this is the former residence of Aunt Ester, keeper of the community's history and morals. Ester died years ago, and her former home is now owned by Joe Barlow, a half-demented oracle who venerates Ester's memory and refuses to sell her former home to a developer. Harmond mistakenly thought he had already bought the property at a sheriff's sale but discovers that it had never come up for auction. This is because Harmond's grandfather, Caesar Wilks— the detested constable in *Gem of the Ocean*—had continued to pay the home's property taxes. When Caesar died, Harmond's father quietly continued paying the taxes. Once Harmond learns of his family's long support of Ester and her house, he finds his racial identity, develops an emotional bond with the neighborhood, and vows to preserve the house himself. When Roosevelt learns of Harmond's change in plans, he conspires with a white businessman to take over the company, tear down the house, and proceed full throttle with redevelopment. Harmond, realizing he may be powerless to prevent Ester's house from being razed, picks up a brush, paints warrior markings on his face, and joins the protest to save the historic Hill and its cultural heritage.

Harmond, a middle-class insider—cut off from the Hill's legacy but open to its appeal—ends up a principled outsider who loses everything materially but gains his racial identity. Harmond was always a warrior, although at first a misguided one who fought solely for his own advancement. Deep down, however, he has a strong ethical streak, and in the end fights for the good of the community. Once he learns of his family's deep, historical connections to Aunt Ester and the Hill, he becomes a race man.

Harmond and Roosevelt are based partly on Hill District residents Wilson had known or known about. One was Robert Lavelle, the Hill's preeminent banker and realtor, whose office—like that of Bedford Hills Realty—was located at the corner of Centre and Herron Avenues. Another was Ronald Davenport, a graduate of Yale Law School and owner of WAMO, the city's Black-oriented radio station. Wilson's old friend and fellow poet Nick Flournoy was an avid golfer who, like Hicks, carried a set of golf clubs in the trunk of his car.[51] As always, Wilson made use of poetic license. Nick Flournoy was an outstanding poet and, Wilson said, one of the finest people he had ever known. Lavelle was a devout Christian with a long history of promoting positive redevelopment and Black home ownership in the Hill. And Ron Davenport had traveled to Mississippi in the 1960s, where he lent his legal talents to the civil rights struggle.[52]

Radio Golf explores some of the contradictions of the Black middle class, a group with whom Wilson regarded with deep ambivalence. Having grown up poor, he harbored a disdain for the affluent Sugar Top section of the Hill.[53] Harmond Wilks and Roosevelt Hicks embody the sort of criticisms made years earlier by Black sociologist E. Franklin Frazier in his study, *Black Bourgeoisie*. As Wilson says, the play is about the Black middle class's failure "to return the sophistication, expertise, and resources they have gained to the communities and the people they belong to. They've forgotten who they are."[54]

Throughout his life, Wilson remained loyal to the grassroots residents of the Hill, but was painfully aware of how much it had deteriorated during his lifetime. During a visit by Charles Isherwood in 2005, Wilson reflected on the decline. "From a community in 1965 that had 55,000 people," he told Isherwood, "we're down to a few thousand. Back then, you had two lumber yards, three wallpaper and paint stores, nine drugstores within a five-minute walk." The community was "poor but vibrant," he said. And he regretted the degree to which it had "been left to the depredations of cultural and political neglect."[55]

From his trips back to Pittsburgh in the 1990s, Wilson had seen that redevelopment was needed, and that it was under way. His friend Jake Milliones was a militant activist and city councilman who led the fight to redevelop the Hill District. But Milliones remained sensitive to the neighborhood's history. He knew how blight had left numerous empty lots and abandoned houses that he, Wilson, and out-of-town visitors found depressing. His campaign gathered the support of Mayor Sophie Masloff and attracted some $75 million in federal grants. Those grants, along with federal Hope 6 funds, let the city begin replacing deteriorating residences with attractive new townhouses. However, Milliones wisely insisted that a significant percentage of the new housing be set aside for those who could not pay market rate, and that there must be no visible difference between units that are market-rate and those that are subsidized. Finally, there was to be no use of eminent domain, the legal tool that in the 1950s allowed city officials to forcibly seize properties.[56] In 1991, when groundbreaking began on the new development, called Crawford Square, Milliones exulted, "We have succeeded in spite of ourselves, and we will continue to revive this community."[57]

Residents felt a sense of renewed pride in their neighborhood's past and a desire to preserve things that made the Hill special. Appreciation of the history was reinforced by the documentary *Wylie Avenue Days*, which appeared in 1991 on WQED, Pittsburgh's public television station. Two years later, another documentary, *Kings on the Hill*, celebrated the era when the Hill boasted two of the finest teams in the history of Negro League baseball. Finally, in 1997 Pittsburgh's Carnegie Museum of Art acquired 4,500 photographic negatives belonging to the extraordinary *Pittsburgh Courier* photographer Charles "Teenie" Harris. The acquisition became the first phase of what would become some eighty thousand negatives, the largest single collection of visual images of any Black community.[58] These documentaries and photographs stimulated residents' pride and desire to preserve their neighborhood's history and legacy.

Despite Milliones's sensitive leadership, redevelopment revived old fears.[59] Residents complained that the new homes were priced beyond their means and that making them available to the general public amounted to a form of gentrification. Others were worried that development would destroy the neighborhood's historical ambience. Milliones defended the project. "We don't want to build another housing project," he said, "having all poor people living in one place."[60] When he died in 1993, Milliones's place on city council was filled by Wilson's old friend Sala Udin, who shared Milliones's vision. Under Udin's leadership, Crawford Square was followed by subsequent developments, including Bedford Hills, immortalized in *Radio Golf* and located diagonally across the street from Wilson's childhood home.[61] In the end, the attractive new construction—virtually the first since the riots of 1968—prompted the *Pittsburgh Post-Gazette* to celebrate what it heralded as "The Rebirth of the Hill."[62]

Radio Golf showed the power of the past to shape the future. In doing so, it won the gratitude of many residents. Sala thanked him for writing dramas that portray "the timelessness of these struggles."[63] Pittsburgh's eternal importance to August Wilson can be seen in the headstone of his burial plot. Located just outside Pittsburgh, it reads humorously but meaningfully:

Wherever You Are

You Are

I'm Here

With his death and the completion of *Radio Golf,* the Pittsburgh Cycle was complete, the circle was closed.

15

Preserving the Legacy

Following August Wilson's passing, Constanza began making plans for the funeral. She called Sala Udin and told him that August wanted the funeral to be held at Saint Paul Cathedral, the mother church of Pittsburgh's Roman Catholic Diocese and the place where the funerals of dignitaries are often held. The bishop was delighted to make the cathedral available but demurred when he learned that August did not want a mass. For that reason, plans changed quickly. The viewing was held on Friday, October 7, at White Memorial Chapel in Point Breeze. A service was held the next day at Soldiers and Sailors Memorial Hall, a large public auditorium that fittingly celebrates the history of the Civil War.

In attendance were August's widow Constanza, his first two wives Brenda Burton Shakur and Judy Oliver, and his children, Sakina Ansari and Azula Carmen. A hundred or so colleagues from the theater world came to pay their respects. These included Claude Purdy, August's longtime friend and collaborator; Kenny Leon, who directed his last two plays on Broadway; and Vernell Lillie, who had staged his first play. Also in attendance were the actors Phylicia Rashad, Charles Dutton, and Ruben Santiago-Hudson, as well as others who performed in his plays. The eulogy was given by Marion McClinton, who had succeeded Lloyd Richards as director of Wilson's next two plays on Broadway. The Reverend Dwight Andrews, former music director at Yale

Repertory Theatre, officiated. Sala Udin, who served as master of ceremonies, reminisced about the times that he, August, and Rob Penny had frequented Pan Fried Fish, a restaurant a few doors from the Wylie Avenue jitney station that ultimately inspired *Jitney!*, the earliest play of the Pittsburgh Cycle to be staged.[1] Other speakers rounded out the service with personal tributes, musical renditions, and readings from Wilson's plays. The overall mood was joyous and celebratory. Wynton Marsalis closed the service by playing "Danny Boy," which brought tears to the eyes of many. Marsalis quickly transitioned to a joyous New Orleans–style closing, "When the Saints Go Marching In," which ended the service with a second line procession out of the hall.[2]

Approximately four hundred attended the service, a number that did not begin to fill the 2,300-seat auditorium. The relatively low turnout surprised the *Pittsburgh Post-Gazette*'s Barbara Cloud, who wondered whether many local white people stayed away because they were still smarting from August's accusatory Drue Heinz Lecture, although his plays continued drawing large audiences.[3] Brian Connelly at the *Post-Gazette* said that while Wilson admitted to a love/hate relationship with Pittsburgh, "if truth be told, a significant chunk of white Pittsburghers feel similarly about him." White people were unhappy, Connelly continued, because Wilson portrayed his hometown as "a hard and racist place," rather than "the friendly, hard-working place we like to be, with solid immigrant values and ethnic traditions."[4]

At the same time, Cloud estimated that white people made up about half of the attendees, which made her wonder how strongly Wilson's plays had connected with local Black people.[5] Indeed, many middle-class Black people felt that Wilson's plays focus too much on street life and far too often employ the N-word. Wilson had saved a letter to the editor from a Black reader in Roanoke, Virginia, who said he left *The Piano Lesson* at intermission, by which point he estimated he had heard the word *nigger* at least twenty times. The writer added, "I remember Stepin' Fetchit, Hattie McDaniel, Rochester. It wasn't funny then, and it's not funny now."[6] Lee Kiburi, a Pittsburgh friend of August, adds that grassroots Black people who have seen a Wilson play often are not impressed because Wilson captures Black dialect so well that they say, "Aw, I could write stuff like that. That ain't nothing."[7]

The low Black turnout may have been because, despite Wilson's fame among theatergoers, many ordinary folks simply had not heard of him. Theater critic Christopher Rawson has a simpler, more likely, explanation: that many Pittsburghers didn't know that the funeral was taking place and that it was open to the public. The first reason may have been an excuse, but the second was plausible, partly because the dominant daily paper, the *Post-Gazette*, had just one blurb about the funeral during the week. Also, Rawson, the paper's theater editor, was in Ireland October 2–9, leading the newspaper's annual week-long theater tour. He had written the paper's two-and-a-half-page obituary in advance; and when word of Wilson's death came, he answered copy editors' questions during an airport stopover. But there was nothing about the funeral in the obituary, and Rawson's usual theater columns didn't run that week, during which time he would have been writing extensively about the funeral and the theatrical stars who would be attending.[8] A friend who did attend said there were groups of people outside, watching arrivals, but never going in because they assumed it was private. Although relatively few Black people turned out for the funeral, Hill District residents clearly cared about their hometown hero.

On a cool, drizzly day similar to the one on which August was born, residents stood outside, lining the route of the funeral procession as it wound its way westward through the Hill before turning eastward out to the cemetery. August was buried later in a private service at Greenwood Cemetery, near the graves of his mother and grandmother.[9] Burial was followed by a special repast for relatives and close friends downtown at the Oyster House, for which August specified four bottles of Crown Royal whiskey for toasting.

August warmly remembered the Oyster House as the place where on Saturdays his father took him and his brother Edwin for fried fish. As a result, whenever August traveled to Pittsburgh, he made it a point to visit the restaurant. During those visits, owner Lou Grippo would regale him with stories of the Hill's past.[10] In the 1930s, Grippo's family delivered ice in the Hill, which gave him entree into all sorts of businesses. It also let him meet a cross-section of residents, including celebrities such as the actress Lena Horne and Gus Greenlee, owner of the Pittsburgh Crawfords baseball team.

August loved hearing stories about life in the Hill, as he had all the years he lived there. The Oyster House remained special to him. When Ed Bradley, host of the CBS show *60 Minutes*, traveled to Pittsburgh in 2002, August took him both to the Oyster House and to Hazelwood, where he had spent his teenage years.[11] Grippo was honored that August chose the Oyster House to serve a special meal for his closest friends.[12]

For days and months after the funeral, August's friends and acquaintances reminisced about times gone by. Thelma Smalls, who had waited tables at Eddie's Restaurant, took a reporter to the restaurant, which had been shuttered since Eddie's death in 2000. "August would come in," Smalls said, "and sit at the counter all day. . . . He was nice, but he was quiet . . . people thought he had issues because he carried all these papers around."[13]

Tributes poured in reflecting on the significance of Wilson and his unique body of work. Ben Brantley of *The New York Times* likened Wilson to other icons in the world of theater. He said that Wilson's dialogs come closer to the great William Shakespeare than those of any other playwright.[14] Charles Isherwood, also of the *Times*, congratulated Wilson for advancing the careers of a generation of Black actors.[15] Christopher Rawson of the *Pittsburgh Post-Gazette* thanked Wilson for breaking down racial barriers and dealing with universal conflicts that, despite the lack of white characters, could nonetheless appeal to white audiences. Indeed, Rawson added, the presence of universal human emotions in Wilson's plays accounts for much of their widespread appeal.[16]

Admirers sought ways to honor Wilson's legacy. Before he passed, he was told that New York's Virginia Theatre would be renamed the August Wilson Theatre, becoming the first Broadway playhouse named for an African American. Chicago and Seattle competed to be the first to stage *Radio Golf* in 2007 and in doing so become the first city to stage the entire Pittsburgh Cycle.[17] Seattle's Repertory Theatre held Wilson Festivals. Atlanta created an "August Wilson Monologue Competition."[18] Cities came up with so many ways to honor Wilson that Rawson said the year 2007 could well be labeled "August Wilson Year."[19]

Surprisingly, Pittsburgh initially lagged behind in finding a way to honor Wilson. The delay may have reflected a perception that Wilson had ambivalent feelings toward the city.[20] He regularly expressed a fondness for Pittsburgh, but while his will donated funds to such places as the Richard Hugo House in Seattle, the Playwrights' Center in Minneapolis/Saint Paul, the Congo Square Theatre Company in Chicago, and Cave Canem poets in New York, it made no comparable donation to a Pittsburgh arts organization.

Nonetheless, Pittsburgh theaters commemorated Wilson by staging a flurry of his plays. The Pittsburgh Public Theater put on *Gem of the Ocean*, accompanied by an exhibition of posters, playbills, photographs, and Wilson-related props. The Public Theater also held a lecture series, "Mondays with the Public," that featured the recollections of artists who had worked with Wilson.[21] The University of Pittsburgh's Kuntu Repertory Theatre performed *Seven Guitars*. The Cultural Trust brought in Charles Dutton to stage a series of monologues titled *Goodnight Mr. Wilson*.[22] Pittsburgh Playwrights continued to produce the August Wilson cycle. Carnegie Mellon University put on its first Wilson play, *The Piano Lesson*.[23] Some urged that CAPA, the Pittsburgh High School for the Creative and Performing Arts, be renamed in Wilson's honor.[24] Others suggested that Pittsburgh hold an annual August Wilson festival, similar to the Shaw Festival in Canada. Much more recognition did come, but later.

Despite the flurry of tributes, Rawson felt compelled to ask: Where is Pittsburgh's signature event honoring "its greatest literary figure"?[25] The Heinz Endowments responded by making a $200,000 grant, matched by a grant from the Pennsylvania Department of Community and Economic Development, to stabilize the New Granada Theater in the Hill, which was suffering from years of neglect. The Pittsburgh History and Landmarks Foundation, a historical preservation group, published a book, *August Wilson: Pittsburgh Places in His Life and Plays*, which provided a short biography of Wilson, a history of the Hill, and a guide to Wilson-related sites.[26]

In the end, one of the city's chief ways of honoring its native son turned out to be an African American cultural center that was still in the planning stages when Wilson died. Milton and Nancy Washington, two leading figures in the cultural life of Black Pittsburgh, had already begun fundraising for the center. Two of the city's main foundations—the Heinz Endowments and the Pittsburgh Foundation—along with Mayor Tom Murphy and the director of the city's Urban Redevelopment Authority, Mulugetta Birru, provided additional monies.[27] It was no small challenge to find a suitable site for the center. Pittsburgh is a city of neighborhoods, and neighborhood loyalties run deep. Emma Slaughter, a Homewood artist, had long sought to establish a cultural center in Homewood, arguing that any center honoring Wilson should be located in an African American neighborhood rather than downtown. Most, however, pushed to use Wilson's name to add a major, nationally known presence to the city's downtown Cultural District. The hope was that doing so would attract tourists and multiracial audiences.[28]

Allison G. Williams, a San Francisco–based African American architect, won the competition for the building's designer. Williams proposed the concept of a sail façade that recalls trading ships on the Swahili Coast of East Africa. The design was iconic and the scale impressive, encompassing some 65,000 square feet, with galleries, a 486-seat theater, and several multipurpose rooms. Missing, however, was the smaller theater that was part of the original plan.

A large, attractive building, the August Wilson Center reflected sponsors' determination, in the words of Sala Udin, to "go first-class." However, going first class is expensive. Construction costs spiraled from $33 million to $42 million, well beyond what the foundations, the city, county, state, and private contributors had pledged. Moreover, construction began just as the nation's economy entered the major economic downturn of 2008. Ultimately an $11 million loan from a bank consortium enabled the center to open, but burdened it with heavy debt.[29] However, on August 29, 2007, construction on the August Wilson Center for African American Culture was finally under way.[30]

In 2007 and 2008—before construction was completed—the August Wilson Center held a series of programs that paid tribute to its namesake. It sponsored "An Evening of Playwrights" as part of what it termed a "First Voice" festival.[31] It screened the documentary *August Wilson: The Ground on Which I Stand*.[32] And it presented an evening of playwrights inspired by Wilson as part of an ongoing series that brought in nationally known performers such as Phylicia Rashad and McKeesport/Homestead native Tamara Tunie. The center opened in 2009, just three months before the passing of Chawley Williams, August's old friend and fellow poet.[33]

After an initial burst of programming, low attendance caused the center to shift to national productions. Doing so put it in competition with already established venues. Management was another problem. The first two directors, Neil Barclay and Andre Kimo Stone Guess, were passionate about the arts but lacked deep experience in marketing and accounting. Financial backers worried when records were not transparent and audits were delayed. Matters came to a head in 2013, when the center could no longer make debt payments. Dollar Bank, which held the mortgage, sought to liquidate the property.[34] In 2014, after a tense, convoluted series of events, including an unceremonious sheriff's sale, three local foundations—the Heinz Endowments, R. K. Mellon, and the Pittsburgh Foundation—bought the center and pledged to preserve its mission while making sure that financial controls were in place.[35] The August Wilson Center reopened under management of the Pittsburgh Cultural Trust.[36]

The whole episode generated racial tensions that degenerated into open public spats. A typical example: "This is my tax money to support a single race. Isn't that racism?" A typical reply: "Public money goes to all sorts of things . . . that mostly white people use, and many black taxpayers pay into that public 'trough.'"[37]

The center continued to be dogged by minor controversies, including its name. The original name was the African American Cultural Center. In 2006, to recognize the death of August Wilson in 2005, his name was added. The resulting name was considered unwieldy and was changed to the August Wilson Cultural Center. Removing the words *African American* sparked additional protests, and so the name was changed to the August Wilson African American Cultural Center, its current name.[38] Today, under the leadership of Janis Burley

Wilson (no relation to August), the center has undergone a happy rejuvenation in both finances and programming, successfully hosting performances and exhibits of African American art of both local and national significance.

While most Pittsburghers focused on the August Wilson Center, a few argued that Wilson's childhood home was equally important. "With all due respect," said Christopher Rawson in 2016, "the August Wilson Center has no more to do with the life of August Wilson than other buildings do with the famous names they bear—the Kennedy Center, say, or Lincoln Center. In contrast, the August Wilson House is at the very heart of its namesake's remarkable life story."[39] Pointing out that visitors from far and wide come to see Wilson's house, Rawson became deeply involved in efforts to preserve it.

Saving the home had long been a family priority. The house adjoined two other properties that, taken together, reflected the Hill's early racial composition. Bella Siger, owner of Bella's Market, resided in the building directly in front of the Wilson/Kittel residence. Next door resided the Butera brothers, who ran a combination watch and shoe repair business from their house. The Sigers were Jewish and the Buteras Italian American, meaning the demographics around the Wilson residence—Black, Italian, and Jewish—perfectly matched the Hill District's dominant ethnic composition of Wilson's youth.

For years, the Wilson family had tried to purchase the three properties. Finally, in 2002 August and his nephew Paul Ellis bought the Butera home, but were unable to acquire Bella's Market and the original Wilson home.[40] However, one day in 2004, August's sister Freda encountered a realtor, who told her the Wilson house would soon be on the market. Freda notified her son, Paul, who moved quickly. On March 11, 2005, Paul purchased the property for $25,000.[41] Freda's children, Paul and Kimberly Ellis, wanted to turn the house into a combination cultural center and residence for visiting artists.[42] All three buildings, however, had badly deteriorated in ways that shocked visitors and raised questions about saving them. The Wilson residence had been unoccupied since the early 1960s, the Buteras's since 2002, and the Sigers's since sometime after that.[43] They all had become eyesores, with broken windows, leaking roofs, buckling walls, and a dangerously tilting chimney. Addicts and the homeless had begun setting up residence inside.

Paul worked to get the houses declared historic landmarks, knowing that such a designation would help in raising funds to restore them. On a beautiful, sunny day in May 2007, the state unveiled a marker declaring the Wilson home a historical landmark. Speakers at the ceremony included August's daughter Sakina Ansari as well as his close relatives Linda Jean, Edwin, Freda, Paul, and

Kimberly. However, the soaring language of the dedication ceremony contrasted with the deteriorated condition of the buildings. A local newspaper wrote:

> The red and maroon façade of the brick house is peeling. Its upper windows are broken. The grocery store that used to fill the first floor is closed. A trash-filled path leads to the back of the house where the Kittel family lived, their apartment's window now filled with gray concrete.[44]

August's nephew Paul worked on getting the house declared a local historic site. In 2008, after several procedural snafus, he succeeded. Two years later, Paul established the Daisy Wilson Artist Community (DWAC), a nonprofit dedicated to interpreting Wilson's literary legacy. The family now wanted the home to become a venue for staging plays, musical performances, community art and craft shows. The DWAC raised $130,000 from local foundations as well as from socially conscious individuals, including city councilman R. Daniel Lavelle and the honors class of Professor Evan Stoddard at Duquesne University.[45] To carry out the restoration, Paul worked with Jeff Slack, an experienced preservation planner with the architectural firm of Rob Pfaffman.[46] Fundraising was hampered because potential donors often confused the August Wilson House with the August Wilson Cultural Center. Over time, however, awareness was aided by national and even international attention. In 2014 the BBC produced a half-hour tribute to Wilson and sent the noted actor Lenny Henry to Pittsburgh to walk the streets and interview local scholars. In 2015 a ninety-minute documentary, *August Wilson: The Ground on Which I Stand*, sponsored by local PBS station WQED, was released as part of the *American Masters* television series.

By 2016, the Daisy Wilson Artist Community had enough money to begin rehabilitating all three homes. Unfortunately, restoration efforts came too late to save the Butera residence. Plans, however, continued to move forward on restoring the Wilson and Siger homesteads. In April, Pfaffman unveiled plans for re-creating the Wilson house as a community arts center, with the goal of restoring both it and the attached Siger home to how they would have looked in the 1950s.[47] This would fulfill what August had told Paul Ellis and Christopher Rawson: "Don't make it a museum—make it useful."

In 2016 preservation efforts began paying dividends. Local playwright Mark Clayton Southers and his Pittsburgh Playwrights Theater staged *Seven Guitars* in the backyard of the Wilson home, the very place where young Freddy Kittel had watched the card playing that later transpired in that play. Theater critics and local audiences raved about seeing the play in such a historic setting.[48] That same year, Denzel Washington traveled to Pittsburgh and made a feature movie of *Fences*, with him and Viola Davis leading the cast. Unfortunately, the Lower and Middle Hill had lost so much of their historic streetscape that filming had to take place in the Upper Hill and the West End.[49] Happily, the film opened to popular and critical acclaim, winning four Academy Award nominations, an Oscar for Davis, a Golden Globe Award, two Screen Actors Guild Awards, and the NAACP Image Award, in addition to others. In 2019 the feature movie of *Ma Rainey's Black Bottom* was filmed on the same Netflix contract.

In his famous speech, "The Ground on Which I Stand," Wilson had called for the strengthening of Black theater. The speech raised awareness of the problem but, according to knowledgeable observers, most Black theaters remain "the same or [less well] funded in comparison to their white peers than twenty years ago."[50]

Local Black theater continued to struggle. In 1992 New Horizon Theatre, the brainchild of Elva Branson, former director of Black Horizons, opened with a name that paid homage to the theater that, back in 1968, Wilson had cofounded. Hoping that New Horizon might nurture the next August Wilson, Elva recruited Rob Penny to chair the Advisory Board and Sala Udin and Joyce Meggerson-Moore to serve on the Board of Directors. Unlike Black Horizons, however, New Horizon was self-consciously not part of the Black Arts tradition. Rather, with Ernest McCarty as artistic director, it aimed to showcase drama that was cultural and artistic rather than explicitly political.[51]

The University of Pittsburgh's Kuntu Repertory Theatre had long carried the torch for Black theater in the city. However, in 2013, after a forty-year run, the theater's founder Vernell Lillie took her last bow and retired. Pittsburgh Playwrights, headed by Mark Clayton Southers, became the city's only venue explicitly dedicated to carrying Wilson's theatrical torch. In fact, in its first decade of existence, Southers's company performed all ten plays of the Pitts-burgh Cycle, and in 2015 began the cycle anew.[52]

Southers, born in 1961 and reared in the Hill, had studied at the Tuskegee Institute before taking jobs at the *Pittsburgh Courier* and US Steel.[53] In 1998, while still with the *Courier*, he attended a theater festival in Grahamstown (now Makhanda), South Africa, where Wilson happened to be giving a master class in playwriting. At the time, Southers was focused on poetry, and so took the opportunity to show Wilson some of his poems. He felt inspired when Wilson said he liked them.[54] The following summer, Southers deepened his ties when Wilson invited him to the Edward Albee Theater Conference in

Valdez, Alaska. Those two meetings motivated Southers to try his hand at playwriting. In December 2002, while still working at US Steel, he took over Penn Theater in Garfield and renamed it the Pittsburgh Playwrights Theatre Company (PPTC). Totally dedicated to the new endeavor, Southers funded the theater largely out of his own pocket.

PPTC then moved into a space over a parking garage across from the Pittsburgh Symphony Orchestra. In 2010 the company acquired its own venue, located across Liberty Avenue from the August Wilson Center. Presentations attracted sizable audiences as well as favorable reviews. Within a year, PPTC was commended by the *Pittsburgh Post-Gazette* for having "established itself as part of the community, drawing large audiences and good reviews."[55] With increased visibility, Southers got support from local foundations as well as from members of his board.

During this time, Pittsburgh produced a unique Wilsonian performer, Wali Jamal, whose performances of Wilson's plays placed him in the rarefied position of being the only actor to have performed all ten of the Cycle's plays, in addition to *How I Learned What I Learned*. The *Post-Gazette* named Jamal a "Wilsonian Warrior" and crowned him the 2018 Performer of the Year for his sterling interpretations of Wilson's works.[56] While still heading PPTC, Southers was asked by the August Wilson Center to head up its theatrical initiatives. Southers was happy to do so because he had recently quit his job at US Steel, unwilling to continue putting up with the racism he encountered there. Southers wanted to make the Wilson Center a place where people came to see a Wilson play, but the center's financial straits left little money for programming.[57] In an effort to keep Wilson's legacy alive, Southers served as a judge for the local August Wilson Monologue Contest and arranged to move his annual performance of Wilson's works to the backyard theater at the August Wilson House.

Flashing ahead to 2025, Pittsburgh has more than become the center of August Wilson studies. The August Wilson House (AWH) was rebuilt for $8 million, starting with a gift of $4.5 million arranged by Denzel Washington, who gave $1 million, as did Oprah Winfrey and Tyler Perry, followed by other cinematic friends. Pittsburgh foundations then followed suit. The AWH sponsors an annual block party, which has drawn crowds of thousands to enjoy performers, games, and vendors. The AWH backyard theater hosts an annual August Wilson play. In service to Wilson's directive that the AWH should be not a museum but "useful," its Art for August program pays local artists $1,000 each, three playwright Fellows have had substantial honoraria,

August in the Schools is developing precollegiate school curricula, and free writing workshops offer poetry, playwriting and creative non-fiction (free for adult students and with well-paid leaders).

And in *Artists Talk August*, thirty-six sessions of ninety-minute podcasts, the AWH has hosted national performers, including Eugene Lee, Montae Russell, Stephen McKinley Henderson, Phylicia Rashad, and Russell Hornsby; regional performers including Wali Jamal, Sala Udin, and Ben Cain; playwrights and directors Todd Kreidler, Ruben Santiago-Hudson, Kenny Leon, Eileen Morris, and Chuck Smith; and such other figures in the arts as David Gallo, George C. White, and Narda Alcorn.

Downtown, the August Wilson African American Cultural Center continues to house performances and exhibits of national scope. But in addition, under the leadership of Constanza Romero Wilson and Sandra Shannon—the latter an expert August Wilson scholar from Howard University—in 2022 it opened *August Wilson: The Writer's Landscape*, an ingenious, beautifully designed fourteen-space exhibit taking audiences through August's life and plays, with interactivity along the way, ending in opportunities to reflect and discuss. It's no surprise that the national August Wilson Society has made Pittsburgh a regular site for conferences. At the other end, CAPA has produced August Wilson plays with the N-words included.

Best of all, perhaps, is that the University of Pittsburgh's library fulfilled its great dream, welcoming the August Wilson Archive, a collection of some 450 boxes of papers and much else gathered by the playwright during a life in which he rarely threw anything away. This transfer was the result of collaboration between the Wilson estate and Kornelia Tancheva, head of the University Library System, who had the staff, plans, real estate, experience, and money to convince Constanza Wilson that Pittsburgh was the best site, compared to the University of Texas, Yale University, and other possible destinations. The rich resources of the archive are available to all—students, scholars, and tourists.

Add all that together—the August Wilson House, the August Wilson African American Cultural Center, the August Wilson Archive, two professional theaters doing his plays—and there is also the Hill District itself. That's where Wilson lived most of his first thirty-three years. It nurtured him, giving him the people, stories, and themes he transformed into his ten plays, plus the additional *How I Learned What I Learned*, an autobiographical prelude and postlude to the cycle. Pittsburgh, Wilson's *Post-Gazette* obituary said, "remained the deep well of memory into which he kept dipping the ladle of his art."

ACKNOWLEDGMENTS

Writing about August Wilson has been enormously satisfying.
Partly, this is because it brought me into contact with many of Wilson's
neighbors, relatives, colleagues, and friends. Numbering almost one hun-
dred individuals, these include Sakina A'la, Ruth Allen, Gail Austin, Natalie
Bazzell, Brenda Berrian, Shirley Biggs, Casey Bowser, Mary Bradley, Elva
Branson, John Brewer, Augustus Brown, Joann Brown, Angeline Burley,
Julia Burley, Brenda Burton Shakur, Johnny Butera, Moses Carper, Samuel
Clancy, Cheryl Fannion Cotton, Doris Cuddy, Ronald Davenport, Betty
Douglass, Herbert Douglas, Ervin Dyer, Maeve Eberhardt, Temujin
Ekunfeo, Freda Ellis, Lynn Ewari Ellis, Barbara Evans, Johannes Fest,
Michael Flournoy, Jeffrey Folino, Sandra Gould Ford, Anthony Fountain,
Daniel Gabriel, Henry Gaston, Betty Jean Goldblum, Tracy Goldblum,
Louis Grippo Sr., Louise Grundish, Nelson Harrison, Frank Hightower,
Earl Horsley, Reginald (Abdullah) Howze, William (Billy) Jackson, Wali
Jamal, Eugene Keil, Louis "Hop" Kendrick, Lee Kiburi, Douglass King,
John King, Anthony Kirven, Linda Jean Kittel, James Knapp, Valerie
Lawrence, Amos Lawson, Eugene Lee, Vernell Lillie, Lutual Love, Noel
McCarroll, Lacy McCoy, Willa Mae Montague Swan (Snook), Greg Mont-
gomery, Joyce Meggerson Moore, Thad Mosley, Nathan Oliver, Gwendolyn
Ormes, Kenneth Owens-El, Carlos Peterson, Ronald Pitts, Curtiss Porter,
Ralph Proctor, Jacqui Sholom Purdy, Christopher Rawson, Gerald (Jerry)
Rhodes, Edward Roberson, Gary Robinson, Betty Rogers, Rob Ruck, Mark
Southers, Marva Scott-Starks, Robert Louis Stevenson, Shelly Stevenson,
William Strickland, Sala Udin, Carver Waters, Troy West, Darzetta
Williams, Melvin Williams, Franki Williams, Barbara Wilson, S. K. Wood-
all, and Albert Zangrilli.

I want to single out a few with whom I spent considerable time and who
were exceptionally important to this book. Julia Burley was the key to unlock-
ing Wilson's childhood years on Bedford Avenue in the Hill. Aunt Julie, as
August called her, was Daisy's closest friend and knew August from the time
he was three years old.

Barbara Wilson, August's sister, was raised in New York by August's Aunt Faye. Over the course of this study, Barbara proved a friend and a steady source of comment, advice, and support.

Frank Hightower, the semiofficial photographer of Black Horizons Theater and a good friend of Wilson, furnished a number of photographic images of August, his friends, and colleagues.

Dr. Carmen DiCiccio, an indefatigable researcher, ferreted out much valuable information from a wide range of sources: city directories, manuscript censuses, deed books, marriage licenses, cemetery records, and many other sources.

Lee Kiburi, the publicity coordinator for Black Horizons Theatre, was both a friend of August and the organizer of an annual tribute to Malcolm X. In the 1960s, Kiburi had been a devoted follower of LeRoi Jones (later Amiri Baraka) as well as a member of the Congress of Afrikan Peoples (CAP), which had been founded in 1970 by Baraka and other Black leaders as the voice of Black cultural nationalism. In 1974, to the consternation of Kiburi and many others, Baraka made a sharp turn away from cultural nationalism. Baraka denounced Black nationalism and embraced Marxism, Socialism, and Mao Zedong thought. Shocked at this development, Kiburi launched an ambitious project chronicling the history of Black nationalism in Pittsburgh in an effort to gain perspective on how such a disheartening development came to pass. Over the next two or more decades, Kiburi interviewed many in the local Black Power movement as well as founder Amiri Baraka. Today, Kiburi's interviews and written material constitute what we have called the Kiburi Archive. It includes interviews of Sakina A'la, Amiri Baraka, Maisha Baton, Mary Bradley, Elva Branson, Moses Carper, Frank Hightower, Vernell Lillie, Curtiss Porter, Rob Penny, Ron Pitts, August Wilson, and Walter Worthington. Kiburi generously made these extraordinarily valuable interviews available to me—an example of "the power of friendship" that nicely complements "the power of place."

Finally, I want to acknowledge my good friend and theater critic Christopher Rawson. Not long after Wilson's passing, Rawson suggested that the two of us undertake a study of Wilson and his ties to Pittsburgh. In 2011, under the auspices of Pittsburgh History and Landmarks Foundation, we copublished a short study, *August Wilson: Pittsburgh Places in His Life and Plays.* But Rawson's busy schedule kept him from working on a planned full-scale biography. However, Rawson has always been encouraging and supportive of my efforts to complete our original task. For that, I am deeply grateful.

CHRONOLOGY

1940	Daisy Wilson (Freddy's mother) meets Fred (Fritz) Kittel (Freddy's father).
1941	Daisy moves into a two-room apartment located in the rear of 1727 Bedford Avenue.
1944	April 21, Charley Burley defeats Archie Moor, World Light-Heavyweight Champion.
1945	Frederick August Kittel, long known as Freddy Kittel and later as August Wilson, is born on April 27.
1949	Daisy teaches Freddy to read, and he obtains a library card.
1950	Freddy attends Letsche Kindergarten/Elementary School.
1951	Freddy attends St. Brigid Parochial School.
1952	Freddy attends Holy Trinity Parochial School.
1952	Louise and Hedley move out, giving Daisy access to two additional rooms.
1955	Freddy attends St. Richard Parochial School.
1956	Urban renewal razes much of Lower Hill District.
1958	David Bedford and the Wilsons move to 185 Flowers Avenue in Hazelwood. Following racial harassment, the family moves to 4378 Sylvan Avenue, across from Gladstone High School.
1959	Freddy wins a scholarship to Central Catholic High School in Oakland; he attends less than a full academic year.
1959	Freddy befriends Greg Montgomery.
1960	Freddy briefly enrolls at Connolley Vocational School in the Hill District.
1960–1961	Freddy attends the ninth grade in Hazelwood's Gladstone High School.
1961	In April, Freddy drops out of Gladstone High School while still in the ninth grade. In May, Daisy finds out that Freddy has not been attending school.
1961	Family moves into duplex at 617 North Murtland Street in Homewood.

1962	Freddy leaves home, joins the US Army for three years, and enrolls in the elite Army Airborne School on May 25.
1963	Freddy receives a general discharge from the US Army as Private Second Class on May 28. Goes to Los Angeles with Hazelwood friend Denny Hollis.
1964	Daisy Wilson and Fred Kittel marry secretly in Butler, PA, on May 1.
1965	With news of his father being near death, Freddy rushes home from California in March.
1965	Fred (Fritz) Kittel passes away on April 5. Freddy is called to identify the body and sign the death papers.
1965	Freddy takes an apartment in a rooming house at 85 Crawford Street (numbers have now changed). He declares himself a poet, buys a typewriter for twenty dollars, adopts August Wilson as a pen name, and sends off several poems to *Harper's Magazine*.
1965	Wilson discovers the blues via the Bessie Smith recording "Nobody in Town Can Bake a Sweet Jellyroll Like Mine."
1966	Halfway Art Gallery is created by the merger of the Hill Art & Music Society and a storefront ministry run by St. Stephen's Anglican Church of Sewickley.
1966	Wilson's first published poems appear in *Signal Magazine*, locally produced and circulated.
1967	Exhibition Catalogue of Halfway Art Gallery publishes Wilson's semiautobiographical poem "Poet." The catalogue also contains Rob Penny's "Doodle-Bug Poem," which introduces Amiri Baraka's nationalist ideology to Pittsburgh.
1968	The first issue of *Connection*, publication of the Centre Avenue Poets Theatre Workshop, is published. It contains Wilson's poem "For Malcolm X and Others," which was later reprinted in 1969 by *Negro Digest*.
1968	The Afro-American Institute (AAI) holds a commemoration of Malcolm X in February. Wilson hands out leaflets for the ceremony, delivers a stirring address, and first meets Amiri Baraka.
1968	Wilson encounters Franki Williams at the Malcolm X commemoration. The two begin dating.
1968	Martin Luther King Jr. is assassinated on April 4, provoking

	riots and fires that decimate the Centre Avenue retail corridor in the Hill.
1968	Wilson begins dating Brenda Burton in the spring.
1968	Wilson accompanies Brenda to New York University to help her get settled. Visits Aunt Fay and meets his sister Barbara.
1968	Post-riot edition of *Connection* takes on strong nationalist flavor.
1968	Wilson's poetry readings are increasingly rejected by public as not "Black" enough.
1968	Rob Penny and Wilson found Black Horizons Theatre, dedicated to promoting Black nationalism.
1969	Wilson angrily quits Black Horizons Theatre and returns to writing poetry.
1969	Wilson marries Brenda Burton in June.
1970	Wilson's daughter Sakina Ansari is born in January.
1971 or 1972	Wilson appointed supervisor of Black studies outreach program, Waumba.
1972	Claude Purdy arrives in Pittsburgh. His theatrical skills bring Wilson back to the world of theater.
1972	Wilson and family evicted from public housing in October for nonpayment of rent.
1973	Frustrated by Wilson's lack of income, Brenda sues for divorce in April.
1973	Wilson's breakthrough poem "Morning Statement," written in simple style, is published.
1973	Rob Penny and Wilson found Ujima Theatre in Hazelwood.
1973	Ujima Theatre stages Wilson play *Recycled*.
1974	Wilson replaces Claude Purdy and Elva Branson as director of Black Horizons Theatre
1976	Ujima Theatre stages Wilson's play *The Coldest Day of the Year.*
1976	Lillie's Kuntu Repertory Theatre stages Wilson's play *The Homecoming*
1977	While rehearsing Ed Bullins's play, *In New England Winter*, Wilson falls out with Vernell and vows to leave Pittsburgh.
1977	Purdy invites Wilson to come to Saint Paul and work together on revising *Black Bart and the Sacred Hills*.
1978	Wilson flies to Saint Paul to join Claude Purdy at Penumbra. Meets Judy Oliver.

1978	Wilson permanently relocates to Saint Paul on April 1.
1978	Wilson discovers *The Art of Romare Bearden: The Prevalence of Ritual.*
1979	Meets Dan Gabriel.
1979	Saint Paul's Penumbra Theatre holds stage reading of *Black Bart.*
1979	Wilson visits Pittsburgh and stops by his favorite jitney station. Writes *Jitney!*
1980	Writes poem "My Father" that signals reconciliation with his dad.
1980	Writes *Fullerton Street*, "Crossroads of the World," set in 1941.
1980	Submits *Fullerton Street* and *Jitney!* to the O'Neill Competition.
1981	Marries Judy Oliver on April 25; legally changes his name to August Wilson.
1981	*Black Bart* staging by Penumbra garners terrible reviews in Saint Paul in July.
1982	*Ma Rainey's Black Bottom* accepted for workshop at the National Playwright's Conference at the Eugene O'Neill Theater Center in July.
1982	*Jitney!* staged in Pittsburgh by Allegheny Repertory Theatre in November.
1983	Daisy Wilson dies of cancer on March 14.
1984	*Ma Rainey's Black Bottom* premieres at Yale Repertory Theatre and then opens on Broadway on October 11.
1985	Wilson writes *The Janitor*, a four-minute play.
1985	*Fences* premieres at Yale Repertory Theatre.
1986	Wilson reads poetry, including "The Founding of the Republic," at New York's 92nd Street Y on November 17.
1986	Reunion of Centre Avenue Poets Theater Workshop with Maisha Baton, Rob Penny, and others.
1987	*Fences* opens on Broadway at the 46th Street Theatre on March 26, wins Tony Award for Best Play and a Pulitzer Prize.
1987	Vernell Lillie's Kuntu Repertory Theatre stages *Ma Rainey's Black Bottom* in September.
1987	Wilson leaves Saint Paul for Seattle.
1988	Wilson delivers controversial lecture, "Blacks, Blues, and Cultural Imperialism," at Pittsburgh's Carnegie Music Hall on March 2.

1988	*Joe Turner's Come and Gone* opens at the Ethel Barrymore Theatre on Broadway on March 27.
1988	Carnegie Mellon University awards Wilson an honorary doctorate.
1988	Appears on Bill Moyers's *World of Ideas* on PBS.
1989	Pittsburgh Public Theater closes season with *Fences* and opens the next season with *Joe Turner's Come and Gone*. Wilson is honored by the mayor, by the local PBS station, and by the Carnegie Library of Pittsburgh. Named Pittsburgher of the Year for 1990 by *Pittsburgh Magazine*.
1990	*The Piano Lesson* opens on Broadway in April; wins Wilson his second Pulitzer Prize.
1990	Moves permanently to Seattle.
1991	Wilson recites poetry at the 92nd Street Y.
1991	*Three Plays by August Wilson* published by University of Pittsburgh Press.
1992	Wilson awarded an honorary doctorate by the University of Pittsburgh and is appointed to the Board of Trustees.
1992	*Two Trains Running* opens on Broadway.
1994	Marries Constanza Romero.
1995	Hallmark's TV version of *The Piano Lesson* occurs in February.
1996	*Seven Guitars* opens on Broadway on March 28.
1996	Wilson delivers famous address, "The Ground on Which I Stand," on June 26.
1996	Rewrites 1982 *Jitney* for professional premiere at Pittsburgh Public Theater.
1997	Public debate in New York City with prominent theater critic Robert Brustein, on February 4.
1997	Marion McClinton returns to direct *Seven Guitars* for Pittsburgh Public Theater in June.
1998	Old friends honor Wilson at a special event at Carnegie Lecture Hall in Pittsburgh on March 16.
1998	Teaches playwriting at Dartmouth College.
1998	Honored at the Edward Albee Theater Conference in Valdez, Alaska.
1999	Wilson returns to celebrate the centennial of the Carnegie Library of Pittsburgh's Hill District branch in March.

1999	Named top Pittsburgh cultural power broker by the *Pittsburgh Post-Gazette.*
1999	Pittsburgh Public Theater stages national premiere of *King Hedley II* on December 15, opening new O'Reilly Theater.
2000	Wilson delivers the Drue Heinz Lecture at Carnegie Music Hall on March 20.
2000	*Jitney* has its New York opening at off-Broadway's Second Stage Theatre on April 25.
2002	*Gem of the Ocean* premieres in Chicago.
2002	*Jitney* wins Olivier Award in London.
2003	Rob Penny's funeral takes place on March 16.
2003	*How I Learned What I Learned* premieres in Seattle in May.
2003	*Ma Rainey's Black Bottom* revived on Broadway with Charles Dutton and Whoopi Goldberg.
2003	Teresa Heinz presents Wilson the $250,000 Drue Heinz Literature Prize in December.
2003	Wilson reads poetry at the 92nd Street Y on December 3.
2004	*Gem of the Ocean* opens at the Walter Kerr Theatre on December 6.
2005	Paul Ellis, Wilson's nephew, purchases Wilson's childhood home, on March 11.
2005	American Century Cycle (Pittsburgh Cycle) completed as tenth play, *Radio Golf,* premieres at Yale Repertory Theatre.
2005	Wilson diagnosed with advanced liver cancer in June.
2005	Pittsburgh theater critic Christopher Rawson publicly announces Wilson's illness on August 26.
2005	Wilson passes away at Seattle's Swedish Medical Center on October 2.
2005	New York's Virginia Theatre is renamed the August Wilson Theatre on October 16.
2005	August Wilson viewing at White Memorial Chapel in Point Breeze occurs on October 7.
2005	Last rites held at Soldiers and Sailors Memorial Hall in Oakland neighborhood on October 8.
2005	Broadway theater named for August Wilson.
2005	Suzan-Lori Parks publishes final interview of Wilson in November.

2006	Groundbreaking ceremony for the August Wilson Center for African American Culture.
2007	*Radio Golf* opens at New York's Cort Theatre on May 8.
2009	August Wilson African American Cultural Center opens.
2016	Directed by Denzel Washington and filmed in Pittsburgh, the movie *Fences* opens.
2017	At last *Jitney* appears on Broadway, directed by Ruben Santiago-Hudson.
2020	Directed by George Wolfe and filmed in Pittsburgh, the movie *Ma Rainey's Black Bottom* opens.
2021	United States Postal Service issues August Wilson stamp.
2023	August Wilson House, his childhood home at 1727 Bedford Avenue, opens to the public. Chief sponsorship by Denzel Washington.
2024	Directed by Malcolm Washington (but filmed in Atlanta), *The Piano Lesson* movie opens.

NOTES

Introduction: The Power of Place

1. Hilary DeVries, "A Street-Corner Scribe of Life in Black America," *Christian Science Monitor*, March 27, 1987.

2. See Shannon, *Dramatic Vision of August Wilson*, 7.

3. At the time of this writing, a search of WorldCat turns up over 2,700 books, articles, dissertations, and videos about Wilson's literary output. A similar search on ProQuest turns up over 40,000 results, mainly newspaper articles and reviews.

4. There is also the awkward way the Hartigan biography began. Originally, it was announced as an authorized biography, a joint project of Hartigan and Constanza Romero Wilson, August's widow. Constanza called a number of August's friends and collaborators in Pittsburgh and the national theater community, asking them to provide Hartigan with help. Some did, at some length, when suddenly calls came from Constanza asking them to stop. The collaboration had broken down. Hartigan was writing alone, and Constanza was holding back papers and information she had for a future authorized biography. The result was that when Hartigan contacted many who were close to Wilson, they refused to talk.

5. Glasco, *WPA History of the Negro in Pittsburgh*, 90–91, 170.

6. For more on Black life in the Shenandoah Valley, see Click, "Slavery and Society in the Shenandoah Valley of Virginia," esp. 33–42. See also Noyalas, *Slavery and Freedom in the Shenandoah Valley*; Koons and Hofstra, *After the Backcountry*.

7. Laurence Glasco, "High Culture in Black America: Pittsburgh, Pennsylvania, 1900–1920," unpublished MS in possession of the author.

8. H. M. Phelps, "Seventh Ward," *Pittsburgh Leader*, November 19, 1905.

9. H. M. Phelps, "Stormy Fifth," *Pittsburgh Leader*, November 5, 1905.

10. H. M. Phelps, "Stormy Fifth," *Pittsburgh Leader*, November 5, 1905.

11. Pittler, "Hill District of Pittsburgh," 23.

12. However, because white people resisted having their children instructed by Black people, desegregation came at the cost of no Black teachers. For examples of the often-harmonious relations between Black people and Jews in Pittsburgh, see Burstin, *Steel City Jews*.

13. Harper, "'Crossroads of the World'"; White, "It Was All a Dream"; Ruck, *Sandlot Seasons*; Buni, *Robert L. Vann of the Pittsburgh Courier*.

14. Glasco, *WPA History of the Negro in Pittsburgh*, 26.

15. "Hundreds of Citizens Seek Bedford Site Homes: Public Response Pleases Hovde," *Pittsburgh Courier*, December 9, 1939, 3.

16. Livingston, "Cool August," in Bryer and Hartig, *Conversations with August Wilson*, 41–42. One time in 1998 while I was visiting in the neighborhood, Charley Hays, an African American longtime resident, extolled the neighborhood: "We didn't have to worry about crime or lock doors," she said. "[It was] one big happy family. I enjoyed my childhood here." Hays, like Wilson, fondly recalled how neighbors would sit on their front stoops, talking and socializing.

In a conversation with Johnny Butera, she spoke fondly of the days when Johnny's father Frank ran a shoe repair shop in the same location, and his mother Antonia worked as a dressmaker.

17. Allen, *Your House of Beauty.*

18. It also was the subject of a major scholarly study by Mindy Thompson Fullilove, *Root Shock.*

19. Calculated from listings in city directories.

20. Ben Brantley, "The World That Created August Wilson," *New York Times*, February 5, 1995.

21. Greg Mims, "Part II: "The Summer of '73: 'Hot' Or 'Cold,'" *Pittsburgh Courier*, July 14, 1973, 1, 5.

22. Gary Rotstein and Tom Barnes, "Rebuilding the Hill," *Pittsburgh Post-Gazette*, December 12, 1993, 1, 6.

23. Effort, "Pittsburgh Profiles."

24. Effort, "Pittsburgh Profiles."

Chapter 1. From Plumtree to Pittsburgh

1. Birth Certificate, Frederick August Kittel, Magee Women's Hospital.

2. Lahr, "Been Here and Gone," 15. The quote is from Donna, the third-born girl.

3. *Seven Guitars*, quoted in Snodgrass, *August Wilson*, 6.

4. Birthdate taken from Daisy Wilson's marriage license, Butler, PA, April 17, 1964. Zonia's first child was Vada. Also known as Nevada, she changed her name to Faye and spent most of her life in New York City.

5. These were "Winter People," released in 1989, and "The Legacy of a Whitetail Deer Hunter," released in 2018.

6. Cooper, *History of Avery County, North Carolina*, 33, 50.

7. The 1850 US Census shows that the states of the Upper South (Virginia, Delaware, Maryland, the District of Columbia, Kentucky, Missouri, Tennessee, and North Carolina) contained two thirds of all mixed-race people in the South. See Williamson, *New People*, 25; Berry, *Almost White*. Anthropologists have long been interested in the Melungeons. See, for example, Schrift, *Becoming Melungeon*; Price, "Melungeons," 256–71; Pollitzer et al., "Survey of Demography, Anthropometry, and Genetics," 388–400.

8. In 1920 Avery County had 10,335 residents. Plumtree had 379. There were moderate class differences along color lines. Mixed-race families included six farmers, one farmhand, seven miners, and one teacher. Of the Black families, two were miners and one (the Cutlers) were farmhands. Zonia grew up in the post office of Plumtree, located in Toe River Township. We know relatively little of Daisy's mother, Zonia, who sometimes appears in records as Zona or Arizona. The 1910 US Census gives Zonia's year of birth as 1901; Zonia's cemetery marker in Pittsburgh gives her year of birth as 1896. In the 1920 US Census, she is listed as a twenty-year-old living with her mother Ella Cutler, her brother Walter, her one-year-old daughter Vada, and two of her mother's grandchildren, possibly the offspring of Walter. Daisy did not resemble Vada, Zonia's first child, who was born in 1917. Daisy did, however, resemble Detroit, Zonia's third-born child. Known as Ray, he was born in 1923 and was light-skinned enough that later he passed as white.

There is no listing for Daisy because the census was taken in January, some two months before Daisy's birth. Avery birth records give Daisy's name as "Daisy Z. Cutler." Zonia had a son, Detroit, born in 1922. See Index to Vital Statistics, Avery County, Births, Toe River Township.

The family was impoverished, as were most families in Avery County. Ella was a widow, which suggest that the six members of the household subsisted on the earnings of Walter, a farmhand. No one in the family could read or write; none of the children attended school. The 1910 census for Toe River Township lists Zonia as the nine-year-old daughter of Ella Cutler, a recently widowed, forty-five-year-old farm laborer. Zonia's fourteen-year-old sister, Gerry, and her twelve-year-old brother, Walter, also did farm labor. Her oldest brother Henry was a twenty-five-year-old widower who worked in the mica mines, and her eighteen-year-old sister Dovie did "odd jobs." In fact, everyone in the Cutler household worked, except nine-year-old Zonia and her three-year-old niece Maude.

9. Julia Burley, interview by the author, May 30, 2012; Application for Marriage License of Daisy Wilson and Fred A. Kittel, May 1, 1964, Butler, PA.

10. Cooper, *History of Avery County, North Carolina*, 51. By the 1950s, mica had been largely "mined out" of Avery County. See Clemons, *View from My Porch*, 52. Clemons married Friel's younger brother, Ivor. Her book provides an informative history of the Tar Heel Mica Company. See also Hardy, *Remembering Avery County*, 39–41; "Centennial Spotlight." In the 1890s, Avery County was the world center of mica production, and had its product showcased at the 1892 Vienna World's Fair.

11. Freda Ellis, interview by the author, May 2008.

12. Ray later married a white woman and "passed" as a Mexican. Freda Ellis, conversation with the author, May 13, 2008.

13. Zonia and Bynum married in 1928 in Carter County, Tennessee, about sixty miles west of Plumtree and a pass-through station for trains bearing mica ore from Avery. Zonia had two children with Bynum: John D., born in 1932, and Franklin, born in 1933. Presumably, Zonia left Daisy and the other children with relatives, for they were not with her in West Virginia. Bynum had been married to Mary Avalonia Young and, between 1916 and 1927, the couple had five children. According to Bynum's grandson, around 1929, Bynum "went up into the mountains to seek work and [was] never heard from . . . again." Bynum's World War I draft registration card of 1917 says he was married at the time and had a child. Mary Avalonia Young was born in 1898 and died in 1992. Their children were Roy (1916–1969), Everette (1918–2002), Earnest (1920–2003), Lucille (1924–1967), Clintress (1925–1968), and William G. (1927–). Kanzada McCombs, communication to "The Wilson Group and Related Surnames" Facebook group. Renee Wilson Gray is the Wilson family's unofficial historian. See also 1930 manuscript federal census of Rock, West Virginia. Marriage License of Bynum Wilson and Zona Cutler, July 9, 1928, for Carter, Tennessee. That Bynum was the father is suggested by the boys' birth dates and the fact that they had the same dark complexion.

14. The entire family, consisting of Bynum, Zonia, and four children—seventeen-year-old Vada (later known as Faye), fourteen-year-old Daisy, eleven-year-old Detroit, two-year-old John D., and newborn Franklin—all crowded into Arthur's car for the long drive back to Pittsburgh. These were the children of Bynum and Zona as listed in the 1940 US Census. Zona's firstborn child, Vida (or Vada, for Nevada) is not with them. Daisy's daughter, Barbara Wilson, who was raised by Vada, says that her stepmother changed her name to Faye and lived in New York. Another child, George, was born two years later. A persistent myth says August's grandmother Zonia walked from Spear to Pittsburgh, a highly improbable journey over rugged mountains with few Black families to take her in and help her on the march. In a conversation with the author, Daisy's oldest child, Freda, confirmed that the family was driven to Pittsburgh.

15. The 1923 Pittsburgh City Directory lists Arthur Wilson as a laborer. He and Minerva

lived at 2324 Fifth Avenue. The family resided variously on Logan, Sinaloa, Clark, and Fernando Streets.

16. Bynum continued to suffer long periods of unemployment. In 1939 he worked only twenty-six weeks and earned a total of $360, the equivalent of about $6,500 today. Based on City Directory records and the 1940 manuscript census.

17. Pittsburgh City Directory, 1940. Zonia's forty-four-year-old brother, Arthur Wilson (the one who drove the family to Pittsburgh), his wife Nerva, and an adopted daughter Aileen Avery shared the house at 1202 Clark Street. Arthur worked as a hotel porter, for which he earned $520 the past year while working fifty-two weeks. See 1940 Census, Ward 3, E.D. 69-33, sheet 13-A. Freda, Daisy's eldest child, says Daisy supported herself working as a janitor in downtown office buildings. See Elkins, "Wilson, August."

18. Lahr, "Been Here and Gone." The information seems to have come from daughter Linda Jean. The reference is to Daisy's grandmother, but probably it was Daisy's mother (Zonia) rather than her "grandmother."

19. Emil J. Kittel (Emil's grandson) and his wife, Melodye Kittel, interview by Johannes Fest, April 25, 2012, Bethesda, OH.

20. Fest visited Teplitz/Teplice to research the Kittel family background.

21. Fred's name of Friedrich Augustus is that of Friedrich Augustus, referred to as Augustus der Starke, or Augustus the Strong.

22. Emil J. Kittel and Melodye Kittel, interview by Johannes Fest, April 25, 2012.

23. The US Army has no record of Fred Kittel being in active service. Aaron McWilliams (reference archivist, Pennsylvania State Archives), communication, November 5, 2012. Based on a review of the Records of the Department of Military and Veterans Affairs (RG-19), Adjutant General, World War I Veterans Service and Compensation File [for Pennsylvania], McWilliams reports that "no record was found for a Frederick August Kittel/Kittle/Kitel."

24. Freda Wilson, personal communication to the author, April 10, 2012.

25. About all we know of Jennie is that in 1927, according to the city directory, she worked as a cook in the Webster Hall Coffee Shop in the city's Oakland neighborhood.

26. City directories show that Fred and Jennie lived in several places, including in 1923 at 491 Norton Street in the old German neighborhood of Mount Washington, a German neighborhood on Pittsburgh's South Side. They purchased an empty lot in Overbrook at 1004 Stewart Avenue on May 30, 1924, from Earl W. Weyman. See Allegheny County Mortgage and Deed Office, Deed Book, vol. 2208, 256. Sometime later, Fred erected a house on the lot. Today the lot is located in the city of Pittsburgh's 32nd Ward.

27. These absences are quite different from Fred's brothers, who appear regularly in the city directories. In 1945 Fred shows up again in the city directory living with his brother Rudolph, who also was a baker, and continued living with Rudolph until 1950. It is not clear what became of Jennie during these years, although it is possible that both were living with Rudolph. Fred was not destitute, however, for in 1954 he purchased an additional piece of property near his home in Overbrook. Fred's brother Emil also was a baker. Emil appears to have done well in the 1920s and early 1930s, but then hit on hard times. During the 1920s, Emil and his wife Anna lived at various locations on the North Side, but then moved to the South Hills, residing at 2515 Kingwood Street, just off Library Road, before buying a house in Overbrook (today Brentwood) in 1926. They purchased a one-and-a-half-story house on an acre of land, just behind Fred and Jennie's home on Stewart Avenue. In 1930 and 1931 Emil bought two additional properties, both in the North Hills. One was in West View and the other near North

Park. Family lore says Emil had a bakery in Squirrel Hill, but in 1935 left the baking trade as well as Pittsburgh, settling in Ohio and working at Wheeling Steel in West Virginia. In 1940 Emil sold his Overbrook house to Fred.

The third brother, Rudolph, also worked as a baker. Rudolph had the steadiest life and work pattern of the three, appearing regularly in the city directories and residing at the same few residences. He first appears in the city directories in 1926, living in Hazelwood and working as a cook downtown at the city's premiere hotel, the William Penn. In 1929 and 1930 he worked as a baker for the Keystone Athletic Club, living first at 3940 Coleman in Squirrel Hill and then in the Englert Hotel in Overbrook. In 1934 Rudolph and his wife Helen moved to 201 Glad Avenue, near the South Side Cemetery in Carrick, a neighborhood next to Overbrook, not very far from where Fred and Emil lived. In 1940 Rudolph bought a house at 1518 Celtic Street in Carrick, and lived there until 1950, when he and his family moved nearby to 214 Quincy Street in Mt. Oliver, where they resided until 1973. Information gleaned from city directories and deed books.

28. Julia Burley, interview by the author, July 30, 2012. Julia says Freda was born while Daisy was living on Clark Street, but the city directory lists a nearby street, Townsend, as her residence.

29. National Register of Historic Places Registration Form, National Park Service Certification, August Wilson House, 1727 Bedford Avenue, March 22, 2013, 5–8.

30. Barbara Wilson, interview by the author, April 28, 2013.

31. Barbara Wilson, interview by the author, April 28, 2013. Barbara says Freddy told her that Floyd "Schoolboy" Barton, the protagonist of *Seven Guitars*, was named in honor of her father.

32. Probably unknown to Daisy, 1727 Bedford Rear had originally been the residence of Reverend Calvin Sackett, a white Baptist minister who opposed slavery and once served as principal of Miller, the city's first "colored school."

33. Measurements by architect Pfaffman and Associates, "August Wilson House: A Project for the Daisy Wilson Artists Community, Inc., Phase 1, Schematic Design," June 17, 2016. The actual measurements were 11 feet 4 inches × 11 feet 4 inches and 11 feet 4 inches × 13 feet 4 inches. Both rooms were 8 feet 3 inches high.

34. Julia Burley, interview by the author, June 17, 2012.

35. Based on interviews with Freda and architect's report seeking national historical status for the house.

36. Historical factors underlay the street's racial geography. Italian and Syrian immigrants had come to Pittsburgh in the early twentieth century, settling around Bedford Avenue near the Pennsylvania Railroad station, located close to downtown. As they moved up economically, they moved out into nicer housing around where the Wilsons resided. Jews, who constituted the Hill's largest ethnic group, arrived about the same time as the Syrians, but settled largely in the southern portion of the Hill, also close to downtown. As their conditions improved, they too began moving out, with some settling on Bedford Avenue east of Crawford Street. African Americans had a different experience. Those who migrated to Pittsburgh in the nineteenth century settled in the Lower Hill near downtown, but the larger number, who came during and after World War I, settled farther away from downtown. Johnny Butera, interview by the author, August 25, 2000. Six or so blocks up the street, the racial composition was quite different. That area was anchored by Bedford Dwellings, a large public housing complex almost entirely African American in composition. August grew up in the racial transition zone between the two.

37. Based on an examination of the 1940 manuscript census.

38. Freda Ellis, interview by Lisa Hazirjian, January 21, 2008 (Property of CAUSE: Center for Africanamerican Urban Studies and the Economy, Professor Joe Trotter, director, Carnegie-Mellon University); Freda Ellis, interview by the author, May 2008.

39. Julia Burley, interview by the author, September 24, 2012.

40. Johnny Butera, interview by the author, August 25, 2000.

41. Glasco and Rawson, *August Wilson*, says that "Doc Goldblum" in Wilson's plays references his neighbor and dermatologist, Dr. Raymond Goldblum. In fact, the character references Dr. Albert Goldblum, a general practitioner and older brother of Raymond. Dr. Orin Goldblum (son of Albert), email message to the author, February 1, 2021.

42. "Charley Burley," *Wikipedia*, https://en.wikipedia.org/wiki/Charley_Burley.

43. Julia Burley, interview by the author, May 26, 2012; Julia Burley, interview by the author, May 27, 2012.

44. Julia Burley, interview by the author, May 26, 2015.

45. Freda Ellis, email message to the author, September 10, 2012

46. Feingold, "August Wilson's Bottomless Blackness," 13; Moyers, "August Wilson," 72.

47. Chris Rawson, "In the Wings: Sunday Doubleheader—August Wilson on TV," *Pittsburgh Post-Gazette*, January 25, 2002; Lou Grippo, interview by the author, August 14, 2013.

48. Lahr, "Been Here and Gone," 102.

49. Lahr, "Been Here and Gone," 16.

50. Julia Burley, interview by the author, July 30, 2012.

51. Julia Burley, interview by the author, July 30, 2012.

52. Julia Burley, interview by the author, May 30, 2012.

53. Julia Burley, interview by the author, May 30, 2012.

54. Julia Burley, interview by the author, October 9, 2012.

55. Emil J. Kittel and Melodye Kittel, interview by Fest, April 25, 2012.

56. Doris Cuddy, interview by the author, October 8, 2012. Extensive searching has produced no indication of what became of "Fred Kittel Jr."

57. Lahr, "Been Here and Gone," 35.

58. Lahr, "Been Here and Gone," 16.

59. Julia Burley, interview by the author, October 29, 2012.

60. Julia Burley, interview by the author, July 30, 2012.

61. Julia Burley, interview by the author, May 26, 27, and 30, 2012; July 25 and 30, 2012; September 23, 2012.

62. Julia Burley, interview by the author, July 30, 2012; Lahr, "Been Here and Gone," 17.

63. Dubner, "August Wilson, R.I.P."

64. Dubner, "August Wilson, R.I.P."

65. Dubner, "August Wilson, R.I.P."

66. Dubner, "August Wilson, R.I.P."

67. Julia Burley, interview by the author, May 26, 2012.

68. Julia Burley, miscellaneous conversations.

69. Today, the institution's large physical plant is still operated by Catholic Charities, but now as Saint Joseph's House of Hospitality for unhoused men.

Chapter 2. Bedford Avenue Outsider

1. Livingston, "Cool August," in Bryer and Hartig, *Conversations with August Wilson*, 41–42. One time in 1998, while the author was visiting in the neighborhood, Charley Hays, an Afri-

can American longtime resident, extolled the neighborhood: "We didn't have to worry about crime or lock doors," she said. "[It was] one big happy family. I enjoyed my childhood here." Hays, like Wilson, fondly recalled how neighbors would sit on their front stoops, talking and socializing. In a conversation with Johnny Butera, she spoke fondly of the days when Johnny's father Frank ran a shoe repair shop in the same location, and his mother Antonia worked as a dressmaker. Johnny had two older brothers, Frank and Louis, and a sister, Rose.

2. Parks, "Light in August Wilson."

3. Julia Burley, interview by the author, May 30, 2012.

4. Rob Pfaffman, architects, draft of application to the US Department of the Interior, National Park Service, Registration Form for the National Register of Historic Places, 2012.

5. Julia Burley, interview by the author, May 26, 2012.

6. Julia Burley, interview by the author, September 24, 2012; May 26, 2012; May 27, 2012.

7. Julia Burley, interview by the author, June 17, 2012.

8. Julia Burley, interview by the author, July 30, 2012.

9. Julia Burley, interview by the author, May 26, 2012.

10. Julia Burley, interview by the author, July 25, 2012; May 27, 2012.

11. Julia Burley, interview by the author, May 27, 2012.

12. Julia Burley, interview by the author, May 30, 2012.

13. Christopher Reynolds, "Mr. Wilson's Neighborhood," *Los Angeles Times*, July 27, 2003.

14. Jerry Rhodes, interview by the author, January 17, 2016.

15. Glasco and Rawson, *August Wilson*, 7; Lahr, "Been Here and Gone," 34. Fitzgerald, "August Wilson," 14; Snodgrass, *August Wilson*, 6.

16. Samuel Freedman, "A Voice from the Streets," *New York Times*, March 15, 1987, A36.

17. Freedman, "Voice from the Streets."

18. Christopher Rawson, "August Wilson, 1945–2005; Pittsburgh Playwright Who Chronicled Black Experience, Pulitzer Prize–Winner Succumbs to Liver Cancer at 60 in Seattle, 'Surrounded by His Loved Ones,'" *Pittsburgh Post-Gazette*, October 3, 2005, A1; Brown, "Light in August," 120. See also Lahr, "Been Here and Gone," 35.

19. Lahr, "Been Here and Gone," 16.

20. Julia Burley, interview by the author, May 30, 2012.

21. Livingston, "Cool August," 25–32.

22. Julia Burley, interview by the author, May 30, 2012.

23. Julia Burley, interview by the author, July 25, 2012. See also Livingston, "Cool August," 39. Julia Burley, interview by the author, October 29, 2012; Lahr, "Been Here and Gone."

24. Lahr, "Been Here and Gone," 17; Julia Burley, interview by the author, May 27, 2012; May 30, 2012.

25. Julia Burley, personal communication to the author, n.d.

26. Moyers, "August Wilson," 72.

27. Wilson, "Ground on Which I Stand."

28. Julia Burley, interview by the author, October 3, 2012.

29. Julia Burley, interview by the author, October 29, 2012.

30. Julia Burley, interview by the author, October 3, 2012.

31. Livingston, "Cool August," 49.

32. Joe Brown, "Staging the Black Experience; Playwright August Wilson and the Persistence of Vision," *Washington Post*, October 4, 1987, F1.

33. Livingston, "Cool August," 48.

34. Julia Burley, interview by the author, July 25, 2012. See also Livingston, "Cool August," 39. Julia Burley, interview by the author, October 29, 2012; Lahr, "Been Here and Gone," 36.

35. Julia Burley, personal communication with the author, n.d.

36. Julia Burley, personal communication with the author, n.d.

37. Lahr, "Been Here and Gone," 17.

38. Linda Jean Kittel, interview by the author, ca. 2001.

39. Johnny Butera, interview by the author, August 25, 2000.

40. Melvin Williams, telephone conversation, July 20, 2019. Williams did well, going on to become a professor of anthropology at the University of Pittsburgh and, later, at the University of Michigan.

41. Jamal, "Union Edge," February 18, 2017. On color-based discrimination, called "colorism," see Russel, Wilson, and Hall, *Color Complex*; Goldsmith, Hamilton, and Darity, "Shades of Discrimination," 242–45; Hunter, "'If You're Light You're Alright,'" 175–93; Keith and Herring, "Skin Tone and Stratification in the Black Community," 760–78.

42. Sister Angelica Little, "Operation Hill District, 1942–1950," Archives of the Sisters of Charity of Seton Hill, Greensburg, PA. The materials, including school records and baptisms, were located by archivist Casey Bowser, July 22, 2019. The 1948 report says that Sarah Degree had converted to Catholicism in 1948. Sarah was the daughter of Sarah Bowden and Joseph Taylor. Born in 1902, she was about fifty years old and lived on Heldman Street. Telephone conversation with Bowser, July 19, 2019.

43. Livingston, "Cool August," 46.

44. Livingston, "Cool August," 45.

45. Church records show that in 1954 Freda, Donna, Linda Jean, and Daisy were baptized in St. Brigid and confirmed in 1955. Freddy underwent confirmation in 1957. Archives of the Sisters of Charity of Seton Hill. Freddy attended to St. Brigid but technically he belonged to St. Benedict the Moor, because that was a Black parish. All Black people were considered members of St. Benedict, regardless of what church they actually attended. He describes St. Benedict as a "tiny, tiny church that does not look too much different than a garage—a two-story garage—because they did have steps going down. See Livingston, "Cool August," 45–46.

46. We know Freddy attended kindergarten at to St. Brigid from the class report of a kindergarten teacher there. Telephone conversation with Casey Bowers, archivist for the Archives of the Sisters of Charity of Seton Hill, July 19, 2019. See also school records of Divine Providence Villa, Central Catholic, in possession of Christopher Rawson.

47. Catechism Roll Book, n.d., courtesy of Casey Bowser and Sr. Louise Grundish, Archives of the Sisters of Charity of Seton Hill.

48. "Analytical Survey of St. Brigid's Parish," ca. 1955, Archives of the Sisters of Charity of Seton Hill.

49. Telephone conversation with Casey Bowser, July 17, 2019.

50. Telephone conversation with Casey Bowser, July 17, 2019.

51. St. Brigid was demolished in 1962. Sala Udin says he met Wilson in 1952, when both were students at Holy Trinity parochial school. Sala Udin, "Growing Up with August," xvii. See also Sala Udin, email message to the author, June 20, 2016; Livingston, "Cool August," 45–46.

52. Glasco and Rawson, *August Wilson*.

53. Grades uncovered by Christopher Rawson and generously made available to me.

54. Udin, "Growing Up with August," xvii.

55. Snodgrass, *August Wilson*, 6. Sala had transferred to St. Richard in 1953 when his family

relocated to Bedford Dwellings public housing complex because of redevelopment. Udin, email message to the author, July 16, 2014.

56. Lyons, "Interview with August Wilson," 207.

57. Lahr, "Been Here and Gone," 16.

58. Brown, "Light in August."

59. Brown, "Light in August," 120.

60. Tony Kirven, interview by the author, April 1, 2016.

61. Tony Kirven, interview by the author, April 1, 2016.

62. Based on interviews with two students at St. Richard: Tony Kirven and Sala Udin.

63. Livingston, "Cool August," 25–32.

64. Tony Kirven, interview by the author, April 25, 2016.

65. Transcript, Central Catholic High School; Samuel G. Freedman, "August Wilson and the Jews," *Jerusalem Post*, October 26, 2005, 15.

66. Tony Kirven, interview by the author, April 1, 2016.

67. Lahr, "Been Here and Gone," 16.

68. Feingold, "August Wilson's Bottomless Blackness," 13.

69. Tony Kirven, interview by the author, April 1, 2016.

70. Julia Burley, interview by the author, July 25, 2012

71. Sala Udin, email message to the author, June 20, 2016.

72. Tony Kirven, interview by the author, April 1, 2016.

73. Tony Kirven, interview by the author, April 1, 2016.

74. Reginald Howze, interview by the author, July 24, 2017.

75. Tony Kirven, interview by the author, April 1, 2016.

76. Tony Kirven, interview by the author, April 1, 2016.

77. Tony Kirven, interview by the author, April 25, 2016.

78. Tony Kirven, interview by the author, April 25, 2016.

79. Tony Kirven, interview by the author, April 25, 2016.

80. See Frazier, *Black Bourgeoisie*. In 1967, in the case *Loving v. Virginia*, the US Supreme Court outlawed prohibitions on interracial marriage. Of course, public attitudes were such that for a long time it remained a rarity. Also see Sollors, *Interracialism*.

81. Tony Kirven, interview by the author, April 1, 2016.

82. Tony Kirven, interview by the author, April 1, 2016.

83. Tony Kirven, interview by the author, April 1, 2016.

84. Ramit Plushnick-Masti, "State Memorializes August Wilson's Childhood Home," *Beaver County Times*, June 1, 2007; Brown, "Light in August," 120.

85. Brown, "Light in August," 120.

86. Tony Kirven, interview by the author, April 1, 2016.

87. Tony Kirven, interview by the author, April 1, 2016.

88. Tony Kirven, interview by the author, April 1, 2016.

89. Tony Kirven, interview by the author, April 1, 2016.

90. Family composition and father's occupation derived from the manuscript censuses of 1910 and 1920. The family lived in Houston's Ward 5, on Maggie Street in 1910, and Schaak Street in 1920. "David Bedford, former schoolmate at Wiley, where he was a famous orator, is in the parcel post division of Uncle Sam's mail service." "Houston" (column), *Pittsburgh Courier*, August 3, 1940, 11.

91. Dave lived variously on Sachem, Clark, Townsend, and Arthur Streets, as well as Centre

Avenue. His picture as a member of the football team appears in the 1925 and 1926 Fifth Avenue High School yearbooks.

92. Commonwealth of Pennsylvania, Board of Pardons, February 8, 1954, David Legion Bedford, No. A-894, Application for Clemency, Pennsylvania State Archives, Harrisburg. It is possible that Bedford returned briefly to Texas. The 1930 manuscript census lists a Black man of the same name and correct age as a teacher at St. John Orphan Home and Industrial Institute in Austin, Texas.

93. The couple resided at 2016 Centre Avenue, near Devilliers Street. Pittsburgh City Directory, 1931.

94. The attempted robbery occurred the evening of Tuesday, August 4, 1931. Bedford, Application for Clemency. See also "Gets Life in Murder of Hill Druggist," *Pittsburgh Courier*, November 21, 1931, 6.

95. Bedford, Application for Clemency, Pennsylvania State Archives; "Gets Life in Murder of Hill Druggist," *Pittsburgh Courier*, November 21, 1931, 6. Dave may also have benefited from political connections. Julia Burley, who years later was active as a ward leader, says she heard that Dave had once been a "big politician." Julia Burley, telephone interview by the author, July 30, 2012.

96. "Pen Rioters on Trial, Object to Lawyers, Differ on Details," *Pittsburgh Courier*, October 31, 1953, 15.

97. Bedford, Application for Clemency, Pennsylvania State Archives; "Gets Life in Murder of Hill Druggist," *Pittsburgh Courier*, November 21, 1931, 6; "DA's Office Fights Paroles for 3 Convicts," *Pittsburgh Courier*, March 20, 1954, 14; Pennsylvania Board of Parole, David L. Bedford, Parole No. 5321-B, June 24, 1964, Pennsylvania State Archives, Harrisburg.

98. August Wilson in Dubner, "August Wilson, R.I.P." Dubner interviewed Wilson in 2000. Hop Kendrick, interview by the author, June 2, 2012.

99. "Wed in Secrecy," *Pittsburgh Courier*, December 3, 1955, sect. 2, 7.

100. Hop Kendrick, interview by the author, June 2, 2012.

101. Hop Kendrick, interview by the author, June 2, 2012.

102. Julia Burley, interview by the author, May 27, 2012.

103. Bedford, Parole No. 5321-B, Pennsylvania State Archives.

Chapter 3. Hazelwood Warrior

1. This is speculation; we have no direct evidence on whether or not Daisy remained on public assistance.

2. Freda Kittel, several informal conversations, 2006.

3. Marva Scott-Starks, interview by the author, June 20, 2013.

4. Marva Scott-Starks, interview by the author, June 20, 2013.

5. "Adults Join in Student Fight at Gladstone High School," *Pittsburgh Courier*, September 13, 1958, 1; "Parent Sues Son's Attacker as Gladstone School Tension Eases," *Pittsburgh Courier*, September 20, 1958, 4; "Hold [White] Man Who Beat Student for Court," *Pittsburgh Courier*, October 25, 1958, 1.

6. Livingston, "Cool August," 42.

7. Freda Wilson, informal conversations.

8. Ruth Allen, interview by the author, October 31, 2012.

9. Marva Scott-Starks, interview by the author, May 1, 2013.

10. Marva Scott-Starks, interview by the author, 13 March 2013.

11. The directory implies that Daisy is a widow by placing her name in parentheses after Fred's name.

12. Marva Scott-Starks, interview by the author, May 14, 2013.

13. Marva Scott Starks, interview by the author, May 14, 2013.

14. Marva Scott-Starks, interview by the author, March 13, 2013.

15. Marva Scott-Starks, interview by the author, May 1, 2013.

16. Julia Burley, interview by the author, October 3, 2012.

17. Marva Scott-Starks thinks it was washed every other day. Marva Scott Starks, interview by the author, May 14, 2013; Earl Horsley, interview by the author, May 14, 2013.

18. Julia Burley, interview by the author, October 3, 2012.

19. Julia Burley, interview by the author, October 3, 2012.

20. Lahr, "Been Here and Gone," 17.

21. Marva Scott-Starks says that "Old Man Horsley" referred to in the play *Fences* was Earl Horsley's grandfather. Earl's father's name was Emmett, but he was called Pete. She does not remember the grandfather's name. She says the Horsleys were from the Hill, which is where no doubt Freddy met Old Man Horsley, who continued to live in the Hill District. It was a remarkable coincidence that Freddy had known Old Man Horsley in the Hill, and in Hazelwood met his grandson. Marva Scott-Starks, interview by the author, June 20, 2013.

22. Earl Horsley, interview by the author, May 14, 2013.

23. Marva Scott-Starks, interview by the author, June 20, 2013.

24. Earl Horsley, interview by the author, May 14, 2013.

25. Parks, "Light in August Wilson."

26. Parks, "Light in August Wilson."

27. Lahr, "Been Here and Gone," 17.

28. Parks, "Light in August Wilson."

29. Earl Horsley, interview by the author, May 14, 2013.

30. Earl Horsley, interview by the author, May 14, 2013.

31. Joann Brown, interview by the author, summer 2015.

32. Marva Scott-Starks, interview by the author, June 20, 2013.

33. Joann Brown, interview by the author, summer 2015.

34. Joann Brown, interview by the author, summer 2015.

35. Snodgrass, *August Wilson*, 6.

36. Earl Horsley, interview by the author, May 14, 2013.

37. Earl Horsley, interview by the author, May 14, 2013.

38. Earl Horsley, interview by the author, May 14, 2013.

39. Earl Horsley, interview by the author, May 14, 2013.

40. August Wilson, "Blacks, Blues and Cultural Imperialism," lecture delivered March 2, 1988, at the "Man and Ideas Lecture Series," Carnegie Lecture Hall, Pittsburgh, Kiburi Collection, donated by August Wilson.

41. Brown, "Light in August," 122.

42. Samuel Freedman, "A Voice from the Streets," *New York Times*, March 15, 1987, A36; Glasco and Rawson, *August Wilson*, 8.

43. Earl Horsley, interview by the author, May 14, 2013; Wilson, "Blacks, Blues and Cultural Imperialism."

44. Wilson, "Blacks, Blues and Cultural Imperialism;" Lyons, "Interview with August Wilson," 207.

45. August Wilson, "Feed Your Mind, The Rest Will Follow," *Pittsburgh Post-Gazette*, March 28, 1999.

46. Feldman and Gartenberg, *Beat Generation and the Angry Young Men.*

47. Tony Kirven, interview by the author, April 1, 2016.

48. Sinclair, "Black Aesthetic."

49. Freedman, "Voice from the Streets."

50. Herbert Douglas, interview by the author, April 30, 2013. In the 1930s, Douglas established an auto-body shop and chauffeur service in Shadyside that employed, among others, the father of Billy Eckstine. His son, Herbert Douglas Jr., later became a track star for the University of Pittsburgh, winning bronze in the 1948 Summer Olympics.

51. Bryer and Hartig, *Conversations with August Wilson*, 206.

52. Livingston, "Cool August," 41–42.

53. Transcript, St. Stephen School. Attendance, grades, and IQ results made available gracious of Christopher Rawson. Freddy's general poor performance is confirmed by his neighbor, Marva Scott-Starks, interview by the author, May 1, 2013.

54. School records in possession of Christopher Rawson.

55. Earl Horsley, interview by the author, May 14, 2013.

56. Transcript, Ninth Grade, Fred August Kittel, Central Catholic High School.

57. Feingold, "August Wilson's Bottomless Blackness," 13.

58. Wilson says he dropped out of Central Catholic in April. See Wilson, "Blacks, Blues and Cultural Imperialism." See also Lahr, "Been Here and Gone."

59. Livingston, "Cool August," 25–32.

60. See, for example, Feingold, "August Wilson's Bottomless Blackness."

61. *Towers*, yearbook of Central Catholic High School, 1960, in the possession of Albert Zangelli.

62. Sala Udin, email message to the author, August 20, 2014.

63. Gene Keil, interview by the author, October 5, 2012.

64. Freedman, "Voice from the Streets," A36.

65. Sinclair, "Black Aesthetic," 96.

66. *Towers*, yearbook of Central Catholic High School, 1960, in the possession of Albert Zangelli.

67. Wilson, "Blacks, Blues and Cultural Imperialism."

68. Wilson, "Blacks, Blues and Cultural Imperialism."

69. Moyers, "August Wilson," 67–80.

70. Savran, "August Wilson," 32.

71. Lahr, "Been Here and Gone"; Livingston, "Cool August," 38–60.

72. Earl Horsley, interview by the author, 14 May 2013.

73. Greg Montgomery, interview by the author, June 13, 2014. Linda Jean clearly came out and interacted at least occasionally. In 1960 she served as an aide at the wedding reception of Earl's sister Earlene. See Toki Schalk Johnson, "Earlene Horsley, W. J. Williams Married in Home of Grandmother," *Pittsburgh Courier*, September 17, 1960, 1C.

74. Earl Horsley, interview by the author, May 14, 2013.

75. Marva Scott-Starks, interview by the author, May 1, 2013; Earl Horsley, interview by the author, May 14, 2013.

76. Greg Montgomery, interview by the author, June 13, 2014.

77. Greg Montgomery, interview by the author, June 13, 2014.

78. Greg Montgomery, interview by the author, June 13, 2014.

79. Greg Montgomery, interview by the author, June 13, 2014.

80. Greg Montgomery, interview by the author, June 13, 2014.

81. Greg Montgomery, interview by the author, June 13, 2014; Earl Horsley, interview by the author, May 14, 2013.

82. Bob Hoover, "Childhood in Hill leads to a Pulitzer for August Wilson," *Pittsburgh Post-Gazette*, June 1, 1987.

83. Greg Montgomery, interview by the author, June 13, 2014.

84. Shirley Biggs, wife of Charles Biggs, interview by the author, October 25, 2012.

85. Moyers, "August Wilson," 66.

86. Lahr, "Been Here and Gone," 18–19.

87. August Wilson, interview with Lynne Hayes-Freeland, "Focus," WAMO radio, September 25, 1987, Kiburi Collection. Wilson says the incident occurred in 1960, which would have placed it when he was fifteen years old. Wilson is a bit mistaken here. School records show that he transferred to Gladstone in December 1960. Hence, leaving at the age of fifteen would imply that he dropped out sometime before April 27, 1961, his sixteenth birthday.

88. Feingold, "August Wilson's Bottomless Blackness," 14.

89. Dates of Freddy's schooling provided by Christopher Rawson from school records.

90. Glasco and Rawson, *August Wilson*, 9.

91. August Wilson, *"How I Learned What I Learned,"* play typescript. Freddy's memory fails a bit here. Claude Lévi-Strauss's *The Origin of Table Manners* first appeared in 1978, well after he had quit school. Nonetheless, the list of readings shows the wide range of his interests.

92. Lyons, "Interview with August Wilson."

93. In the talk, August paraphrased Kiburi's quote as "I dropped out of school but I didn't drop out of life." See Wilson, "Blacks, Blues and Cultural Imperialism."

94. Wilson, *How I Learned What I Learned*. The phrase was originally told by Lee Kiburi to students at CAPA (Creative and Performing Arts Academy) when August traveled to Pittsburgh in 1988 to deliver the "Man and Ideas" lecture at Pittsburgh's Carnegie Music Hall. School records suggest August dropped out of school around the time he turned sixteen.

95. Watlington, "Hurdling Fences," 102–13.

96. Dubner, "August Wilson R.I.P."

97. Earl Horsley, interview by the author, May 14, 2013.

98. "U.S., School Yearbooks, 1880–2012, Westinghouse High School, 1964," Ancestry.com, accessed March 22, 2020.

99. Earl Horsley, interview by the author, May 14, 2013.

100. John Brewer, email message to the author, December 25, 2016.

101. Wilson in conversation with Rick Sebak of Pittsburgh's WQED-TV. *Brain, Space, and Energy: My 1989 Interview with August Wilson*, WQED-TV, March 18, 2024.

102. Lahr, "Been Here and Gone," 19.

103. Feingold, "August Wilson's Bottomless Blackness," 14.

104. Lacy McCoy, interview by the author, August 23, 2014. For background on the reputation of "Bucket of Blood," John Brewer, email message to the author, August 31, 2014.

105. Brown, "Light in August."

106. Lahr, "Been Here and Gone," 19.

107. Frederick August Kittel military records, December 2, 2015, National Personnel Records Center, Saint Louis, MO, letter to the author. Marilyn Elkin says incorrectly that August joined the army in 1963 and left in 1964.

108. Marva Scott-Starks, interview by the author, May 1, 2013.

109. Earl Horsley, interview by the author, May 14, 2013.

110. Marva Scott-Starks says the accident must have occurred while Wilson was in the army because she remembers him being in uniform at the time of the accident. She confirms that Ronnie Culpepper and Vernon Saunders were in the car with Freddy, and that Culpepper was driving. For a while, Saunders was affiliated with the Hill House.

111. Earl Horsley, interview by the author, May 14, 2013.

112. Earl Horsley, interview by the author, May 14, 2013.

113. Lahr, "Been Here and Gone," 19–20. Lahr says Freddy was seventeen when he left the army; he was eighteen.

114. Wilson served under the name Fred August Kittel. National Personnel Records Center, St. Louis, MO, December 2, 2015.

115. The marriage certificate gives the name of Daisy's mother as Zonia Wilson, born Cutler, and her father as "Freil" Vance, whose race it lists as "Negro."

116. This would harmonize with Julia Burley's statement that David Bedford "got" Daisy the house. David apparently was never the owner, for in 1970, Solomon's widow Eva sold the house to Freda Ellis, Daisy's firstborn, for $3,500 (about $22,000 today). In 1978 Freda "sold" the house to Daisy for $1.

117. This is inferred from city directories of the time.

118. Pennsylvania Board of Pardons, September 1964.

119. Fred Kittel and wife to Andrew Levitske et al., July 30, 1964.

120. Court of Common Pleas, Complaint in Divorce, Frederick A. Kittel vs. Daisy Wilson Kittel, August 13, 1964.

121. Lahr, "Been Here and Gone," 20.

122. Perhaps Fred wanted to impress them, for the US Army can find no record of Fred's having served in the military. Aaron McWilliams, Reference Archivist, Pennsylvania State Archives, communication, November 5, 2012, based on a review of the Records of the Department of Military and Veterans Affairs (RG-19), Adjutant General, World War I Veterans Service and Compensation File [for Pennsylvania]. McWilliams reports that "no record was found for a Frederick August Kittel/Kittle/Kitel."

123. Lahr, "Been Here and Gone," 20.

124. Death notice, *Pittsburgh Press*, April 2, 1965.

125. Jennie, recorded as Mary T. Kittel, was on buried January 9, 1964, in what the cemetery lists as a "single grave," w.b., meaning "without a vault." Fred was buried on April 2, 1965, also in a "single grave" with vault designation given as w.b. Cemetery workers pointed out where Fred and Jennie are buried, without headstones, separated by a grave.

126. Freda Kittel, informal conversation.

127. Orphans' Court of Allegheny County, "In the Matter of the Estate of Frederick August Kittel," No. 1590 of Term 1965.

128. Orphans' Court of Allegheny County, "In the Matter of the Estate of Frederick August Kittel," No. 1590 of Term 1965.

Chapter 4. Centre Avenue Poet

1. Bryer and Hartig, *Conversations with August Wilson*, 67.

2. Brown, "Light in August," 122.

3. Brown, "Light in August," 116–27.

4. Brown, "Light in August." 116–27. The 1965 city directory shows a Mrs. Hattie Smith

as rooming house's head. In the play *How I Learned What I Learned*, August says a man took care of the rooming house for free rent. If so, that may have been Sylvester Johnson, the only other resident listed.

5. Bob Hoover, "Childhood in Hill Leads to a Pulitzer for August Wilson," *Pittsburgh Post-Gazette*, June 1, 1987.

6. Hoover, "Childhood in Hill Leads to a Pulitzer for August Wilson"; Livingston, "Cool August," 49.

7. Ben Brantley, "The World That Created August Wilson," *New York Times*, February 5, 1995; Christopher Rawson, "August Wilson, 1945–2005; Pittsburgh Playwright Who Chronicled Black Experience, Pulitzer Prize-Winner Succumbs to Liver Cancer at 60 in Seattle, 'Surrounded by His Loved Ones,'" *Pittsburgh Post-Gazette*, October 3, 2005, A1.

8. Video recording of December 3, 2003, furnished by the 92nd Street Y.

9. Dubner, "August Wilson R.I.P."

10. Shannon, *Dramatic Vision of August Wilson*, 20.

11. The first official document I have found with the name "August Kittel" are his marriage papers to Judy Oliver in 1981.

12. Dubner, "August Wilson, R.I.P."; Lahr, "Been Here and Gone," 20–21.

13. Bryer and Hartig, introduction to *Conversations with August Wilson*, xvii, 49; Wilson, *How I Learned What I Learned*.

14. Lahr, "Been Here and Gone," 21.

15. Elaine Effort, "Pittsburgh Profiles," KQV radio, September 25, 1987, Kiburi Collection.

16. Sala Udin, interview by the author, June 7, 2013.

17. Amos Lawson, interview by the author, May 15, 2013.

18. Rob Penny, interview by Lee Kiburi, August 18, 1998, Kiburi Collection.

19. Rob Penny, interview by Lee Kiburi, August 18, 1998, Kiburi Collection. Penny adds: "At some point the sisters adopted African names, Their African names are [unclear] Marainey and Owash. Her full name is Owashiwawa. You know how Americans are, we shortened these African names."

20. Rob Penny, interview by Lee Kiburi, August 18, 1998, Kiburi Collection.

21. Amos Lawson, interview by the author, May 15, 2013.

22. Amos Lawson, interview by the author, May 15, 2013.

23. Al Zangrilli, interview by the author, June 27, 2013.

24. Al Zangrilli, interview by the author, June 27, 2013.

25. Jerry Rhodes, interview by the author, January 17, 2016.

26. Sala Udin, interview by the author, June 7, 2013; Mike Flournoy, interview by the author, June 16, 2013; Ron Davenport, interview by the author, February 19, 2018; Louis "Hop" Kendrick, "To Tell the Truth: What Happened to the Black Voices of Outrage?" *New Pittsburgh Courier*, December 18, 1999, A7, lists Flournoy as alongside the leading fighters for civil rights. See also *Pittsburgh Courier*, January 15, 1966, 6B (photo); December 24, 1966, 6A (photo); "Black Students Deliver Ultimatum to N.S. College," *Pittsburgh Courier*, May 3, 1969, 1; "Likens Tabor to Nixon on Law n' Order," *Pittsburgh Courier*, August 23, 1969 [running for State Assembly from Homewood]; Carl Morris, "Comment," *Pittsburgh Courier*, September 5, 1969, 13; "Black Political Caucus Next Week," *Pittsburgh Courier*, October 18, 1969, 1; "FLASH!! Nick Flournoy Was Seen in a Shirt and Tie! Can You Believe It??" in Ken Morris, "The Night Owl," *New Pittsburgh Courier*, November 21, 1970, 12; "*Courier*'s Ron Suber Attacked by Man," *Pittsburgh Courier*, October 30, 1976, 1; "Convention Center Talks Reach 'Turning Point,'"

Pittsburgh Courier, July 30, 1977, 1; "Playwright Gears Up For Broadway," *Pittsburgh Courier*, November 22, 1986, 6.

27. Mike Flournoy, interview by the author, June 16, 2013; Gail Austin, interview by the author, June 21, 2013; Moses Carper, interview by the author, November 9, 2007; Sala Udin, interview by the author, June 7, 2013; August Wilson, interview by Lee Kiburi, April 6, 1999.

28. The term *Crossroads of the World* was popularized by WHOD (later WAMO) disc jockey Mary Dee in the late 1940s and early 1950s. Hazel Garland, "Mary Dee Rests: First Female Disc Jockey Is Buried in Pittsburgh," *Pittsburgh Courier*, March 28, 1964, 1. John Clark says a visiting soldier from Washington, DC, coined the phrase just after World War II. Clark, "Wylie Avenue," *Pittsburgh Courier*, March 27, 1954, 16.

29. "Sala Udin: Community Organizer," interview by Jeff Sewald, *Pittsburgh Quarterly* (Fall 2013): 22.

30. Steve Mellon, "A Life on the Hill: The Journey of Sala Udin Mirrors the Experience of Many African American Pittsburghers," *Pittsburgh Post-Gazette*, December 28, 2016.

31. "Sala Udin: Community Organizer."

32. Sala Udin, interview by the author, October 5, 1998; Steve Mellon, "A Life on the Hill: The Journey of Sala Udin," *Pittsburgh Post-Gazette*, December 28, 2016. Sala continued his social and political engagement. He headed House of the Crossroads from 1969 to 1983 and the Multicultural Training Resource Center in San Francisco from 1983 to 1990. He was Pittsburgh city councilman, representing the Hill District, from 1995 to 2006, and then president of the Coro Center for Civic Leadership from 2006 to 2012. Sala also was head of the Pittsburgh chapter of the Congress of Afrikan People (CAP), from 1970 to 1977. In 1974 Baraka and CAP underwent a radical shift away from Black Nationalism and into a radically leftist stance, even changing its name to Revolutionary Communist League (Marxist-Leninist-Mao Tse-tung Thought).

33. Bogumil, *Understanding August Wilson*, 147–48.

34. Sala Udin, interview by the author, June 7, 2013; Darzetta Williams, interview by the author, July 22, 2013; Sala Udin, interview by the author, June 7, 2013; Curtiss Porter, interview by Lee Kiburi, November 28, 2007; James O'Toole, "Chawley Williams, Last Surviving Member of Centre Ave. Poets' Workshop, 28 December 1935–2 December 2009," *Pittsburgh Post-Gazette*, December 4, 2009, 33.

35. Christopher Reynolds, "Mr. Wilson's Neighborhood," *Los Angeles Times*, July 27, 2003; O'Toole, "Chawley Williams."

36. *Pittsburgh Courier*, July 24, 1965.

37. The emotional consequence of that displacement is examined by Mindy Thompson Fullilove in *Root Shock*.

38. *Pittsburgh Courier*, January 16, 1960, and February 18, 1961.

39. Gary Robinson, letter to the author, January 26, 2014.

40. Lyons, "Interview with August Wilson," 1–21.

41. "Robert Creeley, 1926–2005," Poetry Foundation, http://www.poetryfoundation.org/bio/Robert-creeley.

42. Savran, "August Wilson," 34.

43. Glasco, "August Wilson and the Automobile," 103–17.

44. Baudelaire, *Painter of Modern Life*, 400; Tester, *Flaneur*, 6–7; Mazlish, "Flaneur," 52. Wilson, "Man & Ideas" lecture, 1998, Carnegie Music Hall, Pittsburgh, PA, Kiburi Collection, recording donated by August Wilson.

45. Shaya, "Flâneur, the Badaud," 41–77, esp. 51, stresses the difference between the "aristocratic," refined flaneur who walked Paris streets in order to perceive and understand, versus the "badaud," who went out simply to gawk and sensationalize the horrors and tragedies that could be observed on the street.

46. Bryer and Hartig, *Conversations with August Wilson*, 67.

47. Sala Udin, interview by the author, June 7, 2013.

48. Lahr, "Been Here and Gone," 21.

49. Lahr, "Been Here and Gone," 20.

50. Wilson, *How I Learned What I Learned*.

51. Wilson, *How I Learned What I Learned*.

52. Reynolds, "Mr. Wilson's Neighborhood"; Lahr, "Been Here and Gone," 21–22.

53. Frank Hightower, interview by the author, July 7, 1998.

54. Tony Fountain, interview by the author, August 1, 2013.

55. Tony Fountain, interview by the author, August 1, 2013.

56. Amos Lawson, interview by the author, May 15, 2013.

57. Gene Keil, interview by the author, October 5, 2012.

58. "B&M Restaurant Celebrates 5th Anniversary Starting May 31," *Pittsburgh Courier*, May 30, 1953, 23; "B&M Has Home Cooking and Homey Atmosphere," *Pittsburgh Courier*, October 31, 1953, 16; Nate Guidry, "Bessie Mae Rawls, Owned Popular Restaurants in the Hill," *Pittsburgh Courier*, March 28, 2007. Mrs. Rawls established the restaurant with her son, Douglas King, and her daughter, Verna Graham.

59. Among numerous articles, see "'Foe' Gets Prison On Drug Possession," *Pittsburgh Post-Gazette*, December 18, 1969, 2.

60. For the first year or two, Jay Greenfield, a psychologist affiliated with David Lewis, helped run Architecture 2001. Troy West, interview by the author, July 31, 2013.

61. Gail Austin, interview by the author, June 21, 2013; Hoover, "Childhood in Hill Leads to a Pulitzer for August Wilson"; Troy West, interview by the author, July 31, 2013.

62. Willa Mae Montague, interview by the author, February 28, 2015.

63. As a young girl, Montague had scarred her legs roughhousing outdoors in a briar-filled lot with her brothers. She became the prototype for Risa, the waitress in *Two Trains Running* who had scarred her legs to keep the men from sexually harassing her.

64. Willa Mae Montague (now Willa Mae Swan), interview by the author, February 28, 2015.

65. Willa Mae Montague (now Willa Mae Swan), interview by the author, February 28, 2015.

66. Wilson, *How I Learned What I Learned*.

67. Willa Mae Montague (now Willa Mae Swan), interview by the author, February 28, 2015.

68. Willa Mae Montague (now Willa Mae Swan), interview by the author, February 28, 2015.

69. Jerry Rhodes, codirector of the Halfway Art Gallery on Centre, confirms August's version of events. According to Rhodes, Jeanine said to August, "'I told you never bring anybody to our house. He was threatening me and he threatened my kids.' . . . When Chawley came back, he said to August, 'August, I told you: you don't know anything, you don't know anybody. You don't know where anyone lives; you don't have anyone's phone number. I tried to tell you.'" His wife was beside herself. Jerry Rhodes, interview by the author, January 17, 2016.

70. The photograph was taken by Frank Hightower.

71. Brown, "Light in August," 123.

72. Reynolds, "Mr. Wilson's Neighborhood."

73. McKay, *Home to Harlem*, 141.

74. Lyons and Plimpton, "Art of Theater," 66–94.

75. It is not clear exactly when August discovered Pat's Place. In a 1990 interview in the *Phi Kappa Phi Journal*, in Sheppard, "August Wilson," 101. August says he was twenty-three, which would have made this 1968. In an interview with *The Paris Review*, he says he discovered Pat's Place at the age of twenty-one, which would have been 1966. Lyons and Plimpton, "Art of Theater."

76. Hilary DeVries, "A Street-Corner Scribe of Life in Black America," *Christian Science Monitor*, March 27, 1987; Lyons and Plimpton, "Art of Theater."

77. Brantley, "World That Created August Wilson."

78. Lyons and Plimpton, "Art of Theater." At one time, Wilson apparently planned to incorporate this dialogue into *Ma Rainey's Black Bottom*.

79. Sheppard, "August Wilson."

80. For example: "CUTLER Let me worry about what's on the list and what ain't on the list. How you gonna tell me what's on the list?" Or: "CUTLER Boy, ain't nobody studying you. Telling me what to put in my pipe. Who's you to tell me what to do?" See also Lyons and Plimpton, "Art of Theater."

81. Nancy Churnin, "The Academic and the Dropout," *Los Angeles Times*, February 6, 1988, 1.

82. Bogumil, *Understanding August Wilson*, 3, citing Wilson, *Three Plays* (1984), xi.

83. Wilson, *How I Learned What I Learned*. In *Code of the Street*, Elijah Anderson details the prevalence and importance of these often-unspoken codes in North Philadelphia. As Anderson points out, those who congregate are strangers, yet they "know" one another and share the "code" of acceptable behavior.

84. William (Bill) Strickland, interview by the author, June 12, 2013.

85. L. A. Johnson, "Obituary: Edward T. Owens/Long-Time Owner of Popular Restaurant in Hill District," *Pittsburgh Post-Gazette*, July 27, 2000.

86. Johnson, "Obituary: Edward T. Owens."

87. Johnson, "Obituary: Edward T. Owens."

88. Glasco and Rawson, *August Wilson*, 83; Sala Udin, "Tribute to Eddie Owens," Pittsburgh City Council, July 26, 2000.

89. Sala Udin, informal conversation with the author, February 2017.

90. Ervin Dyer, "August Wilson Remembered as a Character in Oddball Hill," *Pittsburgh Post-Gazette*, October 8, 2005.

91. Lyons, "Interview with August Wilson," 216.

92. Reynolds, "Mr. Wilson's Neighborhood."

93. Ralph Proctor, interview by the author, June 24, 2013.

94. Dyer, "August Wilson Remembered as a Character in Oddball Hill," B1.

95. Brantley, "World That Created August Wilson."

96. Wilson, *How I Learned What I Learned*.

97. Kenneth Owens-El, interview by the author, July 13, 2017.

98. Nelson Harrison, interview by the author, July 26, 2013. Harrison maintains an active jazz web page, *The Pittsburgh Jazz Network*, at jazzburgher.ning.com.

99. See Harper, "'Crossroads of the World'"; Whitaker, *Smoketown*.

100. Wilson refers to this performance several times, most notably in his play *How I Learned What I Learned*, which implies a date of 1965 or later. In fact, April 1963 marked Coltrane's last appearance at the Crawford Grill, and set an attendance record for the club. In 1965 he performed at the Civic Arena and made an after-concert appearance at the private Loendi Club, located in the Hill some dozen or so blocks from the Grill. See "John Coltrane Quartet

in Last Three Nights," *Pittsburgh Courier*, December 3, 1960, A18; "Trane Will Whistle in Grill for a Week," *Pittsburgh Courier*, April 13, 1963, 16; "Loendi Club to Host Jazz Festival Stars," *Pittsburgh Courier*, June 19, 1965, 16.

101. Wilson, *How I Learned What I Learned*.

102. Bogumil, *Understanding August Wilson*, 133. Also, 147ff quoting extended interview with Williams.

103. Tony Fountain, interview by the author, August 1, 2013.

104. Nelson Harrison, interview by the author, July 26, 2013.

105. Lahr, "Been Here and Gone," 22; Brantley, "World That Created August Wilson."

106. Feingold, "August Wilson's Bottomless Blackness," 17.

107. Moyers, "August Wilson: Playwright," 63.

108. August Wilson, quoted in Aubrey Hampton, "August Wilson, Playwright," *Organica Magazine*, Summer 1988, 24, quoted in Herrington, *I Ain't Sorry for Nothin' I Done*, 1.

109. Herrington, *I Ain't Sorry for Nothin' I Done*, 1.

110. Brown, "Light in August."

111. Moyers, "August Wilson," 63–64.

Chapter 5. Early Poetry

1. Jerry Rhodes, interview by the author, January 17, 2016; April 22, 2016.

2. Jerry Rhodes, interview by the author, January 17, 2016.

3. August Wilson, "Blacks, Blues and Cultural Imperialism," lecture delivered March 2, 1988, at the Man and Ideas Lecture Series, Carnegie Lecture Hall, Pittsburgh, Kiburi Collection, donated by August Wilson.

4. Gary Robinson, a member, says that the Pittsburgh Organizers gave recovering persons with substance abuse disorders a chance to turn their lives around. As a once-promising young man whose life was turned upside down by one major mistake, Robinson was grateful to Ellis for filling the gallery with books, incense, and artwork that inspired the men to change their lives. Not all participants were able to stop using drugs, but Robinson says they were grateful just to know someone cared. Gary Robinson, letter to the author, January 26, 2014.

5. Jerry Rhodes, interview by the author, January 17, 2016.

6. Bill Strickland, interview by the author, June 12, 2013.

7. Wilson, *How I Learned What I Learned*.

8. Ralph Koger, "Artists Open New Art Gallery in Hill," with accompanying photo by Teenie Harris, in *Pittsburgh Courier*, September 12, 1964.

9. Thomas O'Neil, "Halfway Art Gallery—A Need Fulfilled," *Pittsburgh Post-Gazette*, May 14, 1966.

10. O'Neil, "Halfway Art Gallery."

11. LeRoy Thompson, obituary, *Pittsburgh Press*, June 2, 1989.

12. Jerry Rhodes, interview by the author, January 17, 2016.

13. Jerry Rhodes, interview by the author, January 17, 2016.

14. Jerry Rhodes, interview by the author, January 17, 2016.

15. Issues of *Pittsburgh Point* magazine for February 1967, Calendar of Events. Also, Elaine Weatherley, widow of Rev. Ted Weatherley, who ran the mission and then joined with Ellis in running the Halfway Art Gallery, telephone conversation, March 21, 2014.

16. Ellis, "Comments on the Halfway," catalog, Halfway Art Gallery Exhibition, n.d., in author's possession, gift of Troy West.

17. Halfway Art Gallery Exhibition catalog, n.d., in author's possession; *Church News*, Pittsburgh Episcopal Church, March/April 1967.

18. Gail Austin, interview by the author, June 21, 2013.

19. Bogumil, *Understanding August Wilson*, 17; Wilson, *How I Learned What I Learned*.

20. Jerry Rhodes, interview by the author, April 22, 2016.

21. John O'Mahony, "Profile: August Wilson," *Guardian* (UK), December 14, 2002, 20. See also James O'Toole, "Chawley P. Williams, Last Surviving Member of Centre Ave. Poets' Workshop," *Pittsburgh Post-Gazette*, December 4, 2009, 33.

22. Sala Udin, interview by the author, June 7, 2013.

23. Frank Hightower, interview by the author, June 28, 2013; Amiri Baraka, interview by Lee Kiburi, August 31, 1998; William Strickland, interview by the author, June 12, 2013; Gail Austin, interview by the author, June 21, 2013.

24. Thad Mosley, interview by the author, June 4, 2013.

25. Charles Isherwood, "August Wilson, Theater's Poet of Black America, is Dead at 60," *New York Times*, October 3, 2005, A1. When not dressing like Thomas, August adopted a bohemian style of combining a heavy woolen jacket and black turtleneck sweater.

26. Jerry Rhodes, interview by the author, April 22, 2016.

27. Thad Mosley, interview by the author, June 4, 2013. The poem continues to resonate, garnering the most hits on the Poetry Foundation's website. In 2014, when the Associated Press was describing Peyton Manning's loss in that year's Super Bowl, it said he "went gently into that good Jersey night." That same year, when Roger Federer, at the "ancient" age of thirty-three, entered the Brisbane International tennis tournament, it was said he "did not intend to go gently into that good night." Heinzelman, "Affiliated Poetics."

28. Jerry Rhodes, interview by the author, January 17, 2016.

29. Reginald Howze, interview by the author, July 24, 2017; Shannon, *Dramatic Vision of August Wilson*, 20; Bogumil, "August Wilson's Relationship to Black Theatre," 54.

30. On any number of occasions, Wilson attested to the influence of Berryman on his poetry, later complaining of the difficulty in shaking off his influence. For example, see Sheppard, "August Wilson: An Interview," 103.

31. Barbera, "In Memoriam," 549–51; Young, "Responsible Delight," 161–66; Kameen, *Re-reading Poets*, 133; Hinds and Matterson, *Rebound*, 144; Robert Lowell, "*77 Dream Songs* by John Berryman," *New York Review of Books* 2, no. 8 (1964): 3.

32. Mariani, *Dream Songs*; Barbera, "In Memoriam," 547–53. See also the highly personal but revealing set of insights in Minot, "Speaking in Tongues," 423–34.

33. Christopher Rawson, "August Wilson, 1945–2005; Pittsburgh Playwright Who Chronicled Black Experience, Pulitzer Prize-Winner Succumbs to Liver Cancer at 60 in Seattle, 'Surrounded by His Loved Ones,'" *Pittsburgh Post-Gazette*, October 3, 2005, A1. It is not clear whether August was imitating Chawley directly or developed this practice on his own.

34. Reginald Howze, interview by the author, July 24, 2017.

35. Reginald Howze, interview by the author, July 24, 2017.

36. Jerry Rhodes, informal conversation, 2016.

37. Jerry Rhodes has a personal collection of many of these early, handwritten poems.

38. Rhodes typed up the submissions and ran off copies at the University of Pittsburgh, using paper he "begged" from the staff at the Student Union. Rhodes says Halfway Art Gallery was happy to put its imprint on the publication, and he was happy that the gallery's imprint gave the magazine a certain cachet.

39. "The Halfway Art Gallery: First Annual Exhibition," n.d. [1967], personal donation of Troy West.

40. Samuel Freedman, "A Voice from the Streets," *New York Times*, March 15, 1987, A36.

41. Amiri Baraka, interview by Lee Kiburi, August 31, 1998; Lee Kiburi, interview by the author, June 21, 2013.

42. August Wilson, "True Black Poetry Missing at Forum," *Pittsburgh Point*, May 11, 1967, 4.

43. Lee Kiburi, interview by the author, April 6, 1999.

44. "4 in the Centre Avenue Tradition," *Pittsburgh Point*, May 18, 1967, 6.

45. Rob Penny, interview by Lee Kiburi, 1998.

46. Rob Penny, interview by Lee Kiburi, 1998.

47. Rob Penny, interview by Lee Kiburi, 1998.

48. Rob Penny, interview by Lee Kiburi, 1998.

49. Livingston, "Cool August," 54–55.

50. August Wilson, interview by Lee Kiburi, April 6, 1999.

51. Robert Zavos, "Carmichael Defines Power; Discusses War in Vietnam," *Pitt News*, March 6, 1967, 1.

52. Curtiss Porter, interview by Lee Kiburi, November 28, 2007.

53. Curtiss Porter, interview by Lee Kiburi, November 28, 2007.

54. Curtiss Porter, interview by Lee Kiburi, November 28, 2007.

55. Curtiss Porter, interview by Lee Kiburi, November 28, 2007.

56. Natalie Bazzell, interview by the author, August 30, 2013.

57. Natalie Bazzell, interview by the author, August 30, 2013.

58. Natalie Bazzell, interview by the author, August 30, 2013.

59. Curtiss Porter, interview by Lee Kiburi, November 28, 2007.

60. Curtiss Porter, interview by Lee Kiburi, November 28, 2007.

61. Core members included Sala Udin, Rob Penny, Gail Austin, Norman Johnson, Curtiss Porter, Lloyd Bell, Jake Milliones, and Tony Fountain. Sala Udin, interview by the author, October 5, 1998, and email message to the author, May 29, 2018; Rob Penny, interview by Lee Kiburi, 1998.

62. Rob Penny, "Speakin Briefly on the Centre Avenue Poets Theatre Workshop and Its Founders," *Connection: Journal of the Centre Ave. Poets Theatre* 1, no. 1 (January 1968).

63. Livingston, "Cool August," 50.

64. Penny, "Speakin Briefly on the Centre Avenue Poets Theatre Workshop and Its Founders," 30.

65. Rob Penny, "Consciousness of Revolution," *Connection: Journal of the Centre Ave. Poets Theatre* 1, no. 1 (January 1968): 30.

66. *Negro Digest*, September 1969.

67. Shannon, "August Wilson Explains His Dramatic Vision," 119.

68. Sala Udin, interview by the author, June 7, 2013.

69. Effort, "Pittsburgh Profiles."

Chapter 6. Race Man

1. Curtiss Porter, interview by Lee Kiburi, November 28, 2007.

2. August Wilson, interview by Lee Kiburi, April 6, 1999.

3. Curtiss E. Porter, "Soul 'n Fury: Black Unity Theme," *Pittsburgh Courier*, March 16, 1968, sec. 2.

4. Altman, *Encyclopedia of African-American Heritage*; Woodard, *Nation Within a Nation*.

5. On the New Granada Theatre/Pythian Temple structure, see Albert M. Tannler, "Pittsburgh's African-American Architect Louis Bellinger and the New Granada Theater," unpublished document, Library of Pittsburgh History and Landmarks Foundation.

6. Tannler, "Pittsburgh's African-American Architect Louis Bellinger."

7. Porter, "Soul 'n Fury," March 16, 1968.

8. Curtiss E. Porter, "Soul 'n Fury: Black Unity Theme," *Pittsburgh Courier*, March 23, 1968, sec. 2.

9. Porter, "Soul 'n Fury," March 16, 1968.

10. Porter, "Soul 'n Fury," March 16, 1968.

11. Sababa Akili is probably mistakenly referred to as Sahaba Akib by the *Pittsburgh Courier* (Porter, "Soul 'n Fury," March 23, 1968). Names of CAP leaders are given in Woodard, *Nation Within a Nation*, 169; Porter, "Soul 'n Fury," March 23, 1968.

12. August Wilson, interview by Lee Kiburi, April 6, 1999.

13. Curtiss Porter, email message to the author, July 26, 2019.

14. August Wilson, interview by Lee Kiburi, April 6, 1999.

15. Porter, "Soul 'n Fury," March 23, 1968.

16. Unfortunately, we do not have the text of Wilson's keynote address, just the summary that appeared in the *Pittsburgh Courier*. Wilson, "Ground on Which I Stand," 14.

17. Moses Carper, interview by Lee Kiburi, November 9, 2007.

18. Rob Penny, interview by Lee Kiburi, 1998; Porter, "Soul 'n Fury," March 23, 1968.

19. Rob Penny, interview by Lee Kiburi, 1998; Porter, "Soul 'n Fury," March 23, 1968.

20. Rob Penny, interview by Lee Kiburi, 1998; Porter, "Soul 'n Fury," March 23, 1968.

21. Rob Penny, interview by Lee Kiburi, 1998; Porter, "Soul 'n Fury," March 23, 1968.

22. Moses Carper, interview by the author, November 9, 2007.

23. Porter, "Soul 'n Fury," March 16, 1968.

24. Curtiss Porter, interview by Lee Kiburi, November 28, 2007; Sala Udin, interview by the author, October 5, 1998.

25. August Wilson, interview by Lee Kiburi, April 6, 1999.

26. August Wilson, interview by Lee Kiburi, April 6, 1999.

27. August Wilson, interview by Lee Kiburi, April 6, 1999.

28. Baraka, interview by Lee Kiburi, August 31, 1998.

29. Franki Williams, email message to the author, August 28, 2014.

30. Franki Williams, email message to the author, August 28, 2014.

31. Franki Williams, email message to the author, August 28, 2014.

32. Franki Williams, email message to the author, August 28, 2014.

33. Franki Williams, email message to the author, August 28, 2014.

34. Franki Williams, email message to the author, August 28, 2014.

35. *Pittsburgh Courier*, July 16, 1966.

36. *Pittsburgh Courier*, December 24, 1966.

37. Ribeiro, "'Period of Turmoil.'"

38. *Pittsburgh Courier*, November 4, 1967.

39. *Pittsburgh Courier*, December 9, 1967.

40. *Pittsburgh Courier*, February 17, 1968, and March 16, 1968.

41. Morris, *Black Mood in Pittsburgh*, 3, 5. The advertisement for *The Black Mood in Pittsburgh* appeared in the *Pittsburgh Courier* for April 6, 1968. King had been assassinated on April 4, but

the *Courier* appeared only weekly. The first *Courier* edition mentioning King's assassination and the ensuing riots was the April 13, 1968, edition.

42. Moses Carper, interview by Lee Kiburi, November 9, 2007.

43. Moses Carper, interview by Lee Kiburi, November 9, 2007.

44. Moses Carper, interview by Lee Kiburi, November 9, 2007; Ribeiro, "'Period of Turmoil.'"

45. Amos Lawson, interview by the author, May 15, 2013.

46. Wilson, *How I Learned What I Learned.* The photograph was taken by Frank Hightower, a friend of August, Rob, Sala, and others.

47. Dubner, "August Wilson, R.I.P." Dubner interviewed Wilson in 2000.

48. In 2002 Johnny suffered the same fate as Frank. I attended the funeral of Johnny Butera and observed the sizable number of heartbroken neighborhood residents, past and present, Black and white, who came to pay their respects. Julia Burley was shocked by what happened. "The Buteras," she says, "were good people. They didn't bother nobody." But this has not changed Julia's love of her old neighborhood: "Truthfully," she says, "everybody who lived down there, we got along wonderful." See David Conti, "Businessman Fatally Beaten," *Tribune Review* (Pittsburgh), May 18, 2002; "Watchmaker, 87, Found Dead on Hill," *Tribune Review* (Pittsburgh), May 18, 2002; "A Good Man Gone," *Tribune Review* (Pittsburgh), May 18, 2002; "A Neighborhood Says a Sad Farewell to a Faithful Resident," *Tribune Review* (Pittsburgh), May 18, 2002; Larry Glasco, letter to the editor, *Pittsburgh Post-Gazette*, May 24, 2002.

49. See especially Fullilove, *Root Shock.*

50. Calculated from listings in city directories.

51. Douglas King, personal communication to author, November 2000.

52. Bogumil, *Understanding August Wilson*, 147–48.

53. Brenda Burton Shakur, interview by the author, May 20, 2014.

54. Moses Carper, interview by Lee Kiburi, November 9, 2007.

55. Brenda Burton Shakur, interview by the author, May 20, 2014.

56. Brenda Burton Shakur, interview by the author, May 20, 2014.

57. Faye, according to her niece Barbara, was originally named Nevada Zenobia Cutler/ Wilson, also known as Vida. This would make her the one-year-old granddaughter of Ella Cutler on the 1920 US Census, along with twenty-year-old Arivona/Zona Cutler. Daisy is not listed in the 1920 census because she was born on March 12, 1920, while the census was taken in January and February 1920. Daisy's middle name was Zerola. August's youngest daughter's name is Azula. Barbara's youngest brother, Richard, told her that they wanted to keep the *z*. Barbara adds: "Faye T. Walker celebrated her birthday on Christmas Day. I know she stated she was born in Spear, North Carolina. I vaguely remember her stating that she had found out her birth date. Unfortunately I cannot timeline it. She is older than Daisy, and passed away in December 1999. I attended the funeral with Adair, August did the eulogy. Kimberly sang. We went back to Richard's house in Brentwood. Freda and Edwin were there. Freddy, Richard and Xavier were at the funeral but not at Richard's. Sakina (August's eldest daughter) was also at the funeral. Richard lost two sons, one on the day he buried his mother (March 19) and Xavier who was struck and killed by a train. I think it was close to the revival of *Ma Rainey's Black Bottom*, a sad time."

58. Barbara Wilson, interview by the author, April 28, 2013.

59. Barbara Wilson, interview by the author, April 28, 2013, and September 17, 2018. Like August, Barbara had been raised a Catholic and attended parochial schools. Also important

to Barbara's development was the care she received from Lillian Morrell, a friend of Faye who showered her with love and affection. Barbara regularly went to visit and eat with Mrs. Morrell, whom she still considers her surrogate godmother. Thanks to her, Barbara even got to participate in a cotillion.

60. Michael Wilson, interview by the author, September 2023.

61. Michael Wilson, interview by the author, September 2023.

62. Emmanuel Wilson, interview by the author, September 2023.

63. Emmanuel Wilson, interview by the author, September 2023.

64. Tony Fountain, interview by the author, August 1, 2013.

65. Nathan Oliver, interview by the author, September 2, 2013.

66. Curtiss Porter, interview by Lee Kiburi, November 28, 2007.

67. Tony Fountain, interview by the author, August 1, 2013.

68. Sam Howze (Sala Udin), "An Open Letter to Brothers and Sisters," *Connection: Journal of the Centre Ave. Poets Theatre* (Spring 1968). Perhaps significantly, Chawley Williams and Nick Flournoy were absent from the journal. In 1966 Nick had quit writing poetry and focused on advancing the civil rights movement through CORE. Chawley's absence may have been because drug addiction had taken him out of circulation or because he never made the transition to Black nationalism. Curtiss Porter, email message to the author, July 24, 2019.

69. Curtiss Porter, interview by Lee Kiburi, November 28, 2007.

70. Watlington, "Hurdling Fences," 84. Unfortunately, Wilson gives no clear indication of the year when this appreciation of Malcolm X took place. Shannon, *Dramatic Vision of August Wilson*, 31, says that in 1965 Wilson's friend Clarence Jones presented him an album of Malcolm X speeches. Shannon, *Dramatic Vision of August Wilson*, 181, quoting August Wilson, "The Legacy of Malcolm X," *Life*, December 1992, 89–90. See also Livingston, "Cool August," 57, 84.

71. Brown, "Light in August," 120.

72. Jerry Rhodes, interview by the author, April 22, 2016.

73. "Remembering August Wilson"; Bogumil, "August Wilson's Relationship to Black Theatre," 64n21.

74. Curtiss Porter, interview by Lee Kiburi, November 28, 2007.

75. In 1975 his wife Carol opened Africa Lost and Found Gallery in Oakland. Althea Fonville, "New African Art Gallery Opens," *New Pittsburgh Courier*, August 9, 1975, 17. Ellis died in November 1996, survived by his second wife, Marsha Lyn.

76. Ralph Proctor, interview by the author, June 24, 2013.

77. Troy West, interview by the author, July 28, 2013.

78. Jerry Rhodes, interview by the author, April 22, 2016.

79. Thad Mosley, interview by the author, June 12, 2013.

80. Bill Strickland, interview by the author, June 12, 2013.

81. Moses Carper, interview by Lee Kiburi, November 9, 2007.

82. Temujin Ekunfeo, interview by the author, July 28, 2013.

83. William Strickland, interview by the author, June 12, 2013

84. Mosley thinks it closed because its white financial sponsors pulled out. Thad Mosley, interview by the author, July 20, 2013.

Chapter 7. Black Horizons Theatre

1. Rob Penny, interviews with Lee Kiburi, multiple dates.

2. Rob Penny, interview by Lee Kiburi, August 18, 1998.

3. Christopher Reynolds, "Mr. Wilson's Neighborhood," *Los Angeles Times*, July 27, 2003.

4. Glasco and Rawson, *August Wilson*, 13.

5. August Wilson, interview by Lee Kiburi, April 6, 1999; Effort, "Pittsburgh Profiles."

6. Conner, *Pittsburgh in Stages*, 118–22; "Hill 'Y' Meets New Challenges," *Pittsburgh Courier* July 14, 1984, 1.

7. Christopher Rawson, "O'Reilly Theater: Wilson Again Proves Home is Where the Art Is," *Pittsburgh Post-Gazette*, December 5, 1999.

8. Lee Kiburi, interview by the author, December 8, 2024.

9. Lahr, "Been Here and Gone," 21.

10. The Anna B. Heldman Community Center, two blocks farther up Centre Avenue, was the successor to the Irene Kaufmann Settlement House. A massive five-story building that long had been the Hill's most impressive social institution, the IKS had been established in 1911 by Henry Kaufmann, owner of Pittsburgh's main department store, to help Jewish immigrants adjust to life in the United States. In the 1940s, as the Jewish population left the Hill, the IKS opened its facilities to non-Jews. In 1956, it donated the building and facilities to the Hill District's Black community, who renamed it The Hill House.

11. Moses Carper, interview by Lee Kiburi, November 9, 2007. Udin was not present at the first meeting, but attended the second, and became part of the "core" group.

12. Moses Carper, interview by Lee Kiburi, November 9, 2007.

13. Proctor writes: "The first host was a White woman; the second was a member of the ruling class of Liberia. I protested those choices and 'inherited' the show." Ralph Proctor, email message to the author, October 20, 2019. See also "This Week on Television," *New Pittsburgh Courier*, January 4, 1969, 8. Curtiss Porter, interview by Lee Kiburi, tape 1B. Porter says he is the one who suggested the name *Black Horizons* for the television show, whose popularity ultimately caused the public to refer to "Black Horizon Theatre" as "Black Horizons Theatre," to the displeasure of some original members like Sala Udin. Although the AAI had charged Rob to create Black Horizons as its cultural arm, once the theater was created, the AAI withered away. August said that this was because "we were all doing theater so in essence the Institute sort of dissolved into the theater." August Wilson, interview by Lee Kiburi, April 6, 1999.

14. *The Drama Review: TDR* 12, no. 4 (Summer 1968), https://www.jstor.org/stable/i247894; Neal, "Black Arts Movement."

15. Sanders, *Development of Black Theater in America*, 12.

16. Rob Penny, interview by Lee Kiburi, August 18, 1998.

17. Christopher Rawson, "August Wilson, 1945–2005; Pittsburgh Playwright Who Chronicled Black Experience, Pulitzer Prize-Winner Succumbs to Liver Cancer at 60 in Seattle, 'Surrounded by His Loved Ones,'" *Pittsburgh Post-Gazette*, October 3, 2005, A1; Gail Austin, interview by the author, June 21, 2013.

18. Rawson, "August Wilson, 1945–2005"; Gail Austin, interview by the author, June 21, 2013.

19. Rob Penny, interview by Lee Kiburi, August 18, 1998.

20. Rob Penny, interview by Lee Kiburi, August 18, 1998.

21. August Wilson, interview by Lee Kiburi, April 6, 1999.

22. Rob Penny, interview by Lee Kiburi, August 18, 1998; Livingston, "Cool August," 50; August Wilson, interview by Lee Kiburi, April 6, 1999.

23. August Wilson, interview by Lee Kiburi, April 6, 1999.

24. August Wilson, interview by Lee Kiburi, April 6, 1999.

25. August Wilson, interview by Lee Kiburi, April 6, 1999.

26. Lyons and Plimpton, "Art of Theater XIV." The appendix to Dean and Carra's *Fundamentals of Play Directing* consisted simply of a glossary of theater terms. On the other hand, the book's final chapter, "Rehearsals," advised that the first two rehearsals should be dedicated to "Reading and study of [the] whole play. Dean and Carra, *Fundamentals of Play Directing*, 317. Carra was for many years a professor at Carnegie Mellon in nearby Oakland and kept revising the book, which remained a staple in theater schools.

27. Rob Penny, interview by Lee Kiburi, August 18, 1998.

28. Lee Kiburi, interview by the author, June 8, 2013.

29. Lee Kiburi, interview by the author, June 8, 2013.

30. Lee Kiburi, interview by the author, June 8, 2013.

31. Vernell Lillie, interview by Lee Kiburi, November 15, 2008. It may have been rarely done in Lillie's experience, but it was widely done elsewhere.

32. August Wilson, interview by Lee Kiburi, April 6, 1999.

33. Rob Penny, interview by Lee Kiburi, August 18, 1998.

34. Lyons and Plimpton, "Art of Theater XIV."

35. August Wilson, interview by Lee Kiburi, April 6, 1999. The two plays were directed by Wilson and staged at A. Leo Weil School in 1968. They were subsequently performed at Tougaloo College in Mississippi and at Spirit House in Newark. Rob Penny, curriculum vitae, Archives & Special Collections, University of Pittsburgh.

36. August Wilson, interview by Lee Kiburi, April 6, 1999.

37. Moses Carper, interview by Lee Kiburi, November 9, 2007.

38. Moses Carper, interview by Lee Kiburi, November 9, 2007.

39. For example, on April 12, 1967, the Tuskegee Alumni Association held a *Best of Broadway* music performance there. "'Best of Broadway' April 12, at Weill," *New Pittsburgh Courier*, April 9, 1967, 16.

40. Moses Carper, interview by Lee Kiburi, August 18, 1998, and November 9, 2007.

41. Vernell Lillie, interview by Lee Kiburi, November 15, 2008.

42. Moses Carper, interview by Lee Kiburi, November 9, 2007.

43. Vernell Lillie, interview by Lee Kiburi, November 15, 2008.

44. Rob Penny, interview by Lee Kiburi, August 18, 1998.

45. August Wilson, interview by Lee Kiburi, April 6, 1999.

46. Curtiss Porter, interview by Lee Kiburi, November 28, 2007.

47. Curtiss Porter, interview by Lee Kiburi, November 28, 2007.

48. Tony Fountain, interview by the author, August 1, 2013.

49. Rob Penny, interview by Lee Kiburi, August 18, 1998.

50. Rob Penny, interview by Lee Kiburi, August 18, 1998.

51. August Wilson, interview by Lee Kiburi, April 6, 1999.

52. Sala Udin, interview by Lee Kiburi, October 5, 1998.

53. Sala Udin, Interview by Lee Kiburi, October 5, 1998.

54. Sala Udin, interview by Lee Kiburi, October 5, 1998.

55. Frank Hightower, interview by the author, June 28, 2013.

56. Livingston, "Cool August," 50–51.

57. Betty Douglass, interview by the author, June 20, 2013.

58. Rob Penny, interview by Lee Kiburi, August 18, 1998.

59. Rob Penny, interview by Lee Kiburi, August 18, 1998.

60. Sollers, *Amiri Baraka/LeRoi Jones*, 190.

61. Sakina A'la, interview by Lee Kiburi, October 3, 1998.

62. Sala Udin, interview by Lee Kiburi, October 5, 1998; "Blacks Plan Own Holiday," *Pittsburgh Post-Gazette*, July 1, 1969; David Warner, "Black Arts Festival to Stress Heritage," *Pittsburgh Press*, June 27, 1969; Toki Schalk Johnson, "Black Group Holds Feast of Kwanza," *New Pittsburgh Courier*, January 9, 1971; Frank Hightower, interview by the author, July 7, 1998; August Wilson, interview by Lee Kiburi, April 6, 1999. Black Horizons performed at Manchester Elementary School, Langley High School, Bidwell Cultural and Training Center, and Schenley High School. Examples of college performances included Duquesne University, Washington & Jefferson College, and the University of Pittsburgh. The latter featured a speech by Amiri Baraka and a performance by Baraka's Spirit House Movers. "Sandy Says," *New Pittsburgh Courier*, November 28, 1970.

63. Reginald Howze, interview by the author, July 24, 2017.

64. Curtiss Porter, interview by Lee Kiburi, November 28, 2007; Tony Fountain, email message to the author, December 16, 2014.

65. Curtiss Porter, interview by Lee Kiburi, November 28, 2007.

66. Curtiss Porter, interview by Lee Kiburi, November 28, 2007.

67. Sakina A'la, interview by Lee Kiburi, October 3, 1998.

68. Sala Udin, interview by Lee Kiburi, October 5, 1998.

69. Sakina A'la, interview by Lee Kiburi, October 3, 1998.

70. Lyons and Plimpton, "Art of Theater XIV."

71. Lyons and Plimpton, "Art of Theater XIV."

72. Rob Penny, interview by Lee Kiburi, August 18, 1998.

73. Sakina A'la, interview by Lee Kiburi, October 3, 1998.

74. Sala Udin, interview by Lee Kiburi, October 5, 1998.

75. Bryer and Hartig, *Conversations with August Wilson*, 96.

76. Bryer and Hartig, *Conversations with August Wilson*, 96.

77. Amiri Baraka, interview by Lee Kiburi, August 31, 1998; Penny, curriculum vitae; Curtiss Porter, interview by Lee Kiburi, November 28, 2007; Frank Hightower, interview by the author, August 16, 2013.

78. Bethe Thomas, "Above All, He is a Poet," *Day* (New London, CT), May 19, 1985, B3.

79. Penny, curriculum vitae; Jerry Rhodes, interview by the author, May 22, 2016.

80. Years later, in 1988, Wilson dated his departure from Black Horizons Theatre as 1971. Savran, "August Wilson," 21. In 1969 Wilson withdrew from formal operations at Black Horizons but came around on an informal basis. It may have been 1971 that, in his own mind, he cut all ties with the company.

81. August Wilson, interview by Lee Kiburi, April 6, 1999.

82. August Wilson, interview by Lee Kiburi, April 6, 1999.

83. August Wilson, interview by Lee Kiburi, April 6, 1999.

84. August Wilson, interview by Lee Kiburi, April 6, 1999.

85. Lyons and Plimpton, "Art of Theater XIV"; Savran, "August Wilson."

86. Curtiss Porter, interviews by Lee Kiburi, multiple dates.

87. Rob Penny, interview by Lee Kiburi, August 18, 1998.

88. Rob Penny, interview by Lee Kiburi, August 18, 1998.

89. Elva Branson, interview by the author, May 8, 2017.

90. Frank Hightower, interview by the author, June 28, 2013.

91. Frank Hightower, interview by the author, July 7, 1998.

92. Savran, "August Wilson," 21; August Wilson, interview by Lee Kiburi, April 6, 1999.

93. August Wilson, interview by Lee Kiburi, April 6, 1999.

Chapter 8. Return to Poetry

1. Frank Hightower, interview by the author, December 12, 2013.

2. Barbara Wilson, interview by the author, April 29, 2013, and September 17, 2018.

3. August Wilson, interview by Lee Kiburi, April 6, 1999.

4. Application for Marriage License, Clerk of the Orphan's Court, Pittsburgh, PA.

5. Sala Udin, interview by the author, June 7, 2013.

6. Nathan Oliver, interview by the author, September 2, 2013.

7. See "HDCC Picks New Officers," *Pittsburgh Courier*, December 31, 1966, 3A.

8. Samuel Freedman, "A Voice from the Streets," *New York Times*, March 15, 1987, A36.

9. Freedman, "Voice from the Streets."

10. Brenda Burton, interview by the author, May 20, 2013.

11. Sheppard, "August Wilson," 103.

12. *Connection*, published locally by Oduduwa Productions, 1970. Editor, Curtiss E. Porter; poetry editor, August Wilson. The poem was reprinted in Adoff, *Poetry of Black America*, 491–92.

13. On the changing use and significance of the word *nigger*, see Kennedy, *Nigger*.

14. *Connection*, 1970.

15. Shannon, *Dramatic Vision of August Wilson*, 202.

16. The poem appeared in 1972 in *Black World*, the successor to *Negro Digest*, both national publications.

17. Gail Austin, interview by the author, December 19, 2017; August Wilson, interview by Lee Kiburi, April 6, 1999; Betty Rogers, interview by the author, 2013. This was at Urban Talent Development, a youth education/training and awareness center for teens. Located on Baum Boulevard in East Liberty, the program's mission of encouraging youth participation in the arts would have appealed to Wilson. The two briefly dated, and as he frequently did, August dedicated several poems to Betty and gave them to her. Betty did not save the poems, partly because she was not enamored of August, and also because she had no idea that he would go on to fame and fortune. "I sure wish I had," she says, laughing ruefully. Just as Wilson's poetry differed from that of most others in the Black Arts Movement, the same was true of his manner of speaking. Betty was struck by what she considered August's unusual way of speaking, which she says was different from how most Black people speak, which she describes as "more like an intellectual formulation of words than slang."

18. Virginia Joyce, "FASC Approves Black Studies," *Pitt News* (University of Pittsburgh), June 30, 1969, 1.

19. Curtiss E. Porter and Jack L. Daniel, "Black Paper for Black Studies," 1969, Hillman Library, University of Pittsburgh.

20. Rob Penny, curriculum vitae, Archives & Special Collections, University of Pittsburgh.

21. "Ralph Proctor is Appointed College Aide," *University Times*, May 28, 1969, 3; Ralph Proctor, interview by the author, June 24, 2013.

22. Curtiss Porter, email message to the author, June 17, 2018.

23. Curtiss Porter, email message to the author, June 13, 2018.

24. Frank Hightower, interview by the author, June 28, 2013.

25. Vernell Lillie, interview by the author, November 15, 2013.

26. August Wilson, interview by Lee Kiburi, April 6, 1999.

27. Waumba World was funded by the PACE Foundation (Program to Aid Citizen Enterprise). Curtiss Porter, email message to the author, August 29, 2014. Curtiss Porter remembers it as the Kraal.

28. Shelly Stevenson, interview by the author, August 16, 2013.

29. Ron Karenga, excerpt from "Black Cultural Nationalism," in Gayle, ed., *Black Esthetic*.

30. Matlin, "'Lift Up Yr Self!,'" 103.

31. Shelly Stevenson, interview by the author, August 16, 2013.

32. August Wilson, typed report, n.d., in the August Wilson Collection.

33. August Wilson, interview by Lee Kiburi, April 6, 1999.

34. Vernell Lillie, interview by the author, November 15, 2008.

35. Bill Strickland, interview by the author, June 12, 2013.

36. Frank Hightower, interview by the author, July 7, 1998.

37. Frank Hightower, interview by the author, July 7, 1998.

38. August Wilson, interview by Lee Kiburi, April 6, 1999.

39. Frank Hightower, interview by the author, December 12, 2013.

40. Frank Hightower, interview by the author, November 12, 2013.

41. Elva Branson, interview by the author, May 8, 2017.

42. Elva Branson, email interview by Lee Kiburi, November 28, 2007.

43. Elva Branson, interview by the author, May 8, 2017.

44. Rob Penny, interview by Lee Kiburi, August 18, 1998; Penny, curriculum vitae. *Centre Avenue, A Trip* was performed at the University of Pittsburgh's Studio Theatre. It also was staged that year at the Fifth Avenue High School auditorium and at the Black Arts Festival in Homewood.

45. "Sala's Day Benefit to be Held Here," *New Pittsburgh Courier*, April 15, 1972. The article says Udin had been imprisoned (as Samuel Wesley Howze) at Lewisburg Penitentiary. In 1970 he was indicted in Kentucky for illegally transporting firearms (an unloaded shotgun) and possession of non-tax-paid distilled spirits (moonshine). He was sentenced to five years at a federal penitentiary. He began serving his sentence on February 4, 1972, at Lewisburg Federal Penitentiary. He was paroled after seven months. In 2004 Udin applied for a governor's pardon. In 2006 his request for a pardon was denied. In 2016 he was granted a presidential pardon. See Tracie Mauriello, "Sala Udin Gets Presidential Pardon, 44 Year Later," *Pittsburgh Post-Gazette*, December 19, 2016.

46. Elva Branson, email interview by Lee Kiburi, November 28, 2007.

47. Robert Louis Stevenson, interview by the author, June 26, 2013.

48. Robert Louis Stevenson, interview by the author, June 26, 2013; Samuel G. Freedman, "Wilson's New 'Fences' Nurtures a Partnership," *New York Times*, May 5, 1985, A80.

49. Robert Louis Stevenson, interview by the author, June 26, 2013; Samuel G. Freedman, "Wilson's New 'Fences' Nurtures a Partnership," *New York Times*, May 5, 1985, A80; Elva Branson, email message to the author, June 9, 2017.

50. Christopher Rawson, "Purdy Lends His Energy to 'Iguana,'" *Pittsburgh Post-Gazette*, September 28, 1990.

51. Gwen Ormes, interview by the author, November 6, 2017.

52. Gwen Ormes, interview by the author, November 6, 2017.

53. Rawson, "Purdy Lends His Energy to 'Iguana.'"

54. Elva Branson, email interview by Lee Kiburi, November 28, 2007.

55. Curtiss Porter, interview by Lee Kiburi, November 28, 2007.

56. Sala Udin, interview by the author, June 7, 2013.

57. Curtiss Porter, interview by Lee Kiburi, November 28, 2007.

58. Elva Branson, email interview by Lee Kiburi, November 28, 2007.

59. Elva Branson, email interview by Lee Kiburi, November 28, 2007.

60. Elva Branson, email interview by Lee Kiburi, November 28, 2007; Elva Branson, email message to the author, June 9, 2017.

61. Elva Branson, email interview by Lee Kiburi, November 28, 2007.

62. Curtiss Porter, interview by Lee Kiburi, November 28, 2007.

63. Vernell Lillie, interview by the author, June 7, 2013, and September 6, 2013.

64. Sala Udin, interview by the author, June 7, 2013.

65. Maisha Baton, interview by Lee Kiburi, December 26, 2007.

66. Frank Hightower, interview by the author, November 12, 2013.

67. Elva Branson, email message to the author, June 9, 2017.

68. Elva Branson, email message to the author, June 9, 2017.

69. Imamu Amiri Baraka, "Black Woman," quoted in Matlin, "'Lift Up Yr Self!,'" 102

70. Elva Branson, email interview by Lee Kiburi, November 28, 2007.

71. Sakina A'la, interview by Lee Kiburi, October 3, 1998.

72. Sala Udin, interview by the author, October 5, 1998.

73. Rob Penny, interview by Lee Kiburi, August 18, 1998.

74. Sala Udin, interview by the author, October 5, 1998; Sakina A'la, interview by Lee Kiburi, October 3, 1998.

75. Sala Udin, interview by the author, October 5, 1998; Sakina A'la, interview by Lee Kiburi, October 3, 1998.

76. Sala Udin, interview by the author, October 5, 1998; Sakina A'la, interview by Lee Kiburi, October 3, 1998.

77. Sala Udin, interview by the author, October 5, 1998; Sakina A'la, interview by Lee Kiburi, October 3, 1998.

78. Sala Udin, interview by the author, October 5, 1998; Sakina A'la, interview by Lee Kiburi, October 3, 1998.

79. Rob Penny, interview by Lee Kiburi, August 18, 1998.

80. Elva Branson, interview by the author, May 8, 2017.

81. Brenda Burton, interview by the author, June 7, 2015.

82. Vernell Lillie, interview by the author, June 7, 2013, and June 9, 2013.

83. Sandra Gould Ford, interview by the author, August 26, 2013; Brenda Burton, interview by the author, June 7, 2015.

84. Nadel, *May All Your Fences Have Gates*, 163n9; Nathan Oliver, interview by the author, September 2, 2013; Joe Adcock, "August Wilson: 1945–2005; Playwright Gave Voice to Black Experience," *Seattle Post-Intelligencer*, October 3, 2005, A1; Brown, "Light in August," 124; Bryer and Hartig, introduction to *Conversations with August Wilson*, xv; Feingold, "August Wilson's Bottomless Blackness."

85. Temujin Ekunfeo, interview by the author, July 15, 2013.

86. Christopher Rawson, interview by the author, May 25, 2025.

87. Brenda Burton, interview by the author, June 7, 2015.

88. Bryer and Hartig, *Conversations with August Wilson*, xviii, 14.

89. Hop Kendrick, interview by the author, June 2, 2012.

90. Natalie Bazzell, interview by the author, August 30, 2013.

91. Vernell Lillie, interview by the author, June 7, 2013, and June 9, 2013.

92. Lahr, "Been Here and Gone," 15, 25.

93. Divorce application, Brenda Kittel vs. Frederick Kittel, September 7, 1972, October 7, 1992. Petition filed by indigent person, sheriff's return shows Dpt not found, refiled January 19, 1973, divorce granted April 5, 1973, Common Pleas Court; Feingold, "August Wilson's Bottomless Blackness"; Brown, "Light in August," 124.

94. Quoted in Christopher Reynolds, "Mr. Wilson's Neighborhood," *Los Angeles Times*, July 27, 2003.

95. Brenda Burton, interview by the author, June 7, 2015.

96. Brenda Burton, interview by the author, June 7, 2015.

97. Brenda Burton, interview by the author, June 7, 2015.

98. Elva Branson, interview by the author, May 8, 2017.

99. Michael Louik was an attorney and board member of RAP, a group Packard had founded to help recovering addicts. Louik saved the poem and note from Packard all these years. See poetry appendix.

100. Elva Branson, email interview by Lee Kiburi, November 28, 2007.

101. Elva Branson, interview by the author, May 8, 2017.

102. Sheppard, "August Wilson," 103.

103. August Wilson, interview by Lee Kiburi, April 6, 1999. August told theater critic John Lahr, "For me, it was so liberating." Lahr, "Been Here and Gone," 25.

104. August Wilson, interview by Lee Kiburi, April 6, 1999; Lahr, "Been Here and Gone," 25. Apparently "Morning Statement" has never published in any collection of poetry, only in an article about Wilson published by Lahr in "Been Here and Gone," 25.

105. Barbara Evans, interview with author, July 2, 2018.

106. Arby's Restaurant was, and still is, located downtown at the corner of Liberty Avenue and Wood Street. Richest Restaurant was located at 140 6th Street near Heinz Hall and Penn Avenue.

107. Excerpts reprinted through the courtesy of Barbara Evans.

108. Norwood, "Plain Style in Southern Poetry," 109-24; Norwood, email message to the author, February 5, 2020. See also Vendler, *Music of What Happens*, 75. James Knapp, email message to the author November 11, 2019; Cameron Barnett, email message to the author, November 12, 2019. On the longer history of plain style, in prose as well as poetry, see Hugh Kenner, "The Politics of the Plain," *New York Times*, September 15, 1985. Wilson's 1967 poem "Poet" was also simple and straightforward.

109. Matlin, "Lift up Yr Self!" 106, 116; Sollors, *Amiri Baraka/LeRoi Jones*, 226, 228; Simanga, *Amiri Baraka and the Congress of African People*, esp. chap. 10: "Transition to Marxism"; Woodard, *Nation Within a Nation*.

110. Amiri Baraka, interview by Lee Kiburi, August 31, 1998.

111. Chawley Williams told Maisha Baton that he "had been out of things for a while," presumably meaning his four-year incarceration in the Lexington medical prison in Kentucky.

112. Elva Branson, email message to the author, June 9, 2017; Elva Branson, interview by the author, May 8, 2017.

113. Elva Branson, interview by Lee Kiburi, June 10, 2017.

114. Elva Branson, interview by the author, June 10, 2017.

115. Robert Hurwitt, "Claude Purdy's 'Perfect Play,'" *San Francisco Examiner*, January 8, 1989, E3, courtesy of Macelle Mahala.

Chapter 9. Leaving Pittsburgh

1. Ron Pitts, interview by Lee Kiburi, November 23, 2007.

2. Rob Penny, interview by Lee Kiburi, August 18, 1998.

3. August Wilson, interview by Lee Kiburi, April 6, 1999.

4. Mary Bradley, interview by Lee Kiburi, October 11, 2011.

5. Mary Bradley, interview by Lee Kiburi, October 11, 2011.

6. Mary Bradley, interview by Lee Kiburi, October 11, 2011.

7. Mary Bradley, interview by Lee Kiburi, October 11, 2011; Ron Pitts, interview by Lee Kiburi, November 23, 2007; August Wilson, interview by Lee Kiburi, April 6, 1999.

8. Ron Pitts, interview by Lee Kiburi, November 23, 2007. The cast, as best Pitts can recall, consisted of Robbie Dixon, Greg Jones, Joyce Dixon, Eileen, Kenny Robinson and his brother, plus a few others.

9. Mary Bradley, interview by Lee Kiburi, October 11, 2011.

10. Mary Bradley, interview by Lee Kiburi, October 11, 2011; Ron Pitts, interview by Lee Kiburi, November 23, 2007.

11. Rob Penny, interview by Lee Kiburi, August 18, 1998.

12. Rob Penny, interview by Lee Kiburi, August 18, 1998. The daughter was Joyce. Mary Bradley, interview by Lee Kiburi, October 11, 2011.

13. Mary Bradley, interview by Lee Kiburi, October 11, 2011.

14. Ron Pitts, interview by Lee Kiburi, November 23, 2007.

15. Ron Pitts, interview by Lee Kiburi, November 23, 2007.

16. Mary Bradley, interview by Lee Kiburi, October 11, 2011.

17. Ron Pitts, interview by Lee Kiburi, November 23, 2007.

18. Ron Pitts, interview by Lee Kiburi, November 23, 2007.

19. Ron Pitts, interview by Lee Kiburi, November 23, 2007.

20. August Wilson, interview by Lee Kiburi, April 6, 1999.

21. August Wilson, interview by Lee Kiburi, April 6, 1999.

22. Noel McCarroll, Kiburi Collection, July 30, 2013.

23. Noel McCarroll, Kiburi Collection, July 30, 2013.

24. August Wilson, interview by Lee Kiburi, April 6, 1999.

25. Maisha Baton, interview by Lee Kiburi, December 26, 2007.

26. August Wilson, interview by Lee Kiburi, April 6, 1999.

27. August Wilson, interview by Lee Kiburi, April 6, 1999.

28. Maisha Baton, interview by Lee Kiburi, December 26, 2007.

29. Maisha Baton, interview by Lee Kiburi, December 26, 2007.

30. Ron Pitts, interview by Lee Kiburi, November 23, 2007.

31. Ron Pitts, interview by Lee Kiburi, November 23, 2007.

32. Ron Pitts, interview by Lee Kiburi, November 23, 2007.

33. Ron Pitts, interview by Lee Kiburi, November 23, 2007.

34. Ron Pitts, interview by Lee Kiburi, November 23, 2007.

35. Ron Pitts, interview by Lee Kiburi, November 23, 2007.

36. Shannon mentions 1976 and 1977. For 1976, see Shannon, *Dramatic Vision of August Wilson*, 30. For 1977, see Shannon, "August Wilson Explains His Dramatic Vision," 122.

37. Maisha Baton, interview by Lee Kiburi, December 26, 2007.

38. Shannon, *Dramatic Vision of August Wilson*, 241. Shannon lists the full set of Wilson's unpublished plays, including those written for the Science Museum of Minnesota.

39. Allegheny Repertory Theatre, press release, September 23, 1982, for the premiere of August Wilson's *Jitney* at the Fine Line Cultural Center, Oakland, University of Pittsburgh Theater Archives, Hillman Library. According to the *Pittsburgh Courier,* Johnson had a bit of film experience, having appeared in *Midnight,* the sequel to the Pittsburgh-made film *Night of the Living Dead.* See Walter Ray Watson, "Choreographer Bob Johnson Remembered," *Pittsburgh Courier,* October 11, 1986, 6.

40. "Spotlight on African Art Folk Festival," *Pittsburgh Courier,* May 16, 1970, 3.

41. "BAS Slates Black Week," *Pittsburgh Courier,* November 7, 1970, 8.

42. Greg Mims, "Ailey Dancers Teach Master Class at Local Center," *Pittsburgh Courier,* March 16, 1974, 17.

43. Walter Ray Watson, "Choreographer Bob Johnson Remembered," *Pittsburgh Courier,* October 11, 1986, 6.

44. Watson, "Choreographer Bob Johnson Remembered." I saw BJ dance once, in a solo rehearsal. The performance was so moving, it brought me almost to tears. Johnson's talent and power had to be seen to be appreciated.

45. Johnson does not include the play in his résumé. See Bob Johnson Papers, Archives & Special Collections, University of Pittsburgh. August Wilson, interview by Lee Kiburi, April 6, 1999.

46. Lillie's education options were all in the North. Universities in the South did not admit Black students, but Southern states provided scholarships for Blacks to do graduate work in the North. Vernell Lillie, interview by Lee Kiburi, June 9, 2007, and November 15, 2007.

47. Vernell Lillie, interview by the author, June 9, 2013.

48. Vernell Lillie, interview by Lee Kiburi, April 28, 1998.

49. The company's name, Kuntu, is derived from a Central African word for "way" or "mode," a term popularized by Janheinz Jahn, whose book *Muntu* argued that Africa has a unified cultural aesthetic. Vernell Lillie, curriculum vitae, 1978, Vernell Lillie Papers, box 57, folder 5, Archives & Special Collections, University of Pittsburgh.

50. Vernell Lillie, interview by Lee Kiburi, April 28, 1998.

51. Vernell Lillie, interview by Lee Kiburi, April 28, 1998.

52. The department had relocated from its original office on Craig Street to a suite of offices on the second floor of a building on Forbes Avenue, across from the old police and fire station. Brenda Berrian, interview by the author, September 8, 2013.

53. Brenda Berrian, interview by the author, September 8, 2013.

54. Diana Nelson Jones, "Obituary: Maisha Baton/Nurturing Poet, Playwright, Therapist and Teacher," *Pittsburgh Post-Gazette,* March 28, 2012.

55. Vernell Lillie, interview by the author, June 7, 2013.

56. Vernell Lillie to August Wilson, January 26, 1976, August Wilson Papers, courtesy of the August Wilson estate.

57. Elkins, "Wilson, August." Shannon, *Dramatic Vision of August Wilson,* 35ff, has a summary of the play.

58. Uzzel, *Blind Lemon Jefferson,* 45–46.

59. Herrington, *I Ain't Sorry for Nothin' I Done,* 25.

60. Savran, "August Wilson," 23.

61. "The Homecoming" by August Wilson, courtesy of the August Wilson estate.

62. Vernell Lillie, interview by the author, November 15, 2008; August Wilson, interview by Lee Kiburi, April 6, 1999; Vernell Lillie, interview by the author, June 9, 2013. The play was staged in 1976. Lillie, curriculum vitae.

63. Lillie says she still has a copy of the play, but declines to share it because of its relatively low quality. Sharing it, Lillie says, would be a disservice to August's memory. Vernell Lillie, interview by the author, June 7, 2013, and June 9, 2013.

64. Vernell Lillie, interview by Lee Kiburi, November 15, 2008.

65. Vernell Lillie, interview by Lee Kiburi, April 28, 1998.

66. Vernell Lillie, interview by the author, May 22, 2014.

67. Mary Bradley, interview by Lee Kiburi, October 11, 2011.

68. August Wilson, interview by Lee Kiburi, April 6, 1999.

69. August Wilson, interview by Lee Kiburi, April 6, 1999. Ujima was a failure for Wilson, but for Pitts it was transformative. After finishing his studies at the University of Pittsburgh, Pitts took a job with an optical firm in Columbus, Ohio. There, inspired by his years at Ujima, he joined a theater company that, ironically, also bore the name Ujima. Ron Pitts, interview by the author, February 13, 2015.

70. Elva Branson, interview by the author, May 8, 2017. Rob Penny says it was still functioning "off and on" in 1973, when he and Wilson established Ujima Theater. Rob Penny, interview by Lee Kiburi, August 18, 1998. Years later, the *Pittsburgh Post-Gazette* dated its demise as 1971. Ervin Dyer, "Obituary: Robert Lee 'Rob' Penny," *Pittsburgh Post-Gazette*, March 18, 2003. Curtiss Porter says Black Horizons Theatre ended "about 1972." Curtiss Porter, interview by Lee Kiburi, November 28, 2007.

71. Vernell Lillie, interview by Lee Kiburi, April 28, 1998.

72. Rob Penny, interview by Lee Kiburi, August 18, 1998

73. August Wilson, interview by Lee Kiburi, April 6, 1999.

74. Maisha Baton, interview by Lee Kiburi, December 26, 2007; Maisha Baton, curriculum vitae, Bob Johnson Papers, Archives & Special Collections, University of Pittsburgh; Geri B. Ransom, "Theatre Urge Stages 'Black Happenin','" *New Pittsburgh Courier*, June 6, 1981, A3.

75. Maisha Baton, interview by Lee Kiburi, December 26, 2007.

76. Maisha Baton, interview by Lee Kiburi, December 26, 2007.

77. Maisha Baton, interview by Lee Kiburi, December 26, 2007.

78. Maisha Baton, interview by Lee Kiburi, December 26, 2007.

79. Maisha Baton, interview by Lee Kiburi, December 26, 2007.

80. Maisha Baton, interview by Lee Kiburi, December 26, 2007; Baton, curriculum vitae; Geri B. Ransom, "Theatre Urge Stages 'Black Happenin','" *New Pittsburgh Courier*, June 6, 1981, A3.

81. Maisha Baton, interview by Lee Kiburi, December 26, 2007.

82. Natalie Bazzell, interview by the author, August 30, 2013.

83. Barbara Evans, interview by the author, July 2, 2018.

84. Durham and Jones, *Adventures of the Negro Cowboys*; Love, *Life and Adventures of Nat Love*; Felton, *Nat Love, Negro Cowboy*; Wyman, *Legend of Charlie Glass*.

85. *Jet* magazine, May 27, 1976, 64; Mahala, *Penumbra*, 27.

86. Nolan, *Wild West*, has a chapter devoted to the legend of Black Bart, known as "the gentleman highwayman and poet." When Wilson lived in Los Angeles, he may have seen the 1948 film that celebrated Bart's exploits. See Philip K. Scheuer, "'Black Bart' Arrives," *Los Angeles Times*, February 25, 1948, 18.

87. Script and comments for *Black Bart and the Sacred Hills*, Bob Johnson Papers, Archives & Special Collections, University of Pittsburgh.

88. Rohan Preston, "Claude Purdy Gave August Wilson His Break in St. Paul," *Minneapolis Star Tribune*, July 28, 2009; Nelson Harrison, interview by the author, July 26, 2013; Nelson

Harrison, email message to the author, March 25, 2014; Mahala, *Penumbra*, 21; *Pittsburgh Post-Gazette*, misc. items, February–May 2017.

89. Maisha Baton, interview by Lee Kiburi, December 26, 2007.

90. Lyons and Plimpton, "Art of Theater XIV."

91. Maisha Baton, interview by Lee Kiburi, December 26, 2007.

92. Maisha Baton, interview by Lee Kiburi, December 26, 2007.

93. Elva Branson, interview by the author, May 8, 2017.

94. Maisha Baton, interview by Lee Kiburi, December 26, 2007.

95. *Black Bart*, 125 MS, box 28. Quoted courtesy of the August Wilson estate.

96. James Wilson, in *Actors Talk August*, podcast hosted by Chris Rawson, April 19, 2021.

97. Shannon, *Dramatic Vision of August Wilson*, 26.

98. Herrington, *I Ain't Sorry for Nothin' I Done*, 36–40.

99. Gifted intellectually as well as musically, Harrison went on to earn a PhD in psychology and teach in the Music Department at the University of Pittsburgh. Today, he runs the Pittsburgh Jazz Society, dedicated to the promotion of jazz in Pittsburgh. See https://pittsburgh.jazznearyou.com/pittsburgh-jazz-society.php.

100. Nelson Harrison, interview by the author, July 26, 2013.

101. August Wilson, interview by Lee Kiburi, April 6, 1999.

102. Ron Pitts, interview by Lee Kiburi, November 23, 2007.

103. The play ran June 23–26, 1977. *University Times* (University of Pittsburgh), June 16, 1977. See also Lillie, curriculum vitae; August Wilson, interview by Lee Kiburi, April 6, 1999.

104. Ron Pitts, interview by Lee Kiburi, November 23, 2007.

105. Ron Pitts, interview by Lee Kiburi, November 23, 2007.

106. Justin Maxwell, "August Wilson and the Playwrights' Center," *Minnesota History* (Winter 2006–7): 133–42; Rohan Preston, "Claude Purdy Gave August Wilson His Break in St. Paul," *Minnesota Star Tribune*, July 28, 2009. Purdy later became an expert interpreter of Wilson plays, directing them in Pittsburgh, Houston, San Francisco, and London.

107. Savran, "August Wilson," 22.

108. Thad Mosley, interview by the author, April 30, 2013, and May 23, 2014.

109. Thad Mosley, interview, April 30, 2013.

110. In fact, the Guthrie would not have been a good fit for Wilson. The theater was self-consciously interested only in established playwrights with outstanding national and/or international, reputations. Only after Wilson established himself as a major American playwright did the Guthrie stage his plays. See Daniel Gabriel, interview by the author, July 31, 2014.

111. Elva Branson, interview by the author, May 8, 2017; Jacqui Shoholm-Purdy, Purdy's widow, says that Wilson came with the intention of working with Claude in Saint Paul. Jacqui Shoholm-Purdy, interview by the author, August 25, 2017.

112. Date per Jacqui Shoholm-Purdy, widow of Claude Purdy.

113. Maisha Baton, interview by Lee Kiburi, December 26, 2007.

114. Ron Pitts, interview by Lee Kiburi, November 23, 2007.

115. Sala Udin, interview by the author, June 7, 2013.

116. Ralph Proctor, interview by the author, June 24, 2013.

Chapter 10. Discovering Bearden, Finding His Way

1. Christopher Rawson, "The Power Behind the Plays: August Wilson Has Changed the Way Theater Approaches Race," *Pittsburgh Post-Gazette*, June 6, 1999.

2. Jacqui Shoholm Purdy, interview by the author, August 23, 2017.

3. Jacqui Shoholm Purdy, interview by the author, August 23, 2017.

4. Jacqui Shoholm Purdy, interview by the author, August 23, 2017.

5. Jacqui Shoholm Purdy, interview by the author, August 23, 2017.

6. Jacqui Shoholm Purdy, email message to the author, March 9, 2020.

7. Daniel Gabriel, email message to the author, August 13, 2014; Brown, "Light in August," 124.

8. Brenda Berrian, interview by the author, September 8, 2013; Shannon, *Dramatic Vision of August Wilson*, 27.

9. Effort, "Pittsburgh Profiles"; Maxwell, "August Wilson and the Playwrights' Center," 133–42.

10. Jacqui Shoholm Purdy, email message to the author, January 5, 2020.

11. Shannon, *Dramatic Vision of August Wilson*, 40ff.

12. Bob Hoover, "Childhood in Hill leads to a Pulitzer for August Wilson," *Pittsburgh Post-Gazette*, June 1, 1987.

13. Courtesy of the August Wilson estate.

14. Jacqui Shoholm Purdy, email edits, August 28, 2017.

15. Jacqui Shoholm Purdy, email message to the author, January 7, 2020.

16. Jacqui Shoholm Purdy, email messages to the author, August 23 and 29, 2017; September 6, 7, and 8, 2017.

17. August Wilson, foreword to Schwartzman, *Romare Bearden*, 8.

18. Wilson, foreword to Schwartzman, *Romare Bearden*, 8.

19. Campbell, *American Odyssey*, 1, says that Bearden "filled his canvases with the faces of black people."

20. The family and locals pronounced the boy's name "Ró-mahry"; today many pronounce it "Ro-máre."

21. The grandparents moved to the East Liberty neighborhood. In 1929 Romare graduated from Peabody High School in Pittsburgh.

22. Campbell, "History and the Art of Romare Bearden," 12. Campbell, like others, says that Bearden lived in Lawrenceville. However, the boardinghouse was located at 3142 Penn Avenue, in the heavily industrial area known as the Strip District. Lawrenceville begins at 33rd Street. Technically, then, Bearden spent summers in the Strip District, located near the neighborhood of Lawrenceville.

23. Washington, *Art of Romare Bearden*, 222.

24. Campbell, *American Odyssey*, 284.

25. C. Gerald Fraser, "Romare Bearden, Collagist and Painter, Dies at 75," *New York Times*, March 13, 1988, 36. Bearden's life is beautifully portrayed in Campbell, *American Odyssey*.

26. His collages appeared on the January 1968 issue of *Fortune* magazine and the November 1, 1968, issue of *Time* magazine. Hage, "Reconfiguring Race, Recontextualizing the Media," 36–51.

27. Washington, *Art of Romare Bearden*. For the original exhibition catalogue, see Green, *Romare Bearden*.

28. Quoted in Patton, "Memory and Metaphor," 40.

29. Campbell, *American Odyssey*, 247.

30. Campbell, *American Odyssey*, 246.

31. Campbell, *American Odyssey*, 246.

32. Williams, "Introduction," 10, 17.

33. Wilson, foreword to Schwartzman, *Romare Bearden*, 8.

34. Williams, "Introduction," 17; Campbell, *American Odyssey*, 240.

35. Williams, "Introduction," 17.

36. Christopher Reynolds, "Mr. Wilson's Neighborhood," *Los Angeles Times*, July 27, 2003; Lahr, "Been Here and Gone," 21–22.

37. Reynolds, "Mr. Wilson's Neighborhood"; Lahr, "Been Here and Gone," 21–22.

38. C. Gerald Fraser, in his obituary, terms Bearden "the nation's foremost collagist." See Fraser, "Romare Bearden, Collagist and Painter, Dies at 75."

39. Daniel Gabriel, interview by the author, July 31, 2014.

40. Lyons and Plimpton, "Art of Theater XIV."

41. Christopher Rawson, "August Wilson, Pittsburgh Playwright Who Chronicled Black Experience," *Pittsburgh Post-Gazette*, October 3, 2005.

42. August Wilson, "How to Write a Play Like August Wilson," *New York Times*, March 10, 1991, 5, 17.

43. Wilson, foreword to Schwartzman, *Romare Bearden*, 8–9. See also Fishman, "Romare Bearden and August Wilson," 134.

44. August Wilson, foreword to Schwartzman, *Romare Bearden*, 9.

45. The staged reading was in April or May 1979. Maisha Baton, curriculum vitae, Bob Johnson Papers, Archives & Special Collections, University of Pittsburgh. The staged reading of *Black Bart and the Sacred Hills* in Los Angeles did not draw notice, apparently, for it is not mentioned in Walker, "Politics of Art."

46. Maisha Baton, interview by Lee Kiburi, December 26, 2007.

47. Maisha Baton, interview by Lee Kiburi, December 26, 2007.

48. Shannon, *Dramatic Vision of August Wilson*, 26–27.

49. Daniel Gabriel, interview by the author, July 31, 2014.

50. Jacqui Shoholm Purdy, email messages to the author, August 23 and 29, 2017; September 6, 7, and 8, 2017.

51. Jacqui Shoholm Purdy, email messages to the author, August 23 and 29, 2017; September 6, 7, and 8, 2017.

52. Jacqui Shoholm Purdy, email message to the author, January 7, 2020.

53. Maisha Baton, interview by Lee Kiburi, December 26, 2007. The relationship broke off when the Gabriels went on an extended trip through Europe, Africa, and India, but picked up again once they got back.

54. Daniel Gabriel, interview by the author, July 31, 2014; Jacqui Shoholm Purdy, email edits, August 28, 2017.

55. Daniel Gabriel, interview by the author, July 31, 2014.

56. Daniel Gabriel, interview by the author, July 31, 2014.

57. Daniel Gabriel, interview by the author, July 31, 2014.

58. Daniel Gabriel, interview by the author, July 31, 2014.

59. Daniel Gabriel, interview by the author, July 31, 2014.

60. Jacqui Shoholm Purdy, email message to the author, August 23, 2017.

61. Daniel Gabriel, interview by the author, July 31, 2014.

62. Wilson, *How I Learned What I Learned*.

63. Daniel Gabriel, interview by the author, July 31, 2014.

64. Daniel Gabriel, interview by the author, July 31, 2014.

65. Daniel Gabriel, interview by the author, July 31, 2014.

66. Daniel Gabriel, email message to the author, August 13, 2014; telephone conversations with the author, June 1, 3, and 5, 2020.

67. Wilson later abandoned writing a play about life in a turpentine camp after concluding that he knew too little about life in such camps.

68. Daniel Gabriel, interview by the author, July 31, 2014.

69. Daniel Gabriel, interview by the author, July 31, 2014. Wilson's letters may well have been in the home of Rob's widow, Betty. Rob was an inveterate collector of papers, books, and memorabilia. This collection has recently been transferred to the University of Pittsburgh Archives & Special Collections.

70. Daniel Gabriel, interview by the author, July 31, 2014.

71. Daniel Gabriel, interview by the author, July 31, 2014.

Chapter 11. Breakthroughs

1. We don't know Daisy's reaction, but her friend Julia Burley was thoroughly charmed. Years later, when asked about Judy, Julia called her "the sweetest girl." Daisy resided at 1621 Bedford Avenue, a block down from August's childhood residence at 1725 Bedford. Julia Burley, interview by the author, May 30, 2012.

2. Wilson, *How I Learned What I Learned.*

3. The new venture revived proud memories of the Owl Cab Company, which Knox had owned in the 1940s. See "Owl Cab Bankrupt, Owes $86,000," *Pittsburgh Courier,* December 19, 1959, 1; "New Owners of Owl Cab Study Operation Plans," *Pittsburgh Courier,* May 1, 1960, 9. For newspaper coverage, see the following articles from the *Pittsburgh Courier:* "Silas Knox: Taxing PUC for Ownership of Cab Company," October 1, 1977, 1; "Should a Black Cab Company Be Allowed to Open in the Hill?" October 1, 1977, 7; "Knox Confident He Can Make Cab Company Work," October 29, 1977, 1; "Hearings Set, January 14, 1978, 3; "Fare Hike Won't Hurt Cab Plans," January 21, 1978, 8; "White Cab Companies Trying to Prove Hill Cab Not Feasible," January 2, 1978, 21; "No Need for Hill Cab, Whites Say," March 18, 1978: 1; "Knox Says Cabs Will Be on the Road in Two Months," October 7, 1978, 4; "PUC Stalls Again," February 17, 1979, 6. There were additional articles on Silas Knox's efforts going back to the 1940s.

4. "The Jitney Man" was composed by Earl Hines and Gerald Valentine. It appeared on Bluebird records, a subsidiary of RCA Victor, in 1941, with vocals by Billy Eckstine, another Pittsburgh jazz legend.

5. Garvin, "Flouting the Law, Serving the Poor," 30.

6. In the 1970s, Otto Davis, dean of the School of Urban and Public Affairs at Carnegie Mellon University, conducted a major study of Pittsburgh's jitneys for the US Department of Transportation, and drew favorable conclusions. *Pittsburgh Courier,* April 30, 1977, 1. See also "They Don't Blow Horns Too Loud!" *Pittsburgh Courier,* April 30, 1977. "CMU Studying *Jitney* Habits," *Pittsburgh Courier,* July 15, 1978, 1; Garvin, "Flouting the Law, Serving the Poor."

7. Shannon, "August Wilson Explains His Dramatic Vision," 126.

8. Sala Udin, email message to the author, January 12, 2014.

9. Shannon, *Dramatic Vision of August Wilson,* 56. Shannon cites Brown, "Light in August," 125. The station was located on Wylie Avenue between Roberts and Arthur, although later it moved a few blocks up Wylie, to the corner of Wylie and Erin. In its location at Wylie and Erin, the station was known informally as "Westbrook's," being owned and operated by a man of that name. The

station relocated again in the summer of 2014 when it was destroyed by a fire. See Glasco and Rawson, *August Wilson*, 87. This is probably George Grisham's store, listed in the city directory as George's Pan Fried Fish at 1707 ½ Wylie Avenue. The directory does not list a jitney stand next door or nearby, but these stands were illegal and unlikely to advertise in a directory.

10. Sala Udin, interview by the author, March 19, 2013.

11. Diane R. Powell, "'Jitney' Captures Drama Behind Hill Substitute Taxi-Cab Service," *New Pittsburgh Courier*, November 20, 1982, 7.

12. Herrington, *I Ain't Sorry for Nothin' I Done*, 114. Not all jitney drivers work out of a fixed station. "Line-haul" drivers follow bus routes, honking their horns and picking up passengers who are waiting for a bus. "Freelancers" work bus stations and the airport, but this is rare because of the closer police scrutiny at such places. A popular and gregarious group of drivers hang out at supermarkets, helping customers with their groceries, and sometimes helping elderly customers do their shopping before taking them home.

13. Grantmyre, "'They Lived Their Life and They Didn't Bother Anybody.'"

14. In 1949, Mary Dee, a popular disc jockey, dubbed the intersection "Crossroads of the World." That title is often attributed to Claude McKay, but a search of his publications fails to substantiate that attribution. There is no question that Mary Dee popularized the phrase in the late 1940s. See Laurence Glasco, "Black Radio in Pittsburgh: Search for Identity and Profits," part 1 of a two-part series, *Pittsburgh Courier*, June 18, 2009.

15. Snodgrass, *August Wilson*, 12. Considered one of the greatest heavyweight boxing fights of all time, the fight pitted the "Brown Bomber," the iconic hero of Black America, against Billy Conn, an extremely popular local boxer nicknamed "The Pittsburgh Kid."

16. Herrington, *I Ain't Sorry for Nothin' I Done*, 14.

17. Herrington, *I Ain't Sorry for Nothin' I Done*, 14–15.

18. Savran, "August Wilson," 22.

19. Elkins, "Wilson, August"; Brown, "Light in August," 126; Bob Hoover, "Childhood in Hill Leads to a Pulitzer for August Wilson," *Pittsburgh Post-Gazette*, June 1, 1987.

20. Daniel Gabriel, interview by the author, July 31, 2014.

21. Herrington, *I Ain't Sorry for Nothin' I Done*, 14.

22. The new apartment, like the former, was in the Ramsey Hill neighborhood. Jacqui Shoholm Purdy, email message to the author, January 5, 2020.

23. Daniel Gabriel, email message to the author, August 13, 2014. In 1988 the city directory lists Wilson as living in Minneapolis, at 900 S. Second Avenue, while the 1989 directory lists him as living in Saint Paul, at 472 Holly Avenue.

24. Jacqui Shoholm Purdy, email message to the author, May 5, 2023.

25. Claude and Jacqui wed in Las Vegas. Jacqui Shoholm Purdy, email message to the author, May 23, 2018.

26. Daniel Gabriel, interview by the author, July 31, 2014.

27. Jacqui Shoholm Purdy, telephone interview by the author, August 23, 2017.

28. Mahala, *Penumbra*, 65.

29. Mahala, *Penumbra*, 61; *Minneapolis Tribune*, July 10, 1981, 5C; Hill and Hatch, *History of African American Theatre*, 472, says that Wilson's *Black Bart* also won Penumbra's 1982 Cornerstone Playwriting contest. However, Macelle Mahala cannot confirm that.

30. David Hawley, "Black Bart Is Too Much, Too Soon," *Saint Paul Sunday Pioneer Press*, July 12, 1981.

31. Hawley, "Black Bart Is Too Much, Too Soon."

32. Elkins, "Wilson, August."

33. Herrington, *I Ain't Sorry for Nothin' I Done*, 115; Jim Davidson, "A Home-Grown *Jitney* Spits out Charm, Power," *Pittsburgh Press*, November 3, 1982; Barbara Cloud, "Hill District's Gypsy Cabs Spark Original Play, '*Jitney*,'" *Pittsburgh Press*, October 24, 1982.

34. The play, codirected by Bob Johnson and Beryl Berry, was performed at the Fine Line Cultural Center in the basement of Saint Peter's Episcopal Church in the city's Oakland neighborhood. For reactions, see Diane Powell, "'*Jitney*' Captures Drama Behind Hill Substitute Taxi-Cab Service," *Pittsburgh Courier*, November 20, 1982, 7; Ben Brantley, "The World That Created August Wilson," *New York Times*, February 5, 1995.

35. Sala Udin, interview by the author, March 19, 2013.

36. Herrington, *I Ain't Sorry for Nothin' I Done*, 115.

37. Davidson, "Home-Grown *Jitney*."

38. Donald Miller, "Jitney Characters Try to Cope with Their Bumpy Rides in Life," *Pittsburgh Post-Gazette*, November 5, 1982, 21, 24.

39. Brantley, "World That Created August Wilson."

40. August Wilson, interview by Lee Kiburi, April 6, 1999.

41. Timothy Cox, "'Jitney'—Representing A Realistic Portrayal," *New Pittsburgh Courier*, September 10, 1983.

42. Woodrow L. Taylor, "What Is Happening in the Hill District?" *New Pittsburgh Courier*, September 11, 1976, 1.

43. The station August and Sala frequented was located on Wylie Avenue near the intersection with Roberts Street. The station relocated up Wylie to the corner of Erin Street, where it was known as Westbrook's. The station kept the same telephone number as in the play. Unfortunately, in June 2014 a fire and heavy rains caused the building to collapse and be torn down. Westbrook has opened a new station, located on Centre Avenue.

44. Greg Mims, "Part II: 'The Summer of '73: 'Hot' or 'Cold,'" *New Pittsburgh Courier*, July 14, 1973.

45. Shannon, "August Wilson Explains His Dramatic Vision," 120. Hap Erstein, "Interview with the Playwright," *Palm Beach (FL) Post*, October 9, 2005, 1.

46. Taken from the 1979 script of *Jitney!* Copy in Bob Johnson Papers, Archives & Special Collections, University of Pittsburgh. In the New York version of 2000, Booster picks up his dead father's mantle and takes over the jitney station.

47. Courtesy of the August Wilson estate. Mary Rawson notes that the poem is reminiscent of "Digging," one of the most widely known poems by the Nobel Prize–winning Irish poet Seamus Heaney. The poem describes how Heaney, unlike his father, didn't dig peat, but rather dug with his pen and wrote words.

48. "August Wilson's Jitney: 'All You Got Is Each Other,'" Manhattan Theatre Club, YouTube, January 30, 2017, https://www.youtube.com/watch?v=zjEtKVTc_k0.

49. Daniel Gabriel, interview by the author, July 31, 2014. The characters in *Jitney!* speak in vernacular, but not in the vernacular unique to Black Pittsburgh. Pittsburgh is noted for its regional dialect, known as "Pittsburghese," or "Yinzer-talk," but Wilson's characters do not speak an African American version of Pittsburghese. According to an expert on Black Pittsburgh speech patterns, they speak with linguistic features that are distinctly African American but shared nationally. Maeve Eberhardt, email message to the author, July 24, 2017. Eberhardt, "Identities and Local Speech in Pittsburgh." See Johnstone, Baumgardt, Eberhardt, and Kiesling, *Pittsburgh Speech and Pittsburghese*.

50. Wilson, in *August Wilson: The Ground on Which I Stand.*

51. August Wilson, interview with Lynne Hayes-Freeland, WAMO radio, Pittsburgh, ca. September 25, 1987, Lee Kiburi Collection.

52. Lahr, "Been Here and Gone," 25–26; Shannon, *Dramatic Vision of August Wilson*, 28. As Wilson told Bonnie Lyons, "When I first started writing plays I couldn't write good dialogue because I didn't respect how black people talked. I thought that in order to make art out of it I had to change it, make it into something different. Once I learned to value and respect my characters, I could really hear them." Lyons, "Interview with August Wilson," 215.

53. Samuel Freedman, "A Voice from the Streets," *New York Times*, March 15, 1987, A36.

54. Wilson, interview with Lynne Hayes-Freeland.

55. Herrington, *I Ain't Sorry for Nothin' I Done*, 13.

56. Herrington, *I Ain't Sorry for Nothin' I Done*, 114.

57. Herrington, *I Ain't Sorry for Nothin' I Done*, 15.

58. Elkins, "Wilson, August"; Brown, "Light in August," 125.

59. Daniel Gabriel, interview by the author, July 31, 2014; Savran, "August Wilson," 22–23.

60. Bryer and Hartig, *Conversations with August Wilson*, 123–24; Samuel G. Freedman, "A Playwright Talks About the Blues," *New York Times*, April 13, 1984. Rainey's 1924 performance lasted a week, beginning Monday, October 27, at the Lincoln Theatre on Wylie Avenue, between Junilla and Duff Streets.

61. "Ma Rainey," Rock & Roll Hall of Fame, heeps://www.rockhall.com/inductees/ma-rainey.

62. Harrison, *Black Pearls*, 36.

63. Spencer, "Diminishing Rural Residue of Folklore," 25.

64. Jones, *Blues People*. In his chapter "The City," LeRoi Jones (later Amiri Baraka) talks at length of the emerging market for commercially produced blues recordings in places like New York City and Chicago.

65. "16 Chosen by O'Neill Center for Playwrights Conference," *New York Times*, May 13, 1982, C.25.

66. Joe Brown, "Staging the Black Experience; Playwright August Wilson and the Persistence of Vision," *Washington Post*, October 4, 1987, F1; Brown, "Light in August," 125.

67. April Austin, "Lloyd Richards & August Wilson: A Winning Partnership Plays On," *Christian Science Monitor*, September 18, 1995, 13.

68. *August Wilson: The Ground on Which I Stand.*

69. Brown, "Light in August," 126–27.

70. Brown, "Light in August," 126–27.

71. Julia felt guilty because she and Daisy had started smoking as a way to keep their weight down. "You know how we women are," she says. The next November, during the Great American Smokeout, Julia quit smoking permanently. Julia Burley, interview by the author, May 30, 2012.

72. Barbara Wilson, interview by the author, March 12, 2017.

73. Barbara Wilson, interview by the author, March 12, 2017, and September 17, 2018.

74. Julia Burley interview by the author, October 3, 2012; April 1, 2013.

75. Ellis, "Pride and Pain of Place," xiv.

76. Barbara Wilson, email messages to the author, July 30, 2017, and September 17, 2018.

77. Brown, "Light in August."

78. Frank Rich, "Stage View; Where Writers Mold the Future of Theater," *New York Times*, August 1, 1982, A1.

79. Herbert Mitgang, "Wilson, from Poetry to Broadway Success," *New York Times*, October 22, 1984, C15.

80. Brown, "Light in August."

81. Frank Rich, "Wilson's 'Ma Rainey's' Opens," *New York Times*, October 12, 1984.

82. "Ma Rainey's Black Bottom," *Variety*, October 17, 1984, 156.

83. Cutler's name is an homage to August's grandmother Zonia, whose maiden name was Cutler.

84. Rich, "Stage Review; Where Writers Mold the Future of Theater."

85. Eugene Lee, informal conversation with author, March 10, 2015; Dena Kleiman, "'Joe Turner,' the Spirit of Synergy," *New York Times*, May 19, 1986, C11.

86. Ben Brantley, "The World That Created August Wilson," *New York Times*, February 5, 1995.

87. Robert Brustein, "The Siren Song of Broadway Is a Warning," *New York Times*, May 22, 1988.

88. Freedman, "Voice from the Streets."

89. Shannon, "August Wilson Explains His Dramatic Vision," 129.

90. Chervin, *Short Pieces from the New Dramatists*, 81–82.

91. Audio tape of August at the Poetry Center of the 92nd Street Y, November 17, 1986, courtesy of the 92nd Street Y.

92. Bynum Wilson died in Waterloo, Iowa. Renee Wilson, telephone conversation, April 18, 2019. As the daughter of Franklin, one of Daisy's brothers, Renee has done extensive research on the Wilson family history and genealogy.

93. The reunion was held at the Capricorn East nightclub in East Liberty. Walter Ray Watson Jr., "Playwright Gears up for Broadway," *New Pittsburgh Courier*, November 22, 1986, 6.

94. Samuel G. Freedman, "Wilson's New *'Fences'* Nurtures a Partnership," *New York Times*, May 5, 1985, A80.

95. Freedman, "Wilson's New *'Fences'* Nurtures a Partnership."

96. Daniel Gabriel, interview by the author, July 31, 2014.

97. Ruck, *Kings on the Hill*.

98. The following is based primarily on: "Pittsburgh's Civic Arena: A History of Controversy," Historic American Buildings Survey, Library of Congress, 2010; "That Arena on the Hill," *Pittsburgh Post-Gazette*, July 5, 2010; "History of Black Migration to Pittsburgh" and "The Pittsburgh Courier and the History of Black Migration," in Reich, *Encyclopedia of the Great Black Migration*; "To Make Some Place Special: History of the Civil Rights Movement in Pittsburgh," in commemorative booklet for dedication of Freedom Corner Monument, June 2001, and serialized by *Pittsburgh Courier* in six parts; *Legacy in Bricks and Mortar*; Glasco, "Double Burden."

99. Julia Burley, interview by the author, April 1, 2013.

100. Julia Burley, interview by the author, April 1, 2013. It is possible that August has conflated Troy's struggle with that of Black transit workers, who in the 1940s waged a determined effort to drive Pittsburgh's city buses, a campaign that garnered headlines and, after a long, hard struggle, ultimately prevailed. See, for example, Ralph E. Koger, "Transit Co. 'Opens Doors': Railways Company Agrees to Hire Negro Operators. Victory Achieved After Long and Bitter Campaign for Jobs as Operators on Stret Car Lines Here," *Pittsburgh Courier*, April 7, 1945, 1.

101. Bob Mee, "The Fighter Who Was Too Good for His Own Good, Charley Burley," accessed June 26, 2017, www.boxingnewsonline.net.

102. Dubner, "August Wilson, R.I.P."

103. Franki Williams, several informal conversations with the author, 2015.

104. Brantley, "World That Created August Wilson"; Moyers, "August Wilson," 68.

105. Freedman, "Voice from the Streets."

106. Freedman, "Voice from the Streets."

107. Freedman, "Voice from the Streets."

108. Freedman, "Voice from the Streets."

109. Bob Hoover, "Kuntu's *Ma Rainey* Delivers an Evening of Powerful Drama," *Pittsburgh Post-Gazette*, September 28, 1987; August Wilson, interview by Christopher Rawson, *Sunday Arts Magazine*, WQED, October 4, 1987; Kathleen Healy, RSM, "An Unphotographed Chapter in a Playwright's Homecoming," *Pittsburgh Post-Gazette*, October 12, 1987. Healy was a writer and lecturer at Carlow College in Pittsburgh.

110. Hoover, "Kuntu's *Ma Rainey*."

111. Bob Hoover, "Playwright Has a Quick Trip Home," *Pittsburgh Post-Gazette*, September 28, 1987.

112. August Wilson, interview by Lynne Hayes-Freeland, "Focus," WAMO, recorded by Lee Kiburi.

113. Healy, "Unphotographed Chapter," at the church service on September 27, 1987.

114. August Wilson, interview by Don Marinelli, *Sunday Arts Magazine*, WQED, September 27, 1987, Kiburi Collection.

115. Effort, "Pittsburgh Profiles."

116. August Wilson, interview by Lynne Hayes-Freeland, KDKA, ca. September 25, 1987, Kiburi Collection.

117. August Wilson, "I Want a Black Director," *New York Times*, September 26, 1990, A25.

118. Savran, "August Wilson," 30; Watlington, "Hurdling Fences," 88–89.

119. Sheppard, "August Wilson," 102. Wilson had made the decision of a historical sequence at least by the spring of 1984, as *Ma Rainey* was playing at the Yale Repertory Theatre and Hartford's Lincoln Theatre. Bethe Thomas, "Yale Stage Has Hit in '*Ma Rainey*,' *New London (CT) Day*, April 13, 1984, 20, wrote that Wilson had announced that he intended to create a series of plays about the history of Black people in America.

120. Sheppard, "August Wilson," 102.

121. Glasco and Rawson, *August Wilson*, 3–4.

122. Hoover, "Childhood in Hill Leads to a Pulitzer for August Wilson."

Chapter 12. Grappling with Black Nationalism

1. Gail Austin, interview by the author, December 19, 2017.

2. Eric Pace, "Blacks in the Arts: Evaluating Recent Success," *New York Times*, June 14, 1987, A1.

3. Hilary DeVries, "A Street-Corner Scribe of Life in Black America," *Christian Science Monitor*, March 27, 1987.

4. Samuel Freedman, "A Voice from the Streets," *New York Times*, March 15, 1987.

5. August Wilson, interview by Lee Kiburi, April 6, 1999.

6. Mervyn Rothstein, "Round Five for a Theatrical Heavyweight," *New York Times*, April 15, 1990, A1.

7. Cited by Wilson in reference to Troy in *Fences*. Lyons, "Interview with August Wilson," 205; Shannon and Williams, "Conversation with August Wilson," 246; August Wilson, "Feed Your Mind"; Sala Udin, interview by the author, June 7, 2013.

8. Cited by Wilson in reference to Troy in *Fences*. Lyons, "Interview with August Wilson," 205; Shannon and Williams, "Conversation with August Wilson," 246; Wilson, "Feed Your Mind"; Sala Udin, interview by the author, June 7, 2013.

9. Janice Arkatov, "August Wilson: His Way. 'I'm an Artist First, a Playwright Second and a Black Third,'" *Los Angeles Times*, June 7, 1987, 35.

10. August Wilson, "Blacks, Blues and Cultural Imperialism," lecture, March 2, 1988, Carnegie Music Hall, Pittsburgh, Kiburi Collection; Freedman, "Voice from the Streets."

11. The author was present for Wilson's address and could hear many in the audience inhale.

12. I attended the lecture. Some of these descriptions of audience reaction are based on my personal observations.

13. Wilson, "Blacks, Blues and Cultural Imperialism."

14. Ron Davenport, interview by the author, February 19, 2018.

15. Lee Kiburi, interview by the author, July 22, 2013.

16. Julia Burley, interview by the author, July 25, 2012.

17. Andrea Allinger, "Translating Pictures into Words: The Influence of Romare Bearden on August Wilson," http://fliphtml5.com/avnd/yhoo.

18. Herrington, *I Ain't Sorry for Nothin' I Done*, 79, cited in Allinger, "Translating Pictures into Words."

19. Richard Bernstein, "August Wilson's Voices from the Past," *New York Times*, March 27, 1988.

20. Joe Brown, "Staging the Black Experience; Playwright August Wilson and the Persistence of Vision," *Washington Post*, October 4, 1987, F1. Unfortunately, Bearden died on March 12, 1988, just two weeks before *Joe Turner's Come and Gone* opened on Broadway. Wilson was probably first introduced to Bearden in the 1971 catalogue of an exhibition at the Museum of Modern Art. That catalogue, however, does not contain *Pittsburgh Memories* or *Mother and Child*. However, those two collages, which inspired Wilson's two plays, *Joe Turner's Come and Gone*, and *The Piano Lesson*, were part of the Bearden exhibition at the MoMA. Wilson may have seen those collages on his trip to New York when he stood outside Bearden's residence. On that same trip, he may have visited the Bearden exhibition at the MoMA.

21. See Nabofa, "Blood Symbolism in African Religion," 389–405, and Douglas, *Purity and Danger*. Nabofa, of the Department of Religious Studies, University of Ibadan (Nigeria), writes: "Natural causes are rarely said to be responsible for the cause of most ill health in traditional Africa. Breaking of a taboo, sin and the evil activities of witches and sorcerers are often made the scapegoats. Therefore, when one is seriously sick some kind of sacrificial rites are carried out under the supervision of a diviner, who must have diagnosed and prescribed the cure for the sickness. The principle behind such healing sacrificial rites among the Yoruba of Nigeria is that the sick person must give a part of himself; in other words, he must give out what is precious in himself to a higher power before he may be able to regain his health" (401).

22. Pettengill, "Historical Perspective," 168–69.

23. Said in 1993; see Pettengill, "Historical Perspective," 168–69.

24. Penny, "Review of *Joe Turner's Come and Gone*," *Shooting Star Review* (Summer 1988): 32–33. *Shooting Star Review* was a high-quality local Black publication put out by Sandra Gould Ford. Ford has donated the journal to the Hillman Library at the University of Pittsburgh.

25. *Variety*, June 14, 1989, 86.

26. Elam, *Past as Present in the Drama of August Wilson*, esp. ix–26.

27. Glasco, *WPA History of the Negro in Pittsburgh*, 90–91, 170.

28. For background on the attitudes and cultural values of Pittsburgh's Black community in the early twentieth century, see a four-part series that ran in the *Colored American Magazine* in October, November, and December 1901, and January 1902. The series by the Boston-based magazine praises the social, economic, and cultural accomplishment of Pittsburgh's Black community. See also Mitchell, "Negating the Nadir," 33–47. The reasons for this cultural attitude are spelled out in an unpublished paper by the author, "High Culture in Black Pittsburgh."

29. Bryer and Hartig, eds., *Conversations with August Wilson*, 238.

30. Bryer and Hartig, eds., *Conversations with August Wilson*, 238.

31. Janice Arkatov, "August Wilson: His Way. 'I'm an Artist First, a Playwright Second and a Black Third,'" *Los Angeles Times*, June 7, 1987, 35.

32. Christopher Rawson, "Black Theater Enjoys a Boost Here and Away," *Pittsburgh Post-Gazette*, April 4, 1989.

33. Susan Harris Smith, "Public Theater's Fine, Strong *'Fences'* Raises Emotions, Ovations," *Pittsburgh Press*, June 1, 1989.

34. Smith, "Public Theater's Fine, Strong *'Fences'* Raises Emotions, Ovations."

35. Smith, "Public Theater's Fine, Strong *'Fences'* Raises Emotions, Ovations."

36. George Anderson, "Moving and Mystical: August Wilson's Imaginative Joe Turner's Is Insightful Drama," *Pittsburgh Post-Gazette*, September 16, 1989.

37. A. Vivienne Robinson, "Wilson, 'Joe Turner' Cast Honored in Special Library Ceremonies," *Pittsburgh Courier*, October 14, 1989, B1; David Malehorn, "How I Found August Wilson's Carnegie 'Diploma,'" *Pittsburgh Post-Gazette*, October 9, 2011.

38. Bruce Vanwyngarden, "August Wilson: The Pittsburgher of the Year 1990," *Pittsburgh Magazine*, January 1990, 28–32.

39. "Wilson Named 'Man of Year,'" *Pittsburgh Post-Gazette*, December 29, 1989.

40. Julia Burley, interview by the author, October 9, 2012.

41. Julia Burley, interview by the author, October 9, 2012.

42. Glasco, *WPA History of the Negro in Pittsburgh*, 25.

43. Glasco, *WPA History of the Negro in Pittsburgh*, 25.

44. In 1989 *The Times* of London announced the arrival of *Ma Rainey's Black Bottom* in London, and said, "Britain is about to get quite a flood of Wilson's works." Matt Wolf, "Black and White and Read All Over; August Wilson," *Times* (UK), October 23, 1989. In 2001 the American production of *Jitney*, which was ineligible for a Tony Award because it hadn't played on Broadway, went to London and won the Olivier Award, London's Tony. "*Jitney* at National Theatre," *Africa News*, March 2, 2003, 1. In 2008 a theater in Pretoria was planning a festival of August Wilson plays presented by the actor Charles Dutton and including local talent. "'Backstage Girl' to Take Theatre to Lofty Heights," *Pretoria News*, January 15, 2008, e1. *Fences* staged in Frankfurt, 1992. Leuchtenmüller, *Die Macht der Vergangenheit*, xiv. *Fences* was staged at the Beijing People's Art Theater, September 24, 1996. See Margaret Booker, "Establishing Common Ground: August Wilson's *Fences* in Beijing," *China Today*, May 1, 1997, 58–61, http://chinatoday.sinoperi.com/en19975/607444.jhtml. In 2023 *Jitney* was translated into Italian and produced in Vincenza with hopes of a 2026 tour to the United States. On May 2–12, 1991, *Fences* was staged at Hakuhinkan Theater in Ginza, Tokyo, and May 21–25 at Kochi People's Theater in Kochi Prefecture in the western part of Japan. The play was translated and directed by Hiroko Watanabe, and renamed *The Song That My Father Sang*. For a review, see *Asahi Shinbun*, April 30, 1991. It was recorded in the Past Play Records on the Hakuhinkan Theater website. Director Lou Bellamy reported that the play was well received in Japan: "I think *Fences* is

perhaps his most accessible piece. There's a trope in there that's immediately recognizable to all cultures—that man/son thing. It's so deep that people will come up to me and grab me in Japan, in Germany. 'That's my father.'" See Lisa Kennedy, "*Fences* Director Lou Bellamy Recalls Teaming with Playwright Legend August Wilson," *Denver Post*, Aril 28, 2016, http://www. denverpost.com/theater/ci_21527820#ixzz2HybUpLhp. The May 11, 1991, *Yomiuri* newspaper indicates that the play was staged in two additional cities. Richard Christiansen, "Artist of the Year: August Wilson's Plays Reveal What It Means to be Black in This Century," *Chicago Tribune*, December 27, 1987. Since then, Ayako Kurasawa has translated *Fences*, *Joe Turner's Come and Gone*, *The Piano Lesson*, and *Radio Golf* into Japanese, although none have been produced.

45. Bernstein, "August Wilson's Voices from the Past."

46. Savran, "August Wilson," 37.

47. Moyers, "August Wilson," 72.

48. Watlington, "Hurdling Fences."

49. Brown, "Light in August," 120; Sala Udin, interview by the author, June 7, 2013.

50. Mahala, *Penumbra*, 60.

51. In addition, September 26, 1987, was declared "August Wilson Day" in Pittsburgh

52. August Wilson, address to the Saint Paul City Council, 1987, courtesy of Jacqui Sholm Purdy. Wilson's remarks were published by the Saint Paul Department of Planning and Economic Development.

53. "Playwright's Marriage on Fence," *Philadelphia Tribune*, July 24, 1990, 21; "Couples," *Philadelphia Inquirer*, July 19, 1990, 68.

Chapter 13. The Seattle Years

1. "Playwright's Marriage on Fence," *Philadelphia Tribune*, July 24, 1990: 21; "Couples," *Philadelphia Inquirer*, July 19, 1990, 68.

2. Lahr, "Been Here and Gone," 7; Misha Berson, "Embracing the Legacy of August Wilson," *Seattle Times*, October 30, 2007.

3. Lahr, "Been Here and Gone," April 16, 2001, 7; Berson, "Embracing the Legacy of August Wilson."

4. Megan Rosenfeld, "The Voices of August Wilson; the Playwright Listens—and Stays True—to the People in His Past," *Washington Post*, November 19, 1991, G1.

5. Lee Lescaze, "The Man Behind 'Ma': A Playwright's Journey," *Wall Street Journal*, October 30, 1984, 1.

6. Berson, "Embracing the Legacy of August Wilson."

7. Ben Brantley, "August Wilson Revealed Lives as Sagas of Nobility," *New York Times*, October 4, 2005, E1.

8. "Four Candidates to Receive Honorary Degree in May," (Carnegie Mellon University) *Tartan*, February 23, 1988; Wilson, *Three Plays*; Elkins, "Wilson, August"; "Pitt to Hold Sixteenth Annual Honors Convocation," University of Pittsburgh, Department of University Relations, documenting.library.pitt.edu; Elkins, "Wilson, August." The text of Wilson's Honors Convocation speech at the University of Pittsburgh was printed in the *Pittsburgh Post-Gazette*.

9. Brown, "Light in August," 116–27.

10. Lahr, "Been Here and Gone," 17; Julia Burley, interview by the author, November 14, 2012; Berson, "Embracing the Legacy of August Wilson."

11. Berson, "Embracing the Legacy of August Wilson."

12. Constanza Romero, informal conversation with the author, October 2015; Christopher

Rawson, "August Wilson's Life and Work: A Timeline, 1945–2005," *Pittsburgh Post-Gazette*, June 8, 2012; *Seattle Times* staff, "Timeline: The Life of August Wilson," *Seattle Times*, October 3, 2005.

13. Greg Mims, "Part II: 'The Summer of '73: 'Hot' or 'Cold,'" *Pittsburgh Courier*, July 14, 1973.

14. Mervyn Rothstein, "Round Five for a Theatrical Heavyweight," *New York Times*, April 15, 1990, A1.

15. Program notes for the play. See also Nadel, *May All Your Fences Have Gates*, 163n10; Willa Mae Montague, interview by the author, February 28, 2015.

16. "Braun's Tells NAACP 'We'll Hire Negroes,'" *Pittsburgh Courier*, June 23, 1962, 1.

17. Sean Hamill, "The Real-Life Story Behind August Wilson's Character in His Play about 1968 Violence Is Different—and Compelling," *Pittsburgh Post-Gazette*, April 2, 2018.

18. Christopher Rawson, "August Wilson's Play Results in Case of West Meets West," *Pittsburgh Post-Gazette*, August 2, 1994.

19. April Austin, "Despite Credibility and Good Intentions, Wilson's New Drama 'Two Trains' Disappoints," *Christian Science Monitor*, November 21, 1990.

20. David Richards, "A People Face the Mirror of History," *New York Times*, May 3, 1992, 5.

21. "Fulton Series Gets Broadway's 'Tru,' 'Piano Lesson,' 'Yonkers,'" *Pittsburgh Press*, June 28, 1991; Marilyn Posner, "Mother of the Blues: Public Brings August Wilson's *Ma Rainey* to Pittsburgh," *Observer-Reporter* (Washington, PA), September 20, 1992; "Sideline: Public Coup in Merritt," *Pittsburgh Post-Gazette*, July 28, 1992.

22. Doug Shanaberger, "Curtain Calls: Artist Captured 'Trains' Theme," *Observer-Reporter* (Washington, PA), June 1, 1994.

23. Lynn Elber, "Piano Hits All the Right Notes," *Observer-Reporter* (Washington, PA), February 5, 1995; Christopher Rawson, "Sitting in on '*The Piano Lesson*,'" *Pittsburgh Post-Gazette*, October 3, 1994, C1–C2; local extras included Etta Cox, Hal O'Leary, Mark Connolly, Kathryn Aronson, Bob Gore, Kate Young, Bill Thunhurst, David Doepkin, Ben Cain, Bob Tracy, Harold Surratt, Elva Branson, Lynn Innerst, Alice Eisner, Tommy LaFitte, Todd Ledbetter, Ben Tatar, Glenn Gress, Nate Smith, and Teenie Harris.

24. Elber, "Piano Hits All the Right Notes"; Rawson, "Sitting in on '*The Piano Lesson*.'" The Shadyside setting was on Alder Street.

25. Email communication from Elva Branson, July 5, 2019.

26. Christopher Rawson, "Wilson's History Lesson," *Pittsburgh Post-Gazette*, February 9, 1995, C4.

27. "*The Piano Lesson* (2024 film)," Wikipedia, https://en.wikipedia.org/wiki/The_Piano _Lesson_(2024_film).

28. Patricia O'Haire, "Tuning up 'Guitars' for B'way; The Tales of August: Wilson's New Play about Middle-Class Blacks," *Daily News* (New York), March 27, 1996, 39.

29. Christopher Rawson, "Wilson Succumbs to Liver Cancer," *Pittsburgh Post-Gazette*, October 2, 2005.

30. Ben Brantley, "The World That Created August Wilson," *New York Times*, February 5, 1995.

31. Brantley, "World That Created August Wilson."

32. Brantley, "World That Created August Wilson."

33. Rosenfeld, "Voices of August Wilson."

34. Vincent Canby, "Unrepentant, Defiant Blues for 7 Voices," *New York Times*, March 29, 1996.

35. See Sandra Shannon's interview with August about this in *The Dramatic Vision of August Wilson*, 228–29.

36. Julia Burley, interview by the author, October 3, 2012, and May 27, 2012. Julia says Fred taught Daisy how to play pinochle. He was supposed to teach her as well, but it never happened.

37. Glasco and Rawson, *August Wilson*.

38. Julia Burley, interview by the author, April 1, 2013.

39. Livingston, "Cool August," 56.

40. John Clark, "Hill District Gay, but No Disorder," *Pittsburgh Courier*, June 22, 1946, 33.

41. Christopher Rawson, Review of *Jitney*, *Pittsburgh Post-Gazette*, June 24, 1996, 132.

42. Caroline Abels, "A Fine Opening Act: 'Hedley' Set Records as Public Theater Made Special Effort to Attract Black Patrons," *Pittsburgh Post-Gazette*, January 19, 2000. As usual, Wilson revised *Jitney* as it had many more productions before its New York, non-Broadway opening in 2000, some eighteen years after it first opened in Pittsburgh.

43. Robert Brustein, "The Lesson of 'The Piano Lesson,'" *New Republic*, May 21, 1990, 28.

44. Robert Brustein, "Unity from Diversity," *New Republic*, July 19 and 26, 1993.

45. Gates, "Chitlin Circuit," 44.

46. See Brustein, "Lesson of 'The Piano Lesson,'" and "Unity from Diversity." For Brustein's caustic reply to "The Ground on Which I Stand," see "Subsidized Separatism," *New Republic*, August 19 and 26, 1996.

47. Wilson, "Ground on Which I Stand."

48. Robert Brustein, "Subsidized Separatism," *New Republic*, August 19, 1996.

49. Margo Jefferson, "Oratory vs. Really Talking About Culture," *New York Times*, February 4, 1997, C11.

50. August Wilson, address to the 92nd Street Y, March 17, 1997.

51. Mel Gussow, "Energizing the Future of Black Theater," *New York Times*, March 9, 1998, E1.

52. Hornby, "Two August Wilsons," 291.

53. Christopher Rawson, "Actor Gantt Mines for 'Gold' in *Seven Guitars*," *Pittsburgh Post-Gazette*, June 11, 1997; Christopher Rawson, "Review of *Seven Guitars*," *Pittsburgh Post-Gazette*, June 14, 1997.

54. Abels, "Fine Opening Act."

55. Wilson, dedication page to *King Hedley II*.

56. Tony Norman, "Stage Persona Becomes Chawley," *Pittsburgh Post-Gazette*, January 14, 2000.

57. Tony Norman, email message to the author, March 15, 2017.

58. Tony Norman, email message to the author, March 15, 2017. In 2000 Norman wrote an article on Williams as the prototype for *King Hedley II*. Norman, "Stage Persona Becomes Chawley."

59. Tony Norman, email communication to the author, March 15, 2017; Norman, "Stage Persona Becomes Chawley."

60. Christopher Rawson, "Wilson's Hedley a Thrilling Ride," *Pittsburgh Post-Gazette*, December 16, 1999, B1.

61. Christopher Rawson, "It's Showtime for Our City's Best of Century," *Pittsburgh Post-Gazette*, December 15, 1999, E4.

62. Ben Brantley, "The Agonized Arias of Everyman in Poverty and Pain," *New York Times*, May 2, 2001.

63. Samuel Freedman, "The Mother of an Era: August Wilson's," *New York Times*, February 2, 2003, 1.

64. Charles Isherwood, "At War with Ghosts and History: *King Hedley II*," *New York Times*, March 12, 2007.

65. Hoerr, *And the Wolf Finally Came*.

66. In 2018 the state granted clemency to Wideman's brother Robby for a 1975 killing. "Pa. Pardons Board Votes 5–0 to Grant Clemency to Robert Wideman in 1975 Murder," *Pittsburgh Post-Gazette*, May 40, 2019.

67. "Writer Reviews Roots," *New Pittsburgh Courier*, March 20, 1982.

68. Lahr, "Been Here and Gone," 22.

69. Freda Ellis, interview by Lisa Hazirjian, January 21, 2008 (CAUSE, Carnegie Mellon University). The attack on Stool Pigeon resembles an incident in the same area when August's brother Edwin was attacked by a group of toughs who kicked him in the face, damaging his teeth. Edwin went to Dr. Goldblum, the Jewish doctor in the neighborhood, and then to the hospital where, like Stool Pigeon, he was fixed up. The incident probably took place in the late 1950s, but it certainly could also have happened in the eighties.

70. Rawson, "Wilson's History Lesson."

71. McCollester, "Union Edge: Labor's Talk Radio."

72. Christopher Rawson, "August Wilson Basks amid Pals, Memories," *Pittsburgh Post-Gazette*, March 17, 1998.

73. Rawson, "August Wilson Basks amid Pals, Memories."

74. Christopher Rawson, "Scenes from August Wilson: The Busy Playwright's Been Teaching, Writing and Rewriting," *Pittsburgh Post-Gazette*, March 24, 1998.

75. Christopher Rawson, "August Wilson Helps Hill Library Celebrate Its 100th," *Pittsburgh Post-Gazette*, March 20, 1999.

76. Wilson's lecture also appeared as an op-ed piece in the *Pittsburgh Post-Gazette*. August Wilson, "Feed Your Mind, the Rest Will Follow," *Pittsburgh Post-Gazette*, March 28, 1999.

Chapter 14. Completing the Cycle

1. Herrington, *I Ain't Sorry for Nothin' I Done*, 14–18, 113–30.

2. Samuel Freedman, "The Mother of an Era: August Wilson's," *New York Times*, February 2, 2003, 1.

3. The choice puzzled Claude Purdy, who had directed many of Wilson's plays in regional theaters and might have been the logical replacement, but did not upset him. His widow Jacqui says that as long as Claude was working he was satisfied. Jacqui Shoholm-Purdy, email communication, June 30, 2019.

4. Lahr, "Been Here and Gone," 26–27.

5. Ben Brantley, "Theater Review: Finding Drama in Life, and Vice Versa," *New York Times*, April 26, 2000, E1

6. Don Shewey, "Sharing the Stage with August Wilson," *New York Times*, April 29, 2001.

7. Bob Hoover, "Lynching Rope Replaced with Police Bullets, Playwright Wilson Says," *Pittsburgh Post-Gazette*, 21; Janice Arkatov, "August Wilson: His Way. 'I'm an Artist First, a Playwright Second and a Black Third,'" *Los Angeles Times*, June 7, 1987, 35.

8. August Wilson, "Sailing the Stream of Black Culture," *New York Times*, April 23, 2000, AR1. See also Arkatov, "August Wilson: His Way."

9. Amir Rashidd, in Ervin Dyer, "August Wilson Remembered as a Character in Oddball Hill," *Pittsburgh Post-Gazette*, October 8, 2005.

10. Fred Logan, interview by the author, March 9, 2020; Frank Hightower, interview by the author, June 28, 2013.

11. Hop Kendrick, interview by the author, June 2, 2012.

12. Hop Kendrick, interview by the author, June 2, 2012.

13. Nathan Oliver, interview by the author, September 2, 2013.

14. Nathan Oliver, interview by the author, September 2, 2013.

15. Joe Adcock, "A Moment with . . . Playwright August Wilson, *Seattle Post-Intelligencer*, May 19, 2003.

16. Moyers, "August Wilson," 67.

17. Bogumil, *Understanding August Wilson*, 13.

18. Sillman, "Playwright Wilson Turns Actor in 'How I Learned.'"

19. Wilson, *How I Learned What I Learned*.

20. Stephen Kinzer, "A Playwright Casts Himself to Tell His Angry Story," *New York Times*, May 26, 2003.

21. 92nd Street Y, December 3, 2003. The 92nd Street Y has generously made available videos of Wilson's four appearances.

22. August Wilson, audio of poetry reading at 92nd Street Y, December 3, 2003.

23. Christopher Rawson, "Playwright/Poet August Wilson Wins Heinz Award," *Pittsburgh Post-Gazette*, December 2, 2003.

24. Christopher Rawson, "Heinz Award: August Wilson's Acceptance Speech," *Pittsburgh Post-Gazette*, December 6, 2003.

25. Billy Jackson, interview by the author, July 8, 2014.

26. August Wilson, "Sailing the Stream of Black Culture," *New York Times*, April 23, 2000, AR1.

27. Livingston, "Cool August," 45–46.

28. See Christopher Rawson, "August Wilson's Mythic Character Aunt Ester Explored in Theater Festival," *Pittsburgh Post-Gazette*, November 9, 2009.

29. Patton, *Memory and Metaphor*, 40; Christopher Rawson, "August Wilson's Mythic Character Aunt Ester Explored in Theater Festival," *Pittsburgh Post-Gazette*, November 9, 2009.

30. Samuel Freedman, "A Voice from the Streets," *New York Times*, March 15, 1987.

31. Christopher Rawson, program notes to the 2019 performance of *Gem of the Ocean* by Pittsburgh Playwrights Theatre, 8. In 1839 a Washington newspaper reported that an escaped enslaved man named Jim had revealed, under torture, his plan to go north following an "underground railroad to Boston." See Foner, *Gateway to Freedom*, 6.

32. Plat maps show the school occupied a large lot at 1837–1841 Wylie. In act 1, scene 5, we learn that Ester's mother sent her to live with Miss Tyler/Taylor, whence her last name. On Sarah Degree, see Sister Angelica Little, "Operation Hill District, 1942–1950," Archives of the Sisters of Charity of Seton Hill, Greensburg, PA.

33. In the early 1900s, Black mill workers lived not in the Hill but in Lawrenceville, where they worked at the Crucible, Black Diamond, and Clark mills. Romare Bearden's grandparents took in such workers at their boardinghouse in the 3100 block of Penn Avenue, between the Strip District and Lawrenceville.

34. Richard R. Wright, "One Hundred Negro Steel Workers" in Russel Sage Foundation, ed., *Wage-earning Pittsburgh*. Survey Associates, 1914. Cited by Glasco in "Optimism, Dilemmas, and Progress," 1996.

35. Romare Bearden's grandparents operated a boardinghouse in the Strip that housed some of these men. For a scholarly description of the men, see Wright, "One Hundred Negro Steel Workers," 108–9. Similar breakthroughs occurred at the Clark Mills, the Solar Iron Works, Carnegie Steel, and the McKees Rocks Pressed Steel Car Company, giving Black people a toehold in iron and steel manufacturing. The toehold was both small and vulnerable: In 1900 Black people made up only 2 percent of Pittsburgh's overall industrial labor force, compared to 5 percent of the overall population. Trotter and Day, *Race and Renaissance*, 7.

36. "Investor Comes to the Rescue of Wilson Play," *New York Times*, November 13, 2004, 13.

37. Others placed the blame on shifting audience preferences, in which serious drama was losing out to musicals and lighter fare. See Ben Brantley, "Sailing into Collective Memory," *New York Times*, December 7, 2004, E1; Robert Hofler, "Serious Drama a Hard Sell on Broadway," *Variety*, February 21–27, 2005, 40; and David Rooney, "*Gem* Swims through Rough Seas with Grace," *Variety*, December 13–19, 2004, 45.

38. Charles Isherwood, "August Wilson's 100-Year Memory," *New York Times*, April 27, 2005, E1.

39. Christopher Rawson, "Let's Celebrate the Life That Is August Wilson," *Pittsburgh Post-Gazette*, September 3, 2005.

40. Christopher Rawson, "Playwright Wilson Says He's Dying," *Pittsburgh Post-Gazette*, August 26, 2005.

41. Michelle Norris, "August Wilson, Broadway's Bard of Black Life," *NPR*, October 2, 2007, http://www.npr.org/templates/story/story.php?storyId=14893908.

42. Parks, "Light in August," 22–25, 74–78.

43. Parks, "Light in August," 22–25, 74–78.

44. Parks, "Light in August," 22–25, 74–78.

45. Freda Ellis, interview by the author, spring 2012. There was a rumor that Wilson might win that year's Nobel Prize for Literature, but the 2005 prize was awarded to Harold Pinter on October 13, after Wilson had died.

46. Rawson, "Let's Celebrate the Life That Is August Wilson," and personal communications with the author.

47. Bogumil, *Understanding August Wilson*, 19.

48. Bogumil, *Understanding August Wilson*, 13.

49. Superior Court, King County (Seattle, Washington), Estate of August Wilson.

50. David Rooney, "*Golf* Completes Course," *Variety*, May 14–20, 2007, 56.

51. Bogumil, *Understanding August Wilson*, 186; Ron Davenport, interview by the author, February 19, 2018.

52. Ron Davenport, interview by the author, February 29, 2018. See also Breanna Smith, "Let's Learn from the Past: Ronald Davenport," *Pittsburgh Post-Gazette*, February 23, 2012.

53. Freedman, "Voice from the Streets."

54. Charles Isherwood, "August Wilson's 100-Year Memory," *New York Times*, April 27, 2005, E1.

55. Isherwood, "August Wilson's 100-Year Memory."

56. Michael A. Fuoco, "Return to Glory: Hill District Determined to Regain Lost Greatness," *Pittsburgh Post-Gazette*, April 11, 1999.

57. "Future Looking Up For Hill District; Community Leaders Foresee $250 Million in New Construction," *Pittsburgh Post-Gazette*, November 3, 1997, A11; "Hill District Residents Criticize Plan for Housing Development." *Pittsburgh Post-Gazette*, October 1, 1999, B8; "Milliones: Crawford-Roberts an Economic Magnet," *Pittsburgh Post-Gazette*, December 9, 1992.

58. *Wylie Avenue Days*; Ruck, *Kings on the Hill*; "Photos of Black Experience Pack an Emotional Wallop," *Pittsburgh Post-Gazette*, March 11, 1997, F2.

59. "Hill District Residents Criticize Plan for Housing Development," *Pittsburgh Post-Gazette*, October 1, 1999, B8.

60. "Milliones: Crawford-Roberts an Economic Magnet," *Pittsburgh Post-Gazette*, December 9, 1992.

61. Some argue that the Bedford Hills Redevelopment, Inc., is Wilson's tribute to David Bedford. It may be both.

62. Michael A. Fuoco, "Return to Glory: Hill District Determined to Regain Lost Greatness," *Pittsburgh Post-Gazette*, April 11, 1999.

63. Quoted in Christopher Reynolds, "Mr. Wilson's Neighborhood," *Los Angeles Times*, July 27, 2003. Marimba Milliones continues her father's legacy. As president of the Hill Community Development Corporation, she seeks redevelopment that respects the Hill's history and cultural legacy.

Chapter 15. Preserving the Legacy

1. Sadly, the same day as Wilson's funeral, Councilman Udin's son Patrice was killed in a shooting in the Hill District. See Nate Guidry, "Council Sala Udin's Son Killed in Hill District Shooting," *Pittsburgh Post-Gazette*, October 10, 2005.

2. Bob Hoover, "August Wilson's Final Act," *Pittsburgh Post-Gazette*, October 9, 2005.

3. Barbara Cloud, "United by Admiration for August Wilson," *Pittsburgh Post-Gazette*, October 16, 2005.

4. Brian Connelly, "*Two Trains Running*; White Pittsburghers Unsettled by August Wilson's Vision Should Step Back and Consider His Complete Achievement," *Pittsburgh Post-Gazette*, October 15, 2005, B7.

5. Cloud, "United by Admiration for August Wilson."

6. Letter to the editor from Lanvan Reid, Roanoke, VA, March 10, 1992, courtesy of the August Wilson estate.

7. Lee Kiburi, interview by the author, July 31, 2017.

8. Christopher Rawson, "Obituary: August Wilson, Pittsburgh Playwright Who Chronicled Black Experience," *Pittsburgh Post-Gazette*, October 2, 2005, https://www.post-gazette.com/news/obituaries/2005/10/03/Obituary-August-Wilson-Pittsburgh-playwright-who-chronicled-black-experience/stories/200510030204.

9. Hoover, "August Wilson's Final Act."

10. Lou Grippo, interview by the author, June 27, 2013.

11. Christopher Rawson, "In the Wings: Sunday Doubleheader—August Wilson on TV," *Pittsburgh Post-Gazette*, January 25, 2002.

12. Lou Grippo, interview by the author, June 27, 2013.

13. Ervin Dyer, "August Wilson Remembered as a Character in Oddball Hill," *Pittsburgh Post-Gazette*, October 8, 2005.

14. Ben Brantley, "August Wilson Revealed Lives as Sagas of Nobility," *New York Times*, October 4, 2005, E1.

15. Charles Isherwood, "August Wilson, Theater's Poet of Black America, is Dead at 60," *New York Times*, October 3, 2005, A1.

16. Christopher Rawson, "Wilson Spoke Eloquently Across the Racial Divide," *Pittsburgh Post-Gazette*, October 4, 2005, A1.

17. Christopher Rawson, senior theater critic for the *Pittsburgh Post-Gazette*, inspired the paper to join with the August Wilson House to establish an award to commemorate each theater company that has performed all ten plays of the Pittsburgh, or American Century, Cycle. As late 2024, eighteen theaters, including a collective "Broadway," have performed all ten. Christopher Rawson, "A New Award Recognizes Theaters That Have Staged All 10 Plays of August Wilson's Cycle," *Pittsburgh Post-Gazette*, February 18, 2018, and later interviews.

18. Christopher Rawson, "In the Wings," *Pittsburgh Post-Gazette*, May 31, 2007.

19. Christopher Rawson, "An August Wilson Year," *Pittsburgh Post-Gazette*, January 3, 2008.

20. Christopher Rawson, "Wilson's History Lesson," *Pittsburgh Post-Gazette*, February 9, 1995, C4.

21. Christopher Rawson, "'Gem' Is Good for Those New to Playwright August Wilson," *Pittsburgh Post-Gazette*, May 29, 2006.

22. Christopher Rawson, "Charles Dutton Stirs Laughter, Passion and Memories in 'Goodnight Mr. Wilson,'" *Pittsburgh Post-Gazette*, May 24, 2007.

23. Rawson, "August Wilson Year."

24. Joe Smydo, "Rename CAPA After Playwright August Wilson?" *Pittsburgh Post-Gazette*, October 21, 2005.

25. Christopher Rawson, "In the Wings," *Pittsburgh Post-Gazette*, April 12, 2007.

26. Glasco and Rawson, *August Wilson*.

27. Elizabeth Bloom, "The Rise and Fall of the August Wilson Center," *Pittsburgh Post-Gazette*, February 8, 2014.

28. Christopher Rawson, "How Best to Honor a Playwright Who Honored His Hometown?" *Pittsburgh Post-Gazette*, October 30, 2005.

29. Bloom, "Rise and Fall of the August Wilson Center."

30. Christopher Rawson, "August Wilson Center," *Pittsburgh Post-Gazette*, August 30, 2007.

31. Christopher Rawson, "Reunion and Scenes Honor August Wilson with Strong Playwrights, Actors," *Pittsburgh Post-Gazette*, October 20, 2007.

32. Christopher Rawson, "An August Wilson Year," *Pittsburgh Post-Gazette*, January 3, 2008.

33. James O'Toole, "Chawley P. Williams: Last Surviving Member of Centre Ave. Poets' Workshop," *Pittsburgh Post-Gazette*, December 4, 2009.

34. Bloom, "Rise and Fall of the August Wilson Center"; Trip Gabriel, "Pittsburgh Center Honoring Playwright Finds Itself Short on Visitors and Donors," *New York Times*, November 23, 2013.

35. "Dollar Bank Sells August Wilson Center to Three Pittsburgh Foundations," *Pittsburgh Post-Gazette*, November 5, 2014.

36. Patty Tascarella, "August Wilson Center Transition Plan Revealed," *Pittsburgh Business Times*, December 4, 2014.

37. Two email comments about the article: "August Wilson Center in Downtown Pittsburgh Rescued: In 11th Hour Deal, Local Foundations, Aided by City and County, Will Buy Building for $8.49M," *Pittsburgh Post-Gazette*, September 29, 2014.

38. Sharon Eberson, "August Wilson Center Restores 'African American' to Its Name," *Pittsburgh Post-Gazette*, March 21, 2019.

39. Christopher Rawson, "An Ambitious Renovation of August Wilson's Boyhood Home Will Be Good for Pittsburgh and the Arts," *Pittsburgh Post-Gazette*, April 24, 2016.

40. It was built in 1920 and occupied some 3,700 square feet. Pittsburgh property tax records, accessed June 28, 2017.

41. Martin, "August Wilson's Home."

42. Rawson, "Ambitious Renovation of August Wilson's Boyhood Home Will Be Good for Pittsburgh and the Arts."

43. The 1962 city directory lists 1727 Rear as "vacant." Unfortunately, in 1963 the city directory ceased giving information by street address so we cannot be sure that it was never occupied afterward.

44. Ramit Plushnick-Masti, "State Memorializes August Wilson's Childhood Home," *Beaver County Times* (Beaver, PA), June 1, 2007.

45. "Nephew Working to Preserve Wilson Home," *Pittsburgh Post-Gazette*, July 13, 2007; Rich Lord, "Council Oks Historic Status for Wilson Home," *Pittsburgh Post-Gazette*, February 21, 2008; "Pittsburgh Cultural Trust," May 8, 2014, http://daisywilson.org/blog.html (link no longer valid); Diana Nelson Jones, "August Wilson's Residence Could Be Nationally Recognized: Writer's Childhood Home Considered for Historic Designation," *Pittsburgh Post-Gazette*, October 1, 2012.

46. Diana Nelson Jones, "August Wilson's Childhood Pittsburgh Home Joins National Register: Playwright's House on Bedford Avenue Dates to 1840s," *Pittsburgh Post-Gazette*, May 28, 2013. Pfaffman and his firm had excellent credentials. He had served as board chair of the Rachel Carson Homestead and designed both the Legacy Apartments in the Hill District and the Carnegie Library of Pittsburgh's Hill District branch.

47. Sharon Eberson, "Celebrations to Mark First Phase of August Wilson House Restoration," *Pittsburgh Post-Gazette*, April 17, 2016.

48. Sharon Eberson, "Stage Review: There's Power in the Place as August Wilson's '*Seven Guitars*' Comes Home," *Pittsburgh Post-Gazette*, August 8, 2016.

49. See the map of filming locations in Sharon Eberson, "Building '*Fences*': Actors Discuss the Denzel Washington-Directed Film Version of August Wilson's Play," *Pittsburgh Post-Gazette*, December 22, 2016.

50. Macelle Mahala, author of a history of the Penumbra Theatre, email communication to the author, September 11, 2019. Mahala cites an article from *American Theatre* magazine on the twentieth anniversary of the speech as well as a study of the equity of funding for the arts. See Weinert-Kendt, "Ground on Which He Stood." See also Surdna Foundation, *Not Just Money: Equity Issues in Cultural Philanthropy*, 2017, https://heliconcollab.net/our_work/not-just-money/.

51. Elva Branson-Lee, email message to the author, June 25, 2017.

52. Sharon Eberson, "Pittsburgh Playwrights' '*Fences*' Inspires Local Artist," *Pittsburgh Post-Gazette*, April 27, 2015.

53. Christopher Rawson, "Joe Turner's Come Again," *Pittsburgh Post-Gazette*, August 25, 2005.

54. Mark Southers, interview by the author, June 20, 2017.

55. Anna Rosenstein, "Stage Review: 'Dorothy 6' Sparks Up Emotions of a Steelworking Clan," *Pittsburgh Post-Gazette*, September 17, 2004.

56. Sharon Eberson and Christopher Rawson, "2018 Post-Gazette Performer of the Year: Wilsonian Warrior Wali Jamal," *Pittsburgh Post-Gazette*, December 13, 2018.

57. Mark Southers, interview by the author, June 20, 2017.

BIBLIOGRAPHY

Archives
Archives of the Sisters of Charity of Seton Hill, Greensburg, PA
August Wilson Collection
August Wilson Estate
   August Wilson Papers.
Library of Congress, Washington, DC
National Personnel Records Center, Saint Louis, MO
Pittsburgh History and Landmarks Foundation
University of Pittsburgh
   August Wilson Archives
Bob Johnson Papers
Theater Archives, Hillman Library

Periodicals
Africa News
Asahi Shinbun
Beaver County Times
Chicago Tribune
Christian Science Monitor
Colored American Magazine
Day (New London, CT)
Daily News (New York)
Denver Post
Guardian (UK)
Jerusalem Post
Los Angeles Times
Minneapolis Star Tribune
Minneapolis Tribune
Negro Digest
New Pittsburgh Courier
New York Times
Observer-Reporter (Washington, PA)
Palm Beach Post (Florida)
Philadelphia Inquirer
Philadelphia Tribune
Pitt News
Pittsburgh Business Times
Pittsburgh Courier

Pittsburgh Leader
Pittsburgh Point
Pittsburgh Post-Gazette
Pittsburgh Press
Pretoria News
Saint Paul Sunday Pioneer Press
San Francisco Examiner
Seattle Post-Intelligencer
Seattle Times
Star Tribune (Minneapolis)
Star Tribune (Saint Paul)
Tartan (Carnegie Mellon University)
Times (London)
Tribune Review (Pittsburgh)
University Times (University of Pittsburgh)
Wall Street Journal
Washington Post
Yomiuri

Primary Interviewees and Personal Correspondents
A'la, Sakina
Allen, Ruth
Austin, Gail
Barnett, Cameron
Bazzell, Natalie
Berrian, Brenda
Biggs, Shirley
Bowers, Casey
Branson-Lee, Elva
Brewer, John
Brown, Joann
Burley, Julia
Burton Shakur, Brenda
Butera, Johnny
Carper, Moses
Cuddy, Doris
Davenport, Ron
Douglas, Herbert
Eberhardt, Maeve
Ekunfeo, Temujin
Ellis, Freda
Evans, Barbara
Fannion-Cotton, Cheryl
Flournoy, Mike
Fountain, Tony
Gabriel, Daniel

Gould Ford, Sandra
Grippo, Lou
Harrison, Nelson
Hightower, Frank
Horsley, Earl
Howze, Reginald
Jackson, Billy
Keil, Gene
Kendrick, Hop
Kiburi, Lee
King, Douglas
Kirven, Tony
Kittel, Freda
Kittel, Linda Jean
Knapp, James
Lawson, Amos
Lillie Blanton, Marsha (Hasani)
Lillie, Vernell
Logan, Fred
Mahala, Macelle
McCoy, Lacy
McWilliams, Aaron
Montague, Willa Mae (now Willa Mae Swan)
Montgomery, Greg
Mosley, Thaddeus
Norman, Tony
Norwood
Oliver, Nathan
Ormes, Gwen
Owens, Kenneth-El
Pitts, Ron
Porter, Curtiss
Proctor, Ralph
Rawson, Christopher
Rhodes, Jerry
Robinson, Gary
Rogers, Betty
Romero, Constanza
Scott-Starks, Marva
Shoholm Purdy, Jacqui
Southers, Mark
Stevenson, Robert Louis
Stevenson, Shelly
Strickland, William (Bill)
Udin, Sala
Weatherley, Elaine

West, Troy

Williams, Darzetta

Williams, Franki

Williams, Melvin

Wilson, Barbara

Wilson, Emmanuel

Wilson, Freda

Wilson, Michael

Wilson, Renee

Zangrilli, Al

Primary and Secondary Sources

Adoff, Arnold. *The Poetry of Black America: Anthology of the 20th Century*. Harper & Row, 1973.

Allen, Lillian. *Your House of Beauty: The Long Hard Struggle*. Amazon Books, January 1, 1998.

Altman, Susan. *Encyclopedia of African-American Heritage*. Facts on File, 2001.

Anderson, Elijah. *Code of the Street: Decency, Violence, and the Moral Life of the Inner City*. W. W. Norton, 1999.

August Wilson: The Ground on Which I Stand. PBS, February 20, 2015. https://www.pbs.org/wnet/americanmasters/august-wilson-the-ground-on-which-i-stand-about-the-film/3610/.

Baldwin, James. *The Fire Next Time*. Dial, 1963.

Barbera, Jack V. "In Memoriam: John Berryman." *Journal of Modern Literature* 2, no. 4 (1972): 547–53.

Baudelaire, Charles. *The Painter of Modern Life and Other Essays*. Phaidon, 1970.

Berry, Brewton. *Almost White*. Macmillan, 1963.

Bigsby, Christopher. *The Cambridge Companion to August Wilson*. Cambridge University Press, 2007.

Birchard, Carl, and William B. Weinstein. "The Curtaineers: A Study of an Interracial Dramatics Project of the Irene Kaufmann Settlement of Pittsburgh from Its Inception, November 1943 to February 1948." Master's thesis, University of Pittsburgh, 1948.

"Black Theatre." Special issue, *The Drama Review: TDR* 12, no. 4 (1968).

Bogumil, Mary. "August Wilson's Relationship to Black Theatre: Community, Esthetics, History and Race." In *The Cambridge Companion to August Wilson*, edited by Christopher Bigsby. Cambridge University Press, 2007.

Bogumil, Mary. *Understanding August Wilson*. Revised ed. University of South Carolina Press, 2011.

Brown, Chip. "Light in August." *Esquire*, April 1989, 116–27.

Brustein, Robert. "The Lesson of 'The Piano Lesson.'" *New Republic*, May 21, 1990.

Brustein, Robert. "Subsidized Separatism." *New Republic*, August 19, 1996.

Brustein, Robert. "Unity from Diversity." *New Republic*, July 19 and 26, 1993.

Bryer, Jackson R., and Mary C. Hartig, eds. *Conversations with August Wilson*. University Press of Mississippi, 2006.

Bryer, Jackson R., and Mary C. Hartig. Introduction to Bryer and Hartig, *Conversations with August Wilson*, vii–xvi.

Buni, Andrew. *Robert L. Vann of the Pittsburgh Courier: Politics and Black Journalism*. University of Pittsburgh Press, 1974.

Burstin, Barbara. *Steel City Jews: A History of Pittsburgh and Its Jewish Community, 1840–1915*. Closson, 2008.

Campbell, Mary Schmidt. *An American Odyssey: The Life and Work of Romare Bearden*. Oxford University Press, 2018.

Campbell, Mary Schmidt. "History and the Art of Romare Bearden." In *Memory and Metaphor: The Art of Romare Bearden, 1940–1987*. Studio Museum of Harlem. Oxford University Press.

Chervin, Stan. *Short Pieces from the New Dramatists*. Broadway Play, 1985.

"Centennial Spotlight: 'There's Gold in Them There Hills': Mica Mining in Avery County." *Avery Journal-Times*, December 2, 2011. https://www.averyjournal.com/news/history/centennial-spotlight-theres-gold-in-them-there-hills-mica-mining-in-avery-county/article_2bfcb7b0-735f-578d-914a-86669f05cb71.html.

Click, Patricia C. "Slavery and Society in the Shenandoah Valley of Virginia, 1790–1830." Master's thesis, University of Virginia, 1974.

Connection. General editor, Curtiss E. Porter; poetry editor, August Wilson. 1970.

Conner, Lynne. *Pittsburgh in Stages: Two Hundred Years of Theater*. University of Pittsburgh Press, 2007.

Cook, Philip J. "Crime in the City." In *Making Cities Work: Prospects and Policies for Urban America*, edited by Robert P. Inman. Princeton University Press, 2009.

Cooper, Horton. *History of Avery County, North Carolina*. Biltmore, 1972.

Darity, William A., Jr., ed. *International Encyclopedia of the Social Sciences*. 2nd ed. Macmillan Reference USA, 2008.

Dean, Alexander, and Lawrence Carra. *Fundamentals of Play Directing*. 1941. Reprint, Holt, Rinehart and Winston, 1965.

Douglas, Mary. *Purity and Danger*. Penguin, 1966.

Dubner, Stephen J. "August Wilson R.I.P." *Freakonomics*, October 21, 2005. https://freakonomics.com/2005/10/august-wilson-rip/.

Durham, Philip, and Everett L. Jones, *Adventures of the Negro Cowboys*. 1965. Reprint, Dodd, Mead, 1966.

Eberhardt, Maeve. "Identities and Local Speech in Pittsburgh: A Study of Regional African American English." PhD diss., University of Pittsburgh, 2009.

Effort, Elaine. "Pittsburgh Profiles." KQV Radio broadcast, recorded by Lee Kiburi, September 25, 1987.

Elam, Harry J., Jr. *The Past as Present in the Drama of August Wilson*. University of Michigan Press, 2006.

Elkins, Marilyn. "Wilson, August." In *The Oxford Companion to African American Literature*, edited by William I. Andrews et al. Oxford, 1997.

Ellis, Kim. "Pride and Pain of Place." In Glasco and Rawson, *August Wilson*.

"Establishing Common Ground: August Wilson's *Fences* in Beijing." *China Today*, no. 5 (1997): 58–61. https://chinatoday.sinoperi.com/en19975/607444.jhtml.

Feingold, Michael. "August Wilson's Bottomless Blackness." In Bryer and Hartig, *Conversations with August Wilson*.

Feldman, Gene, and Max Gartenberg, eds. *The Beat Generation and the Angry Young Men*. Citadel, 1958.

Felton, Herold W. *Nat Love, Negro Cowboy*. Dodd, Mead, 1969.

Fishman, Joan. "Romare Bearden and August Wilson." In *May All Your Fences Have Gates: Essays on the Drama of August Wilson*, edited by Alan Nadel. University of Iowa Press, 1994.

Fitzgerald, Sharon. "August Wilson: The People's Playwright." *American Visions* 15, no. 14 (2000): 14.

Foner, Eric. *Gateway to Freedom: The Hidden History of America's Fugitive Slaves*. Oxford University Press, 2015.

Frazier, E. Franklin. *Black Bourgeoisie*. 1957. Reprint, Free Press, 1965.

Fullilove, Mindy Thompson. *Root Shock: How Tearing Up City Neighborhoods Hurts America, and What We Can Do About It*. New Village, 2016.

Garvin, Glenn. "Flouting the Law, Serving the Poor." *Reason*, June–July 1985.

Gates, Henry Louis, Jr. "The Chitlin Circuit." *New Yorker*, February 3, 1997.

Gayle, Addison, ed. *The Black Aesthetic*. Doubleday, 1971.

Glasco, Laurence. "August Wilson and the Automobile: A Peculiar Relationship." In *Pittsburgh and the Great Migration*, compiled by Kim Cady. History Press, 2023.

Glasco, Laurence. "Double Burden: History of Blacks in Pittsburgh, PA." In *City at the Point*, edited by S. P. Hays. University of Pittsburgh Press, 1989.

Glasco, Laurence. "High Culture in Black America: Pittsburgh, Pennsylvania, 1900–1920." Unpublished manuscript in possession of the author.

Glasco, Laurence. "Optimism, Dilemmas, and Progress: The Pittsburgh Survey and Black Americans" in Maurine Greenwald and Margo Anderson, eds., *Pittsburgh Surveyed: Social Science and Social Reform in the Early Twentieth Century*. University of Pittsburgh Press, 1996.

Glasco, Laurence A., ed. *The WPA History of the Negro in Pittsburgh*. University of Pittsburgh Press, 2004.

Glasco, Laurence A., and Christopher Rawson. *August Wilson: Pittsburgh Places in His Life and Plays*. Pittsburgh History & Landmarks Foundation, 2015.

Goldsmith, Arthur, Darrick Hamilton, and William A. Darity Jr. "Shades of Discrimination: Skin Tone and Wages." *American Economic Review* 96, no. 2 (2006): 242–45.

Grantmyre, Laura. "'They Lived Their Life and They Didn't Bother Anybody': African American Female Impersonators and Pittsburgh's Hill District, 1920–1960." *American Quarterly*, December 2011, 983–1011.

Green, Carroll. *Romare Bearden: The Prevalence of Ritual*. Museum of Modern Art, 1971.

Greenwald, Maurine W., and Margo Anderson, eds. *Pittsburgh Surveyed: Social Science and Social Reform in the Early Twentieth Century*. University of Pittsburgh Press, 1996.

Hage, Emily. "Reconfiguring Race, Recontextualizing the Media: Romare Bearden's 1968 Fortune and Time Covers." *Art Journal* (Fall 2016): 36–51.

Hampton, Aubrey. "August Wilson, Playwright." *Organica*, Summer 1988.

Hardy, Michael. *Remembering Avery County*. History Press, 2007.

Harper, Colter. "'The Crossroads of the World': A Social and Cultural History of Jazz in Pittsburgh's Hill District, 1920–1970." PhD diss., University of Pittsburgh, 2011.

Harrison, Daphne Duval. *Black Pearls: Blues Queens of the 1920s*. Rutgers University Press, 1988.

Hartigan, Patti. *August Wilson: A Life*. Simon & Schuster, 2023.

Heinzelman, Kurt. "Affiliated Poetics: John Berryman and Dylan Thomas." *Southwest Review* (2015): 572–88.

Herrington, Joan. *I Ain't Sorry for Nothin' I Done: August Wilson's Process of Playwriting*. Limelight Editions, 1998.

Hill, Errol, and James Hatch. *A History of African American Theatre*. Cambridge University Press, 2003.

Hinds, Michael, and Stephen Matterson, eds. *Rebound: The American Poetry Book*. Rodopi, 2004.

Hoerr, John. *And the Wolf Finally Came: The Decline of the American Steel Industry*. University of Pittsburgh Press, 1988.

Hofler, Robert. "Serious Drama a Hard Sell on Broadway." *Variety*, February 21–27, 2005.

Hornby, Richard. "The Two August Wilsons." *Hudson Review* 53, no. 2 (Summer 2000).

Howze, Sam (Sala Udin). "An Open Letter to Brothers and Sisters." *Connection*, Spring 1968. Afro-American Institute, Pittsburgh.

Hunter, Margaret. "'If You're Light You're Alright': Light Skin Color as Social Capital for Women of Color." *Gender and Society* 16, no. 2 (2002): 175–93.

Jamal, Wali. "The Union Edge: Labor's Talk Radio." Pittsburgh (broadcast), February 18, 2017.

Jet magazine. May 27, 1976, 64.

Johnstone, Barbara, Daniel Baumgardt, Maeve Eberhardt, and Scott Kiesling. *Pittsburgh Speech and Pittsburghese*. Wakter De Gruyter, 2015.

Jones, LeRoi (Amiri Baraka). *Blues People: Negro Music in White America*. William Morrow, 1963.

Kameen, Paul. *Re-reading Poets: The Life of the Author*. University of Pittsburgh Press, 2011.

Keith, Verna, and Cedric Herring. "Skin Tone and Stratification in the Black Community." *American Journal of Sociology* 97, no. 3 (1991): 760–78.

Kennedy, Randall. *Nigger: The Strange Career of a Troublesome Word*. Vintage Books, 2002.

Koons, Kenneth E., and Warren R. Hofstra, eds. *After the Backcountry: Rural Life in the Great Valley of Virginia, 1800–1900*. University of Tennessee Press, 2000.

Lahr, John. "Been Here and Gone: How August Wilson Brought a Century of Black American Culture to the Stage." *New Yorker*, April 16, 2001.

Legacy in Bricks and Mortar: African-American Landmarks in Allegheny County. Pittsburgh History & Landmarks Foundation, 1995.

Leuchtenmüller, Thomas. *Die Macht der Vergangenheit: Einführung in Leben und Werk August Wilsons*. Königshausen und Neumann, 1997.

Love, Nat. *The Life and Adventures of Nat Love*. 1907. Reprint, Arno Press, 1968.

Lyons, Bonnie, and George Plimpton. "The Art of Theater XIV: August Wilson." *Paris Review* 41, no. 153 (1999): 66–94.

Lyons, Bonnie. "An Interview with August Wilson." In Bryer and Hartig, *Conversations with August Wilson*.

"Ma Rainey's Black Bottom." *Variety*, October 17, 1984, 156.

Mahala, Macelle. *Penumbra: The Premier Stage for African American Drama*. University of Minnesota Press, 2013.

Mariani, Paul. *Dream Songs: The Life of John Berryman*. Farrar, Straus and Giroux, 1990.

Martin, Michel. "August Wilson's Home: A Place in History." *Tell Me More*, NPR, April 21, 2008.

Matlin, Daniel. "'Lift Up Yr Self!' Reinterpreting Amiri Baraka (LeRoi Jones), Black Power, and the Uplift Tradition." *Journal of American History* 93, no. 1 (2006): 91–116.

Maxwell, Justin. "August Wilson and the Playwrights' Center." *Minnesota History* (Winter 2006–2007): 133–42.

Mazlish, Bruce. "The Flaneur: From Spectator to Representation." In Tester, *Flaneur*, 52.

McCollester, Charles. "The Union Edge: Labor's Talk Radio." Pittsburgh (broadcast), February 18, 2017.

McKay, Claude. *Home to Harlem*. 1928. Reprint, Northeastern University Press, 1987.

Minot, Stephen. "Speaking in Tongues: John Berryman and the Lure of Obscurity." *Sewanee Review* (Summer 2003): 423–34.

Morris, Carl. *The Black Mood in Pittsburgh*. New Pittsburgh Courier, 1968. Pennsylvania Room, Carnegie Library of Pittsburgh.

Moyers, Bill. "August Wilson: Playwright." In Bryer and Hartig, *Conversations with August Wilson.*

Nabofa, M. Y. "Blood Symbolism in African Religion." *Religious Studies* 21 (1985): 389–405.

Nadel, Alan, ed. *May All Your Fences Have Gates: Essays on the Drama of August Wilson.* University of Iowa Press, 1994.

Neal, Larry. "The Black Arts Movement." *Tulane Drama Review* (Summer 1968). http://nationalhumanitiescenter.org/pds/maai3/community/text8/blackartsmovement.pdf.

Nolan, Frederick. *The Wild West: History, Myth & the Making of America.* Arcturus, 2003.

Norris, Michelle. "August Wilson, Broadway's Bard of Black Life." NPR, October 2, 2007. http://www.npr.org/templates/story/story.php?storyId=14893908.

Norwood, Nick. "The Plain Style in Southern Poetry." *Southern Literary Journal* (Fall 2010): 109–24.

Noyalas, Jonathan A. *Slavery and Freedom in the Shenandoah Valley During the Civil War Era.* University Press of Florida, 2021.

Parks, Suzan-Lori. "The Light in August Wilson: A Career, a Century, a Lifetime." *American Theatre*, November 1, 2005. https://www.americantheatre.org/2005/11/01/the-light-in-august-wilson-a-career-a-century-a-lifetime/.

Patton, Sharon F. *Memory and Metaphor: The Art of Romare Bearden, 1940–1987.* Oxford University Press and The Studio Museum in Harlem, 1991.

Penny, Rob. Review of *Joe Turner's Come and Gone. Shooting Star Review* (Summer 1988): 32–33. Hillman Library at the University of Pittsburgh.

Pettengill, Richard. "The Historical Perspective: An Interview with August Wilson." In Bryer and Hartig, *Conversations with August Wilson.*

Pittler, Alexander. "The Hill District of Pittsburgh: A Study in Succession." Master's thesis, University of Pittsburgh, 1930.

Pollitzer, William S., et al. "Survey of Demography, Anthropometry, and Genetics in the Melungeons of Tennessee: An Isolate of Hybrid Origin in Process of Dissolution." *Human Biology* (September 1969): 388–400.

Price, Edward T. "The Melungeons: A Mixed-Blood Strain of the Southern Appalachians." *Geographical Review* (April 1951): 256–71.

Pugh Mitchell, Patricia. "Negating the Nadir: The Smoky City Newspaper Series." *Western Pennsylvania History* (Winter 2006–2007): 33–47.

Reich, Steven A., ed. *Encyclopedia of the Great Black Migration.* Greenwood, 2006.

"Remembering August Wilson." PBS *NewsHour*, April 6, 2001.

Ribeiro, Alyssa. "'A Period of Turmoil': Pittsburgh's April 1968 Riots and Their Aftermath." *Journal of Urban History* 39, no. 2 (2012): 147–71.

Rooney, David. "*Gem.* Swims Through Rough Seas with Grace." *Variety*, December 13–19, 2004, 45.

Rooney, David. "*Golf* Completes Course." *Variety*, May 14–20, 2007, 56.

Ruck, Rob, dir. *Kings on the Hill: Baseball's Forgotten Men.* Video. San Pedro Productions, 1993.

Ruck, Rob. *Sandlot Seasons: Sport in Black Pittsburgh.* University of Illinois Press, 1987.

Russel, Kathy, Midge Wilson, and Ronald Hall. *The Color Complex: The Politics of Skin Color Among African Americans.* Harcourt, Brace, Jovanovich, 1992.

"Sala Udin: Community Organizer." Interview by Jeff Sewald. *Pittsburgh Quarterly*, Fall 2013, 22.

Sanders, Leslie Catherine. *The Development of Black Theater in America.* Louisiana State University Press, 1989.

Savran, David. "August Wilson." In Bryer and Hartig, *Conversations with August Wilson*.

Schrift, Melissa. *Becoming Melungeon: Making an Ethnic Identity in the Appalachian South*. University of Nebraska Press, 2013.

Shannon, Sandra. "August Wilson Explains His Dramatic Vision: An Interview." In Bryer and Hartig, *Conversations with August Wilson*.

Shannon, Sandra. *The Dramatic Vision of August Wilson*. Howard University Press, 1995.

Shannon, Sandra G., and Dana A. Williams. "A Conversation with August Wilson." In Bryer and Hartig, *Conversations with August Wilson*.

Shaya, Gregory. "The Flâneur, the Badaud, and the Making of a Mass Public in France, circa 1860–1910." *American Historical Review* (February 2004): 41–77.

Sheppard, Vera. "August Wilson: An Interview." In Bryer and Hartig, *Conversations with August Wilson*.

Sillman, Marcie. "Playwright Wilson Turns Actor in 'How I Learned.'" *All Things Considered*, May 23, 2003.

Simanga, Michael. *Amiri Baraka and the Congress of African People: History and Memory*. Palgrave MacMillan, 2015.

Sinclair, Abiola. "Black Aesthetic: A Conversation with Playwright August Wilson." In Bryer and Hartig, *Conversations with August Wilson*.

Snodgrass, Mary Ellen. *August Wilson: A Literary Companion*. McFarland, 2004.

Sollors, Werner. *Amiri Baraka/LeRoi Jones: The Quest for a "Populist Modernism."* Columbia University Press, 1978.

Sollors, Werner, ed. *Interracialism: Black-White Intermarriage in American History, Literature, and Law*. Oxford University Press, 2000.

Spencer, Jon Michael. "The Diminishing Rural Residue of Folklore in City and Urban Blues, Chicago, 1915–1950." *Black Music Research Journal* (Spring 1992): 25–41.

Tester, Keith, ed. *The Flaneur*. Routledge, 1994.

Trotter, Joe W., and Jared N. Day. *Race and Renaissance: African Americans in Pittsburgh Since World War II*. University of Pittsburgh Press, 2010.

Udin, Sala. "Growing Up with August." In Glasco and Rawson, *August Wilson*.

Uzzel, Robert. *Blind Lemon Jefferson: His Life, His Death, and His Legacy*. Eakin, 2002.

Vance Clemons, Fran. *View from My Porch: A Look Back at Plumtree*. Published by the author, 1968.

Vanwyngarden, Bruce. "August Wilson: The Pittsburgher of the Year 1990." *Pittsburgh Magazine*, January 1990, 28–32.

Vendler, Helen. *The Music of What Happens: Poems, Poets, Critics*. Harvard University Press, 1988.

Walker, Victor Leo. "The Politics of Art: A History of the Inner City Cultural Center, 1965–1986." PhD diss., University of California, Santa Barbara, 1989.

Washington, M. Bunch. *Art of Romare Bearden: The Prevalence of Ritual*. Abrams, 1973.

Watlington, Dennis. "Hurdling Fences." In Bryer and Hartig, *Conversations with August Wilson*.

Weinert-Kendt, Rob. "The Ground on Which He Stood: Revisiting August Wilson's Speech." *American Theatre*, April 21, 2016. https://www.americantheatre.org/2016/04/21/the-ground-on-which-he-stood-revisiting-august-wilsons-speech/.

Whitaker, Mark. *Smoketown: The Untold Story of the Other Great Black Renaissance*. Simon & Schuster, 2018.

White, Jonathan J. "It Was All a Dream: Pittsburgh Musician's Local 471: Collective Memory and Alternate Truths." PhD diss., University of Pittsburgh, 2020.

Williams, John A. Introduction to Washington, *Art of Romare Bearden*.

Williamson, Joel. *New People: Miscegenation and Mulattoes in the United States*. New York University Press, 1984.

Wilson, August. "Blacks, Blues and Cultural Imperialism." Lecture delivered March 2, 1988, at the Man and Ideas Lecture Series, Carnegie Lecture Hall, Pittsburgh. Recorded by Lee Kiburi.

Wilson, August. "Feed Your Mind, The Rest Will Follow," *Pittsburgh Post-Gazette*, March 28, 1999, 21.

Wilson, August. Foreword to *Romare Bearden: His Life and Art*, edited by Myron Schwartzman. Harry Abrams, 1990.

Wilson, August. "The Ground on Which I Stand." *American Theatre*, June 20, 2016. https://www.americantheatre.org/2016/06/20/the-ground-on-which-i-stand/.

Wilson, August. *How I Learned What I Learned*.

Wilson, August. "The Legacy of Malcolm X." *Life*, December 1992.

Wilson, August. *King Hedley II*. Theatre Communications Group, 1999.

Wilson, August. *Three Plays*. University of Pittsburgh Press, 1991.

Wilson, James. In "Actors Talk August." Podcast by Chris Rawson in collaboration with Pittsburgh's City of Asylum, April 19, 2021.

Woodard, Komozi. *A Nation Within a Nation: Amiri Baraka (LeRoi Jones) and Black Power Politics*. University of North Carolina Press, 1999.

Wright, R. R., Jr. "One Hundred Negro Steel Workers." In *The Pittsburgh Survey: Wage-Earning Pittsburgh*, edited by Paul Underwood Kellogg. Russell Sage Foundation, 1914.

Wylie Avenue Days. Video. WQED Multimedia, 1991.

Wyman, Walker. *Legend of Charlie Glass, Negro Cowboy on the Colorado-Utah Range*. River Falls State University Press, 1970.

Young, Kevin. "Responsible Delight: Reevaluation: John Berryman." *Kenyon Review* 21, no. 2 (1999): 161–66.

PHOTO CREDITS

Figure 1. Courtesy of North Carolina State University.

Figure 2. MSP285.B033.F06.I01, Allegheny Conference on Community Development Photographs, 1892-1981, MSP 285, Library and Archives Division, Senator John Heinz History Center.

Figure 3. Photograph by John R. Shrader. MSP285.B033.F05.I08, Allegheny Conference on Community Development Photographs, 1892-1981, MSP 285, Library and Archives Division, Senator John Heinz History Center.

Figure 4. Courtesy of Julia Burley.

Figure 5. Courtesy of the Sisters of Charity of Seton Hill Archives, Greensburg, Pennsylvania.

Figure 6. Photograph by Richard Sanders. MSP285.B022.F10.I01, Allegheny Conference on Community Development Photographs, 1892-1981, MSP 285, Library and Archives Division, Senator John Heinz History Center.

Figure 7. Courtesy of Laurence Glasco.

Figure 8. Courtesy of Laurel Roberts.

Figure 9. Courtesy of Julia Burley.

Figure 10. Courtesy of the Siger family.

Figure 11. Courtesy of Laurence Glasco.

Figure 12. Photograph by Cbaile19, used under Creative Commons license.

Figure 14. Courtesy of JaQuay Carter.

Figure 15. Map by Carlos Peterson. Reproduced by permission from the cartographer.

Figure 16–25. Courtesy of the Charles "Teenie" Harris Archive, Carnegie Museum of Art, Pittsburgh.

Figure 26. Courtesy of Frank Hightower.

Figure 27. Reproduced from *Dateline Pittsburgh*.

Figure 29. Courtesy of Frank Hightower.

Figure 37. Courtesy of Julia Burley.

Figure 38–39. Courtesy of Frank Hightower.

Figure 40. Courtesy of Shirley Biggs.

Figure 43–46. Courtesy of Laurence Glasco.

INDEX

Note: Page numbers in *italics* indicate figures.